*ENGINEERS AT WAR*

# ENGINEERS AT WAR

RICHARD CROUCHER

MERLIN PRESS
LONDON

© The Merlin Press 1982
This edition first published by
The Merlin Press,
3 Manchester Road,
London E14


British Library Cataloguing in Publication Data
Croucher, Richard
    Engineers at war
    1. Industrial relations — History
    2. Engineering — History
    1. Title
    331'.042        HD6976.E52


ISBN  0-85036-27009
ISBN  0-85036-271-7  Pbk

Cover design by Peter Kennard

Typesetting by Heather Hems
The Malt House,
Chilmark, Wilts.

Printed by
Whitstable Litho Ltd.,
Whitstable, Kent

# CONTENTS

*The photographs on plates 1–9 are reproduced by kind permission of the Radio Times Hulton Picture Library, and those on plates 10–12 are from the TUC.*

# PREFACE

This book has been written for two main reasons. First, because there is a need to consider this important period in the light of the governmental archive material available in the Public Record Office—a need that has grown rather than diminished with the publication of the various volumes of the official history of the war. Official historians, perhaps more than others, need to be interrogated and challenged now that this documentary evidence is available and while there is still a wealth of human memories to be tapped. Second, there has been a need for a history that begins to examine the origins, in the decade 1935-45, of the present system of workplace trade union representation. This need is not felt only by academics, whether they be labour historians or industrial relations specialists. It is also felt by the descendants of the shop stewards of that generation. At a time when trade-unionists and shop stewards in particular are under exceptionally strong adverse pressures, there is a need to make sense of the past; an increasing number of activists are coming to realise this. Although this book is not designed solely for them, I hope it will be of use to them.

The bulk of my research was done from 1972 onwards, when the public records up to 1945 were first made available. Some of this time was spent at the Centre for the Study of Social History at the University of Warwick, where I incurred debts to Royden Harrison and James Hinton. But this book would never have been written if I had not been able to attend the Institut für Europäische Geschichte, Mainz, in the Federal Republic of West Germany. It was in the Mainz Institute in the summers of 1978 and 1979 that I was given the time and full facilities to write it. During that time, kindly granted me by Professor Dr K.O. von Aretin, I was

i

very much helped by Claus Scharf and his colleagues in the
Institute. I have also to thank the Berks., Bucks. and Oxon.
district of the Workers' Educational Association for allowing
me the time from my normal work as an industrial tutor.
A list of all those who helped me along the way would be
long indeed, but I must mention Peter Caldwell who first
discussed the topic with me, Richard Storey at the Modern
Records Centre at Warwick who gave me a lot of help, and
Spencer Phelan who travelled a part of the way with me.
Apart from them, I would like to add—but space will not
allow it—all the shop stewards and activists who have
discussed these issues with me at different times.

*Wolverton*
*July 1980*

# INTRODUCTION

The main purpose of this book is to challenge an idea—it might be better called a 'common-sense' assumption—popular amongst historians: that the Second World War was, in Britain, a period of unprecedented national unity in which industrial class conflict was to all intents and purposes suspended 'for the duration'. Indeed, many people who lived through these years have assured me, despite my youthful protests, that the very idea of, say, stopping work was unthinkable under the circumstances. When such statements were probed critically, however, it invariably transpired that a statement of *value* rather than of *fact* was being made. People were saying that if there had been industrial disputes then there ought not to have been. This sort of statement is not one that historians might be expected to make, as they are supposed to be diligent seekers after objective historical fact, but similar values can be detected behind much of the historical writing on domestic affairs in the period. When reading books on the Second World War years, it is very often difficult to resist being enticed into the atmosphere of nostalgic patriotism which they evoke. Today the nation may be divided, but then things were different: everyone knew the job that had to be done. All agreed that Nazism was a terrible nightmare and that the Axis simply had to be defeated. Almost nobody, therefore, had any reservations about pulling together to win the war. In any case, the political consensus was very much a reformist one, and was thus far from unattractive to the left; national unity on these terms was perhaps not too repugnant.

So far historians have not tackled the sometimes tricky task of waking themselves or their semi-somnambulant readers from their comfortable patriotic doze, quite possibly for fear of the unpredictable reaction which might result. Those who would doubt the assumptions on which the traditional historical view is based have drawn back from the task of anatomising the industrial class conflict of the war years. This book attempts to fill a small part of the gap by studying the history of engineering workers in the decade of rearmament and war, with the specific purpose of examining the nature and evolution of industrial battles. Hence the ambiguous title.

The traditional view is not, of course, entirely mistaken: the war years *were* in many respects years of unprecedented national unity. But this is a partial one-dimensional truth which does not capture the ambiguity of working-class attitudes of the time.[1] Just as working people were determined to defeat Nazism in the war with the Axis, they were equally determined to root it out wherever it appeared, albeit in diluted form, in the factories. Foremen and managers who were seen as 'little Hitlers' were given just as short shrift as the foreign enemy. Engineering workers, along with many others, shared an historical experience which prompted them to suspect their employers' motives in every sphere. This experience and the consciousness which was its result could not be spirited away by a declaration of war. As some contemporary commentators pointed out (generally in private), the engineers were fighting a war of their own which had begun long before September 1939. Admittedly, the interaction of class and national allegiances frequently produced ideas and actions which may appear to us internally contradictory and illogical. But this cannot be accepted as an excuse for ignoring or failing to understand them with all their apparent contradictions and inconsistencies, nor should it lead us simply to reduce them to variants of patriotism.

The attempt to reconstruct workers' material conditions, their mentalities and the conflicts to which these contributed, has been a difficult and only half-successful one. There have been a number of important obstacles on the way. The most significant of these has been the dense fog of propaganda and historical apologetics which began during the war itself, often contemporaneously with the events it shrouds. During the period of rearmament, newspapers, newsreels and radio constantly hammered home, to a largely anti-war audience, the message that Britain had to arm itself to keep up with the foreign threat. Newsreel sequences showing the build-up of the Luftwaffe, for example, carried the implicit and sometimes explicit implication that Britain was falling behind. In this way, popular opinion was moulded during the 1930s into a shape that was more acceptable to government. During the war the messages became much more pointedly patriotic. The development of this propaganda could no longer be entrusted to agencies with any shred of independence from government, and the change was expressed in the formation of a whole new ministry misnamed 'Information'. The ministry attracted some able literary minds, and profoundly influenced the production of news and propaganda alike. Women and men were shown 'doing their bit' in factories while servicemen and women were portrayed doing theirs; the inter-relationship of the military and the industrial war efforts was shown in all its complexity in a massive ideological offensive. At the same time began the production of 'instant history' which became increasingly intense as the war drew to a close. Thus 'news', 'propaganda' and 'history' were fused together in a potent and highly influential combination. To take an example: J.B. Priestley's *British Women Go To War* (n.d., probably 1944) was typically attractive in conception and execution. With its cleverly individual (yet universal) studies of a whole range of women making their different contributions to the war effort, complete with idealised full-page colour plates, it presents a cosy and congratulatory picture of the women's devotion to duty, against which active discontent becomes quite inconceivable. The pervasive influence of such writers, who exercised their 'common-touch' talents with the support and encouragement of the state, was collectively very considerable.

The other side of this history is, of course, the history of wartime censorship. This is a difficult story to uncover. Those who wielded the censor's blue pencil have not been over-anxious to publicise their activities, while the informal channels developed and used so adroitly in Britain generally leave little documentary trace. But the contrast between internal government documents and public statements is great enough to allow us to say that much was suppressed 'in the public interest'. Fat Ministry of Labour files on particular disputes have only to be set beside insignificant newspaper reporting of the same events to see the effects of the censor's formal and informal work. In many cases, for example, it is only possible to read of returns to work in the newspapers, while photographic coverage of disputes was even more rare than that of other matters. But propagandists and censors clearly played important roles in constructing the historical consensus, but the state was not prepared to let the matter rest there. There had to be an 'official' history of the war effort on the home front. This was clearly a politically sensitive task with considerable implications for the future direction of historical writing on the topic. The government therefore paid the subject some attention, and we should do likewise.

The official history of the war is historiographically crucial to the conventional wisdom, and the circumstances of its making are correspondingly significant. The volumes of interest to us are the War Production series within the war's Civil Series. These books were written by historians who were brought into the ministries with which they were concerned during the war, were given free access to official documents and to the appropriate civil servants in London and the regions, and an 'inside' view of the workings of the state. They also wrote under the convention of revealing neither their documentary nor their personal sources. As a result, the official histories occupy both a privileged and a specific position within the historical literature, having at once a unique insight into the workings of ministries that cannot possibly be matched by 'unofficial' historians denied these advantages and an entirely predictable tendency to see questions from the point of view of government.

Directed by Professor M.M. Postan, a Cambridge economic historian, the resultant histories appeared at various dates scattered across the post-war years. These solid blue volumes, making up a pleasantly uniform row, their spines embossed in gold with the crown above their titles, are as scholarly and thorough as their pedigree and appearance suggest. Their subject is the administration of the economic war effort, terms of reference which reduce even conventional industrial relations matters to something of a side issue. The purpose of the most important volume from our point of view, entitled *Labour in the Munitions Industries* (1957), is stated by the editors to be the study of labour 'as a factor of production within the industries controlled by the supply Ministries'.[2] Although Mrs P. Inman set about her allotted task with rather more humanity than the austerity of this definition suggests, the framework laid down for her was as clear as it could be. Labour was to be studied primarily as a *commodity*, a 'factor of production' alongside other factors of production such as machine tools and raw materials. However, this history was not written by 'typical' official historians. Mrs Inman was one of only three women to have taken part in writing one of the volumes in the Civil Series, and she collaborated with James B. Jefferys, the trade union historian who wrote *The Story of the Engineers* (1945). Yet this promising partnership produced a book which, though amongst the best of its kind, constituted little more than a twitch in the blue ranks. Very much preoccupied with problems of labour supply, it contains only one chapter (12), of some fifty pages, entitled 'Morale and Industrial Relations', which deals with social relations within the munitions industries. As Mrs Inman outlines in her preface, she and her collaborator were mainly concerned with the 'labour budget' in the first part of the work, and with the effective use of labour in the factories in the second. It is hardly surprising, then, that reading this book does not help very much when trying to reconstruct the war years 'from below', and that the hopes, fears and aspirations of working people which underlie industrial conflict are revealed only occasionally and incidentally. Yet even the history of government labour policy pure and simple demands some assessment of working-class reactions to render it fully comprehensible. Labour may have been, objectively speaking, a 'factor of production', but it had the peculiar quality of thinking and reacting in ways which constrained governments and managers alike.

The official history has been extremely influential, providing a source of ready-made yet impeccably authoritative judgments for almost a quarter of a century. It is high time that the subject be revisited. The influence of the official history cannot be exorcised simply by attempting to argue with it, but the shape and direction of this work have been to some extent determined by the official history. We have attempted to redress the balance by jumping hard (some will say too hard) on the other end of the historical scales, and to write an 'unofficial' history, but this very process has its own disciplines; any argument necessarily constrains the debaters. We have not set out here to write a complete history of the engineering shop stewards who played so important a part in the history of industrial relations in the war years, although we hope that a contribution to that history will be made in the following pages. We do have, in James Hinton's *The First Shop Stewards' Movement* (1973), a history of engineering shop stewards during the First World War, but there is as yet no satisfactory history of the shop stewards during the Second World War, a fact that has hampered and limited this work. Nevertheless, we do have enough evidence about the evolution of shop floor organisation to allow us to assess rather more precisely what point had been reached by the end of the war, which is the starting point for most standard 'industrial relations' analyses.

An understanding of the trajectory of workplace trade-unionism in this period can also help to explain the historical processes which led to the political 'revolution' of 1945. So far, historians have tended to explain the massive Labour victory of 1945 in largely parliamentary and non-industrial political terms, focusing on high politics, shifting Cabinet allegiances and so on, in fine Oxbridge tradition. Reading these accounts, it is frequently necessary to remind oneself that politics does not only go on in Parliament (indeed, class politics are often rather distorted on entry to those august chambers), nor even in the conventional 'political sphere' encompassed by political parties. It is also, of course, carried on in workshops and on housing estates. Yet accounts of the 1945 election generally ignore industrial politics. They recognise the importance of developments in the services and in other social spheres, but flounder as soon as they approach industry. This is true even of the best historians in the field. Paul Addison, in his influential book *The Road to 1945* (1975), posits a 'new consensus' in British governing circles emerging in the war, and uses government reports on popular 'morale' to indicate the social changes going on at the popular level. But in order to explain fully the changes which were going on, it is necessary to descend to the level of the workplace. Britain was, above all, a nation *at work* in these years, and it seems therefore perverse to ignore the course of industrial conflict in plotting the road to 1945. We may get our hands dirty in the factory, but we stand to learn a great deal there about the forces from below which generated the 'new consensus' at the top. The difficulties involved in understanding workers' industrial experience should not deter the political historian from paying a good deal of attention to the subject. After all, it was not only the returning servicemen who voted Labour in 1945.

We consider these matters in a specific context, that of the engineering industry. The industry was of great importance because, even more than the First World War, the Second fully deserved the title of 'The Engineers' War'. By 1939, warfare had become very much a motorised, armoured and airborne affair. Weaponry determined military strategy and tactics to an extent that would have been almost unimaginable in 1914. Indeed, it is possible to argue convincingly that the Second World War was decided at least as much in the metalworking factories of the industrialised world as in open combat. The industry was also important because it absorbed previously unheard-of numbers of men and women into its workshops, making it by far the largest manufacturing industry at the peak of the war effort. These considerations brought engineering out of the category of a mere industry and made it *the* employer of wartime labour. It was for these reasons that the state took an extremely active interest in engineering. The problems of the maximisation of labour supply and the full mobilisation of productive resources received great attention, but difficulties with workers who for one reason or another refused to accept managerial or state priorities were paid even greater heed. Government observation and surveillance of shop floor affairs reached an unprecedented level; in common with other combatant states, Britain monitored the morale of its industrial 'troops' very closely, and it is this that has made our study possible.

The intervention of governments in industrial affairs, and especially in workplace relations between managements and trade unions, required a large measure of sensitivity to the particular situation in each sector of the economy. The government departments appreciated the specific nature of any given industry, and it is important that we do the same. The coal owners and the Miners' Federation, to take one example, had quite different traditional relationships from those obtaining between the engineering employers and the Amalgamated Engineering Union. The patterns of profit and investment, of wage payment and working practices, and of both formal and informal methods of resolving disputes, varied widely between the two industries, as indeed they did even between different areas and districts within them. The differences are so manifest that they need no further stress. It is to the industrial context, then, that we have first to turn if we are to understand the conflicts of wartime.

*Acronyms used in this book*
ABCA Army Bureau of Current Affairs
AEU Amalgamated Engineering Union
AID Aircraft Inspection Department
ASE Amalgamated Society of Engineers
ASSNC Aircraft Shop Stewards' National Council
CI Communist International
CPGB Communist Party of Great Britain
CSEU Confederation of Shipbuilding and Engineering Unions
CWC Clyde Workers' Committee
E&ATSSNC Engineering and Allied Trades Shop Stewards' National Council
EEF Engineering Employers' Federation
ETU Electrical Trades Union
EWO Essential Works Order
ILP Independent Labour Party
JPC Joint Production Committee
JWC Junior Workers' Committee
MAP Ministry of Aircraft Production
NAT National Arbitration Tribunal
NUDAW National Union of Distributive and Allied Workers
NUFW National Union of Foundry Workers

NUGMW National Union of General and Municipal Workers
NUWM National Unemployed Workers' Movement
RCP Revolutionary Communist Party
ROF Royal Ordnance Factory
RSL Revolutionary Socialist League
SBAC Society of British Aircraft Constructors
TAG Tyneside Apprentices' Guild
TGWU Transport and General Workers' Union
WIL Workers' International League

*Notes*

All references to LAB, AVIA, CAB, MH and similar acronyms relate to the abbreviations used in the indices to public records in the Public Record Office. References which give only a date relate to standard reports from local officials of the Ministry of Labour to London Headquarters, and the names of senders and recipients are not therefore repeated. See Bibliographical Note, p. 387, for a fuller explanation of sources.

The following abbreviations are used in the notes: *NP (New Propellor)* and *DW (Daily Worker)*. The place of publication of all books and pamphlets cited is London, unless otherwise stated.

1    It is interesting to note that recent historians of the Third Reich have been at pains to point out the continued existence of class conflict throughout the Nazi period, albeit in attenuated and distorted forms. See T.W. Mason, *Sozialpolitik im Dritten Reich. Arbeiterklasse und Volksgemeinschaft* (Opladen, 1977). Most of the debate to which Tim Mason's work has given rise has been in German, which is perhaps why a similar approach has not been adopted to look into the British situation. A comparative study of the similarities and differences would help to isolate the specific features of the British and German wartime experiences.

2    M.M. Postan's introduction to P. Inman, *Labour in the Munitions Industries* (1957).

CHAPTER 1

# REARMAMENT

The disparate complex of metalworking undertakings known
as the engineering industry, the basis of wartime arms production, established itself as a major British manufacturing
industry during the second half of the nineteenth century.
Engineers were concerned with the demanding processes
needed to cut, shape and assemble metal into a wide variety
of products. British textile machinery, machine tools, loco-
motives, marine engines and ships formed the basis of the
industry's world dominance, and had a reputation for quality
that enabled the British masters to make full use of the
opportunities offered by free trade.[1] British craftsmen
acquired skills which allowed them to travel all over the
world and to find employment wherever metal was worked.
Indeed, it is impossible to begin to penetrate the 'labour
aristocratic' mentality of the skilled engineers who formed
the industry's elite, without first understanding the key role
which they saw themselves playing within the 'workshop of
the world'.

By the outbreak of the First World War, the metal
industries as a whole employed just over one and three
quarter million people. Despite growing German and
American competition, British engineering was still expanding. Much of the growth was due to the rise of the great arms
firms: Vickers, Beardmore's, Armstrong-Whitworth, John
Brown's and Cammel Laird's built enormous factory-palaces
for munitions production in Scotland and the North of
England, spawning around them a whole number of sub-
contracting firms to provide specialised tools and components.
The First World War saw these firms become even larger and
more important, bloated by the rich inflow of government
arms contracts. By mid-1918 the munitions industries,

1

employing some two millions and dominated by the giant private companies, sprawled across the British economy.

After a very brief post-war boom, the engineering industry entered a period of slump and restructuring that lasted until rearmament began in the mid-1930s. The general tendency for trade in manufactured goods to decline heightened the problems involved in the transition to peace production, as many firms searched in vain for orders. But as the older sections of engineering declined sharply, throwing thousands out of work, other 'new' sections grew up. Thus, despite widespread unemployment, the total number of people employed edged marginally upwards from 985,000 in 1924 to 1,104,000 in 1935.[2] General engineering and railway carriage and wagon work showed a net loss of labour between 1924 and 1935, but electrical engineering and motor vehicles and cycles increased their labour forces, while the aircraft industry had just started the rapid growth that distinguished it in the late 1930s. Looking at the converse of the employment situation—the numbers unemployed—very similar conclusions can be drawn, and Table 1 also shows the enormous toll of human waste exacted by the slump in shipbuilding. The 1935 census showed the geographical consequences of these trends. A southward shift in the industry's centre of gravity was taking place, with the Midlands and South-East becoming more important as the 'new industries' set up there, while Scotland and the North of England suffered as their staple industries slid into decline.[3] During the decade from 1935, the expansion of the aircraft industry led a general revival, but from its base in the southern half of Britain.

While governments had shown very little interest in the question of the manufacture of arms during the 1920s, the changing international situation forced them to intervene more actively in the 1930s. The decline of heavy engineering capacity and the actual decay of some crucial plant made governments fear that rearmament would become unnecessarily difficult if they did not intervene. At the same time it was quite evident that the RAF would have to be expanded enormously if it was to become a viable branch of the armed forces. Orders were therefore placed with the big

Table 1 *Percentage of insured workers unemployed by industry, 1929–39*

| | 1929 | 1930 | 1931 | 1932 | 1933 | 1934 | 1935 | 1936 | 1937 | 1938 | 1939 |
|---|---|---|---|---|---|---|---|---|---|---|---|
| General engineering; engineers in iron+steel founding | 9.9 | 14.2 | 27.0 | 29.1 | 27.4 | 18.4 | 13.6 | 9.6 | 5.8 | 7.0 | 6.6 |
| Electrical engineering | 4.6 | 6.6 | 14.1 | 16.8 | 16.5 | 9.6 | 7.0 | 4.8 | 3.1 | 4.7 | 4.4 |
| Construction and repair of motors, cycles and aircraft | 7.1 | 12.1 | 19.3 | 22.4 | 17.6 | 10.8 | 9.0 | 6.9 | 5.0 | 7.2 | 4.4 |
| Shipbuilding and repair | 25.3 | 27.6 | 51.9 | 62.0 | 61.7 | 51.2 | 44.4 | 33.3 | 24.4 | 21.4 | 20.9 |

Source: *British Labour Statistics, Historical Abstract, 1886–1968* (Department of Employment and Productivity, 1971), pp. 314–5.

arms firms to keep key plant active, and there was a steadily growing demand for aircraft throughout the 1930s. By far the most striking development resulting from government orders was the mushrooming of the aircraft industry, which grew from a small and unimportant group of luxury concerns into *the* arms industry of the Second World War. Hawkers and A.V. Roe were the Second World War heirs to the thrones occupied by Vickers and Beardmore's in the First War. Between 1936 and September 1945, state capital committed to aircraft, aero-engine building and plant alone amounted to over £220 millions.[4] The main method of supervising this enormous growth was the 'shadow' scheme, under which established specialist firms gave the benefit of their expertise to other engineering companies when, as very often happened, expansion necessitated the building of new factories. The state bore the cost of building and equipping the new units, which were managed by private firms. The result was the growth of a number of modern, well equipped factories designed specifically for aero-engine production; between 1935 and 1940, Coventry alone saw the opening of six such large new factories, in a frenzy of building which transformed the Midland town's industrial geography.[5]

Those firms which were able to benefit from government orders were able to register sizeable profits quite quickly, deriving them from 'cost-plus' contracts. Aircraft shares rocketed upwards on the Stock Exchange in 1931 and again in the spring of 1933, maintaining their strength right through to the end of the war.[6] Between 1932 and 1935, aircraft firms had the distinction of earning the highest rate of return on capital employed in any branch of engineering, while aircraft profits rose from £767,146 in 1935 to £2,310,004 in 1938 (see Table 2 for more information).[7] These profits were made almost exclusively by those firms known as 'the ring', who were the sole recipients of RAF contracts through their membership of the Society of British Aircraft Constructors (SBAC). Up until 1937, the small aircraft firms outside 'the ring' made consistent losses.[8]

The aircraft industry was not the only profitable sector of engineering, but it led recovery with its heavy demand for large amounts of electrical equipment and components.

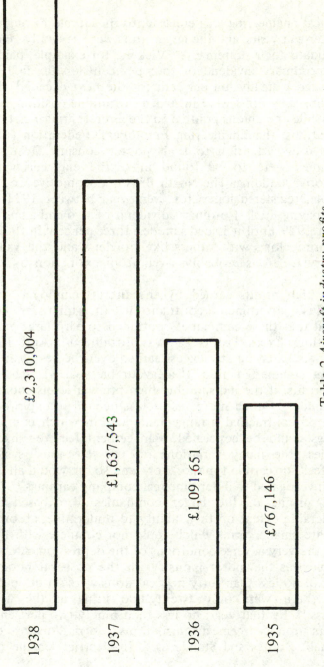

£2,310,004

£1,637,543

£1,091,651

£767,146

1938

1937

1936

1935

Table 2 Aircraft industry profits

Electrical engineering was consistently profitable throughout the inter-war years, and the larger firms were generally able to consolidate their supremacy.[9] Vickers, for example, paid its lowest ordinary dividend of four per cent less tax in 1934, but issued a steady ten per cent for the next decade.[10] Not all engineering firms were in such a favourable position, however. While the unions pointed to the aircraft firms in national negotiations, the Engineering Employers' Federation (EEF) always drew attention to their poorer cousins. Most such companies were to be found in textile engineering and locomotive building. The North British Locomotive Co., for example, registered losses for every year between 1921 and 1937, paying its last ordinary dividend of two and a half per cent in 1929 until it issued a modest three per cent in 1942.[11] This firm, along with others like Fowler's and the Vulcan Foundry Co., was probably saved from extinction by tank orders.

The high profits earned by the aircraft employers from 'cost-plus' government contracts in the inter-war years ensured that these companies continued to earn large profits in wartime. Excess Profits Tax was introduced in April 1941, but it was based on any excess earned over the best year in a pre-war 'standard' period. If a favourable year was selected, then profits at the indisputably high pre-war levels could be maintained.[12] Much more research is needed to explore the jungle of contractual arrangements within which company earnings could be concealed. Management fees for shadow factories, the many variations on the 'cost-plus' system, fixed fees for certain types of work and so on, would all have to be investigated to determine real company earnings.[13]

The profits of the larger companies were based to a considerable extent on their ability to undermine, absorb or eliminate smaller firms which could not compete with them under the very adverse conditions of the depression. A classic example was the motor industry: in the post-war boom of 1919-20, no less than forty new car firms were set up, but by 1938 there were only twenty-two firms in the whole business.[14] By that year, no less than ninety-two per cent of the cars produced came from six firms (Morris, Austin, Ford, Vauxhall, Rootes and Standard).[15] In electrical engineering, four giant companies controlled over a third of the invested capital in the late 1930s. Similar tendencies prevailed in every section of the industry. In aircraft, however, the nature of the concentration process was quite distinctive. The Hawker Co., through its financial interests in many of the other air-craft manufacturers, stood at the centre of the industry.[16] But the aircraft manufacturers were not only linked by the Hawker connection; they were also welded together by the Society of British Aircraft Constructors, formed during the First World War for the defence of their collective interests against the Royal Aircraft Factory at Farnborough, and constituting a tremendously powerful pressure group with excellent connections with government departments.[17] The government received (or at least hoped to receive) a mini-mum guaranteed level of quality, while the SBAC shared out the government contracts between its member firms. There is no doubt that the high profits earned on aircraft contracts throughout the decade 1935-45 owed a good deal to the activities of this society, about which we still know too little.

The rationalisation and concentration of the aircraft industry at the level of the company was paralleled by the rationalisation of production on the shop floor. It was in the newer branches of engineering that the division of labour was pushed to its furthest extent. On the machining side, plant became more modern as an increasing number of American and German machine tools were imported, and flow production methods were widely adopted in motors and electrical engineering.[18] Motor manufacturers followed the examples of the American-owned firms, Ford and Pressed Steel, who introduced radically new production methods in their Dagenham and Oxford plants built in the late 1920s. Machine-fed power presses, flow-line machining and improved methods of internal transport all heralded the way forward in these plants. Yet it remained apparently difficult for the British engineering employers to realise fully the potentials of such methods. True mass production was difficult to achieve with such highly complex products as aero-engines, which were usually in any case designed on an experimental basis. Only radical reorganisation and massive investment could see these problems overcome, even in wartime.[19]

It was not until the second half of the war that anything approaching mass production was applied to aero-engine machining. In the heavy engineering centres of the North, machining operations were often time-consuming and difficult, and not conducive to mass production. In the marine engineering industry, for example, the degree of standardisation was minimal; jobs tended to be 'one-offs' and the skilled machinist could take days, weeks and even months over individual components. Machine tools were often antiquated even in the war years; an official historian accurately described technology in these factories as 'persistently regressive'.[20] The majority of machines in some works dated from before the First World War or even earlier, while one firm had machinery reaching its seventieth anniversary in 1942. This sort of plant could not be run at acceptable speeds in wartime, and caused constant bottlenecks despite special shift arrangements to ensure maximum use.[21]

On the assembly side of the industry, machine-regulated conveyors became increasingly widespread during the inter-war period, so that by the beginning of the war they were standard equipment in the larger motor and radio plants.[22] The aircraft factories were less advanced in this area: it was not possible to produce aircraft on power-driven assembly lines. Nevertheless, dramatic changes went on in methods of aircraft assembly between 1935 and 1945. Despite the growing complexity of aircraft (and in particular the move from fighters to bombers) and the change from wooden to metal construction, fabrication could still be broken down into the main sections (fuselage, wings, etc.) before final assembly.[23] The typical method of construction involved fitting sub-assemblies onto fuselages and wheeling them through large shops on trolley rails, with final assembly taking place in large halls adjacent to the airfields which the aircraft companies used for flight testing.[24] As *The Aeroplane* said, it was usually 'light accurate work of varied character'.[25] If there were problems with aircraft building, there were even greater difficulties with such heavy work as naval gun-mounting. Naval guns could weigh up to fifteen hundred tons and take three years to mount, requiring the use of cranes, heavy lifting tackle and so on; under these circumstances flow-line assembly was clearly out of the question.[26]

The rationalisation of production between the wars led to a very considerable dilution of the traditional engineering skills. As complex processes requiring the multi-faceted abilities of the journeyman fitter and turner were broken down into their constituent operations, semi-skilled 'handymen', boys and women could take over the skilled man's work. This process had gone on at a rapid rate during the First World War, but it was consolidated and advanced in these years. The official historian of the Amalgamated Engineering Union states that by 1933 fifty-seven per cent of the workforce in the factories of firms in the Engineering Employers' Federation were 'semi-skilled'.[27] Much of the 'dilution' in the industry was effected by women and young 'trainees'. A good deal of it was informal and was carried out by using 'apprentices' and 'trainees' as general dogsbodies; in this way the feelings of foremen and workers alike against women in the shop were less likely to be aroused.

In this context it was inevitable that the importance of apprenticeship as the route of entry to the skilled trades declined in importance. Employers were bound by the terms of their indenture agreements with parents to provide apprentices with a general training in their chosen trade, whereas trainees needed only to be taught an operation or small range of operations on a few machines. Moreover, as *The Aeroplane's* editorial candidly admitted in 1936: 'As union men have to be paid union rates, the only solution is to take on trainees'.[28] By 1933 the federated employers took on only 52,741 apprentices as compared with 78,161 in 1929, thereby ensuring a shortage of skilled labour in the late 1930s.[29] Nevertheless, although they were given very little training, and that 'on the job', trainees were adequate for many jobs in the newer factories. Mr Booth of the new Rootes Securities No. 1 shadow factory in Coventry complained to his colleagues in the local Engineering Employers' Association that the trainees in his polishing shop had 'not even as much engineering knowledge as a labourer', but he had no less than forty-eight of them in one gang of 133.[30] The work was often boring and monotonous, with very little

9

discretion allowed to the worker—'very high speed production
to the stop watch', as one toolmaker called it[31] —and the
emphasis laid on speed. This type of work, repetitious and
frequently 'machine-paced', lent itself to systems of
'scientific' work study such as that devised by the industrial
consultants of the Bedaux Company. These oppressive
systems became increasingly popular amongst managements
in the inter-war years because of the spectacular speed-ups
which they could achieve by cutting out unnecessary movements, tea breaks, and so on. For the same reason, they
earned the hatred of those who had little choice but to work
under them. 'Scientific' work study was often used in the
radio industry, for example, in which large numbers of girls
were employed. One girl described her work in these terms:

> I work on a conveyor belt under a point system like M. Bedaux's,
> and we make radio sets. The sets are placed on the conveyor and
> move rapidly along, therefore I cannot leave my bench because if
> I do, I find that there are several sets awaiting my return, and that it
> is impossible to get these out and cope with the others which still
> continue to come up the belt.[32]

This girl worked from eight in the morning to seven at night
when trade was good, with no breaks except for lunch; she
commented (not surprisingly): 'The general opinion is that
we are entitled to more consideration.'[33] Automation and
sophisticated systems of piece-working combined to make
such work both monotonous and intense.

The extent of the dilution of the traditional skills varied
considerably according to the branch of the industry concerned. It is most easily measured by looking at the proportion of women employed in each sector, although this by
no means represents the absolute limits of the process. By
mid-1939 no less than 40.69 per cent of those employed in
electrical apparatus and cables were women, and 9.5 per cent
of those in motor vehicles, cycles and aircraft. In marine
engineering, on the other hand, women made up only 2.1 per
cent of the workforce.[34] These differences were also reflected
locally, with the 'new industry' towns of the Midlands and
South having a relatively high proportion of semi-skilled

workers.[35] The skilled men regarded these developments as serious threats to their position within engineering, because the existence of a large pool of semi- and unskilled labour menaced both their jobs and the rates of pay established by restricting the supply of skilled labour through apprenticeship. Members of the Coventry district of the AEU, interviewed by their District Secretary, Walter Givens, as to the situation in their factories in 1931, pointed consistently to this problem. As H.J. McElvey from Armstrong-Siddeley complained: 'The same disease was attacking this firm as others, i.e. displacing fully paid labour by machines and boys and cited a case in middle machine shop where five heavy semi-autos from Herberts had been introduced and five men discharged. He believes that the firm has taken a dead set against employing anyone on the full rate.'[36] His colleague, P.E. Crump, employed on engine-fitting in the same firm, gave a similar statement, saying that the majority of the two hundred employed in his shop were under twenty, and that they had a lot of difficulty in getting decent piece prices on new work 'as Hewitt the ratefixer wanted to give boys' prices always'. He added that the shop was 'getting a rotten hole'.[37]

The rapid progress of technological change in the inter-war years also led to an increase in piece-working, particularly in the 'new industry' areas. By 1940, sixty per cent of all workers in engineering were operating under one or another variant of payment-by-results, and this figure increased during the war.[38] Increasingly, only maintenance workers, toolmakers and others whose work was extremely difficult to quantify and whose resistance to piece-work was strong remained on time rates, and during the war many such workers moved on to rates related to the piece-workers with whom they worked. The spread of piece-work, in the context of localised shortages of labour and the introduction of new work on which 'loose' rates were often fixed, led in some areas to the steady upward 'drift' of earnings. The best example of this occurred in Coventry, where a large number of engineering firms were concentrated and employers bid against one another for labour. From Table 3 it is clear that inter-district differentials were growing, and they widened

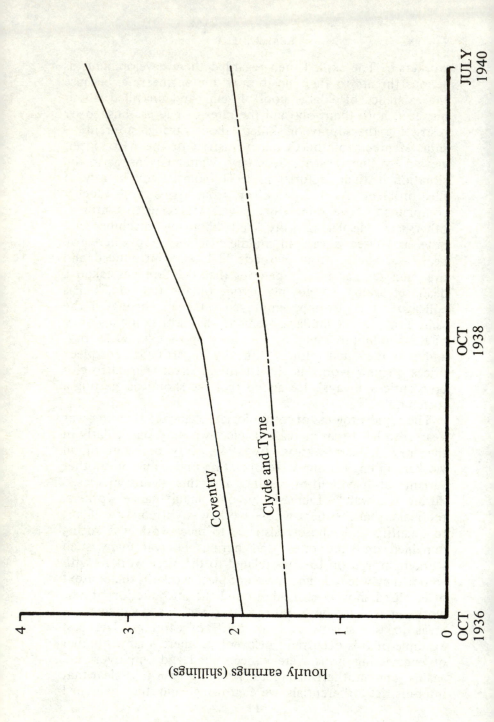

still further in wartime. The basic rate and the minimum piece-work earnings of twenty-five per cent above it were of much less interest to engineers in the South and Midlands than to those in Scotland and the North-East, an important contrast with great significance for the emphasis which workers in these areas put on national and local negotiations.

In 1938 the skilled fitter's earnings established him as a member of the aristocracy of labour; the average adult male was earning somewhere between £3 and £3.10s. a week at this time.[39] Even in the northern centres, the skilled men (assuming that they were in work, of course) were relatively prosperous when compared to other working people. Semi-skilled engineers, labourers and women (the Engineering Employers' Federation classified them in that order) were less well paid. London engineering labourers earned an average rate of 50s. 3d., for example.[40] But on the whole, workers throughout engineering were well up in the earnings league by the end of the 1930s.

Engineers' working conditions were also fairly typical of British industry during the period 1935-45; that is to say, they were by international standards poor. Even German and Italian workers, despite their lack of independent trade unions, often enjoyed higher standards of welfare. British engineers were not usually in a position to make direct comparisons, but trade-unionists often drew attention to the failure to maximise gains made during the First World War. While factory workers were generally prepared to allow that accidents were often difficult to avoid, they found the employers' approach to compensation and rehabilitation lacking in humanity. Injured workers, it was felt, were just a nuisance for employers. Hence the lack of provision for them in terms of compensation, insurance and light work. The only benefit an injured worker could be sure of was a 'whip-round' from his workmates. Treatment of the dead was thought to be little better. An ex-shipyard worker from Clydeside spoke to me with bitterness about a riveter who had fallen off the stocks to his death in the yard and whom the foreman had put on a cart, covered, and delivered without ceremony to his wife in a nearby house. To this man, the management's attitude was clear: dead riveters were of

13

no use to them.[41] Many managers would no doubt have vigorously rejected such accusations of callousness, but they were a very real part of workshop lore. When improvements did take place during the war in terms of welfare, canteens, nurseries, clinics and so on, it was very often not the employer but their own Ernie Bevin who derived the credit. Employers themselves gained very little from these changes in terms of the goodwill of their employees.

Technological change and an increased tempo of work were two of the factors which underpinned a consistently high accident rate in engineering. The industry had always been dangerous, although it had normally ranked behind coal-mining and building in terms of the human cost of production. In 1935 the metal industries as a whole had accounted for 18.3 per cent of all recorded industrial accidents, and the upturn in activity brought an increase both in the gross number of accidents and in the accident rate per worker.[42] The Chief Inspector of Factories ascribed this trend not only to the rusty skills of those re-entering factories after years of unemployment, but also to the indecent haste with which employers introduced new machinery, often before it was adequately fenced or guarded.[43] The degree of risk in different branches of engineering is shown in the Chief Inspector's reports. The figures—which are not entirely reliable guides to the volume of accidents, because of the persistent problem of under-reporting—show that the heavier occupations (locomotive-building, ordnance and munitions and marine engineering) carried a much greater risk than the lighter trades. This is perhaps understandable with tasks such as turning locomotive axles or marine propellor shafts under tremendous pressure, where one mistake could dislodge the enormous component from the lathe and even send it hurtling across the shop.[44] The electrical engineer could meet sudden death from an electrical shock, although on average he was only likely to be unable to earn full wages for three days (the period which constituted an official reportable accident) once in just under forty years. While locomotive engineering was the most dangerous trade, young workers were those most prone to accidents. By 1938 (when youth accident differentials had narrowed somewhat), young

14

persons under eighteen were seven per cent more likely to have an accident than adults.[45]

During the first half of the war, and especially in 1940, the accident rate increased alarmingly. Until 1944 the Chief Inspector stopped publishing comprehensive statistics similar to those published before the war, while the Royal Society for the Prevention of Accidents, who kept statistics for these years but who had been completely taken over by the Ministry of Labour, refused to release their figures when requested.[46] The Chief Inspector's reports do allow us to say, nonetheless, that during 1940 there was a gross increase in accidents of some forty per cent, that a disproportionate number of these were suffered by workers new to the industry, and that the upward trend in the gross number of accidents was not reversed until 1943.[47] The long hours worked by the 'green' labour flooding into the shops in the first half of the war proved expensive not only in terms of physical exhaustion but also in the number of accidents reported.

If the statistics for accidents are unreliable, those for health problems are almost non-existent. Only a very few diseases that were quite specific to certain trades were recognised for the purposes of state benefit, and these by no means reflected the health problems within the industry.[48] Moreover, some problems had long-term effects that could not be easily measured: in 1935 the report of the Chief Inspector expressed apprehension as to the ultimate effects of the widespread introduction of conveyors, with their largely unmeasurable strains on the whole human system.[49] No specific ailment could be directly attributed to working on them, but the stress and enervation induced were none the less real. Another widespread hazard was noise. The first impression on walking into a boiler- or press-shop was of an ear-shattering din, a state of affairs accepted by many as a fact of industrial life; but the problem of noise was a very general one, even in the comparatively quiet aircraft factories.[50] Stress-related ailments, as well as deafness, were the result. The steady introduction of more and more chemical substances also represented a considerable and little-recognised hazard. 'Dope' and chemical adhesives were widely used in aircraft-building for treating and gluing fabrics

15

and wooden components; pressings were anodised in chromic acid baths, which could produce chrome 'holes' in the flesh; cheap mineral oils were used universally as coolants, followed by toxic de-greasing agents and so on. Most such substances, despite the asphyxiation (from which one often rapidly 'recovered'), dermatitis and cancer which they could cause, were effectively ignored by legislation, with the result that the associated ailments increased. In the case of the very common dermatitis, which was notified to the Factory Inspectorate on a purely voluntary basis (a system which invited employers to encourage visits from the Inspectors), there was a steady rise in the number of cases notified in the late 1930s.[51] These problems were to become even more acute during the war, and were an important cause of discontent amongst the women who came into the industry in those years.

In common with almost all other manual workers in the early 1930s, engineers had very little respite from their arduous work during the summer. Holidays with pay were virtually unknown in industry, and trade unionists called summer shutdowns 'lockouts' because wages were so low that engineers clamoured to be allowed to work in these periods. This was one of the issues taken up by the shop stewards in the years 1935-37, with the result that the engineering employers conceded the principle of holidays with pay during the 1937 national negotiations, thereby allowing well organised factories to push for more. This was an important step forward, although wartime holidays were of course very restricted. In the long run, engineering workers would not have to anticipate their 'lockouts' with foreboding, but could look forward to them with some limited amount of financial security.[52]

Workers' general welfare, both inside and outside of working hours, had started to interest a minority of 'progressive' engineering employers immediately after the First World War. Before 1914 very few British employers since Owen had made any provision for their employees' welfare outside of work, but after state encouragement during the war a number—and especially those employing large numbers of women—had begun to take an interest. This interest was

16

fostered and developed by journals like *Industrial Welfare* and *Labour Management,* which advocated more sensitivity to labour as a unique commodity, while looking favourably on the Italian *Dopolavoro* and later the German *Kraft Durch Freude* movements. As a result, the number of medical departments, rest rooms, factory libraries, sports clubs and so on probably increased slowly between the wars. Nevertheless, these remained small-scale developments. Perhaps the most important changes occurred in the late 1930s, when the increased demand for labour in the Midlands and South led many employers building new factories to specify canteens and playing fields in their plans. In 1939, for example, *Industrial Welfare* published a typical picture of a rather clinical-looking canteen recently built at Vickers' Weybridge factory: it occupied the whole of the first floor of a large building, seated three thousand, and apparently served a good choice of meals with a full lunch costing a shilling.[53] Nurseries were very rare before the war: by 1938 there were only one hundred and four in the whole of Britain, very few of them run by employers.[54] During the war, as his biographer Alan Bullock has made known, Ernest Bevin's appointment as Minister of Labour made a considerable difference to the quantity and quality of nurseries for the children of munitions workers. He appreciated this need very quickly: arriving at the Ministry in May 1940, Bevin soon so impressed his lieutenants Gould and Leggett with the need to develop a comprehensive system of nurseries that they surprised their colleagues at the Ministry of Health by their 'emphatic' insistence only a few weeks later on Bevin's willingness to join with them in an application for Treasury funds.[55] By 1942 Bevin's name was intimately linked with nursery provision. Nevertheless, as with many wartime improvements, the reality was not as rosy as it was painted, and the contrast with the pre-war situation was the most flattering perspective to adopt.[56] Nurseries were conceived of as a temporary measure and were under the responsibility of local authorities rather than attached to factories; in fact, most children of war workers never saw the inside of one.[57]

The Factories Act of 1937, which came into force in July of that year, was hailed by some contemporaries as ushering in a new era in workplace health, safety and welfare, a viewpoint shared by some historians.[58] The Act, the first full consolidation and revision of minimum standards enacted since 1901, did bring the law rather more into line with the actual industrial conditions of the late 1930s. New sections covered several important matters that were not dealt with at all in the 1901 Act:[59] the construction and sale of new machinery, the training and supervision of young persons working dangerous machinery, the condition of ropes, chains and lifting tackle, precautions to be taken where dangerous fumes were present, the supply of drinking water, washing facilities, clothing, accommodation, the protection of eyes, and so on. This impressive list of areas in which the new legislation intervened for the first time had, according to the Chief Inspector of Factories, made the 1937 Act better-known than its predecessor[60] to trade-unionists and factory occupiers alike. In fact, however, the effects of the new Factories Act were probably more long- than short-term, because its approach was more piecemeal and persuasive than general and punitive. Discrete problems were discerned from which a whole range of exemptions could be granted, rather than general duties laid down (as in some earlier legislation and the Health and Safety at Work Act of 1975). Many accidents were therefore simply not covered by the Act; one official of ROSPA estimated in 1942 that three quarters of the total number of accidents were not covered because they involved handling goods, falls, hand tools, collisions and falling objects.[61] In any case, the penalties allowed for in the Act were low: the maximum fine for any offence was £100.[62] The three hundred and twenty factory inspectors of all grades in the country had to put up an excellent case to justify the maximum fine: in 1938 the average fine for breach of regulations causing death or injury was just under £18.[63] It is hardly surprising, then, that serious problems remained. The protection of eyes, a particular problem in engineering, where swarf and tiny metallic particles flying off work at high speed in close proximity to the operator's face were commonplace, is a good example. Dr Minton, an eminent industrial oculist, estimated in early 1941 that some quarter of a million eyes were injured each year in British industry.[64] Even allowing for a certain amount of professional hyperbole, the estimate is a staggering one. In another article, Minton argued that a large part of the problem was not (as employers often contended) 'carelessness', but the fact that goggles and visors, even when supplied, were not 'suitable' as required under the 1937 Act and were therefore discarded.[65] Swarf in the eye (usually picked out by a mate), castings and tools falling on the toes, and a touch of deafness, were facts of workshop life, as those entering the industry were soon to find.

Improving these conditions was a slow process and in many cases still continues today. Their existence is the all-important background to an understanding of the engineering workers' position. These risks were part of being an engineer: this was what was implied in the workshop saying that you were not a fitter until you had lost a finger. But it should not be supposed that this statement implied a passive acceptance of injury. Many thought that the responsibility for death and injury at work lay with the employer, and looked to unionisation to curb his power. As workers at Briggs' Bodies wrote to the TUC in 1937:

> One poor fellow was crushed to death last night owing to the anarchy prevailing in methods of work. Men and women are so afraid of losing their bread and butter that they dash about here and there without any regard for the safety of themselves or any others, this was how the man was killed, he was crushed by an overhead crane, the crane man had to hustle so fast, that he had no time to look out for anyone who might be in the way. We are crying out for organisation. . .[66]

The Briggs' workers' statement implied a sophisticated analysis of the underlying causes of accidents, which focused on the pressure for production rather than on the individual worker, and linked this with the need for effective union organisation. Many other workers coming into the industry in wartime were to come to similar conclusions, as we shall see.

Workplace trade union organisation had always been central to craft unionism in engineering, from the middle of the nineteenth century. The Amalgamated Society of Engineers (ASE), the proud 'New Model' union founded in 1851, had no full-time officers in the modern sense of permanent paid officials; its strength lay not so much in its national presence, important though this was, as in its ability to ensure that only time-served men who were earning the full district rate worked at the trade. This had to be enforced, if it was to be effective, in the shops themselves. The national union was only useful, the engineers argued, to the extent that it reflected the needs of the craftsmen in the localities, who claimed a determining voice in the ASE by dint of their status as journeymen. The ASE was a highly democratic union, with an Executive which was late to develop as a central authority and which could always be overruled in individual questions by a Final Appeal Court elected directly from the rank and file. Its membership was used to electing workshop deputations to take matters up with the masters, and expected a full participative democracy within their own union.

During the 1890s the employers launched a serious techno-logical drive to modernise their plant under the pressure of foreign competition. Repetition machines such as capstan lathes and new types of milling and grinding machines were brought into the workshops, with significant effects on the traditional skills of the turner. This put severe pressure on the craftsmen's policy of restricting the supply of labour by keeping non-skilled men off 'their' machines, and was accompanied by a managerial offensive which culminated in the national lockout of 1898. The ASE's delegate meeting accordingly accepted a motion designed to strengthen work-place organisation by allowing shop stewards to be elected within the shops, under the local direction of the District Committees.[67] At first the shop stewards did little more than collect subscriptions, but they gradually began to take up a wide range of issues and to become a force in the union. But while the shop stewards were beginning to grow in numbers and strength, the ASE's Executive became weaker, as a result of the terms of settlement of 1898 which laid down for the first time a national Procedure for the Avoidance of Disputes. This procedure specified the stages which negotiations had to pass through before any strike action could become 'constitutional' and the Executive saw it initially as the best way of negotiating with the employers, given the setbacks suffered after the 1898 lockout. Several districts disagreed violently in the years before 1914, and this led to important strikes in which the District Committees and shop stewards condemned the supposed collaboration of their Executives with the employers and argued for 'local autonomy' in determining trade policy.[68]

With the introduction of new technology, the First World War brought a tremendous increase in the rate of dilution of the traditional skills, and in these years the shop steward system flowered into a widespread response to the massive new problems faced by the engineers. Through their local and national organisations, the shop stewards became a power within the factories well before their official recognition by the engineering employers in an agreement of 1919. The stewards led a rising craft militancy which stood for the maintenance of their relatively privileged position within the industry and their immunity as skilled men from conscription, but they had increasingly to come to terms with two major developments. The first was the factor which had helped to stimulate their growth: the tendency to integrate their Executive in the national war machine, which led to a sharpening of the clashes between the shop stewards and the Executive already evident before the war. The other was the fact that craft trade-unionism in engineering had been deeply undermined by technological progress. In particular, their refusal to admit semi-skilled men and still less women to their ranks led to the growth of the Workers' Union and the National Federation of Women Workers within the engineering industry.

It was only in the face of disaster, and then without enthusiasm, that the Amalgamated Engineering Union (as the ASE became by amalgamation with some other craft societies in 1920) decided to admit semi-skilled men in 1927. The traditions of craft trade-unionism died hard, despite the unionisation of many of the semi-skilled workers during the First World War, and many engineers continued to look on the non-skilled workers with a mixture of nine parts

Engineering Union

AMALGAMATED SOCIETY OF ENGINEERS.

This is to Certify that the Beaver, | If State Approved insert Reg. No.

following the occupation of ___ Branch

was admitted a member of ___

Class ___ in accordance with Rule No. ___ on the ___

day of ___, at the age of ___ years and

___ months, and is now a member of Class ___ to which

he was transferred on the ___ day of ___ 19 .

He is entitled to the following Benefits ___

as per Rule No. ___

He was then* ___ *married and is now* ___ married.

He has been granted this card by consent of the ___

Branch or Branch

Officers, as provided by rule, on the ___

day of ___

IN WITNESS WHEREOF we have subscribed our Names and affixed the Seal of our Branch.

PRESIDENT.

SECRETARY.

* If single insert "un" before the word "married."

This card must be signed by the President, or Vice-President, and the Secretary; likewise the member on travel.

Member's Signature

SEAL.

If previously on Travel, state here No. of Card [ ]

6

## DECLARATION IN CASE OF DEATH.

This is to certify that ___

has signed a Declaration Form dated the ___

day of ___ 1 , and

No.'d ___ in the Declaration Book of

the ___ Branch, in the presence of Witnesses, autho-

rising the payment of all money due to

him from the Society at his death to

___ residing

at ___

___ Secretary.

REGISTRATION SEAL

AEU membership card from early 1920s, showing deleted Amalgamated Society of Engineers heading condescension to one part fear. This fear was exacerbated after the Executive's old nightmare of another national lock-out was realised in 1922. After this disastrous thirteen-week lockout, substantial wage cuts were inflicted, and AEU membership dropped by twenty-five per cent on the 1920 total.[69] Effective shop steward activity was largely extinguished, as the lockout had provided the employers with an ideal opportunity to re-employ selectively. The employers could be well satisfied, because they had re-established their 'right to manage' and need brook no 'interference' in the running of their factories. Engineers showing signs of discontent could simply be shown the door. Within the unions the Executive became stronger in relation to their membership, as all had to huddle together in the cold wind of the employers' offensive. As union membership dropped, Executives amalgamated with other unions, creating more developed official structures. The classic example was the Transport and General Workers' Union (TGWU), which was formed by the amalgamation of a large number of unions including the Workers' Union, whose engineering membership had slumped almost to vanishing point prior to the amalgamation.

Life on the shop floor had become extremely difficult for trade-unionists by the end of 1922, and the defeat of the General Strike made it even harder. It was a brave man indeed who would try to negotiate under the circumstances, and the atmosphere in the workshops was one of fear. There is very little documentary evidence relating to what went on in the factories in these years, but a notebook kept by the conscientious Coventry District Secretary of the AEU, Walter Givens, has survived. It contains a survey which he carried out to discover the state of the union in the relatively prosperous Midland town's engineering shops in 1930, and shows just how difficult things had become. The members interviewed in the comparatively buoyant motor, cycle or related engineering trades reported that at best there were 154 members among the nine hundred eligible to join in their areas.[70] Only two of the many interviewed responded favourably to Givens' question about the possibility of electing a steward, and not one existing steward was mentioned. The response of H.J. McElvey from Armstrong-Siddeley was typical: 'He was not in favour and reasons given were that you can't trust the men, even amongst our own members you do not know who you are talking to.'[71] Such was the distrust in the engineering factories. Workers' solidarity had been broken and trade-unionists isolated from the majority and even from one another by the threat of the sack.

Givens' notebook gives a clue to the survival of slightly more substantial organisation in one particular factory employed on a different type of work. This was at Armstrong-Whitworth Aircraft's factory at Baginton, in the countryside to the south of Coventry. The aircraft industry was marginally better off than the rest of engineering, and the demand for skilled labour still quite high. But even this sector could not entirely escape the common problems. Minutes of a meeting held at the AEU offices to elect shop stewards for the works in 1930 recorded an attendance of some forty members. In Givens' opinion, to give adequate coverage seventeen stewards should have been elected, but only eight were in fact prepared to accept the risk that went with a shop steward's card. On the detail section, for example, brothers Martin, Ingram and Ward were nominated, but the first two declined and, despite an appeal to the meeting, nobody could be persuaded to help the experienced J.H. Ward (the ex-President of the Coventry Minority Movement) in the considerable task of representing one hundred and eighty men and boys.[72] Nevertheless, the mere fact of electing those shop stewards was more than could be achieved at most factories. Only a high proportion of skilled men and a relatively prosperous industry could support such levels of organisation, which were elsewhere impossible.[73] To be known as a steward—some tried to operate secretly, just collecting subscriptions and fighting quiet rearguard actions in a whole range of subterranean ways—was to court dismissal. For many engineers, trade union membership had been reduced to the maintenance of a habit, and branch meetings to a persistent and quietly defiant routine.

Most employers and managers were only too pleased to see the restoration of the 'right to manage', but there was a small minority who thought that some system of workplace representation should be allowed to exist so long as it increased the management's ability to communicate effectively with the workforce. These managers shrewdly perceived ways in which shop stewards could be made into something approaching an arm of management itself. The militant engineers' bulletin *The Engineer* claimed in 1927 that the Vickers shop stewards had been the victims of such wiles, and that the stewards had become simply 'go-betweens'.[74] It seems likely that a similar situation existed at Leyland's Lancashire factory. At first sight it is surprising to see the shop stewards' committee there printing a glossy journal in 1927, until we read the introduction, written by the managing director and complimenting the stewards on the fact that no serious matters of contention had been discussed in the past year.[75] Some employers had works committees which performed a similar function to these shop stewards. The railway companies, who had some experience in shaping systems of workplace representation to their own ends, had such joint worker-management 'asking machines', as one manager called them, which proved highly effective managerial tools.[76] These systems were current in 'progressive' managerial circles during the 1930s; contributors to *Industrial Welfare* stressed the usefulness of shop stewards in solving production problems and creating 'good morale'—providing, one such writer was at pains to point out, that the managers were always thanked for their concessions; otherwise relations might be soured.[77] Nevertheless, they remained the theories of a minority, ridiculed (as they themselves admitted) by most production managers and foremen.

From about the beginning of 1934 there was a real change in the nature and tone of industrial relations in the engineering industry. Uneven and hesitant as it was, it was nonetheless quite noticeable. The effect of seeing old mates, even in ones and twos, coming back into the shops, was out of all proportion to the numbers involved. The iron workshop discipline of the previous few years, when it was not unheard of for men to be sacked for laughing at work, slowly began to dissipate. Smoking in the shops began to be allowed again, a more liberal attitude was taken towards spoilt work, and workers were allowed more choice over which shifts they worked. This thaw in the workshop regime did not occur uniformly: there were some factories where discipline did not relax at all until the war, and sometimes only slightly then. So much depended on the factory's particular traditions, economic position and size that it is difficult to generalise, but in many shops internal relations were beginning to change. This could be partly attributed to a more assertive mood on the part of the working engineers as the labour market improved slightly. The old traditions had clearly lurked only just beneath the surface and required only a very little encouragement to bring them out. A resurgence of independent trade union activity was a feature of these years in many industries: in the miners' struggles against company unionism, in the revival of the rank and file movements amongst busmen which had clung on since the end of the First World War, as well as in the docks and building trades. In the engineering industry it took the form of a renaissance of the shop steward system. From the beginning it was clear that the impetus came from the rank and file themselves, who were determined to have independent representation free from all managerial influence. An attentive managerial student of shop steward activity wrote of the newly elected shop stewards at his northern factory that they 'shewed a deplorable lack of tact in negotiations', because of the pressure they were under from their members. The shop stewards, he said, '. . . had frequently to meet and rebut accusations of weakness and even treachery; in many situations they found they had to change the outlook of their fellow-workers, a task they found very difficult. Occasionally, they feared the workers they represented'.[78] The author of the article thought that the stewards were 'weak' when questioned by their members about their progress in discussions with management, and saw the problem as a lack of verbal skills on their part. He does not seem to have fully understood (though as a meticulous observer he actually recorded it) the stewards' members' fierce wish that their representative should actually represent them and not be a 'go-between' or 'gaffer's messenger'. It was precisely because of this fierce wish that the shop stewards could become effective advocates of their members' grievances.

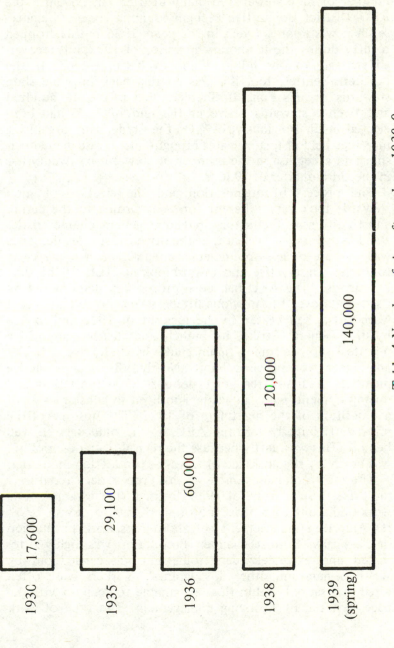

Table 4 *Number of aircraft workers, 1930–9*

1930    17,600

1935    29,100

1936    60,000

1938    120,000

1939
(spring)    140,000

Pressure from below led to the election of an increasing number of shop stewards in many districts. In Coventry the AEU District Committee recognised an average of eighty-seven new stewards a year in the years 1935-7; this dropped to fifty during the temporary recession of 1938, but recovered strongly to one hundred and twelve in 1939.[79] In the northern centres, too, life was coming back into the shop stewards' organisations. In Sheffield, fifty of the one hundred and twenty stewards active at the end of 1936 had been elected in the previous year.[80] On the Clyde, daily organising meetings held at factory gates brought an increase in membership and a net rise in the number of stewards by twenty-five in the third quarter of 1936.[81]

The process of organisation and the election of shop stewards took very different forms according to the nature and traditions of the factory, but some general characteristics stand out. First, it is clear that the drive for specific demands was a more or less spontaneous one, which in many cases took the conservative and inward-looking AEU of the time by surprise. The AEU had been profoundly demoralised by its defeats over the previous fifteen years. Forced to accept wage cuts, then beaten in the lockout of 1922 and rocked by the General Strike, its branch and district committee minutes show a union maintained by defensive tenacity and sheer working-class habit. Nearly all its most active members had suffered long periods of victimisation and unemployment, while its leadership lived in constant fear of a repetition of the nightmare of 1922. The upsurge of the mid-1930s initially left the AEU, at the official level, well behind. This was partly because the revival of trade-unionism was begun by the unskilled of the mass production industries.

The most notable example of this process occurred during the Pressed Steel strike of 1934. Pressed Steel established its works adjacent to Morris' motor works at Cowley in 1928. Its American management set about presswork production in classically 'Fordist' manner. Production was highly automated and extremely dangerous, and was carried out by Welsh miners and other 'immigrants'. Workers were often hired and sacked within the day, unable to keep up with the pace required by a driving management. The type of work involved did not in general need the skills of the AEU man, who could often find work at Morris' works on the other side of the road. When the revolt came, it was the TGWU who were the beneficiaries.

The immediate cause of the strike was the short wages paid to men in the press shop, although the difficulty of getting compensation for accidents was also an important issue. The strikers were men from the depressed areas, with a high proportion of ex-Welsh miners, together with the women in the shop. They demanded minimum earnings of 1s. 8d. per hour, and the right to shop steward representation. The strikers elected their own deputation to see the management, but initially to no avail.[82] Mass meetings were held at which hundreds of TGWU forms were filled in, while a broadsheet entitled *The Conveyor,* described by the *Oxford Mail* as 'the organ of the TGWU', was issued.[83] The TGWU seized with both hands the opportunity presented to them, paying strike pay despite the fact that the overwhelming majority of the strikers were not, strictly speaking, entitled to it.[84] Speakers were sent to all the motor firms in Britain; workers at a Chiswick factory sent cash for the strike fund, the Firestone union branch sent a message of support and money, collections were taken after a mass meeting of railway workers at Swindon, mass meetings were addressed at Fords and Briggs' Bodies with promises of support, while a number of workers at the unorganised Morris Motors just across the road at Cowley promised to lead a strike there if Morris supplied blackleg labour.[85] While the TGWU was in the thick of this ferment of activity, the AEU and the National Union of Vehicle Builders declared the strike 'unconstitutional'.[86] It is hardly surprising, then, that the TGWU established its first major stronghold in the motor industry when the Pressed Steel strikers won their dispute.[87] The 'unorganisable' mass of semi-skilled workers—super-exploited in the 'slave shop', the 'coolies' of their own leaflets, Welshmen and local women alike—had made a major breakthrough. By March 1938 there were forty TGWU shop stewards at Pressed Steel, representing some two and a half thousand members.[88] In November 1938 the management counter-attacked by sacking Tom Harris, the TGWU convenor, for 'insubordination', and the craft unions regained some ground when, although a strike for his reinstatement failed, the first crucial step had been taken.[89] The initiative had come from the rank and file, and the TGWU had been quick to respond.

The Oxford strikers were mostly Welsh, Scottish and Irish workers who had travelled to Pressed Steel to find work. They were separated from the AEU and NUVB men by their background as well as by their work. A management document of 1938 shows that at that time there were twenty-three TGWU shop stewards, whose average length of service with the company was fifty-six months. The biographies of three new stewards on the Morris 8 section are quite revealing:

E.A. O'Neill. 3, Gidley Hill, Horspath, Oxford. Aged 32 years. Married. Commenced with this company on the 27th January 1931 as a sanitation attendant, and was employed continuously until 22nd January 1932, when he was suspended owing to shortage of work. Reinstated on the 14th October 1933 as a polisher on the Composite Door Section, and has been employed practically continuously since that date, apart from short periods owing to low schedules. He is at present employed as an operator in the Morris 8 section. This man is a native of Glasgow, and was employed as a polisher at Morris Radiators for two years prior to joining this company.

Wm. Thos. Owen. 71, Bailey Rd., Cowley, Oxford. Aged 29 years. Married. Is a native of Neath, Glamorgan. Has been employed continuously in the Morris 8 section as a straightener since 3rd September 1934. This man was obtained from the Aldershot Training Centre, being an ex-Army Vacational [sic] student.

Trevor Rees. 9, Benson Rd., Headington, Oxford. Aged 34 years. Single. Native of Swansea. Originally commenced with this Company as a straightener learner on the 3rd June 1931, and was so employed until 9th December 1933, when he was suspended owing to shortage of work. He was reinstated on the 31st October 1934, and worked practically continuously until the 12th May 1935, when he was suspended on the closing down of the 4-door Morris 8 HP Conveyor, Night Shift. Finally reinstated on the 19th August 1935, and has been employed continuously since that date.[90]

All three of the TGWU stewards were typical, in that they were in their late twenties or early thirties and came from Wales and Scotland. Two of them had suffered considerable insecurity of employment, and all of them were engaged on semi-skilled work. These were hardly the type of time-served, often local, men who ran the AEU and NUVB. Here was a rank and file who had been treated as disposable menials, to be hired and fired as required, and who had reasserted the trade union traditions of their towns of origin just as soon as economic circumstances allowed it.

The Pressed Steel strike also demonstrated the vital importance of the left, which was characteristic of many of these organising strikes of the mid-1930s. The key personality on the left was Abe Lazarus. Lazarus, nicknamed 'Firestone' for his part in the dispute at that factory in the previous year, was an excellent speaker and member of the CP, whose experience on the Great West Road stood him in good stead in this type of dispute. His understanding of tactics was of great assistance to the strikers, who had come out without any well laid plans; he and his comrades worked day and night to get support for the Pressed Steel workers, helping with the broadsheets, with picketing and with the business of the strike committee.[91] Lazarus could not be called typical, but the involvement of the left was a common feature of strikes of these years. The development of important rank and file movements in the late 1930s, with their own papers such as *The Conveyor* and *New Propellor,* owed much to their influence.

In some factories shop steward organisation was established without strike action. At Siemens electrical engineering works in South-East London, with some five thousand employees, the largest factory in the South East, the left began to organise the plant through the imaginative tactics which so often characterised their agitation. Charlie Wellard, then a CP member in his mid-twenties working in the toolroom, contacted the existing stewards who were 'sleeping' in the early 1930s, who would then latch on to a particular issue when it arose. Short-time working gave them their opportunity. Apprehensive as to how to present the introduction of short time, the management agreed to Wellard's proposal to produce a leaflet on the assurance that it would state management's explanations. The leaflet was produced by Wellard and others and posted in every shop, arousing such interest that workers fought each other to see it.

The leaflet announced a meeting, attended by some two thousand workers. Charlie Wellard, 'scared out of my wits', stood up and stated the management's reasons for short-time working, then, growing in confidence as he spoke, introduced a man called Owen. Owen had a large family, it was explained, and could not afford to feed them and pay the rent on what he would earn. This signalled the end of the meeting: the workforce was in uproar. Wellard remembers that 'the management thought that the revolution had started'. One week later, short time was ended and hundreds had been recruited into the union 'while they were still warm'. Within a short time the stewards were producing a very professional journal, with a circulation which eventually reached some three thousand; they played an active role in the apprentices' strike of 1937 and in lobbying Parliament for holidays with pay. Soon after, by linking up with their fellow stewards in Johnson and Philips', Elliot's, Harvey's, Pitter's Tool and Gauge and others, they formed an unofficial South-East London shop stewards' organisation, issuing regular leaflets that reached not only their members but others in the community at large. By 1937 they were distributing copies of leaflets like *Message to South East London Housewives,* pointing out the need for paid holidays and for women to support the boys then on strike, and making themselves into what Charlie Wellard called a 'public institution'. The South-East London shop stewards set up a 'travelling improvements committee' to deal with the problems faced by working people not only at work but also with landlords and councillors, and pressurised MPs and the trade unions to take up both individual cases and wide issues. Their correspondence and literature give the impression of trade-unionism reaching out of the workshop and into the working class in a way that in turn strengthened their factory work.[92]

The Communist shop stewards of the 1930s like Charlie Wellard rapidly became extremely important within the factory trade union movement, becoming convenors, senior shop stewards and so on. This was partly because they had proved so effective in building the shop steward system in the first place; they had been prepared to go where wiser men feared to tread and had reaped the reward. It was also because the shop steward system was completely 'open': in the very early stages of its development after the Depression, there were no well established hierarchies within which one had to operate for years before being considered as a candidate for the convenor's job. In many factories those who wanted the job could have it. The left-wingers did not 'infiltrate' the shop floor organisation; rather, they grew with it, at its head.

Despite the popular image of shop stewards developed from the First World War and derived from the press portrait of them, most did not feel particularly confident in their ability to negotiate with management. One manager wrote of shop stewards in his factory in somewhat patronising terms—which nevertheless reflected the cultural differences between himself and the stewards in question—that they (the shop stewards) admitted they were hampered 'by inadequate vocabularies, and by inexperience of conditions outside of their own firm', and felt that they needed training in negotiating skills.[93] But the generation of shop stewards elected in the 1930s had very little opportunity for formal trade union education outside of the occasional summer school. Nor did they have any established facilities, precedents or agreements to work from, so that it was not unusual for stewards to be intimidated by feelings of inadequacy when speaking to management above the level of foreman. This was rather less true of the left-wingers among them. Whatever their other shortcomings, they at least had an idea of their role derived from their political affiliations. Where others found the opposing pressures of management and their members difficult to reconcile, they unequivocally defined themselves as workers' representatives. Moreover, they often possessed skills which were rarely acquired outside of political parties. Trade-unionists who had served a political and agitational apprenticeship in the Labour Party, the Communist Party or the National Unemployed Workers' Movement (NUWM) were often able to speak in public, write leaflets and conduct the sort of close argument frequently needed in negotiations.

Indeed, many of the Communist activists in particular had very impressive credentials in these respects. They were frequently highly skilled men, and this gave them a strong advantage in establishing themselves both amongst their fellows and with the management. They had very often been brought up in left-wing families and were married to like-minded women. This domestic element was especially important. Trade union activity always meant evenings and weekends outside of the home, and often entailed financial insecurity; here the crucial role of shop stewards' families could hardly be overstated. They were also sustained by their contacts with other trade-unionists inside and outside their own workplace. A whole book could be written on this subject. In many areas groups of left-wing shop stewards emerged informally during the late 1930s; some idea of the sort of individuals involved can be gained by briefly looking at the records of a few of the left-wing engineers active in the Manchester district at this time. Similar pictures could also be painted for Coventry, London, Sheffield and other areas.

Many of the activists in the Manchester area spent a lifetime in the labour movement. Bill Abbott, for example, a patternmaker member of the AEU, joined the Communist Party in 1926 and became active in the Openshaw branch of the NUWM in 1928. He later found work at A.V. Roe's Newton Heath factory, where he worked closely with Ernie Jones, a CP sheet metal worker, and won the TUC's Tolpuddle badge for recruiting five hundred workers into the union. One of the few men willing to stand up to the formidable Roy Dobson, works manager and old colleague of A.V. Roe himself, he was eventually sacked, later to become convenor of the important Metro-Vickers factory. Bill Abbott remains active although now retired.[94] One of his contemporaries was Arthur Walmsley, one of three brothers active in Manchester industry in this period. Said to be a 'very highly skilled tradesman', Arthur was one of a whole family of trade-unionists who had been active in the CP since the early 1920s. He found work at Gardners in 1933, which he played a part in the long fight to organise, eventually becoming chairman of the works committee there.[95] Eddie Frow, now a well known labour historian, was then a toolmaker who had joined the CP in Leeds in 1924. In 1930 he visited

Russia to work with the Communist International, and on his return became a member of the NUWM. By 1938 he had recruited a large number of workers to the union at Salford Electrical Instruments, and was shop stewards' representative on the Manchester District Committee of the AEU.[96] Such men, all in their late twenties or early thirties, had already accumulated a good deal of experience within the labour movement, and were soon branded by managements as 'agitators' and 'troublemakers'.

Although the managerial view tended to minimise the real grievances among their workers, there was some basis for the often expressed view that the Communist Party was 'behind' shop steward organisation. Ever since its 'Bolshevisation' in the early 1920s, the CP had placed much more emphasis on the importance of organising workers at the point of production than had the Labour Party. The workplace was all-important in Communist theory as the place where workers' sense of collective interest reached its peak, and it had a centrality in their thinking comparable to that of Parliament in Labour Party theory. From 1935 the CP began to adopt policies and a rhetoric which made it much easier for them to work together with and influence members of the Labour Party, Cripps' Socialist League, the waning Independent Labour Party (ILP) and other left groups. Putting the harsh sectarianism of the earlier 'class against class' period behind them, they worked towards the building of the widest possible unity to defeat the apparently inexorable progress of fascism. The local Labour Party activists (many of whom were also active in the engineering unions) were prepared to join with them to this end, especially after the re-election of the 'National' government in 1935. In the summer of 1937, when the journal *The Aeroplane* 'exposed' a 'cell' operating within De Havilland's Edgware aircraft works, they claimed that there were nine Communists in the cell, with a group of ten left sympathisers comprising members of the ILP, the Socialist League and the left of the Labour Party, and four 'IWW types' who were prepared to work with the others in industrial action.[97] Despite the hostility of our source, it would seem likely that *The Aeroplane* was about right, despite its dark murmurings about 'enemy influences' and so on. The CP activists had seized the initiative in the aircraft industry in particular, and were able to influence fellow stewards in industrial matters while other political organisations offered no serious industrial perspectives.

The CP's political influence was not generally attributable to any very widespread support amongst engineering workers for what the party stood for; in so far as they recruited workers' political sympathy, it was more a matter of what they so effectively campaigned *against*. By the late 1930s it was becoming appallingly clear that fascism represented a very real and militant threat to peace and to workers' rights to organise themselves politically and industrially. In some areas, like South Wales and the East End, the CP and anti-fascism became almost indistinguishable and developed into popular movements reminiscent of similar ones in France and Spain. But even in these areas a good deal of the CP's support was built on the solid foundations of agitation within actual battles in 'The Fed' (the South Wales Miners' Federation) and in the rent strikes endemic in the East End. These battles were the base on which political consciousness was built. To participate one did not need to agree with Communist politics, although one was liable to be exposed to them in due course. Indeed, it was quite possible to be involved in these discrete struggles without being at all in sympathy with Communist politics. Just after the beginning of the war, for example, Quintin Hogg wrote to the *Oxford Mail* to complain that the CP-controlled NUWM would gain from the formation of an unemployed association in 'the other Oxford'. A member of the association wrote in reply:

> I am as bitterly opposed to the people he mentions politically as himself, but they are apparently honourable men whose sole aim in this matter is to be of service to their fellows who have fallen on evil days, which is to their credit, and I and others not of the same faith have no hesitation in associating ourselves with them in our effort to provide employment.[98]

If this applied to the organisation of the unemployed (always considered a 'dangerous' political matter), it applied even more in the confines of the workshop, where social relations were less public.

The influence of the CP amongst the shop stewards largely depended on how far it was able to relate to the industrial needs of those stewards and the members whom they represented. The CP had always been in favour of linking up shop stewards from the various plants within a concern and of developing district and national organisations of shop stewards, on the grounds that this would strengthen trade union organisations. As we have already seen, shop stewards themselves felt that they needed to know more of conditions in other factories—comparison was very often the mother of negotiation. The AEU Executive, on the other hand, was firmly opposed to unofficial action of any sort, and in particular, to stewards linking up across districts. The union was just beginning to emerge from a difficult period in which membership had fallen, and precipitate action might provoke the employers into another 1922 lockout. In any case, shop stewards were under rule responsible to their District Committees; to whom would they be responsible in bodies which transcended districts?[99]

These conflicts were to be a feature of engineering in general throughout the next decade and beyond, but they occurred initially and most significantly within the aircraft industry. In aircraft, the industrial climate was again beginning to favour effective trade union organisation, and it was in that branch of engineering that the CP set out to found a movement of shop stewards. They did this by building on the needs of a group of aircraft workers who were actually on strike, and extending their intervention through the base thereby established.

On Saturday 9 March 1935, seven hundred of the workers at Hawker's Brockworth factory, members of the AEU, stood in a field in a bitterly cold wind to hear a report from the shop stewards on the progress made during the first day of their strike. Their demands for the removal of a non-unionist from their department, for an increase in pay and for the abolition of the long-hated 'premium bonus' system were, they had decided, to be upheld until they were met by the management.[100] Already, by dint of careful preparation by the CP members, the shop stewards were able to report that the Hawker factory at Kingston was prepared to come out

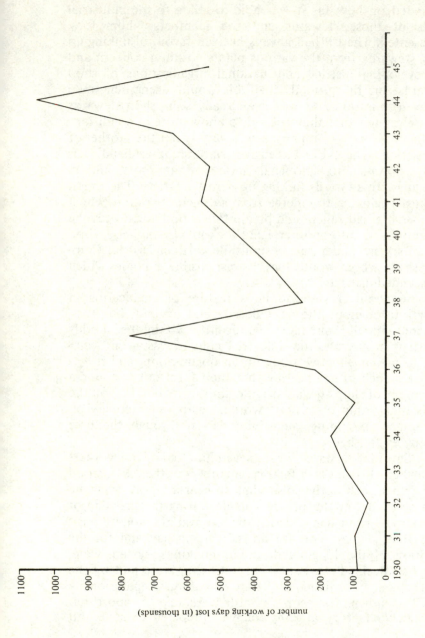

Table 5 *Stoppages of work in metal, engineering and shipbuilding industries, 1930–45*

on strike with them for similar demands.[101] Over the week-end the shop stewards circularised all the aircraft factories in the country to ask for financial support, and met the stewards from Kingston to discuss tactics.[102] On Monday 11th, the strikers' ranks were swelled by many other workers at Gloucester. The women were addressed by the Women's Organiser of the TGWU, and many of the remaining non-unionists stopped work and joined the union.[103] The strike was tightening up organisation, and regular mass meetings were held to keep the members informed of developments. On Wednesday 13 March then, the strikers must have been surprised to hear that the Executive Council of the AEU was advising its members to return to work so that a works conference could be held under the Procedure for the Avoidance of Disputes. The Brockworth AEU members stayed out on the advice of their stewards, and were joined the next day by just under half of the Kingston factory.[104] Meanwhile, the Bath branch of the NUWM gave its support and affirmed its opposition to blacklegging, and on the following Monday 'excellent' financial support was claimed by the shop stewards, contributions having been raised from many aircraft factories.[105] On the Tuesday, management agreed to meet three stewards from Brockworth, together with three from Kingston, thereby apparently conceding the principle of joint negotiations.[106] This meeting reached no agreement, as the management argued that they were power-less to ensure that a man joined the union.[107] On Wednesday 20 March the Executive Council of the AEU sent some of its members down to a mass meeting at Brockworth to argue for a return. They were prevented from entering the meeting by pickets, but on the Friday the stewards reported that they had agreed to a works conference immediately after a return to work, as the non-unionist had left, and the management had agreed to allow everyone to go back to work together (instead of in stages, as they had claimed production required); an immediate works conference was to be held on the other grievances. The stewards at Brockworth and Kingston re-commended acceptance, and mass meetings at the two factories accepted unanimously.[108]

Although the Brockworth strike had ended without all of

the strikers' objectives being obtained, it had important results. The trade union membership rose from seventy per cent to almost one hundred per cent, and management agreed at a works conference to modify the bonus system. Although these developments might not seem particularly substantial in themselves, the spirit of the strikers caused the AEU's Organising District Delegate to praise them as the finest body of trade-unionists he had ever been associated with.[109] It is not, however, in the domestic dimension so much as in the national one that the dispute was most significant. It was the midwife of the first shop stewards' movement worthy of the name since that of the First World War. The strike had occurred in the factories that formed the core of the most important aircraft firm. The Communists had been able to use their network of contacts nationally to coordinate joint action and organise support. The CP members had carefully prepared the way for the dispute in both Hawker factories, as well as in the unions themselves; the *Daily Worker* had been adopted as the official organ of the strike committee, and Tom Roberts, the CP's Industrial Organiser in the Midlands, had been involved throughout.[110] The CP ensured that these advantages were not lost, and acted very quickly to set up a national movement of aircraft stewards. Soon after the Hawker strike, contemporaries spoke assuredly (and with justification) of an aircraft shop stewards' *movement*, characterised by shared aims and permanent inter-factory organisation. During the pre-war years at least, it was merely a sectional movement within the engineering industry, involving only about one in ten engineering workers, but it formed the cutting edge of militancy within the AEU and to this extent had a much wider significance.

During the Hawker dispute the shop stewards had appealed for support to the rest of the aircraft industry through a duplicated sheet entitled *The Propellor*.[111] Four days after the strike had ended, a meeting of London aircraft stewards was called, which in its turn called two national conferences at which a programme of immediate demands was drawn up.[112] *The Propellor* then became *New Propellor,* organ of the Aircraft Shop Stewards' National Council (ASSNC), costing one penny, printed in London and edited by Peter Zinkin of the CP.[113] The first two issues of the paper described its aims and objects, and those of the ASSNC, which were, broadly, to achieve full trade-unionism and a separate national agreement for aircraft workers. If the circulation figures printed in the paper itself are to be believed, then its readership expanded rapidly: by August 1937, forty-nine factories took fourteen thousand copies, and by October 1938 there were fifty-one factories taking twenty thousand copies. By 1938, then, the paper claimed a circulation which was the equivalent of roughly one in six aircraft workers.[114]

From the winter of 1935 to the autumn of 1939, the ASSNC and *New Propellor* were swept along in a groundswell of shop floor activity that made the aircraft industry into easily the most strike-prone branch of engineering, and rapidly brought many factories up to ninety per cent trade-unionism and above.[115] The ASSNC and its lively and interesting paper played a considerable part in this wave of union activity. The paper was undoubtedly very close to the workshops; indeed, both concept and format were designed to ensure this. Unsigned contributions from supporters in different factories formed the bulk of the paper, an editorial commented on the general position, a column entitled 'The Money We Make for Others' gave aircraft firms' profits, while cartoons and jokes ensured that the overall impression was not too dry. The ASSNC and its paper also played an important part in drumming up support for major disputes: in the second issue of *New Propellor,* the secretary of the ASSNC described how this worked in the case of a strike for union recognition at Blackburn Aircraft's Brough factory. He first heard of the dispute late on the evening of Wednesday 25 September 1935, and quickly produced a letter on the dispute for circulation to all of the shop stewards on his list. A special meeting of the ASSNC's Executive, the 'acting committee', called for the Friday night decided to take collections in the London area and to call a special national conference. During the seventeen days of the strike, £628.10s.6d. was collected, a formidable total for an unofficial organisation, giving each of the two hundred and

41

seventy strikers over two pounds.[116] *New Propellor* officially supported eight other disputes in this way between 1935
and the outbreak of war, collecting several thousand pounds
for them.[117]

Although the prestige and influence of *New Propellor* were
mainly founded on its immediate usefulness to trade-unionists
active in the aircraft industry, it was also related to the way
in which it was able to engage in topical political debate with
the aircraft employers. The Baldwin and (from May 1937)
Chamberlain governments were the targets of some criticism
both explicitly and by implication, as rearmament involved
the Conservative government pouring money into various
schemes for the expansion of aircraft production. The safeguards for the use of public money in this context were
reckoned by many to be quite inadequate, and the issue
emerged as a public debate which on occasions verged on
becoming a national scandal.[118] Both the industrialists and
their political allies were the targets of *New Propellor's*
criticism, and as war drew closer its views corresponded
increasingly with those held by the majority of workers.
The left-wing paper had from the start a large anti-fascist
dimension which gave it a distinctive political as well as trade
union form. Building outwards from the trade union battles,
*New Propellor* argued that aircraft workers should adopt a
critical attitude to the political activities and allegiances of
their employers, and watch where their products were sold.
In this period it was by no means taken for granted that
rearmament was directed against Germany; it was often
suggested on the left that the large volume of trade with
Germany indicated that rearmament was directed against the
Soviet Union. There was undoubtedly a wide scope for such
arguments, because the aircraft employers themselves made
public statements which tended to support them. Indeed, in
some ways it could be said that the aircraft employers
played a substantial part in raising political consciousness
amongst their own employees.

The left was able to draw attention to the regularly
expressed and unquestionably anti-Communist and imperialist
views of the aircraft employers as epitomised by the journal
*The Aeroplane.* This paper was avowedly anti-Chamberlain

and put a point of view which can only be described as proto-fascist. *New Propellor* and the *Daily Worker* took full advantage of the idiosyncratically extreme right-wing views of the editor of *The Aeroplane,* C.G. Gray, in exposing the views of the aircraft employers. Lest *The Aeroplane's* position be thought to be exaggerated here, an illustration of its political stance can be taken from a debate which the paper conducted with *New Propellor* and the *Daily Worker* in early 1938. During this debate, in which the *Daily Worker* implied that the aircraft manufacturers were taking too little care with aircraft instrumentation because the Air Ministry and the employers had a close relationship, C.G. Gray took the opportunity of replying to allegations made against his paper:

> The *Daily Worker* accuses this paper of being pro-Nazi. The chief reason why I am pro-Nazi is that I admire so intensely the team spirit, and the spirit of patriotism which pervades everything in Germany. There is a happy medium between the wage slavery of unbridled capitalism and the national slavery of unbridled communism. And National Socialism seems to have found the happy medium in a way that suits the German temperament. It might not suit us here but we shall arrive at the same sort of thing in our own way.[119]

Readers of the paper, some of whom at least were aircraft workers (as the letters columns show), could read such views regularly and could see that Gray was not over-anxious to refute the left's suggestions. Politically aware aircraft workers had the issues presented to them in a particularly stark fashion through the constant arguments carried on between the aircraft industry's papers from 1935 until 1940, when *The Aeroplane* changed its editor and became a solely technical journal.

*The Aeroplane* was an especially brazen example of pro-Nazism in an employers' journal, and aircraft shop stewards were unusually well organised and equipped to point out the political sentiments of their employers. But their anti-fascist activity was not only at the level of propaganda and political debate. The advent of the Spanish Nationalist rebellion against the Republican government raised the spectre of fascism in a wide context, as many within the labour movement began to appreciate that the destruction of trade union rights and a descent into barbarism were a very real possibility which could soon affect Britain. The Spanish Civil War was also a conflict in which air power (mostly deployed on the side of the Nationalists) played a pivotal role. Had it not been for the use of Nazi planes, Franco's Moorish troops would never have been able to take part in the uprising, which would almost certainly have been still-born as a result. The new-found industrial strength of the aircraft shop stewards was deployed in Britain to ensure that British-made aeroplanes were not sent to the Nationalists. In the summer of 1937 the shop stewards at De Havilland's, aware of the destination of their products, informed their management that if another De Havilland plane left for the Nationalist forces there would be a strike. The stewards may have been bluffing, but no more planes were sent and within three days the National government had adopted their policy of 'non-intervention'.[120] Although the policy of non-intervention has been criticised by many historians as simply a betrayal of the Spanish Republican government (as it undoubtedly was), it could also be said to have represented a curb on the aircraft employers' previous activities, achieved through shop floor agitation.

Outside the aircraft industry, the state of shop floor trade union organisation did not allow similar threats to be made. The development of trade-unionism was uneven, and the threat of the sack remained very real for most engineering workers. In most cases, therefore, support for the Republic was expressed largely in terms of voluntary backing rather than industrial solidarity. Many engineers joined the International Brigades (including Phil Edwards, a worker from De Havilland's who died in Spain just after the shop stewards had made their intervention at home);[121] others organised collections for food ships or worked in their spare time repairing motor cycles for use as ambulances for Voluntary Industrial Aid. Support for Spain was both intense and wide-spread amongst engineers, and was not simply the concern of a coterie of Oxbridge intellectuals. In April 1938 the AEU's Executive Committee called on members to support Voluntary Industrial Aid for Spain by giving their skill to help the

Republic, and this expression of commitment from the AEU at the official level evoked a wide response.[122] A meeting in Manchester to launch the scheme attracted one hundred members, while Oxford men from the AEU and the NUVB produced motor-cycle ambulances from mid-1938 until the very end of the Spanish Civil War. As late as June 1939 there were still a couple of dogged motor-cycle repairers working in a Manchester garage.[123]

The general, if uneven, revival of shop floor trade-unionism in the late 1930s was perhaps not particularly remarkable given the increasing expenditure on arms production. The prominence of left-wingers amongst the shop stewards may have been equally predictable given the history of workplace representation in Britain. But upsurges in the British labour movement, in the 1880s, 1910s and again in the 1930s, brought an almost entirely unexpected broadening of membership, with workers previously thought to be among the most 'backward' sections of the working class exploding into incandescent militancy. In the upturn of the 1930s, it was the engineering apprentices who played this role.

Engineering apprentices' grievances were usually regarded by adult engineers as real enough but without hope of solution. They themselves had suffered similarly, and the trials and tribulations of an apprenticeship were regarded as facts of life. The apprentices' complaints were manifold, ranging from their being treated as children (one leaflet from Aberdeen was headed: 'We Are Nobody's Baby')[124] through being made to lose time served when changing employer, to being cuffed and sworn at by chargehands and foremen. But the lads' most important grievance related to wages. Indeed, *Challenge,* the paper of the Young Communist League (YCL), went so far as to say that apprentices were worse off in 1937 than they had been half a century earlier because rises in the cost of living had not been matched by wage increases.[125] It is difficult to assess the validity of this claim without more information than we at present have about apprentices' wages, but it is certainly true that employers had always justified paying apprentices the 'small rate' by arguing that the boys cost them more than just a

45

wage, since they were under an obligation to train them and to accept the broken tools and scrapped work which went with that obligation. Even when boys 'came out of their time' (that is, finished their apprenticeships), and were fortunate enough not to be sacked, they were not paid the full rate until they had worked another year at the 'loosing rate' (the intermediate rate between the last year of the apprentice's rate and the journeyman's rate). Nor were apprentices entitled to special wage supplements, like the 'dirty money' paid for working in ships' holds which had carried oil or phosphates, for example.[126] All of these things made the apprentices feel that they were being used as cheap labour.

From the mid-1930s journeymen's wages left those of apprentices behind, as national negotiations yielded increases which the apprentices did not share. It was when the 1936 increases brought the skilled men three shillings a week extra, that the Executive Committee of the AEU presented the engineering employers with a case for some increase to apprentices. The Employers' Federation agreed to strictly informal talks, but these led nowhere despite the employers' later claims that apprentices' wages were the subject of national negotiations.[127]

The apprentices' other major grievance was the lack of adequate training, and in their view, the employer was breaking indentures by not providing it. Proper training was an important thing to a boy; if he could emerge at the end of his time having worked on a wide variety of work, and had received adequate technical training, then he could get a job almost anywhere: abroad, as a sea-going marine engineer, or in another factory or yard. If, on the other hand, he was poorly trained and was then sacked at the end of his time, he would find life quite difficult. Crucial as these things were, there was an even more vital aspect to the training question: the element of craft pride. As *Challenge* said: 'The Clyde boys are going to hit hard and obtain the chance to become brilliant mechanics, a chance which their employers deny them.'[128] Not only were the boys demanding a pay increase and union representation, they were also determined to be given the opportunity to develop into craftsmen who could take a pride in their work.

The apprentices' vitality in pursuing their cause under their slogan of 'All for one, and one for all' came as an invigorating surprise to many journeymen engineers, as it did to their employers. Their strikes of the spring and autumn of 1937 were central to the development of trade union organisation as a whole, marking a watershed between the dark years of the Depression and the growing strength and confidence evident in the months immediately preceding the war. If the apprentices could strike successfully, then anything was possible. For generations of apprentices, 'serving your time' was regarded as a necessary evil which boys had to go through, a sort of extended ritual ordeal on the road to journeyman status. The apprentice's indentures 'bound' him to his employer, and invariably emphasised the duties of the parents and the boy himself. Above all else, the indentures stressed that the arrangement was terminated by any indiscipline on the apprentice's part; strike action was strongly and specifically included. When the boys actively challenged their indentures, they were supported by their families. Moreover, because the main route to apprenticeship was by introductions by fathers, uncles and elder brothers, the very real sympathy and support shown for the lads by the adults was experienced through, and strengthened by, family relationships. The young engineers' families had a financial and emotional interest in the boys' battle for higher wages and decent treatment, and this both strengthened their resolve and intensified their action within the workshop community. The strikes were not individual and sectional affairs; they were an integral part of a wider movement and were experienced as such. It was with some justification, then, that *New Propellor*'s special issue covering the boys' strikes carried the banner headline: 'YOUTH MAKE HISTORY!'.[129]

It is worth noting here that although *New Propellor* was undoubtedly correct in its assessment of the importance of the apprentices' action, very little of this history has filtered through into the textbooks and standard works. Nor has it been effectively preserved by word-of-mouth tradition in the trade union movement, except in a few areas. The apprentices'

## YOUNG AIRCRAFT WORKERS' NUMBER

# NEW PROPELLOR

### OCTOBER, 1937

## EVERY AIRCRAFT WORKER

### AIMS AND OBJECTS

(a) To establish and maintain 100 per cent. trade unionism in all aircraft factories. To elect shop stewards in each department of the factory, such shop stewards to form a Works Committee.

(b) The enforcement of all trade union agreements.

(c) To co-ordinate the activities of all workers in the aircraft factories and the trade union branches in order to secure higher wages and better conditions. To secure through the trade unions a national agreement relative to rates of pay and conditions of employment.

(d) To publish a Monthly Bulletin for all aircraft workers.

### IMMEDIATE DEMANDS

1. An immediate wage advance of 2d. per hour on the basic rate, the consolidation of the war bonus into the basic rate, and the establishment of a minimum rate of wages for adult workers of 1/4½ per hour.

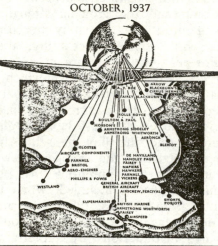

## A TRADE UNIONIST

2. Where a system of payment ☐ results prevails, the workers s☐ be able to earn at least 33⅓ cent. above the basic rate of wa☐ and the abolition of all "☐ systems."

3. No change in workshop cust☐ and practice shall be made u☐ negotiations have been comple☐ with the Shop Committee, sub☐ to the approval of those concern☐ In all factories, records of all pie☐ work shall be available for ☐ spection by the Shop Stewards a☐ Works Committee.

4. Forty-hour week, with no reduct☐ in pay.

5. A minimum outworking allowa☐ of 7s. 6d. per day.

6. The restoration of the cuts in ov☐ time and piece-work rates of ☐ made in 1931.

7. Payment for all statutory holiday☐

8. Every Aircraft Worker a Tra☐ Unionist.

Volume 2. No. 11.　　ORGAN OF THE AIRCRAFT SHOP STEWARDS' NATIONAL COUNCIL　　One Pen☐

# YOUTH MAKE HISTORY

YOUNG aircraft workers and engineers have made history. After years of official effort and negotiations with the trade unions, by a series of strikes called and conducted in an exemplary manner by the youth themselves, and supported by the adult trade unionists, the Engineering Employers' Federation has at last been forced to concede the principle of trade union recognition to the youth.

In this the magnificent youth conference, which we report inside, and the threat of national strike action which the youth made at this conference, played an important and decisive part.

From this it is clear that had the trade unions pursued a more vigorous policy, this question would have been settled long ago. It should also show us that such questions as the amendment of York Procedure, machine rates, aircraft agreement, etc., could also be secured if the trade unions pursued this

vigorous policy. A change is necessary and a growing number of full-time officials and active trade unionists are of this opinion : it is up to us to make this decisive change and support all those officials and others who are doing their bit in this direction.

WHILE trade union recognition has been gained for the youth, and in some areas wage increases have been secured as a result of strike action, there are areas, such as London, where no increase has been given. We would warn the youth to keep up the pressure and get their wage increases now and for a speedy conclusion to negotiations.

But there are many other problems which face young aircraft workers, and now that trade union recognition has been secured there is no reason why every young aircraft worker should not be in his trade union. The more young aircraft worker trade unionists, the better possibilities of good results from negotiations, and the better shall we be able

to get improvements in our own factorie☐ This is but the first stage of the fight; trad☐ union organisation will ensure that th☐ second stage is as successful as the first. Jo☐ up now.

We believe that youth committees, workin☐ in close conjunction with and represented o☐ the adult works committees, will be of advan☐ tage to both sections, and such committee☐ have been elected in a number of works.

IN the article on the position at A. V. Ro☐ we draw attention to the necessity o☐ defending our shop stewards and fighting fo☐ their retention in the factories, whatever th☐ reasons employers may give for their di☐ missal. This is an elementary principle o☐ trade unionism, and now that the threats t☐ those who carry the brunt of the fight in th☐ workshops is again appearing, we have n☐ hesitation in calling upon every aircraf☐ worker to do his duty both in the shop an☐

(Continued on page 2)

Special issue of *New Propellor*, on the apprentices' strike, October 1937 strikes nevertheless contain many important lessons for trade-unionists. Not the least of these is the most general, perhaps, in that the strikes shocked many at the time because they showed that, far from being prey either to apathy or to youthful inexperience, the apprentices were more than capable of organising themselves and of prosecuting their aims largely without the help of their elders. The strikes constitute an important episode in British labour history, showing that the much-vaunted virtue of experience in industrial matters is often less important than enthusiasm and determination.

The strikes may be grouped into two waves.[130] The first, which was limited to Scotland, began in April and forced the employers to pay attention to the hazy and ill-defined 'informal talks' which had ostensibly been going on before the stoppage. The second started in Salford in September and continued into October, when apprentices realised that the national negotiations were still not yielding any tangible results. This wave spread to most of the engineering factories in Lancashire and Yorkshire, Birmingham, Coventry and (finally) London, but almost entirely by-passed Scotland and the Tyne. Local employers' associations made settlements on wages as need dictated, and national negotiations were revived once again. In December the AEU won the right to negotiate for apprentices on a national and local basis, although the right to shop steward representation was not conceded.[131]

It is not surprising that the apprentices' movement first began on the Clyde. The northern centres were the stronghold of apprenticeship because of the shipbuilding and marine engineering industries' need for fully skilled labour.[132] During February and March 1937, the apprentices began their agitation for an increase in wages and improved training facilities. A committee was elected from most of the shipyards and engineering shops on the Clyde to present the demands to the employers, who refused to entertain them, causing a strike to break out on 24 March.[133] At first the movement was a small one, with just a few hundred lads out, but the apprentices took advantage of the yards being grouped fairly closely together by reviving a tactic which had last been used in the Forty Hours strike of 1919. They assembled each morning to form a large picket which travelled up and down between the Clyde yards, trying to muster more support. Having at one point swelled their ranks by enlisting the Fairfield, Govan, boys, the picket moved on to Stephens' Linthouse yard and hammered on the huge steel entrance doors. The hammering began to be returned from the other side of the doors, and the Stephens' boys opened the gates to come streaming out with a great cheer to join their mates.[134] By 5 April there were about 3,700 apprentices and trainees involved, representing something between a third and a half of the local boys in engineering and shipbuilding. The next day they were joined by the apprentices at John Brown's.[135] If, up until this stage, it had been possible for the local employers to assume that the strike would attract no more than minority support among their apprentices, any such hope had to be abandoned with the fall of the biggest yard on the river to the besieging youthful army. This was the turning point of the strike—from a stoppage that could still be passed off as a localised attack of adolescent impetuosity to what was obviously a serious movement of national importance. By 8 April the Greenock shipyards were also included, and local union officials approached the local employers for a conference on the matter. The employers replied that there must be a general resumption of work before any talks could be contemplated, and that in any case there was a national application under consideration. The Chief Conciliation Officer of the Ministry of Labour reported to London that the union officials were 'completely flabbergasted' at this news, and stated that they simply did not believe that there had been any intention on the employers' part to negotiate nationally before the strike had started.[136] The apprentices had already achieved something in compelling the employers to refer to the national negotiations which they had not previously been much concerned with.

As time went on, the apprentices developed and indeed refined the internal organisation of their strike. By the first week in April they had a central strike committee (chaired by Stuart Watson of the Young Communist League), elected by a general committee of one hundred and sixty shop and yard delegates. The central executive met and issued a strike bulletin, distributed to all the lads by a cycle corps of one hundred and fifty boys.[137] By the beginning of the following week, the committee had formulated a set of demands that were intended to consolidate and extend the strike. They decided to press for a uniform scale for all trades, recognition of the right of apprentices to be represented by the trade unions, and (at the request of the AEU District Committee) the setting of a definite quota for apprentice recruitment by each employer.[138] The programme was clever and well thought out: it clarified the apprentices' attitude to trade union membership (which had not been officially adopted as one of their initial aims), unified all types of young workers divided by their various trades and skills by seeking a uniform scale of wages and, most importantly, it enlisted the support of the adults by requiring a definite quota for apprentices.

By the second week in April there were well over eleven thousand apprentices and trainees out on strike in the West of Scotland, and the local shop stewards were beginning to organise support for them.[139] On 11 April a meeting of shop stewards from all unions set up a committee to help the lads in every way possible, deciding to recommend an overtime ban and a one-day strike to the District Committees.[140] By 13 April the strike was beginning to spread beyond the Clyde, to Edinburgh, Tees-side and Belfast.[141]

The stoppage was expanding geographically, but it is interesting to see that the apprentices determined not to allow it to expand in other directions. They drew the line at the involvement of girls and women. On 7 April five hundred women had come out on strike at Barr and Stroud's for an extra penny an hour.[142] In the words of the Conciliation Officer: '. . . they offered to join the apprentices' movement, but were informed that they would be more of a hindrance than a help in view of the fact that they were not apprentices but only learners.'[143] The argument was spurious, as there were already boys on strike who were not apprentices as such. The girls went away feeling understandably 'rather hurt' by the boys' attitude, particularly as they were referred to the organiser of the NUDAW, whose status with the

51

engineering employers was simply non-existent.[144] A girls' movement for improved wages did not begin until early November, well after the end of the apprentices' strike.[145] However, this incident must have seemed of little importance to the boys themselves, as they gained more and more support from their fathers, uncles and elder brothers. The District Committees agreed to support the shop stewards' call for an overtime embargo and a one-day strike timed for Friday 16 April, while the shop stewards at Howden's had already called their members out on strike when a man was asked to touch apprentices' work.[146]

On the morning of Friday 16th, Clyde engineers walking about Clydeside saw a number of chalked slogans on the walls of the factories and shipyards. Among the messages were: 'Don't Let Us Down!', 'Don't Scab Today!', and with a touch of apprentice humour: 'Don't Work Today, Daddy!'[147] Strike instructions were received very late by some shop stewards, so that at John Brown's, for example, the men had to pass the picketing lads to attend a meeting, but they soon accepted their stewards' recommendation and walked out again to youthful cheers. Overall, the strike was quite solid, with about one hundred and fifty thousand out in all.[148]

With hindsight, the April 16th strike may be seen to have been the highpoint of the stoppage. The overtime embargo was less well observed than the one-day support strike: on the lower reaches of the river it was hardly adhered to at all, while the Boilermakers' Society had never even tried to enforce it.[149] At the very end of April there was an apparent strengthening of the strike when the unions agreed to pay benefit to those lads who were members of a union prior to having stopped work (about ten per cent) although some unions recruited by offering strike benefit without this condition.[150] The boys had a central fund, and donations to it had been 'both widespread and generous'.[151] It had helped them to maintain what the Conciliation Officer thought a 'rather astonishing solidarity' by turning down on 19 April an offer of one penny an hour.[152] Eleven days later, however, the fund seems to have run down to almost nothing, and the offer of official strike benefit must therefore have seemed timely.[153] The offer was not quite as straightforward as it might have seemed, though, as the officials had decided that the time had come to end the strike in favour of national negotiations. They accordingly decided to call a meeting of the boys to which they would put a motion for a return to work on the basis of an immediate national approach to the employers for the Clyde demands (now generally known as the Apprentices' Charter, as *Challenge* and the YCL had christened it). The Conciliation Officer thought it unlikely that the boys would accept the recommendation: 'It is very doubtful if the boys will return to work on the somewhat vague guarantees which are proposed. After all, they began this strike without the trade unions and there is a mood amongst them to carry it on without the trade unions until their full demands are obtained.'[154] The apprentices' committee were prepared for the officials' proposals, and the meeting was stormy. The officials said they would withdraw the offer of financial assistance unless the boys agreed to return. The apprentices' committee agreed to accept this suggestion only if no individual firms were negotiated with, if a national approach was made immediately, and if the charter was the basis for negotiations. This was accepted on the officials' side, and the boys agreed to go back to work, although the officials did not escape some criticism from *Challenge*.[155]

The summer of 1937 saw a lull in strike activity which was paralleled by the employers' refusal to budge in negotiations. Frustration built up among the apprentices during these months, while the YCL and the CP agitated and prepared for a second explosion of militancy.[156] Between the return of the Clyde apprentices at the beginning of May and the autumn there had been a number of smaller strikes. The Edinburgh apprentices' strike, 'carefully nursed' by the Scottish union officials until the Clyde dispute was almost over, ran from 29 April to 14 May, ending on the same basis as the Clyde strike.[157] There were also strikes at Stockton and Lincoln (6-20 May) and Aberdeen (18 May-9 June).[158] In September, apprentices in Manchester showed that the employers could simply not afford to procrastinate in the hope that the boys would cool off. Yet this wave of strikes was started, as the earlier one had been, as no more than an almost imperceptible ripple on the surface of industrial relations; this ripple was soon to develop into a tidal wave of militancy.

During the second week of September 1937, some apprentices stopped work at a small engineering shop in Salford because their employer would not give them an increase of three shillings a week. By 14 September apprentices and trainees were out at Gardner's Peel Green factory, at A.V. Roe's factories, at Crossley Motors and at Mather and Platt's machine tool works.[159] By the following day there were about a thousand more boys out, as a result of another 'flying picket' moving from works to works.[160] On that day, Wednesday 15th, a committee was set up on Clyde lines, with two delegates from every shop on strike, and elected a deputation to visit the Manchester and Salford Trades Council, which was meeting that evening. The delegates were heard with great sympathy, and the Council members unanimously instructed their sheet metal worker secretary, W.J. Munro, to seek financial aid from the two hundred-odd affiliated branches.[161] However, the Manchester strikes were not quite as well organised as the Clyde stoppages had been. As the *Manchester Guardian* commented: 'The strike does not yet show any of the smooth organisation nor any of the clarity about objects that distinguished the Glasgow youths' strike.'[162] The newspaper's comment was to some extent borne out over the next week; although more apprentices stopped work that Friday, factories began to negotiate individually with the employers (a temptation that the Clyde lads had been able to resist).[163] By this time the strike committee itself was arguing for a ten-day 'armistice', under which they would agree to return to work pending the outcome of local negotiations, and by Wednesday 22nd a number of factories had returned on this basis.[164] The day before the armistice was due to end, the Manchester employers conceded a two shilling a week increase to all boys, and although this was received with mixed feelings there were no further stoppages.[165]

The Manchester events had stimulated further strikes in Hebden Bridge, Leeds and Halifax, and by 30 September Coventry's apprentices were also stopping work.[166] The initiative was taken by a large group of boys working together on detail-fitting at Armstrong-Whitworth Aircraft's Baginton factory.[167] On 27 September these lads struck for an increase of three shillings a week and recognition of the right of trade unions to represent them. On the following day apprentices at the same firm's Whitley (Coventry) factory also struck. That Wednesday there were mass meetings at all Armstrong-Whitworth's factories in the town, which voted to black all apprentices' work, to levy themselves two shillings per head for the boys' fund, and to have an hour and a half's down-tools in their support on the following day. The down-tools was 'a great success'.[168] The strike spread to five other engineering factories, and Courtauld's rayon plant.[169] This last stoppage is of particular significance in view of the Clyde apprentices' decision not to encourage the support of non-apprentice girls. No less than eight thousand girls and women stopped work at Courtauld's as the apprentices' demonstration moved from the city centre towards Herbert's works along the Foleshill Road. Their support for the apprentices showed that, as a battle to abolish low pay, the dispute had an appeal that was not limited to the engineering industry, and is reminiscent of the way in which some American car towns like Flint and Detroit were gripped by 'union fever', bringing waitresses, truck drivers and many others into the union at the same time on the other side of the Atlantic.

Another interesting feature of the Coventry strike was the boys' fierce reaction to the hostility of the *Midland Daily Telegraph*. Eight hundred boys marched to the paper's offices to demand an adequate statement on the strike, and to refute the suggestion made in one edition that they were 'impetuous'.[170] The paper does not seem to have changed its editorial policy, but the incident shows the apprentices' heightened awareness of the need to be given a good press if local opinion was to be swayed against the employers rather than against their own 'impetuousness'. After a Sunday march through the town and a meeting in the market place attended by two thousand apprentices and journeymen, the Engineering Employers' Association conceded increases of between one and three shillings per week, and trade union recognition. Several shop stewards were suspended from work for instructing members not to touch jobs normally done by apprentices at Armstrong-Whitworth Aircraft, but a ban on overtime and a ban on recruitment to the works was decided on until they were reinstated.[171]

While the Coventry apprentices were on strike, moves were being made to set up a national federation of apprentices' committees. In the first week of October the Clyde and Manchester boys met and circularised other districts, attracting fifty-six delegates to a conference held in Manchester on Sunday 10 October under the presidency of Brother Harrison of the Manchester and Salford Trades Council. The conference heard that the employers were still not conducting meaningful national negotiations, and decided to call for national strike action on Monday 18 October if the demands of the Apprentices' Charter were not met.[172] In the event, the employers did meet the unions on Thursday 14 October, and conceded their right to negotiate for apprentices. They also agreed to another meeting in one month, provided that the unions agreed to prevent any further stoppages. Although some further strikes did take place in London between 20 October and 6 November, this was effectively the end of the 1937 strikes as a national movement.[173]

The London boys' strikes started at Johnson and Philips', and on the day after they came out a mass picket of about a thousand boys stood outside the gates of Siemens. The picket allowed the adults in, but stopped the boys. The boys' strike committee was chaired by a sympathetic local priest, the Reverend Hannigan, but the boys showed the same militancy and refusal to follow trade union constitutionality as their Scottish counterparts. After a mass picket at which they rejected the advice of the AEU Executive to return to work, they held a meeting at which, Charlie Wellard recalled, 'You could almost feel the air boiling. . . I think that's the finest meeting I've ever been at in my life.'[174] The strike won the boys two shillings from the local engineering employers, but it also helped an adult worker, Paddy Sheeley, the convenor at Harvey's, to stop management from victimising him.[175]

By December 1937 the AEU had secured the right to negotiate for young workers not covered by indentures from the EEF, although the right to shop steward representation was not conceded even in their case. The wages of 'junior male workers' were also to be related to those of adults, so that they would not slip behind as they had done in 1936-7.[176] These national advances do not do justice to the effect of the strikes, however. Many employers' associations had concluded local wage agreements which gave the boys large increases. These increases allowed them to think of themselves, in many cases for the first time, as wage-earners whose contribution to the family budget could be taken seriously. But it was not only a matter of economics. The boys had shown that they were capable of effective collective action, and the 1937 strike transformed their status in negotiating terms. No foreman could afford to treat apprentices' problems with the contempt that they had previously shown. The apprentices had become a force in the engineering factories, and they were to use their strength in a number of large strikes stretching over the next two decades. Although each generation of apprentices to some extent had to relearn the experience of the 1937 strikes, the myth that indentures could be effectively enforced to prevent stoppages had been largely scotched. Indeed, the apprentices could be said to be amongst the more 'privileged' people working in the industry, since many of them could eventually expect regular employment and some of the better jobs. And in other sectors of the industry and amongst the growing number of non-skilled engineers, some significant stirrings were evident.

The level of shop floor organisation outside of the aircraft industry varied greatly from factory to factory and even shop to shop before about 1941, when a certain minimum of informal organisation could be expected. Most of the factories that were as well organised as the aircraft plants at this time were to be found in other 'new industry' works. In some factories, such as Pressed Steel, Oxford, Salford Electrical Instruments, or Siemens, London, shop stewards steadily built up the range and number of issues that they raised with management, to the point where collective bargaining was relatively advanced. All this called for a lot of slow, patient work by the shop stewards, and in some of these well organised plants the results were impressive. The nature of the process at Siemens, London, can be seen in the pages of the shop stewards' printed journal. The journal, which clearly reflects the influence of the Communist Sam Wellard, shows a gradual broadening of the type of issues which the stewards were able to take up in the late 1930s. In one of the 1935 numbers the main matters reported on were the employment of unskilled labour on toolroom machines, back pay for five workers on being reclassified as toolmakers, payment for a shop steward suspended from work, reinstatement of a girl sacked for fighting, and a wages dispute in the battery shop.[177] The importance of the toolroom as the centre of union activity and the prominence of cases involving individuals or small groups is quite marked. Between 1935 and 1937, no doubt partly through publicising their successes in the pages of their lively journal, the stewards were able to develop membership to an exceptionally high level, approaching hundred per cent. Another issue of the journal shows that the questions they were able to take up in 1937 were wider also in terms of the number of workers involved. The matters dealt with included an increase for capstan setters in one department, the provision of adequate sanitation in another, a number of problems relating to the cable shop, the factory holiday rota, apprentices' wages, a wage increase in the milling shop, and two sectional piece-work disputes.[178] The stewards were clearly moving out of their base amongst the stalwarts of the toolroom and into the production areas, and were broadening their influence in every sense.

Factories like Siemens were exceptional, however. In the majority of factories, raising grievances with the management meant one could confidently expect retaliation in the form of badly paid, heavy or dirty work, suspension or dismissal. Perhaps the worst in this respect was the motor industry, which was characterised by a high degree of instability in employment. Before 1939 motor cars were basically produced to order, and this meant not only seasonal employment with an enforced three-month 'holiday' in the summer before the Motor Show, but periodic lay-offs throughout the year. 'Troublemakers' would be the last to be taken on and the first to be laid off. Many trade-unionists had thought that Austin, Morris and Fords would never be organised under this regime.[179] Although in many of the motor, electrical and general engineering factories the skilled men were union members, the large numbers of non-time-served workers were generally non-union. During the late 1930s the general workers' unions (the Transport and General Workers' Union and the National Union of General and Municipal Workers) made strenuous efforts to establish themselves amongst these workers. A satisfactory history of these unions in engineering has yet to be written, but some preliminary indications of the nature and scope of their influence must be attempted here.

During the second half of the 1930s, the general unions managed to expand their engineering membership considerably. This was particularly true of the TGWU. In May 1935 the TGWU's *Record* noted the successes registered in the Midlands area (the spring and summer were, of course, the open season for factory gate meetings), and by June 1936 claimed good progress in the AEU-dominated aircraft industry.[180] By the outbreak of war the Metal, Engineering and Chemical Trade Group, formed only just over seven years previously, had grown to such a size that it was bigger than the docks group.[181] This growth was achieved by a very energetic approach to recruitment. Both general unions were better geared to recruit than the AEU. Throughout the decade 1935-45, the general unions were in a more competitive position when recruiting non-skilled workers than the AEU: they both had provision in their rule-books for collectors separate from the stewards, who handled every aspect of recruitment; the benefits offered to the members for their subscriptions were superior to those offered by the AEU for section 5 (non-skilled) members; prospective members did not have to attend the branch before they were accepted; and they were not given a different-coloured card because they were not fully skilled.[182] Just a quick glance at the TGWU's *Record* will show how it was used not only as a newspaper for members, but also as a recruiter. The AEU *Monthly Journal* was rather more an information bulletin for established members. Within the tradition of William Allan (founder and, for a period beginning in 1848, General Secretary of the ASE), it printed reports from each organiser, items about engineering technology, votes for union positions and so on, which were of interest to the craftsman member but of little interest to the potential semi-skilled member. In practice, too, the general unions and especially the TGWU showed that they were willing to make some sacrifices to enrol more members. During the strike of Pressed Steel, Oxford, in 1934, strike benefit was paid out despite the fact that the great majority of strikers were not strictly entitled to it since they had only just joined. The contrast with the craft union at the works could not have been starker: the NUVB only paid out strike benefit to its members over two years after the end of the dispute, much to the disgust of its Oxford members.[183] The general unions were willing to make their concessions to prospective members in order to break into the engineering industry, but the craft unions were not concerned with making concessions to non-apprenticed men. The whole philosophy of craft-unionism was concerned with keeping these people out, and applications for membership were often still scrutinised closely to determine whether the applicant had in fact served his time to the trade. Even when the semi-skilled had been recruited, they were still not regarded as full members of the union by the skilled engineers of the old school; in the summer of 1939 some members of the unskilled section 5 of the AEU alleged that they had been prevented from starting at A.V. Roe's Chadderton works because they were not fully skilled. The District Committee instructed the stewards to accept any man with an AEU card in future, but that it should have been necessary for them to do so shows how far from extinction the old attitudes were.[184]

The general trade-unionists had to establish their unions within engineering almost entirely from scratch, against some opposition from the craftsmen's organisations. They had frequently to contend with the journeymen's condescension, and in return they defined themselves as against a caricature of a conservative, deferential AEU man. Many ex-stewards painted these pictures of the AEU men, when interviewed. Harold Taylor, who had moved to Armstrong-Whitworth Aircraft from the Coventry buses, where he had joined the TGWU, portrayed the union at the aircraft factory in these terms:

> There was a couple of the old AEU stewards. . . the old chaps were finding it difficult, they were still doffing their caps at the boss, and we had started not to doff our caps. We were demanding seats when they called us in to give us some information or tell us something, we were able to say 'Well, are we going to stand here all bloody day, or are you going to give us a seat, because if you're keeping us standing we're not going to stop.' And then we found chairs being spread out. But they thought 'God, you shouldn't have said that to him, it was sacrilegious'.[185]

But if the TGWU stewards displayed this lack of deference both to management and to the AEU men, it was largely because they had yet to establish their right to be there at all. Even where the general unions had established their right to coexist in the workshops with the AEU (and in some cases the AEU and NUVB men were actually encouraging the un-skilled to join the TGWU and NUGMW), this was a far cry from establishing their right to be considered equal as trade-unionists. They were there on sufferance, as unions that organised anybody, with no special claim to expertise in engineering. It was for this reason that the AEU persisted throughout this period in refusing, if they could possibly avoid it, to allow general trade-unionists to lead the factory organisation. A convenor's job was skilled work, they reasoned, and should be done by a skilled man. In fact, of course, there were very few occasions in the 1930s when the general unions could claim enough numerical support to put the convenor's job within their reach. The Manchester District Secretary was able to state proudly at the beginning of the war that whatever 'encroachments' may have been allowed in the South, the general unions had made very little progress in the northern aircraft industry.[186] Even amongst women, where the general unions had a free hand except for some desultory opposition from the NUVB in car trim shops, the results of their efforts in global terms were not very great: in 1935, two per cent of the women in engineering were in unions, and by 1940 this had only increased to six per cent.[187]

By the beginning of the war, then, the general unions had succeeded in gaining a foothold in the engineering industry, but their membership remained patchy and their stewards were still struggling for recognition by both the employers and the craft unions. The level of trade union organisation amongst the non-skilled workers throughout engineering, and the relatively disparate nature of their problems, made it impossible to build an equivalent to the ASSNC and *New Propeller* outside of the predominantly skilled and AEU-dominated aircraft industry. An attempt to do this, through a paper called *The Conveyor* which was based initially on the AEC factory in Southall, began in January 1937 with an initial subscription of £16 collected from stewards in a number of different districts, but it seems to have faded out in the summer of 1938 after constant appeals to increase the paper's circulation.[188] The potential for the rapid expansion of circulation based on common problems and steadily advancing union organisation did not exist.

In the two years or so preceding the outbreak of war, the trade union movement within the different branches of the engineering industry became more homogeneous as more and more shop stewards were elected in all types of factories. For a number of reasons the aircraft factories and the ASSNC therefore became less isolated and atypical. The first and perhaps most important reason related to the economics of the industry. Unemployment was generally decreasing and a shortage of skilled labour was becoming acute in some areas, largely because of the expansion of the arms industries as a whole, led by aircraft. The bargaining position of all engineers and especially skilled men, was becoming steadily greater everywhere. In any case, the aircraft industry was beginning to include the motor-car firms enlisted under the shadow scheme to produce aero-engines, while at the same time creating a growing demand for the thousands of components which went to make up an aeroplane. In some ways, then, it is already becoming possible in these years to speak of the arms industries in general rather than as a set of different branches. Second, the aircraft shop stewards, recognising these changes and anxious not to come into too direct a conflict with the Executive of the AEU, had already decided in the summer of 1937 not to organise a national strike for a separate aircraft agreement but instead to throw themselves behind the national engineering claim.[189] The significance of this change of tack can hardly be over-

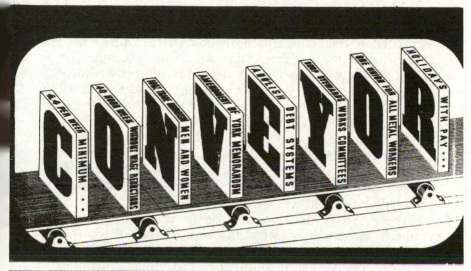

Volume I. No. I      JANUARY, 1937      Price One Penny

# WHAT IS THIS?

THE CONVEYOR is not an "opposition" paper. The object of this paper is to express the desires of the rank and file throughout the metal and engineering industry.

Most trade unionists recognise that it becomes increasingly impossible to get the unofficial voice heard or the unofficial hand seen through official channels. Branches are rebuked because they communicate their views to other branches. Shop stewards are forced to call meetings to discuss the attitude of officials to the so-called unofficial strikes which increase in proportion to the hellish speed-up which is characteristic of the modern production shop.

In another column there will be found a sample of profits published during the past year. A glance will show how fat the parasites of engineering are growing at the expense of the workers. In every large engineering town one hears the remark : What are the unions doing about wages?

True, there have been increases; but, on the other hand, thousands recognise that, with more sagacity and courage, more could have been forced from the employers. Equally true is the despondent note which can

be heard. A fear that if we do not act quickly " we shall miss the boat."

Many of us are old enough to remember the last war period and its Munitions of War Acts. Thousands more are conscious to-day that the world is rapidly approaching a new world war which only the organised might of the workers can crush. Yet we see very little organised effort on the part of the majority of officials of the trade union movement towards such organised resistance.

And because of such episodes THE CONVEYOR makes its appearance, the cost of the first issue subscribed for by engineers all over the country. The columns are open to all who wish to further the cause of the working class exploited in the industry.

It shall be a medium by which the rank and file shall express their opinions. Its aim will be to build workshop organisation and 100 per cent. trade unionism throughout the industry.

Some reactionary officials will frown and they will demand that the members shall not buy it and read it. The rank and file will build the paper and will behold it as a beacon of light, a guide in the struggle for better conditions, increase in wages, shorter hours and 100 per cent. trade unionism.

First issue of *Conveyor*, aimed at engineering workers in mass production works emphasised for its effect on the future development of the shop stewards' movement; aircraft shop stewards who had previously emphasised the distinctive features of their work and 'gone it alone' were now reminded by the ASSNC that their fellow trade-unionists in the industry as a whole needed their help if the national claim was to be successfully prosecuted. The way was thereby paved for a formal broadening of the movement beyond the core aircraft sector. In 1939 the metal, engineering and shipbuilding industries had registered the second highest number of working days lost through strikes for a decade, at 332,000. Within this total the aircraft industry at 40,394, accounted for about one-eighth of the days lost.[190] Aircraft were still providing a disproportionately high number of days lost through strikes, but within the context of a general upward trend.

The ASSNC's decision to drop its claim for a separate aircraft agreement reflected the wish of the CP to avoid a head-on clash with the Executive of the AEU. The defeat of the busmen's 'Coronation' strike had brought disciplinary action by the TGWU against the Communists on the Central Bus Committee, and it seems likely that the CP wished to avoid a similar setback within the AEU. From this point on it became increasingly apparent that left-wing opposition within the AEU was being actively discouraged, in favour of a more conciliatory approach to the Executive which emphasised the wish of the left to respect the union's machinery and not to be seen to be breaking ranks by trying to build a 'divisive' rank and file movement.

The CP's accommodation to the AEU's official apparatus, which became so apparent from 1937 onwards, derived from the more general policy of building a British popular front. Emphasis had to be placed, it was felt, on building a broad movement which pulled as many trade-unionists as possible into the defence of existing democratic freedoms in the face of the fascist threat. Within this political perspective, divisive arguments with trade union officials had to be avoided.[191] When trade-unionists were being imprisoned and murdered in Italy, Germany and Spain, it was felt to be essential to build a broad basis of awareness that trade-unionism itself was in imminent danger of destruction. The weaknesses of this policy were to become apparent only later, when the trade union officials were called on to prevent any form of industrial action in wartime while the CP was actively defending trade union rights come what may. But in some ways the strengths of the policy were more immediately obvious. The AEU as a union was solidly anti-fascist, and was able to mobilise the shop floor to take industrial action in defence of the Spanish Republic even when the Civil War was almost at an end. In early 1939, for example, thirteen London engineering factories jointly implemented a ban on overtime and demonstrated with workers from eight building sites, stopping work at four p.m. to march to Downing Street and the Spanish Embassy.[192] Such demonstrations showed that the political development of at least a section of the trade union movement was outstripping its industrial growth. It was this near-unanimity of anti-fascist sentiment that constituted one of the major strengths of shop floor trade union organisation.

By the outbreak of war, the whole complexion of the AEU at official level was beginning to change, as the men who had been forced into a conciliatory stance by the Depression years gave way to some aggressive, left-leaning officers. This was symbolised by the election of Jack Tanner to the important post of National President of the union in 1939.[193] Tanner, who took over from the more middle-of-the-road Jack Little, had a long history of rebellion within the AEU. In 1913 he had thrown up his job as a skilled fitter and walked from Ostend to Barcelona, becoming a syndicalist in the process. In 1920 he attended the second Congress of the Communist International as a representative of the Shop Stewards' and Workers' Committee Movement. Although he never joined the CP, he was active in the CP-dominated Metalworkers' Minority Movement right up until its dissolution. In the early thirties these activities had brought him into conflict with the Executive Committee. The trajectory of his trade union career epitomised the development of the union in these years, as it moved decisively to the left. By the middle of the war, Communists had become very prominent if not predominant at official level within the AEU, with Berridge, Scott, Hannington (elected National Organiser in 1942) and Crane all occupying important full-time posts.

To many activists, if not to the Chamberlain government, it was quite apparent that the fall of Spain which the British left had fought hard to prevent presaged a second major war in Europe, despite the abortive Munich negotiations. It was simply a question of when, rather than whether, it would finally begin. When it came, trade union organisation in the engineering industry was stronger than at any time since the end of the First World War. In spite of marked weaknesses in terms of low membership outside of the aircraft sector, and the practical non-existence of women and apprentice members, great strides had been made towards the goal of full unionisation. More importantly, the 'frontier of control' was being pushed back rapidly, as managements were having to treat with shop stewards on an increasing range of negotiating issues. Industrially, engineering workers already presented quite a strong front to the employers compared to the situation of only a few years previously, when collective action was unimaginable outside a very few exceptional workplaces. Politically, they were pervaded with a 'Popular Front' consciousness of the threat that fascism posed to trade-unionism which, although not as well-defined and widespread as the equivalent feeling in France, deserves to be considered alongside it.

## NOTES

1 Shipbuilding is considered here only when its industrial relations were vital to engineering. It is really worth a separate study, as its economics and the traditions of its workforce are quite distinct from those of engineering.

2 J.B. Jefferys, *The Story of the Engineers* (1945), p. 198.

3 Ibid., p. 199.

4 W. Hornby, *Factories and Plant* (1958), p. 214.

5 See F.W. Carr, *The Coventry Labour Movement, 1914-1939* (unpublished PhD thesis, Warwick, 1979).

6 *Labour Research*, June 1934; in May 1945 Hawker-Siddeley 5s. shares still gave a yield of £9.0s.6d., despite fears of a post-war slump; this put them second only to De Beer's in *The Economist*'s survey of leading shares (*The Economist*, 5 May 1945).

7 *Labour Research*, Oct. 1936, Aug. 1939.

8 R. Fletcher, *Air Defence of Britain* (1938), p. 4.

9 A. Plummer, *New British Industries in the Twentieth Century* (1937), pp. 46-7.

10 J.D. Scott, *Vickers* (1962).

11 R.H. Campbell, 'The North British Locomotive Co. Between the Wars', p. 210 (in *Business History*, vol. xx, no. 2, July 1978).

12 *Labour Research,* no. 29, p. 82.
13 See the highly critical remarks on the pre-war situation made by Keith Middlemas, in *Politics in Industrial Society* (1979), ch. 8.
14 D.G. Rhys, *The Motor Industry: An Economic Survey* (1972), p. 9; G. Maxcy, 'The Motor Industry' in P. Cook (ed.), *The Effects of Mergers* (1958), p. 365.
15 G. Maxcy, op. cit., p. 367.
16 In 1937 Hawker-Siddeley owned or controlled Armstrong-Siddeley Motors, Armstrong-Whitworth Aircraft, A.V. Roe, Hawker Aircraft, Gloster Aircraft and Air Service and Aircraft Technical Services (A. Plummer, *New British Industries in the Twentieth Century* (1937), p. 98).
17 *The Aeroplane,* 12 February 1936. See the same journal on 3 June 1936, reporting SBAC's control of Civil Aviation, with Imperial Airways, through the Airworthiness Board.
18 Motor manufacturers were the most active group of British industrialists in importing American machine tools during the war (W. Hornby, *Factories and Plant* (1958), p. 328). See also W.F. Watson, 'The Working Mechanic's View', in C.T. Cramp (ed.), *The Worker's View. A Symposium* (1933), p. 16.
19 *The Aeroplane,* 8 March 1940.
20 W. Hornby, op. cit., p. 55.
21 Ibid.
22 R.A. Leeson, *Strike* (1973), p. 126, Z.E. Lambert and R.J. Wyatt, *Lord Austin. The Man* (1968), pp. 142–5; P.W.S. Andrews, *The Life of Lord Nuffield. A Study in Enterprise and Benevolence* (Oxford, 1955), p. 197. See also the picture facing p. 225. *The Conveyor,* Jan. 1937.
23 *The Aeroplane,* 1 April 1936 (description of Saunders-Roe), 8 March 1940.
24 Ibid.
25 Ibid., 22 Jan. 1936.
26 J.D. Scott, op. cit., pp. 220–1.
27 J.B. Jefferys, op. cit., p. 207.
28 *The Aeroplane,* 10 June 1936.
29 Engineering and Allied Trades Federation, *Forty-Hours Week. Analysis by the Federation of the Case Presented by the Trade Unions* (April 1934), p. 7.
30 *Minutes* of the Coventry Engineering Employers' Association, July, Nov. 1939.
31 Notebook of Walter Givens, Coventry District Secretary of the AEU, p. 20 (Coventry District Office, AUEW).
32 *Challenge,* 25 Nov. 1937.
33 Ibid.
34 P. Inman, *Labour in the Munitions Industries* (1957), p. 80.
35 This can be seen in the number of 'metal machinists' per toolmaker and setter as given in the 1931 census: Coventry: 5.6; Manchester: 9.4; Newcastle: 22.1 (1931 census, *Occupational Table* (1934), pp. 236–7, 316–7, 364–5). Because the term toolmaker was not used in the Scottish census, a comparative figure for Glasgow has to be obtained by looking at the proportion of metal machinists who were women. The results are: Coventry 18%; Manchester: 3.4%; Newcastle: 3.5%; Glasgow: 4.8% (Ibid., and *Census of Scotland* (1932), p. 106).
36 Walter Givens' Notebook, p. 15.
37 Ibid., p. 16.
38 J.B. Jefferys, op. cit., p. 210.

39  These figures are taken from G.D.H. Cole and Raymond Postgate's *The Common People, 1746–1946* (first published 1938; 1961 edition used here), pp. 642–7; still the best and most sensitive analysis of wage statistics for the 1930s.

40  Ibid., p. 644.

41  Private information.

42  *Industrial Welfare,* Nov. 1936, p. 38.

43  *Report* of the Chief Inspector of Factories, 1936, Cmd. 5514, p. 8.

44  A description of the processes involved in locomotive-building and ordnance manufacture is contained in interesting articles in the *Daily Telegraph,* 29, 30 and 31 Oct. 1928, surveying Beardmore's Parkhead Forge.

45  *Report* of the Chief Inspector of Factories, 1938, Cmd. 6081, p. 9.

46  'Interview with Mr Winbolt of ROSPA', 30 Jan. 1942. Industry Raw Materials, Mass Observation Archive.

47  *Report* of the Chief Inspector of Factories, 1940, pp. 4, 6; 1942, p. 6; 1943, p. 5.

48  H.B. Morgan, 'Scheduling of Industrial Diseases', in *Industrial Welfare,* Feb. 1938, pp. 62–3. Morgan pointed out how the registering of industrial diseases was strongly influenced by the legal definition of a disease as a sort of 'accident', and the subsequent distortion of reality which this involved.

49  *Report* of the Chief Inspector of Factories, 1935, p. 42.

50  H.C. Weston, 'Noise in Industry', in *Industrial Welfare,* Jan. 1938.

51  *Report* of the Chief Inspector of Factories, 1938, p. 82.

52  See Hansard V series, vol. 338, July 1937, col. 1554; Hansard, vol. 344, Feb. 1939, col. 531, on the number of workers enjoying paid holidays; J.B. Jefferys, op. cit., pp. 242–3.

53  *Industrial Welfare,* Jan. 1939, p. 41.

54  S. Ferguson and H. Fitzgerald, *Studies in the Social Services* (1954), p. 190.

55  Z.L. Puxley to Mr de Montmorency, 29 May 1940, MH/55/695.

56  The comparison with Germany was less flattering (see *Labour Management,* Jan. 1942, pp. 14, 15).

57  S. Ferguson and H. Fitzgerald, op. cit., pp. 190, 203, 207, 211.

58  See, for example, the Chief Inspector's annual *Report* for 1939; p. 1 and J.B. Jefferys, op. cit., pp. 212, 215.

59  J. Owner, *Redgrave & Owner's Factories, Truck and Shops Act* (16th ed., 1945), pp. 61–2 ff.

60  *Report* of the Chief Inspector, 1939, p. 1.

61  'Interview with Mr Winbolt of ROSPA, 30 Jan. 1942, Industry Raw Materials, Mass Observation Archive.

62  J. Owner, op. cit., p. 355.

63  *Report* of the Chief Inspector, 1938. Calculated from tables.

64  *Picture Post,* 4 Jan. 1941.

65  *Industrial Welfare,* Aug. 1939, p. 305.

66  Letter from twelve Briggs' Workers dated 6 Nov. 1937, TUC Library. A study of industrial workers' attitudes to health and safety matters would be extremely useful in determining how far workers accepted the 'compensation' approach adopted by most unions; this is still a much ignored area.

67  B.C.M. Weekes, 'The Amalgamated Society of Engineers, 1880–1914. A Study of Trade Union Government, Politics and Industrial Policy' (unpublished PhD thesis, University of Warwick, 1970).

68  R. Croucher, 'Local Autonomy in the ASE, 1889–1914' (unpublished MA thesis, University of Warwick, 1971).

69   J.B. Jefferys, op. cit., p. 227.
70   Walter Givens' Notebook, pp. 13–21.
71   Ibid., p. 15.
72   Ibid., p. 17. On J.H. Ward's impressive career as a trade-unionist, see R. Croucher, 'The Coventry Minority Movement', in *Bulletin* of the Society for the Study of Labour History, Spring 1976.
73   Trade union organisation seems to have been relatively good in other aircraft factories at this time; a joint committee of aircraft workers from different factories was set up in Southampton in 1929 (A. Clinton, *The Trade Union Rank and File* (Manchester, 1977), p. 172.
74   *The Engineer*, no. 3.
75   Leyland Shop Stewards' *Journal*, 1927.
76   See, for example, *Wolverton Express*, 8 Sept. 1939, reporting the delegates' collection for a respected manager who was retiring from the LMS works there.
77   'Shop Stewards in a Modern Factory. An Experiment in Promoting Industrial Co-operation', in *Industrial Welfare*, June 1936. 'Some Difficulties of a Personnel Manager. How to Start in a New Firm', in *Labour Management*, March 1939, no. 225, p. 45.
78   'Day-to-Day Problems of Shop Stewards', in *Industrial Welfare*, Nov. 1936, pp. 15–16.
79   *Minutes* of the Coventry District Committee of the AEU, 1935-9.
80   *The Conveyor*, Feb. 1937.
81   AEU *Monthly Journal*, Oct. 1936.
82   Dudley Edwards, *How Trade Unionism Came to Pressed Steel* (Oxford Militant pamphlet, 1979), p. 11.
83   *Oxford Mail*, 19 July 1934.
84   *The Conveyor*, Sept. 1934.
85   Bulletin of the Strike Committee, no. 6, 24 July 1934.
86   D. Edwards, op. cit., p. 6. The NUVB eventually paid strike benefit to its members who came out in support of the press shop workers two years after the strike (*Minutes* of the Oxford branch, NUVB, 2 Sept. 1936).
87   D. Edwards, op. cit., p. 16.
88   Management document, dated 29 March 1938, kindly lent to me by Roger Seeley of the TGWU 5/60 branch, who is working on a history of the branch.
89   TGWU document, 'Oxford Inquiry' (to all members of Area Committee no. 5, Inquiry held re loss of membership, 5/60 branch, in Oxford on 31 June 1939). This document, also lent by Roger Seeley, shows that the General Executive Council had come in for much criticism for not giving financial aid to Harris, and the AEU had been recruiting members as a result. At this meeting Murphy, the Area Secretary, revealed that Harris was being paid an amount by the GEC after all. Some stewards claimed that the attitude of the CP had also had a bearing on the TGWU's loss of membership because the CP had encouraged the AEU stewards to recruit amongst TGWU members.
90   List of TGWU shop stewards dated 28 April 1938, kindly lent by Roger Seeley.
91   D. Edwards, op. cit.
92   Talk given by Charlie Wellard at Goldsmith's College, London, 1980. The South-East London shop stewards' papers are in the National Museum of Labour History's archives.
93   'Shop Stewards in a Modern Factory', *Industrial Welfare*, June 1936.

94 There is a series of revealing passages on Abbott and Dobson in S. Phelan, 'The Avro Conspiracy' (Ruskin College Oxford Labour Studies dissertation, 1979).
95 Information kindly supplied by Mr John Smethurst.
96 Interviews with Eddie Frow. See also on all of these people and many others Ralph Hayburn's interesting thesis, 'The Responses to Unemployment in the 1930s, with special reference to South-East Lancashire' (un published PhD thesis, University of Hull, 1970).
97 *The Aeroplane,* 2 June 1937.
98 *Oxford Mail,* letter from Q. Hogg, 12 Dec. 1939. Reply from M. Yeatman, 18 Dec. 1939.
99 The Executive frequently made these points through the AEU *Journal;* see May 1935, p. 16, for example.
100 *The Citizen* (Gloucester), 9 March 1935.
101 Ibid., 8 March 1935.
102 Ibid, 11 March 1935.
103 Ibid.
104 Ibid., 14, 15 March.
105 Ibid., 18 March.
106 Ibid., 19 March.
107 Ibid.
108 Ibid., 25 March. Tom Roberts, 'The Importance of the English Aircraft Strike', in *Communist International,* vol. 12, 13 July 1935. This latter account has to be treated with caution, but is interesting in that it praises the idea of shop-stewardism, presumably for the benefit of foreign readers of the English language edition of *Communist International.*
109 AEU *Journal,* May 1935.
110 T. Roberts, op. cit.
111 *New Propellor,* vol. 1, no. 1, Oct. 1935.
112 T. Roberts, op. cit.
113 *NP,* vol. 1, no. 1; interview with Harold Taylor, 12 April 1976.
114 *NP,* Aug. 1937, Oct. 1938. The number of aircraft workers (120,000) for 1938 is the figure given by *Labour Research* in August 1939. The paper was distributed on a sale or return basis by bulk orders placed through shop stewards' committees.
115 Precise figures will always be unreliable here because of the difficulty of disentangling aircraft from other firms, but a look at the Ministry of Labour's Disputes Books confirms the key role of the aircraft firms in disputes. Trade union progress is detailed in 'Nine Months' Progress', in *NP,* March 1936.
116 *NP,* Nov., Dec. 1935. Number of strikers taken from LAB 34/50.
117 See strike fund acknowledgements in *NP.*
118 K. Middlemass, op. cit., pp. 246–7, and *passim.*
119 *The Aeroplane,* 19 Jan. 1938.
120 *NP,* Aug. 1937.
121 *NP,* Sept. 1937.
122 *Manchester Guardian,* 7 April 1938.
123 *Minutes* of the Manchester District Committee of the AEU, 18 Aug. 1938. *Minutes* of the Oxford branch of the NUVB, 6 July 1938, 11 Jan. 1939. *Minutes* of the Manchester District Committee of the AEU, 8 June 1939.
124 *Challenge,* 27 May 1937.
125 Ibid., 15 April 1937.
126 Ibid., 29 April 1937.

127  J.B. Jefferys, op. cit., pp. 244–5.
128  *Challenge*, 8 April 1937. See also J. Gollan, *Youth in British Industry* (1937), p. 67, on the sacking of apprentices at twenty-one.
129  *NP*, Oct. 1937.
130  A total of 173,552 working days were lost through apprentice and trainee strikes during 1937.
131  J.B. Jefferys, op. cit., pp. 244–5.
132  J. Gollan, op. cit., p. 65.
133  *Challenge*, 8 April 1937.
134  *Engineering Apprentices. Record of the Progress of the Movement among Engineering Apprentices for the Improvement of their Conditions of Employment: 1936-1937*, 24 March 1937, LAB 10/80. *Challenge*, 8 April 1937.
135  Reports of 5, 6 April in LAB 10/76.
136  8, 9, 15 April 1937, LAB 10/76.
137  *Challenge*, 8 April 1937.
138  7 April, LAB 10/76.
139  9, 12 April 1937, LAB 10/80. *Challenge*, 15 April 1937.
140  *DW*, 12 April 1937.
141  *Engineering Apprentices. Record of the Progress* etc.
142  *DW*, 8 April.
143  7 April, LAB 10/76.
144  Ibid.
145  *Challenge*, 11 Nov. 1937.
146  14 April, LAB 10/76. *DW*, 16 April 1937.
147  *DW*, 17 April.
148  17 April, LAB 10/76.
149  Ibid., 29 April 1937. There were extensions of the stoppage to Lanarkshire structural firms at this time (26 April, LAB 10/76).
150  The woodworkers recruited four hundred members because they followed this policy (23 April, LAB 10/76).
151  20 April, LAB 10/76.
152  Ibid.
153  1 March, LAB 10/76.
154  30 April, LAB 10/76.
155  *DW*, 4 May 1937. *Challenge* said: '. . . it is our opinion that the union leaders' advice was unwise. Instead of advising a return, they should have called for an extension of the strike all over the country for the Charter, and this would have been the best method of forcing the employers to give in', (6 May 1937).
156  At the beginning of June the Clyde apprentices adopted a green, red and blue badge: green for the Catholics, blue for the Protestants and red for the Communists. In the middle of that month they launched a Clyde apprentices' paper. (*Challenge*, 3, 15 June.)
157  *Engineering Apprentices. Record of the Progress* etc., p. 3, LAB 10/80.
158  Ibid.
159  Ibid., p. 3.
160  *Manchester Guardian*, 15 Sept. 1937.
161  Ibid., 16 Sept.; *Challenge*, 16 Sept. L. Bather, *A History of Manchester and Salford Trades Council* (Manchester PhD, 1956), pp. 208, 267.
162  *Manchester Guardian*, 16 Sept.
163  *Manchester Guardian*, 23 Sept.
164  Ibid.

165 Ibid., 2 Oct., *DW*, 2, 3 Oct.
166 *Engineering Apprentices. Record of the Progress* etc., p. 3, LAB 10/80.
167 *Minutes* of the Coventry District Committee of the AEU, 13 July 1937.
168 *NP*, Oct. 1937.
169 Ibid.
170 Ibid.
171 Ibid., Oct. 1937.
172 Ibid.; *Challenge*, 14 Oct.
173 *Engineering Apprentices. Record of the Progress* etc., p. 4. See also J.B. Jefferys, op. cit., p. 245.
174 Talk given by Charlie Wellard at Goldsmith's College, London, 1980.
175 Ibid.
176 J.B. Jefferys, op. cit., p. 245.
177 *Journal* of the Siemens Shop Stewards' Committee, no. 20, 1935, pp. 1, 2-4, 5, 9.
178 Ibid., no. 31, pp. 6-8, 10, 13-17, 19, 23-5.
179 Various interviews, including Dick Etheridge of Austin.
180 *The Record,* May 1935, June 1936.
181 A. Bullock, *The Life and Times of Ernest Bevin,* vol. 1(000), p. 525.
182 These matters were the subject of complaint by a member of the AEU Manchester district in 1944 (*Minutes* of the Manchester District Committee of the AEU, 22 June 1944).
183 Roger Seeley, *From Carriages to Cars. A Study in Change with Partial Reference to the Oxford Branch of the NUVB* (Ruskin College, Oxford, Labour Studies dissertation, 1976), p. 36. *Minutes* of the Oxford Branch, NUVB, 2 Sept. 1936.
184 *Minutes* of the Manchester District Committee of the AEU, 8 June 1939.
185 Interview with H. Taylor, 12 April 1976.
186 *Minutes* of the Manchester District Committee of the AEU, 24 Sept. 1939.
187 *Labour Research,* Sept. 1935, p. 196; May 1940, p. 72.
188 Not to be confused with *The Conveyor,* the journal of the Pressed Steel shop stewards, published in 1934, which is entry no. 719 in the *Warwick Guide to British Labour Periodicals* (ed. R. Harrison *et al.*). The *Warwick Guide* contains no reference to this journal; I have used the copies for January 1937, June 1937 and July 1938, by courtesy of Eddie Frow at the Library of the Working Class Movement, Manchester.
189 *NP*, May 1937. The ASSNC had timed a national strike to begin on 25 May, but decided that the meeting of the EC with the EEF timed for 26 May should not be prejudiced (ibid.) For the history of the demand and the influence of internal CP politics on this decision, see my thesis, pp. 48-58. It seems likely that the decision was influenced by the busmen's 'Coronation Strike', in which the unofficial Central Bus Committee came into sharp conflict with the TGWU Executive. For the Communists, a similar defeat in the AEU would have had serious results for their industrial work.
190 P. Inman, op. cit., p. 393. Figures for aircraft strikes calculated direct from Ministry of Labour Disputes Books (LAB 34/54).
191 See, for example, an important article by 'PJ' entitled 'Why We Don't Want Rank and File Movements' in the internal CP journal *Discussion*, Jan. 1936 (Maitland-Sara Collection, University of Warwick).
192 *Labour Research,* March 1939, p. 66.
193 *Evening Standard,* 5 May 1952.

# CHAPTER 2

# FROM PHONEY WAR TO PEOPLE'S WAR

The astonishing inertia of the Chamberlain government in the months between the declaration of war in September 1939 and its fall after the disastrous Norwegian campaign in May 1940 reflected its failure to make adequate preparations for mobilisation in the late 1930s. The mood in these months of 'Phoney War' was predominantly one of expectancy: Britain was waiting for the war to start rather than preparing to carry it strongly to the enemy. Germany was less backward, however, and by mid-September had successfully overrun Poland with a devastating Blitzkrieg. Temporarily satisfied by this considerable conquest, the German forces were content to pass the winter without further major military initiative. Many people in Britain feared attack from the air more than anything else during this period; large-scale evacuations in anticipation of massive air-raids were organised, only for the children to return home when the Luftwaffe bombers failed to appear. So far, it was a gentleman's war as far as Chamberlain's government was concerned. When the suggestion was made to Sir Kingsley Wood that the RAF should attempt to set fire to the Black Forest by bombing it, he replied indignantly that the forest was private property, adding: 'Why, you will be asking me to bomb Essen next.'[1] *The Aeroplane* revealed a similar conception of the purpose of the war, when it saw fit to castigate the government for restricting the export of aeroplanes when Britain was 'supposed to be fighting a war for commercial purposes'.[2]

Initially at least, the electoral truce concluded between the main political parties tended to restrict public discussion of the purpose, aims and conduct of the war. The Communists might have been expected to break this silence, but they found themselves in a difficult position. Having initially supported the war (Harry Pollitt wrote a pamphlet entitled *How To Win The War*), they were compelled to reverse their position on instructions from the Communist International which made it clear that the war was an imperialist one. The CP was for some time taken up at national level with the internal discussions which followed the CI's intervention, and was lumbered with a 'line' that was out of step with that of their allies of Popular Front days.

The Wehrmacht's spectacular successes in Scandinavia effectively removed the Chamberlain government, whose complacent reliance on the Royal Navy's supremacy at sea and utter failure to conduct the war efficiently were there for all to see. The Coalition government formed under Churchill in May 1940 held out some hope that the central direction of the war effort was at last in competent hands: with Churchill unexpectedly at the head of the Coalition, and Ernest Bevin at the Ministry of Labour, there was for the first time a look of conviction about the Cabinet. But despite a major success at birth, the Coalition government had inherited an extremely grave military situation. Almost immediately it had to contend with another disaster. France, Britain's major ally, whose defences had appeared almost impregnable, soon proved to be as vulnerable to Blitzkrieg tactics as Poland had been. With France beaten, Britain would stand alone against the German Reich.

During the next year the invasion of Britain was a constant haunting possibility. Some thought that it would come immediately after Dunkirk, many felt that it would only happen after the end of the blitz, and although the Battle of Britain had clearly deterred the Germans, there was still felt to be a real threat right up until the invasion of the Soviet Union in June 1941. A new period in the history of the war had opened with Dunkirk: a large section of the governing class had been completely discredited and ordinary people felt it was necessary to clear them out—they still lurked in the government—and to start the business of fighting the war themselves. National safety was too important to be entrusted to governments any more, it was felt.

Despite efforts to mobilise the economy for war, the depth of the crisis led to considerable criticism of Britain's unpreparedness. The Chamberlain government had in fact begun to mobilise labour and to extend the shadow factories and Royal Ordnance Factories, but the process was a slow one. The government had been much impressed by the experience of the First World War, when severe industrial problems had been created by allowing recruitment to the forces to carry on without regard to industry's need for skilled workers (although this concern did not prevent the recruitment of many miners to the forces). Consequently, they had drawn up a Schedule of Reserved Occupations in 1938, and from November 1939 employers could apply for the 'deferment' of men who would otherwise have been called up. By the end of 1940, over two hundred thousand men had been granted deferment at their employers' request. Skilled engineers were within the category of reserved occupation, and so the call-up, which proceeded progressively, starting with the youngest and reaching the forty to forty-one year-olds only by July 1941, did not affect the structure of the engineering workforce as radically as it had done in the First World War.[3] Nevertheless, many men not in a skilled category were called up and their places taken by men not yet called up, or by women.

Nationally, unemployment remained remarkably persistent, at over one million until April 1940. As late as July 1941 it still stood at two hundred thousand.[4] Pools of unemployment tended to be most common in the old 'depressed areas' and especially the mining regions. In the centres of war production, labour was in short supply. The result was a very considerable migration from mining areas to the booming munitions factories of Birmingham, Coventry and London. After an initial period of lay-off—Pressed Steel and Morris laid off four thousand five hundred men in Oxford at the end of September 1939, for example—to reorganise their lay-out and to re-tool for war work, it was extremely easy to find work at factories in these months.[5] All types of people with no engineering experience whatever were taken on: butchers, bakers, housewives—people from every conceivable background were coming in to the factories to earn the good wages that were reputedly available.

Some knowledgeable commentators were taken by surprise

when they saw the extent to which the engineering industry had already been turned over to arms production by the outbreak of war. This was especially true in the Midlands, where the Ministry of Labour's Chief Conciliation Officer reported that less disturbance than expected had been necessary, because of the large amount of government work being carried on 'just below the surface'.[6] Subcontracting of component manufacture and sub-assembly work had already pushed the limits of the aircraft industry further and further into engineering and sheet metal factories.[7] The traditional and always somewhat artificial boundaries between different sectors of the engineering industry were being gradually eroded as work was farmed out to whoever could undertake it. During 1940 a good deal of new productive capacity was brought into operation, with the second group of shadow factories coming into service; and large-scale Royal Ordnance Factories built to maximise the use of female and unskilled labour were commissioned. Very often, the cement was hardly dry on the new shop floor before machines were being laid out and set up for production.[8]

The new factories were built to the most modern specifications, with flow-lines, assembly tracks and automatic machine tools widely utilised to allow the maximum use of semi-skilled labour. At the Rootes No. 2 shadow factory in Coventry, for example, automatic machinery was used in every possible operation: on one job, the installation of modern bar automatics reduced a standard machining time from forty minutes to just four and a half.[9] The aircraft industry was constantly striving to rationalise production methods, but mass production remained extremely difficult to achieve. At Gloster Aircraft, 'one of the finest production shops in the country', Hurricanes were being made in a way which *The Aeroplane* considered to be 'something approaching mass production', but this was only true of some of the most efficient units.[10] A well known expert on engineering technology was voicing his concern at the lack of standardisation of aircraft parts which he considered to be a major retarding factor in expanding aircraft production.[11] From the summer of 1940 and the appointment of Beaverbrook to the Ministry of Aircraft Production, medium-term programmes of technological innovation were in any case to be strictly subordinated to the demands of immediate production. Everything was sacrificed to producing aeroplanes. This, too, brought its own sort of radical change in the workshops, tending to break down traditional job demarcations, to pull more and more people into the productive process and to intensify existing problems.

By 1940 Coventry was a munitions town which demonstrated the social impact of these developments in an unusually clear way. With three shadow factories already in operation in the town and three more which opened on its outskirts during the first year of war, it was experiencing an enormous expansion in population. Housing estates were extended and hostels set up for war workers, but these measures proved insufficient and billeting had to be introduced. Between 1931 and 1939, the city's population had already expanded by 42,148 through immigration alone in a total population (in 1939) of 229,500.[12] Most of the incoming workers were from the area around Cardiff and Newport, the Lancashire cotton towns, Clydeside, Greater London and the coal-mining districts of Northumberland and Durham (in descending order of importance).[13] The overwhelming majority of these immigrants (eighty per cent) entered the engineering factories, showing a marked aversion for the Warwickshire pits to the north of the town. Most of them were young single men.[14] During 1940 these areas continued to provide the highest proportion of incoming workers, but a steadily increasing proportion of new workers were women. By 1941 approximately five immigrants in every fourteen entering the factories were women, since Coventry had a below-average population of spinsters and widows, soon absorbed by the expanding factories.[15]

The local engineering employers had been anxious to obtain young men from the depressed areas during the early 1930s, but found in the 'boom' circumstances of late 1939-40 that the immigrant workers in general were not as pliable as they had earlier thought. Some had already worked under piece-work in the mines, but many had probably had little previous work experience at all. They nevertheless developed a very determined collective approach to problems. In the areas they came from, trade unionism was an aspect of local and national culture that had deep roots outside of the workplace. Just after the war started, for example, the Rootes Co. complained to their colleagues in the Coventry Engineering Employers' Association that one particular gang was causing continual trouble in the polishing shop of their No. 1 shadow factory adjacent to the Humber works in Stoke Aldermoor. The gang comprised one hundred and thirty-three men, of whom no less than forty-eight were trainees from the depressed areas who had, as Rootes's Mr Booth contemptuously remarked, 'not even as much engineering knowledge as a labourer in the shop'. They did, however, have the audacity to refuse to man certain disputed jobs, and after a number of clashes with them Booth decided to break the gang up. Whether this solved the problem or spread it is unknown.[16] In other areas, such as Slough, employers complained about the behaviour of young workers from the depressed areas who were taking advantage of the increasingly tight labour market to change jobs 'at the drop of a hat' and to kick against managerial discipline.[17] In due course these young workers (and especially those from Scotland, Ireland and Wales) were to play an increasingly important part in the engineering unions in the Midlands and London, as a cursory glance at shop stewards' names will show.

The new workers in munitions had good reason to feel that they needed the protection of trade union membership during 1940. At first, during the Phoney War, the hours worked in engineering had increased only slightly, with more shops working overtime than before the war. This situation persisted more or less generally until the fall of France. After Dunkirk, the sky was the limit as far as overtime was concerned: many workers were on double shifts, and summer holidays were not observed at all. In fact, the lessons of the First World War in terms of the diminishing returns on hours spent at work were largely ignored, and exhaustion became common. The Chief Inspector of Factories, pointing out the short-sightedness of long hours of 'extravagant proportions', linked this with the very high accident rate of 1940.[18] The accident rate amongst young workers and women increased dramatically during 1940 and 1941: by 1941 it had almost quadrupled amongst adult women, when compared to 1938. The unions had become aware of the dimensions of this problem, and had pushed the advantages of union participation in accident-prevention committees and their support in obtaining compensation.[19] The TGWU was particularly well aware of the potential of this situation. At Gloster Aircraft, the shop stewards publicised to a packed meeting in the canteen a settlement of £4000 which had been obtained from the company for Miss D.M. Price, who had her fingers severed by the descending cutter of an inadequately guarded power press. The 'splendid settlement' was publicised in *The Record* as an important aspect of the union's service to members.[20]

The new entrants to the industry could often find themselves at the bottom of the wages pile, and this was a matter of concern to all the engineering unions, who were opposed to undercutting established rates through the dilution of the traditional engineering skills. As the rate of technological change increased, so the content of 'skilled' engineering work of the past became such that it could be carried out by unskilled operators. Complex operations were broken down into their constituent parts and into a number of repetitive tasks on a flow-line basis; this was the classic 'dilution'. Very often, however, the situation was not as clear-cut, and entirely new operations would appear for which there was no existing equivalent. The AEU's main aim—to protect the rates of its largely skilled membership against the impact of dilution—proved extremely difficult to achieve, but in 1940 it signed an agreement with the engineering employers, entitled the Extended Employment of Women Agreement, which provided for the payment of the full skilled rate for women who replaced skilled men. In the workshops, the resultant problems were very apparent: when, for example, a turner's job was done by a dozen women on repetition work, should they all be paid the full rate? The employers generally refused to comply, as the women were not able to do the skilled turner's work; yet a skilled job had disappeared.

The only way to deal with such difficulties was to try to ensure that the women and semi-skilled men involved were in trade unions and pushing for the rate themselves. The AEU refused to recruit women until 1943, and most of them had therefore to join one of the general unions. Although not signatories to the 1940 Agreement, these unions were prepared to try to apply it, but they combined this with another line of attack of their own. The TGWU in particular called for the grading of jobs as well as the rate for the job. This approach had the great merit of appealing to the woman labourer, for example, who earned less than her male counterpart simply by reason of her sex. It also appealed to the semi-skilled man, who would have his status recognised in a semi-skilled grade rather than being categorised as unskilled. On one point, however, all the unions were unanimous: dilution should not be used to create a pool of cheap labour within engineering. The early adoption of policies which had at least this degree of unanimity paved the way for a campaign of considerable momentum on women's and semi-skilled wages by 1943-4.[21] At this point, however, the process of dilution was still in a relatively early stage, and recruitment was the union's first priority.

The general consensus amongst engineering trade-unionists was that it was 'catch-as-catch-can' in the factories, especially in the new shadow units, where nobody could establish any exclusive rights to recruit. The toolmakers would join the AEU, and the sheet metal workers one of their two unions, but after that the field was open. The activists spared no effort and used a good deal of imagination in bringing the many non-unionists into the union. Jock Wallace recalls recruiting in factories along London's Great West Road; the AEU set up a Western Area Organising Committee and went about the job with enthusiasm:

I volunteered to do the jobs at night time. Day workers were always contactable. . . during the day. But it was always a difficulty to make recruitment on nights. Some of the factories, like one Brentford factory. . . we entered the gates and were escorted off the premises by the Police. Little did they know that the other half of our group were scaling the railings at the back to get entry onto the site. This was a highly successful job because we recruited about sixty per cent of the night shift on that first go. Unfortunately, they couldn't get out, they had to stop there all night, some sleeping under hedges within the factory site. . . the police were on the main

80

gate, you see, and there was a patrol going round. We were very lucky to get in on that score because that particular spot had been left unguarded. We got out on the days, but two of the lads were caught, interviewed by the police, and it was due to the fact that they had shown up the Police by their own weakness, I believe, that the whole case got dropped.

At Sunbeam Talbot's the organising committee had a 'friend at court' in the wife of Ted Bramley (Secretary of the London District of the Communist Party); she had already started to talk to some people about the union, and when some organisers arrived in the nine p.m. night shift break the ground was already prepared for them. Within a short space of time they had built a strong shop stewards' committee at the Ladbroke Grove plant.[22] Other trade-unionists did not stop at organising in the factory: Jock Gibson, a young CP member and TGWU steward, met incoming workers at Coventry station, handing out leaflets and applications for membership.[23]

It was at this time that trade-unionism started to make inroads into the car factories, now employed on war work, which had previously proved extremely difficult to organise because of the seasonal fluctuations in employment. At Austin's Longbridge complex a group of AEU members had been meeting together since about 1937 in the canteen, with the experienced Micky George, a veteran of the 1929 strike at Longbridge, and George Fowler, a toolmaker to whom everyone turned for advice. At first there were just seven or eight people meeting on a Monday night straight after work, but this expanded at the beginning of the war, and two women workers, Gertie and Freda Nokes, employed in the Aero factory, played an important part in bringing the women into membership.[24] At Morris Radiators, Oxford, it was the transfer of skilled men from the Wolverton railway works that brought trade-unionists to the factory. Working in the toolroom, one Wolverton man was put with one Oxford man on making aircraft oil-coolers. The Wolverton men were all skilled, and all unionised. They insisted on retaining their union cards and their old, higher rate of pay. Their legitimate demands seem to have provided just the first step towards initiating trade union activity in the Morris works, previously regarded as a union 'blackspot'.[25]

The booming Midlands munitions towns, swollen with war workers, offered great potential for the energetic trade union organiser. Coventry and Birmingham had been centres of the Workers' Union, and had a tradition—albeit under threat of extinction during the Depression years—of unskilled trade-unionism. In Coventry these opportunities were seized by the exceptionally able new District Secretary of the TGWU, Jack Jones. Appointed only a few weeks before the outbreak of war, the young Secretary had only recently returned from fighting for the Spanish Republic. The leftward-leaning Jones soon grasped the importance of developing his shop stewards, the cadre of the union's industrial army. In an era when trade union education hardly existed, he gave his stewards practical training. Harold Taylor, one of these men, remarked on his flair for this work:

> Jones really started to promote a new kind of shop steward. . . people who can benefit from a little weekend down the office. . . and we used to do negotiating sessions. . . we didn't realise we were being taught how to negotiate and not to get irate and how to take advantage of situations where the management were losing their page and things like that. Jack Jones was a brilliant man, even at that young age. In fact, I thought he was much older, he was so able.[26]

By 1944 these sessions had become quite formalised and included sessions on the history of the trade union movement in engineering and the provisions of the Factories Act and workmen's compensation, all given by Jones himself.[27] As early as December 1939 he was noticed by the Chief Conciliation Officer as making the TGWU 'more prone than they were to be aggressive, and to threaten strike action'.[28] By 1944 the new District Secretary had built up the TGWU's local organisation to such an extent that he was shortlisted for the post of National Secretary of the union's metal, engineering and chemicals trade group.[29]

Jones helped Jock Gibson, Harold Taylor and other young TGWU shop stewards to take advantage of the recruitment possibilities of Coventry, but it also has to be remembered that the TGWU had kept a toehold in the local engineering industry during the Depression. In the northern districts, and especially in Scotland, the AEU had long maintained almost exclusive control over engineering factories. In mid-1940, however, the TGWU made an important breakthrough in Scotland. The new aero-engine factory set up at Hillington just outside Glasgow was designed to employ large numbers of women and semi-skilled, and the CP members who led the way in organising the plant were determined to break down craft exclusiveness there. The logic of their argument at Hillington must have been quite apparent: if the AEU was to be the only engineering union, then the factory would remain largely unorganised. In September 1940 the newly formed factory committee decided to ask the TGWU to recruit the women,[30] and in the following month matters came to a head when a supervisor insisted that women should either be in the AEU (which was clearly impossible), or in no union at all.[31] The result was a strike in the foundry which successfully established the TGWU's right to organise the women, and laid the foundations for the important part that the Scottish arms industries were later to play in the TGWU's wartime expansion.[32]

While the general unions brought their considerable experience to bear on the new possibilities opening up before them, the craft unions were maintaining their traditional vigilance over workshop affairs. Thus, despite the extreme pressure on engineers to work any hours necessary, the shop stewards at Beardmore's Parkhead Forge, Glasgow, threatened to strike because an AEU member refused to pay a fine for not observing the stewards' rule that all overtime be reported to them.[33] Their threat, redolent of the craft trade-unionists' attitude that strict control should be maintained over overtime, shows how persistent some AEU shop stewards could be despite powerful pressure to abandon their old practice.

The craftsmen also insisted on the importance of workshop rituals, despite the changes occurring in the factories and the exigencies of war production. Sometimes their purpose was patriotic, as when the royal family was greeted in a Coventry factory in August 1940 by cheering 'accompanied by hammer blows on metal'.[34] They were being greeted, in other words, with the old custom of 'ringing in', practised on almost any occasion of importance and described by the journeyman engineer Thomas Wright in the middle of the nineteenth century.[35] In this particular context 'ringing in' was to be encouraged by the management as a sign of loyal enthusiasm, but there were other less innocuous instances when it turned against an unpopular foreman or manager.[36] When these rituals involved 'time wasted', like the 'footings' drunk at apprentices' expense when they became journeymen, then managements tried to suppress them. In 1943 a factory paper wrote of a managerial attempt to suppress a strange custom: 'And so the Ancient Ceremony of the Suspension of the Matrimonial Utensil of Lowly Purpose, which has graced engineering establishments since the day when Stevenson's "Rocket" went the way of all flesh, has been banned.'[37] In this case the management seemed to have successfully suppressed the disorderly but no doubt enjoyable 'Ancient Ceremony', but in many others they failed or did not even try, for fear of being derided as spoilsports. These touchstones of the engineers' collective identity generally survived, despite the disapproval, tacit or explicit, of managements.

The perpetuation, and in some cases revival, of these customs may also be seen as an affirmation of the continuity of workshop life despite the very considerable upheavals going on at the time. It is quite probable that many of those involved in 'ringing in' the King had not been in the factory for more than a year, yet they participated in an old engineering ritual. This consciousness of the importance of continuity was also reflected in trade union matters. A determination to defend existing rights and practices was evident, despite the managerial offensive that was beginning.

Despite the impression transmitted by some historians and nurtured by others, engineers did not suddenly fly into the arms of waiting managers on the declaration of war. By and large, trade-unionists saw no reason to imagine that these same managers had suddenly changed their industrial ways on patriotic grounds. The determination to hold on to such gains as had been made was particularly marked in some areas. In Scotland, Galbraith, the Ministry of Labour's Chief

Conciliation Officer, drew the attention of London Head-quarters to the 'state of sensitiveness' on the Clyde in March 1940. He cited as evidence two important strikes: one at Beardmore's Parkhead Forge over the sacking of two men, and one at Albion Motors over the introduction of a non-unionist into the shop.[38] All the indications were that the Clyde engineers had no intention of giving an inch, a feeling that was soon to be confirmed.

Shop stewards had still to fight for the right to operate; managements were by no means reconciled to their continued existence within the factories. Companies very rarely, there-fore, conceded operational facilities to shop stewards. In Coventry two factories secured elementary facilities by appealing over the heads of management to Beaverbrook, but in spite of this the AEU District Committee was unable to secure promises of notice-board and meeting rights from the local employers.[39] In some cases, existing 'privileges' were withdrawn. At A.V. Roe, Manchester, the stewards had for some time had a joint committee of the various plants which met in company time to negotiate with manage-ment, but a period of prolonged hostilities was opened by the withdrawal of this right on account of the amount of travelling time involved and the disparity of conditions between the different units.[40] Galbraith saw these problems of ill-defined shop stewards' rights as the source of many disputes over victimisation in his region, and much evidence points to his judgment having more than a local validity.[41] During 1940 and especially after the Phoney War months, managements felt politically confident enough to challenge the shop stewards' right to operate in the workshops. They sacked a number of shop stewards, assuming that engineers would not dare strike to defend them, in view of the grave military situation. Stopping work in 1940 called for a good deal of collective resolve. Workers denied their annual summer holidays could call their strikes 'holidays' in an attempt to justify them, but the government replied in the language of coercion. Harold Taylor, an ex-soldier working at Armstrong-Whitworth Aircraft, recalled being surprised to see troops being brought into Baginton to man anti-aircraft guns there during a strike in 1940; their presence could, of course, be interpreted in more than one way.[42] During the summer of 1940 laws were passed that could be used against strikers.

Yet despite the fact that these pressures reinforced the general reluctance to stop work, strikes only tailed off in the months of June, July and August, a period of excruciating national anxiety. In fact, the number of strikes in the metal, engineering and shipbuilding industries during 1940 exceeded the corresponding figure for 1939. The number of days lost through strikes declined by almost half, on the other hand.[43] But the effect of the critical war situation was not to reduce the number of strikes; it was rather to keep them short. John Perryman, a London shop steward, has argued that it was in any case CP policy to keep strikes short at this time because of the likelihood of police harassing shop stewards and the possibility of prosecution.[44] It is difficult to say how relevant this policy was to the length of strikes, but managements were only too prepared at the time to lay the blame for strikes at the feet of Communists. Indeed, they sometimes argued that anyone who was concerned with trade union rights at such a time must be politically motivated. Although this view neglected the existence of grievances amongst the factory rank and file, and the determination of many non-CP trade-unionists to maintain their organisation, it contained a grain of truth.

The CP had taken up a clear position on the need to defend shop floor union organisation, and had made it a central part of their policy. After some initial problems with Harry Pollitt's and John Campbell's objections, the CP had adopted the Communist International's line that the war was an imperialist conflict in which workers could have no interest.[45] Historical parallels were drawn by the engineer and ex-leader of the unemployed, Wal Hannington, in his *Industrial History in Wartime,* to show that the shop stewards of the First World War had been forced to defend and advance workers' rights despite the role of the trade unions at the official level, and articles were published by Hannington and Campbell in *Labour Monthly* reminding stewards of their duty in this respect.[46] Both publicly and on the shop floor, the CP was stressing that the trade union officials were cooperating with the government and as a result could not be relied upon. The Communist analysis was fairly accurate, to the extent that it stressed how the officials had become more integrated at national level into the structure of the state through participation in a large number of tripartite bodies. Its analysis ignored the price extracted by the unions for their cooperation, but it stiffened their resolve to defend victimised shop stewards in cases which were less than fully supported by either local or national full-time officers.

The Chamberlain government had done little to cultivate the trade unions at national level, and had in fact completely failed to win the confidence of their leaders. Indeed, this has been identified by some writers as the primary cause of that government's defeat in the House of Commons on 7 May 1940.[47] Churchill did not make the same mistake, appointing Ernest Bevin, General Secretary of the TGWU, as Minister of Labour. Bevin's presence alone ensured that the radical action required in view of the serious military position could be taken with the active cooperation of the trade union leaders.

The first priority in May 1940 was to frame the necessary statutory instruments to give the ministers the power to achieve maximum mobilisation of the country's productive resources in the shortest possible time. On 22 May Attlee introduced an extension of the Emergency Powers Act in the House of Commons. The next day, *The Times* said of the new Act (the Bill had been passed in one day) that: 'It is doubtful whether such powers have ever been in the hands of the Executive since the seventeenth century.'[48] Attlee had explained to the House of Commons exactly what the new Act was intended to do: it was to give the Minister of Labour the power to direct any person to perform any service required of him. Workers could be moved, and the Minister could prescribe wages, hours and conditions of work. Excess Profits Tax was to be levied at a rate of one hundred per cent over the pre-war 'standard' years so that employers could not (formally, at least) enjoy larger profits than before the war. In addition, the minister was to control key establishments immediately, and others as soon as practicable.[49] An important set of regulations was immediately promulgated under the new Act. They were collectively known as Regulation 58A, and had two main industrial features: they delegated the Minister's power of direction to National Service Officers, and they required Inspectors of Labour Supply to ensure that wages and conditions in controlled factories were good enough to compel people to work in them. But Regulation 58A also had an explicitly political dimension. The Home Secretary was empowered to suppress organisations 'which have had associations with the enemy or are subject to foreign influence or control and which may be used for purposes prejudicial to the national security'.[50] The reference to organisations subject to foreign influence or control could of course include the Communist Party, with its links with the Communist International, and indeed was more relevant to it than to the British Union of Fascists. The fusion of the political and the industrial aspects of ministerial direction in the same regulation augured ill for the Communist Party, with its strength in industry, and leading Communist stewards were to be arrested and even imprisoned under the regulation.[51]

The Emergency Powers Act and the related new regulations gave the Minister of Labour and the Home Secretary sweeping powers, but they did little more than create a framework and an atmosphere within which Bevin could start to build a labour policy. The two main foundations were the Conditions of Employment and National Arbitration Order (known by its number, Order 1305) and the Essential Works Order. Order 1305 aimed at preventing industrial stoppages by strengthening existing procedures and backing them up with compulsory arbitration. If a dispute occurred, either party was entitled to refer it to the Minister of Labour, who would in turn simply refer it to the existing joint machinery for settlement by negotiation. If there was a failure to agree within the procedure, then the Minister was to refer the problem to the National Arbitration Tribunal, whose decision would be binding on both parties. Only if the Minister failed to refer the dispute to the National Arbitration Tribunal within the prescribed time was a strike or lockout legal. Also, the Order empowered the Minister to enforce 'recognised terms and conditions' within each district on any employer who was not observing them, as some compensation for the effective withdrawal of the right to strike.[52] In practice, as Wal Hannington pointed out, some shop stewards thought this right had not been entirely withdrawn and argued that the process of giving twenty-one days' notice of strike action was sufficient to ensure a strike's legality.[53] Behind the shop stewards' legal interpretation was an assertion of value, an argument that it was not right to completely remove the right to stop work. This did not derive from any haziness in the Order itself: Order 1305 quite clearly stated that procedure should be followed, and that where there was a procedure in existence there could not be a legal strike.

Order 1305 had grown organically out of the close relationship that Bevin enjoyed with senior trade union officials. On 22 May he had met the National Joint Advisory Council of union officials and employers, and on 4 June they voluntarily signed an agreement promising to use the constitutional machinery (and therefore not to take 'unconstitutional' strike action), and to use arbitration in the event of failure to agree at the highest level of procedure. This agreement formed the basis of Order 1305. The Order, then, stemmed directly from the official trade union response to the national crisis and Bevin's initiatives in dealing with it.[54] Indeed, similar pressures lay behind the Extended Employment of Women Agreement, which provided for the dilution of skilled engineering work by women provided that they were paid the skilled rate where they replaced skilled men.[55] This agreement was signed on 22 May. The new government, unlike its predecessor, understood the potential to be realised by harnessing the trade union officials to the war machine; by doing so, they ensured that the officials would act resolutely against strikes. In return, Bevin ensured that certain minimum standards were enforced, and that direct government consultation with unofficial elements such as shop stewards would not be allowed to undermine the authority of the head offices.

All forms of industrial action therefore took on a new character and a new significance from this point onwards.

There was now no possibility of an official strike, and indeed the trade union Executives usually treated strikes as emergencies, straining to put them out with all the vigour of a team of fire-fighters tackling an incendiary bomb. But this was not always the case: there were occasions, especially later in the war, when even Executives felt that industrial action could strengthen their hand in difficult negotiations, and did not therefore rush to end them. Similarly motivated, local officials could sometimes be strategically out of the office for a while, and on at least one occasion a local official was to support a strike openly. The fact remains, though, that trade union officials were generally opposed to industrial action in wartime.

In the political atmosphere of 1940 there were many who defined industrial action as 'sabotage', so it was not necessary for anyone to stress the need to negotiate if at all possible before taking action. Indeed, there was a small but significant trend towards suspicion of anyone who might be remotely likely to be involved in sabotage of any sort. Few people thought there were many such offenders, but under the circumstances most were prepared to see anyone suspected of 'sabotage' dealt with severely. The police and government departments were extremely active during this period in trying to detect any such cases. It is not always clear either what direction these 'sabotage' inquiries mainly followed (and hundred-year restrictions on access to the public records will not help here), nor what was the division of labour between government departments, police, secret services and managements. All that is apparent is that there was a good deal of activity, of which only the tip is visible to the historian, which both took advantage of and stimulated a very broad definition of industrial sabotage.

During June and July 1940, the full-time security officer at the Woolwich Arsenal began to suspect a number of 'Communists' of 'sabotage'; he found it difficult to produce very much concrete evidence in support of his accusation, but thought it possible that they had put sand in a grinding machine. Of the seven men named, three were dismissed more or less straight away, and the other four were earmarked for a similar fate. The official concerned was not especially worried about their colleagues' reaction because: 'At present we have a good deal of information to suggest that they are hanging themselves by pursuing a policy that the bulk of the working people abominate.'[56] The policy in question was, of course, the Communist insistence that the war was an imperialist dogfight, and it may be that this was as important as the sabotage accusation in getting them the sack. Three weeks later the official was confirmed in his opinion that his action had met with the approval of the other employees, when the skilled shop stewards' committee informed him that they were in favour of all of the men's dismissal, and that in fact: 'If they are not removed it may well be that their colleagues will take the law into their own hands.'[57] The accusations of Communism and sabotage were inextricably intertwined in this case. For some, it appears, one was proof of the other.

Cases of sabotage in which political motivations were at least superficially absent seem to have made up the bulk of cases. The Ministry of Information monitored court cases brought for the offence and collected data on its incidence. Between October 1940 and October 1941 it discovered eight cases involving twelve people. All concerned quite young men: the oldest was only thirty-one, while five were under twenty-one. Almost all of them had as their ostensible objective temporary or permanent release from their work. In January 1941, for example, a Bristol youth of seventeen 'messed up' the fuse box at a factory, causing a power failure to some fifty workers, because, he said, he wanted a night off. He was sentenced to three months' imprisonment. In October 1940 a fitter was fined £100 for deliberately scamping work on an aircraft, in order to obtain his release from the firm so that he could find a better-paid job. In the following month, a young engineer was bound over for two years for an unspecified act of 'sabotage' committed because, he claimed, he wanted his release to join the Army.[58] The last two instances, superficially at least, are fairly typical, and show workers trying to get themselves sacked from controlled establishments because they were unable to move in any other way. To have people actually trying to get dismissed was hardly conducive to good discipline within a works, and left management powerless. How could such people be punished? However justified the charge of sabotage was, the motive behind it seems to have been usually nothing more political than the desire to change jobs. When it involved destruction of company property companies were able, with the backing of magistrates, to punish the offender, but such cases were very few. Even the Ministry of Information was unable to unearth many cases. As a real threat to production within British industry, sabotage was to all intents and purposes irrelevant.

The same could not be said, however, of the shop stewards in engineering, and this was recognised both by government and employers. The employers of course, had always been reluctant to allow any interference with their untrammelled right to manage, and had certainly not yet become reconciled to the presence of shop stewards in their factories. There is some evidence to suggest that the government, or at least some government departments, were not averse to providing firms with information which encouraged them to be selective about whom they took on or continued to employ. The management at Rolls-Royce, for example, had checked up with the Air Ministry on a man who was leading an unofficial strike at their Crewe factory in 1939, and found that the man concerned was on an Air Ministry blacklist for 'causing' a strike at Fairey Aviation.[59] Surveillance of activists intensified during the war itself. The manager of a radio factory in southern England noted that the police kept a 'strict watch' on Communist movements and meetings, which were reported to him by Air Intelligence.[60] In a Clyde shipyard, a boy rivet-heater grew so annoyed with being watched at work by a detective that, instead of throwing the rivet to his mate on the stocks, he threw it at the man, and was sacked as a result.[61] From these scattered instances it seems possible to infer that both Air Intelligence and the police were involved in this sort of surveillance, and that they had a fairly close relationship with employers.

The arrest and sacking of shop stewards during 1940 became a matter of acute concern not only to *New Propellor* and the *Daily Worker*, but also to union District Committees. In early August John Mason, a Sheffield shop steward, was arrested under Regulation 18B and interned; a campaign was initiated for his release by the Communist papers, which drew increasing attention to the use of Regulation 18B against stewards.[62] The campaign to obtain Mason's release for 'impeding the war effort' continued through 1940, with the Engineering and Allied Trades Shop Stewards' National Council (E&ATSSNC) pointing out the need for the Executive of the AEU to defend all victimised shop stewards.[63] Mason's case was unusual in that Regulation 18B had been used against him, but it was by no means atypical in that he was a left-wing shop steward who had been punished for his activities. Whether this was for his industrial or political role or for both is unclear; as *New Propellor* pointed out, the nature of the charge against him was rather vague.[64] The E&ATSSNC and *New Propellor* were in no doubt, however, that Mason's internment was part of a general tendency for shop stewards to be picked out for punitive treatment. They were not surprised, but they were concerned, and they equated the wave of victimisations with the first steps towards fascism and the suppression of free trade-unionism.[65] Effective shop floor trade-unionism would be vital to compensate for the weakness of union leadership, but at the same time it guaranteed that the shop stewards would become prime targets. With shop stewards suppressed, the way could be open to fascism through 'regimenting' the working class.[66] The theory was expounded by J.R. Campbell and Wal Hannington, but in so far as it drew on engineers' fears about the conscription of labour and the victimisation of their workplace representatives, it was not exclusively a Communist one.

More than one shop steward was to feel the ripples sent out by the arrest of John Mason. Jock Wallace, who had already been the subject of police interest, recounts his experience:

> The police came down the following morning [following a meeting at Napier's Action works]. Called me up to the office. Two police-men, Sergeant Andrews of the CID, I'll remember that as long as I live. He had something to do with Johnny Mason because he kept on about it. I said to him, 'Fair enough, put me away down to Epsom, or wherever it is.' I said, 'I'll have some very good

Cartoon depicting the victimisation of John Mason, *New Propellor*, 15 February 1941

companions there, don't keep saying that.' They were under instructions to keep me in the office on this night until I signed this document. Little did I know that the Party had got to work and there wasn't a thing going on in the factory, and they were getting ready to spread it all round West London. This was the machinery we had in those days.[67]

The police had clearly hoped that the arrest and imprisonment of Mason would facilitate their task of trying to stop shop stewards from holding meetings. It is quite apparent that the police were showing an intensity of interest in shop steward activity that they had previously reserved for the National Unemployed Workers' Movement during the 1930s. Almost every ex-shop steward who spoke about this period mentioned being watched, followed or interviewed formally by the police. The precise methods and objectives of this campaign will remain obscure until the public records on the subject are available, but it already seems likely that the fears of the E&ATSSNC were not as far-fetched as they might at first seem.

The engineering employers needed little prompting to begin taking advantage of the political climate to get rid of 'troublemakers'. Victimisation is as old as workplace representation itself, and possibly even older. An ugly motif running through trade union history, it flows from the conflict between management's tendency to identify the steward with the union as a whole and the engineers' view of the steward as representative of their collective interests. But during 1940, when engineering workers were reluctant to stop work, some managers took the opportunity to 'settle accounts', and the rate of sackings rose sharply. For example, the Coventry District Committee of the AEU spent a good deal of time discussing such cases that year: in January the convenor at the Standard Aero shadow factory was sacked; in March, nine men were suspended from SS Cars; in July, two shop stewards were sacked from the Alvis Co.; in the same month, a man called Matthews was dismissed from the Coventry Gauge and Tool works for, the employers openly admitted, his 'Communistic tendencies'; in September, another convenor was sacked from the Standard Aero.[68]

This list is probably far from exhaustive, but it was quite long enough for the Coventry District Committee. The sacking of the third convenor at the Standard Aero brought a response from them and the local shop stewards.

Trade-unionism in the Standard Aero shadow factory was a rather delicate growth in 1940, and the management seem to have been determined that it should not develop any real roots. When in January 1940 the convenor had been sacked, the company, not recognising the union, had refused to discuss the matter at a works conference.[69] In April there was a strike of inspectors in the factory which received financial support from all over the district, bringing the problems at the new factory to the attention of the local shop stewards.[70] Yet trade-unionism was still not established there by September, when Horace Wilcocks, the new AEU convenor and member of the Labour Party, reported to the District Committee that the company was challenging his right to act as convenor by dictating when and where shop meetings would be held.[71] Having tried to negotiate with the company, Wilcocks insisted on holding a meeting at what the Conciliation Officer of the Ministry of Labour described as an 'inconvenient' time, and was sacked.[72] Two hundred and fifty workers came out on strike on 26 September, of whom fifty were non-unionists.[73] Billy Stokes and Cyril Taylor, the AEU Divisional Organiser and District Secretary respectively, met the strikers with other officials and appealed to them to return to work as the company were insisting they would not negotiate until they did so. About one hundred of the strikers went back, among them some sheet metal workers, some toolmakers, and some women.[74] By the next day the District Committee of the AEU had pledged its support for the strike (largely because the Communist faction were in the majority at a small meeting), and were calling for district-wide support. A deputation was elected to the AEU Executive in London to demand action over the victimisation of shop stewards, failing which a ballot was to be taken for district strike action.[75] The TGWU District Committee was also supporting the strike.[76]

These events made the 'holiday' a matter of more than passing importance. The local officials had tried to end the

96

strike, but had been only partially effective; the District Committee, on the other hand, was determined that the officials, not only locally but also at national level, should support them in their stand against the sacking of stewards for carrying out their functions. The Conciliation Officer thought the position 'serious', and remarked on the officials' 'embarrassment'.[77] Their embarrassment was compounded when Taylor described by the *Daily Worker* as 'not only not pulling his weight' but as 'positively obstructive', was censured by the District Committee for failing to carry out their policy.[78] The local officials could clearly not give any support to the idea of district-wide strike action at this juncture, but the shop stewards at an important local aircraft factory decided to rattle their sabres. The shop stewards at Armstrong-Whitworth Aircraft, amongst whom Joe Steele, a leading Communist and member of the District Committee delegation to London, was influential, decided to call a meeting of the district's shop stewards to discuss 'matters of vital importance to all workers'.[79] The meeting discussed the Standard Aero dispute, though what it decided is unknown.[80] In any event, it seems to have had some effect, since the Standard management agreed at a works conference held soon afterwards to reinstate Wilcocks.[81]

Wilcocks' reinstatement did not prevent other employers from taking disciplinary action against their shop stewards, but managements had been shown that the patience of the shop stewards in the district was not infinite. Indeed, the organisational achievement in generalising interest in the dispute beyond the factory concerned was considerable, and showed both the agitational ability of those involved and the general level of concern in the district with the problem of victimisation. If Wilcocks, Steele and others had come out of the dispute smelling of roses, the same could not be said of the local officials. They appeared to have exercised a very limited amount of control over the activities of their members, shop stewards and District Committee. This temporary loss of control had been noted by the Ministry of Labour and the *Daily Worker*; the initiative had clearly laid with the militants throughout the dispute. Nor was it they, but Taylor, who was rebuked for his non-accountability to the union! Such a situation could not have been regarded with equanimity by the AEU nationally or the Ministry of Labour. If local officials could have their position undermined, then the Executive—who had met Steele and his colleagues themselves and no doubt heard some criticism—could have theirs similarly subverted. Before long they could find themselves in a position similar to that of their colleagues of the First World War. They could feel the ground moving beneath their feet.

In the next important dispute over the sacking of a convenor, the Executive of the AEU cooperated closely with the Ministry of Labour to ensure that their position was not put at risk as it had been in Coventry. Despite the clear evidence of concerted action on the part of the local engineering employers' association against their members, the Executive of the AEU resisted any suggestion that procedure be circumvented. The Ministry of Labour backed them in their stand, and treated the dispute as a 'test case' for their whole industrial relations policy.

The Clydeside strike took place against a very different background to the Coventry dispute. If Coventry had been a boom town in the late 1930s, with workers flooding in to find employment in the shadow factories, then the Clyde, with its overgrown shipyards and half-empty engineering shops, had remained a slump town. In some ways the inter-war years had been a period of cold storage in which many of the features which had earned the area its famous political reputation and 'Red' designation had been relatively well preserved. The rich popular political culture of the First World War largely remained. The Communist Party was of course the major left force on the Clyde, with around one thousand members in the late 1930s, but it was certainly far from having the left-wing ground to itself. The ILP was comparably strong; indeed, even in national terms its membership had been equivalent to that of the CP until the mid-1930s. But on Clydeside it retained a real working-class base despite its national decline from about 1930, as well as its famous four MPs elected in 1935. During the period of the Popular Front, the ILP grew increasingly critical of the CP, arguing that the revolution in Spain should not be put off until after the Civil War had been won; in return, the CP denounced the ILP as 'Trotsky-fascist'.[82]

The ILP and CP were rooted in the local political culture, within which there was no shortage of varieties of leftism and sharp discussion. The CP, ILP and the many fringe groups including Guy Aldred and Angelica Balobanova and their friends, the Anarchists and the remnants of the Socialist Labour Party, could always attract a critical audience to argue on a street corner, on Glasgow Green, in the pubs, or in one of the many left-wing haunts. Disputations on socialist theory could become almost mediaeval in their scholasticism. In February 1939, for instance, the Socialist Labour Party held a meeting in Glasgow. *The Socialist* directed its readers' attention to the impeccable orthodoxy of the diatribe with which the audience was harangued: 'Holding close to the principle of the class struggle, the speaker disentangled in fine fashion the knotty problems, and made it clear to the audience that they could do the same if only they would apply themselves to a diligent study of SLP literature, which would render them immune from the wiles and lures of labour fakers.'[83] A quarter of a century earlier, such a speech would have been less surprising. Yet the paper claimed that many stayed on the eve of the Second World War to discuss socialist politics and the SLP. The sort of climate in which people retained an interest in SLP politics ensured that there was a critical and politically aware milieu on the Clyde which went well beyond membership of the CP. This was to prove important in the trade union battles to come.

Trade-unionism on the Clyde, largely unchallenged by the floods of new labour diluting craft exclusiveness in the Midlands, retained many of its older forms and a strong element of the 'ASE mentality'. Craft traditions of control over working conditions remained exceptionally strong in Scotland. It is not surprising, then, to find the Ministry of Labour's Chief Conciliation Officer, Mr Galbraith, reporting to headquarters in December 1939 that the Communist Party had taken advantage of 'a growing measure of unrest' in local factories by setting up 'an organisation not unlike the Clyde Workers' Committee of the last war'.[84] This organisation sent

99

out a circular to all branches, asking them to send contributions to help fund the committee, whose main object was to defend established working conditions. Several branches voted money, but little more was heard of the committee until a strike at the British Auxiliaries factory later in the year.[85]

This dispute broke out at the beginning of September 1940, just as events were about to come to a head in Coventry. The management of the British Auxiliaries Co., a firm making components for the marine engineering and aircraft industries, had dismissed two AEU convenors in the previous four months, and the local Engineering Employers' Association was operating an embargo on engineers who had been employed at their works. The last straw for the engineers there was the sacking of another convenor, a Communist Party member called Cunningham, only a few days after a short strike had ended to allow negotiations on allegations made against him to begin.[86] The management claimed that Cunningham had 'interfered' with a woman working at the factory, an incident dismissed by the *Daily Herald* as nothing more than a 'jocular spar'.[87] A letter from the girl's mother, Mrs R. MacBrayne, to the works manager at British Auxiliaries, Mr Bruce, painted a different picture:

> On three occasions during last week alone, he made himself objectionable to her and put his arms about her so that she slapped his face on Wednesday, and did so again on Thursday. On Saturday at noon she came home in such a state that she said she would not return to her work where that man was. He had used language to her that she is not accustomed to hearing, and passing [sic] insulting remarks about her figure. She has had this kind of thing to put up with since the beginning of the year.[88]

The letter ended by asking Bruce to take the matter up, which he did by sacking Cunningham. The shop stewards later threatened to reveal 'some rather unsavoury information' about the woman, who was married but separated from her husband, but no revelations appear to have been made in public, at least in writing.[89] Whatever the truth about the relationship between Cunningham and the woman, it is clear that the introduction of women into an almost all-skilled male workshop could bring its problems.

The strike initially broke out on 10 September, and for a while Galbraith left it substantially alone. After a fortnight, however, it became clear that the problem was deep-seated and that it would not simply end as some others had done, after a short 'protest' period. This was already more than a 'protest' matter; it quickly became a determined fight for a principle: the principle of the protection of stewards from sacking. On the employers' side, the principle involved was that of adherence to procedure (which Galbraith sarcastically called 'the received word'): the matter had not been through procedure, and therefore the men could not strike. Galbraith's first attempt to conciliate with the North Western Engineering Employers' Association rested on trying to circumvent procedure, and it failed. He proposed that the employers' association should recommend a return to the status quo pending negotiations, but the employers would have none of it: 'They were far from enthusiastic about any such suggestion, and seemed to be tremendously overwhelmed with the dangers which lurked in any suggestions of this kind.'[90] A second initiative by Galbraith, this time probing into whether a small committee of inquiry might be acceptable, was also rejected by the employers' association. These rebuffs make it clear that the employers' association had decided to press the principle of a return to work before negotiations would begin. Thus, despite the fact that the firm concerned was a small one, the large engineering employers in the district were behind it and were in no mood for compromise.

Soon after the rejection of Galbraith's feelers to the employers, the Executive Committee of the AEU took up a similar stand to the employers in insisting on procedure being followed, and instructed William Irvine, the Divisional Organiser, to secure a resumption so that negotiations could begin.[91] Meanwhile, British Auxiliaries further exacerbated the situation by sending the strikers' employment books to the labour exchange, informing the manager that they should be directed to essential work (which they knew the employers' embargo prevented them from obtaining) as they were no longer employed by the Govan firm.[92]

Bevin took up a position that put him firmly on the side of constitutionality. He decided to send a telegram advising the Lord Provost of Glasgow, Dollan, not to intervene in the dispute when he offered to do so, as he was sure that the strike should be settled through the normal machinery of negotiations.[93] At the same time, however, his public statements in the press and on the radio at Sunday lunchtime had given the strikers food for thought and, they considered, some justification for their action. Towards the end of October Hector McAndrew, the secretary of the strike committee, tried (without success) to enlist Bevin's support by writing to him a letter using some of the Minister's public statements as a lever:

> In the press reports you say you will not tolerate the word 'can't' and any man who uses this word is a friend of HITLER'S and a traitor to DEMOCRACY, well on your own words, Mr. Bevin, the MASTERS FEDERATION ARE TRAITORS for keeping 250 men and boys on the street who are most anxious to get back to work in the nation's interests.[94]

McAndrew's letter, powerful as it was, did not deter the Ministry of Labour from pursuing its policy of supporting the official trade union line. Towards the end of the strike, Leggett, Bevin's right-hand man, wrote to Jack Tanner of the AEU making it clear that the ministry would not intervene in the dispute (despite Galbraith's earlier moves), because it had become a 'test case' in which the government did not wish to let the AEU Executive down.[95]

Unlike most other wartime disputes, the British Auxiliaries strike lasted long enough for the strikers to make their action into a *cause célèbre* amongst trade-unionists throughout Scotland. Every Monday they held meetings, with their wives present, at which they reaffirmed their determination to hold out until Cunningham was reinstated.[96] At one of these meetings Cunningham himself made a speech advising a return to work, but he was howled down from the floor for this breach of trade union principle; to have returned would have meant doing so without their convenor.[97] By the end of the month the men's morale, according to Galbraith, was beginning to wane, and some of them were 'very anxious to return'; but at the same time appeals for support to other trade-unionists were beginning to bring results.[98]

The strikers had won this support by distributing a leaflet throughout the district with collecting sheets attached, which Galbraith obtained and sent to London. This document is worth quoting in full both because of the response it evoked and because of the way it argued the men's case:

### British Auxiliaries Shop Steward's Committee
### Go To It

We went to it—some of us enlisted and the others worked excessive overtime etc. The management went to it and have disrupted every means we have in power for redress of any injustice. And they have encroached on our AEU status by taking up a dictatorial attitude in refusing to discuss our case when we had already resumed work in accordance with all legal procedure.

### Our Case

Our shop convenor has been sacked for his trade union activities. The men have taken an extended holiday pending his reinstatement. We have been forced to take this action as this is our third convenor to be got rid of in four months. We want to take part in our country's war effort, and we are willing to work in any factory. The Masters' Federation has closed its doors to us, i.e. preventing us from being employed elsewhere.

Why are honest shop stewards being persecuted and victimised? Because they are maintaining trade union rights and conditions.

We appeal to you to send resolutions to Mr. Bevan [sic] demanding that this management be put in its place, and once and for all stopping all recurrences of this trouble elsewhere.

We need your financial aid immediately. Please help.

Treasurer A. Turnbull.[99]

The appeal brought widespread financial support, and even, in at least one factory in the East of Scotland, a weekly levy in support of the strikers.[100] But the West of Scotland Shop Stewards' Committee felt that more positive action was required to settle the matter, and at the end of October they threatened to spread the stoppage to the whole of Clydeside.[101] The employers were taking district action in attacking existing organisation, it was argued, and the nature of the required response was clear. This threat was taken seriously by the Ministry of Labour. Galbraith thought it unlikely that the committee would be able to initiate a genuine district-wide strike that pulled all local factories in, but felt that it could 'make a good show' at Beardmore's Parkhead Forge, the factories of the North British Locomotive Co., Albion Motors, and Rolls-Royce Hillington.[102] This would have represented a very serious extension of the dispute, had it taken place; the factories he referred to were not even medium-sized enterprises, but very large works which were crucial to the war effort. In the event, however, no such strike occurred, because the British Auxiliaries dispute soon came to an end.

The story of the strike ends with a finely ironical twist. The ex-convenor at Beardmore's Parkhead Forge, David Kirkwood MP, who had been responsible for the Beardmore engineers 'breaking the front' of the Clyde Workers' Committee against dilution during the First World War, appeared on the scene.[103] At the invitation of the Communist Party, Kirkwood offered the District Committee of the AEU a document giving himself the right to negotiate a settlement on their behalf, a document which some committeemen agreed to sign. Accordingly, he went ahead and proposed to the employers that Cunningham should be reinstated for a fortnight after a full return to work. But the management was in no mood to compromise when men were dribbling back into the factory, and rejected his proposal. The rest of the men went back to work without their convenor.[104]

The British Auxiliaries dispute had attracted considerable publicity, and had developed into *the* important case as far as all parties with an interest in industrial relations were concerned. The Ministry of Labour therefore determined to stand firm with the local employers, and not to allow the emergency to push them into circumventing the Procedure for the Avoidance of Disputes by setting up any sort of machinery that might detract from the authority of the trade union officials. The strike led the Ministry of Labour to begin, nevertheless, to question whether their labour policy was adequate in every respect. For Galbraith in particular, the dispute had been a trying one in which entrenched positions had been taken by both sides, and all that could be done was to hang on till the bitter end after initial notions of ignoring procedure had been rejected. He thought it possible that action could be taken to reduce the number of occasions on which such desperate set-piece battles were fought, and his proposed solution set head-quarters officials thinking along lines that were of great importance in the development of government labour policy. It was becoming clear to them that firms needed to be encouraged to develop communications structures through which workers' grievances could be aired before they became so strong that they led to strikes. These structures (which were not far removed from the ideas of *Industrial Welfare* and *Labour Management* of the 1930s) would have the added benefit of drawing on workers' knowledge of pro-duction matters, which might both improve production and bring workers to a closer understanding of management's problems. In a letter to Jack Tanner of the AEU in November 1940 Leggett wrote in connection with the British Auxiliaries strike that he thought that more firms should follow Beard-more's example by setting up consultative machinery for reviewing these problems.[105] It is already possible, then, to see at this early stage in the war the conception of the Joint Production Committees that were later to play an important part in wartime industrial relations.

If the British Auxiliaries dispute had caused the Ministry of Labour to re-think its labour policy, then it is also true that the affair brought the West of Scotland shop stewards to question their own leadership. Some active trade-unionists thought that crucial trade union principles had been abandon-ed for the sake of particular political interests. Here, too, the strike was in a sense the starting point for later develop-ments, since this disagreement was subsequently to become wider. For this reason it is worth looking a little more closely at the debates going on amongst the local shop stewards during and immediately after the British Auxiliaries dispute.

During the strike, Galbraith recounted an incident which showed that a gap was emerging between the members of the AEU District Committee who wanted Cunningham to be unconditionally reinstated and those who were prepared to offer a compromise. In Galbraith's view, the split emerged because the CP feared they would have their national position in the AEU damaged if they did not try to end the stoppage as quickly as possible. Since the beginning of the strike, the Executive of the AEU had been pressurising the District Committee to secure a return to work, and having been frustrated on this score for some time they threatened the district that their delegates to the forthcoming National Committee would have their credentials withdrawn if they did not follow the Executive's instructions. According to Galbraith's source, the local Communist committeemen received instructions from outside the area to acquiesce to the Executive's instruction. The results of this initiative were to be seen when the Conciliation Officer was trying to mediate between the local employers and three members of the District Committee, and the leading Communist on the District Committee fell embarrassingly out of step with his colleagues.

The District Committee's deputation consisted of three men: Tommy Sillars, a well known Communist and delegate elect to the National Committee, J. Cloakie and J. Grey. Sillars led off for the union side, roundly castigating the employers for their slavish attachment to procedure, and so on. But at the end of his presentation, Cloakie and Grey were surprised to hear Sillars propose that Cunningham should be reinstated after having been formally suspended for one week. The AEU delegation had to request an adjournment to clarify their position. On their return they collectively withdrew Sillars' suggestion.[106] Some time later in another letter to London Galbraith wrote that the CP were 'not exactly in very good odour' among local shop stewards because they had been seen to offer a compromise for ulterior, political motives.[107] The supporters of the strike were determined to defend existing rights and conditions, and did not feel that 'outside' questions should enter the discussion.

On Saturday 14 November a similar debate took place at the West of Scotland Shop Stewards' Committee, which had put district strike action in support of the British Auxiliaries men on the agenda. The agenda had clearly been overtaken by events, since the dispute was over. However, there was a

106

faction at the meeting that thought they should proceed with preparations for a district-wide strike, but in support of the national pay claim. Inflation during 1940 had been high, and many local engineers depended on plain-time rates. Discussion on the proposal revealed 'a very sharp cleavage of opinion', but the leaders of the committee prevailed when they argued against such a strike.[108] The *Daily Worker* justified the decision thus: '. . . on the date suggested, it would be difficult for a united move to be made. It was therefore decided not to take a holiday for the time being.'[109] Galbraith, on the other hand, thought that the real reason for the leadership of the committee arguing in this way was not simply a tactical one. He reported that these delegates had argued that it was strategically more appropriate to use the official union machinery.[110] Precisely what they meant by this is not clear, but presumably they advocated use of the Procedure for the Avoidance of Disputes. A minority of stewards on the committee had felt that this action would not bring the relatively large increase required.

At the beginning of 1941 the CP continued to follow a fairly moderate line; at a meeting of two thousand engineers held in St Andrew's Hall, Glasgow, called by the West of Scotland Shop Stewards' Committee, the 'left' shop stewards, who had no reputation as militants, made speeches 'of the reasonable kind'.[111] It is clear that the CP was far from exercising a monopoly of militancy and, indeed, seemed to have adopted a deliberate policy of soft-pedalling industrial issues. Some shop stewards in the area were beginning to find themselves at odds with the CP for not being militant enough. The feeling that trade union rights and existing conditions had to be defended went deep amongst the Clyde shop stewards, and was not merely a 'cover' for political activity against the war. Indeed, some stewards had begun, as we shall see, to question the CP's tactics, and were later to become very critical of them.

During the autumn of 1940 it became apparent that defending members' rights and conditions in the 'total war' involved a good deal more than the traditional and time-honoured duty to support shop stewards under threat. The Luftwaffe's primary aim had become the reduction of Britain's productive resources prior to invasion, and German air attacks brought industrial workers serious risk of death and injury on a large scale. Nobody at the time underestimated this risk; indeed, if anything, it was overestimated. The popular view in the 1930s, nurtured by government, radio and newsreels, was that a second large-scale war would inevitably lead to massive destruction from the air, with thousands of civilians slaughtered by bombs. Clearly nobody relished such a fate, whatever their desire to expedite production. Very few factories had their own deep shelters; workers usually had to use makeshift shelters of one sort of another, 'Anderson' (corrugated iron), or public ones. In Coventry, for example, only one works had its own deep shelter in 1940.[112] Adequate warning was therefore crucial, or workers could find themselves on the way to public shelters while bombs were falling. But after only a short experience of air-raids very considerable hold-ups in production were caused by the air-raid warning system. The fact that sirens sounded over large areas when bombers were only active in a part of it, the frequency of false alarms and the long waits between the first 'alert' siren and the 'all clear' even during brief raids, led to workers spending long periods in shelters. By the end of August, London was having about half a dozen warnings per twenty-four hours, and the opinion was spreading that they could in fact be ignored. Clearly, this could be dangerous, and a story circulated about Cardiff docks carrying on during raids, whereupon a German bomb dropped into a hold, killing seven men whose remains had to be brought out in pails.[113] Although constant warnings were tedious and bred a certain amount of complacency, people were also well aware of the dangers.

In early September the government saw the need to act on this problem, and adopted a scheme already thought up by some enterprising employers to minimise production delays caused by people taking shelter when the 'alert' was sounded. The system, as suggested and actively promoted by the government, was supposed to be discussed with representatives of the workpeople so that details could be worked out and agreed—a task often carried out by stewards. It involved 'roof-spotters' raising the alarm when they could actually see bombers approaching, and reporting on the size and composition of the enemy aircraft for plotting purposes.[114] A large group of factories in the North of England operated the system in the following 'fool-proof' (as they claimed) way: trained observers were positioned in several observation posts at strategic points on the roof of each factory block. Each observer was linked to a central controller by phone. When aeroplanes were seen approaching, the central controller was notified, whereupon he decided when to sound the factory sirens. Most workers would immediately take shelter, but certain 'key men' remained until the shops were clear, when they, too, went to the shelters.[115] In October 1940 the popular *Picture Post* carried an article which touched on workers' feelings about the whole problem of sufficient notice of air-raids and the spotter system. The writer thought that there were two points of view in the factory. One was that workers had the 'right' to take as much risk as the servicemen. The other was that:

> Maximum production in a factory calls for the utmost concentration from the worker, especially on rapid jobs requiring an accuracy of half of one thousandth of an inch. The soldier's job, they say, is to be prepared for risks. He is trained and disciplined for months to just this end. The factory worker's job is to concentrate on his lathe or drill, so as to produce efficient work as quickly as possible. . . [the workers] would tell you that if they are working a ten-hour shift and assured of adequate warning, they can work cheerfully and fast. Whether they can work at top speed if they are always thinking of whether there will be an adequate warning, is a subject which causes a lot of controversy. At any rate, they know the Government wants to get more production. And they don't want anything to interfere with that.[116]

Despite the last sentence (which was almost obligatory, on patriotic grounds for a widely read magazine), it is clear that this logic could be used by those who preferred the safety of the shelters after the 'alert', or by shop stewards anxious to ensure that their members felt no pressure on them to stay at work too long.

In fact, stewards had taken up the question of sirens even

before the spotter system had been brought into operation. In July, shop stewards at a large engineering factory in the West of Scotland complained that sirens were not being sounded at all until bombs were actually being dropped. They complained both to the management and to their respective union District Committees.[117] Later, the shop stewards in many factories became seriously perturbed by spotter systems, both in general and in their operational detail. *New Propellor* devoted a good deal of space to shop stewards outlining the results of discussions with their firms, and the November 1940 issue, for example, contained no less than seven such reports.[118] Some of them (such as that from Simms Motor Units) showed that stewards had insisted on their members being allowed to take shelter when the public sirens were sounded.[119] Another report stated that workers in Avery's Heavy Machine shop had collectively decided to stop work immediately the 'danger imminent' was sounded, and did so, despite the management's alternative plans.[120] These developments caused managements serious problems. As the editorial of *Labour Management* said: 'The immediate problem we have here at home. . . is how to ensure workers do not stop work on the "alert". This is a real test of the quality of industrial relations in each undertaking.'[121] As many shop stewards had long suspected, 'good industrial relations' could be equated with continuing to work, come what may. The managerial point of view could be considered, in the abstract, as implying that workers should be 'militarised' and exposed to similar risks to those run by servicemen. One reply to the argument—namely that highly skilled work was not comparable to a soldier's work—has already been quoted, and another response, that of *New Propellor,* amounted to a hoot of derision. Quoting an imaginary worker from Avery's, *New Propellor* said:

Ten years ago you was all out o' work and on the Means Test. Bunch o' loafers. It's soldiers in the front line now. Got to work under spotters. Huh! When this lot's over you'll all be spotting for jobs. Once it was stop-watches. Now it's spotters. Huh! You make me sick! Spotters you said? Bah! Any mug can spot when they ain't aimin' at the factory. The only reason they ain't hit you yet is they ain't been aiming' at yer, yer twerps. Spottin's all right if the spotters can see at 300 miles an hour.[122]

Such responses ensured that the managerial preference for the 'military' argument was kept under control in most workplaces. Indeed, the effect of air-raids was generally to subvert managerial control over work, since the whole question of the amount of time to be spent at work was now inevitably up for discussion. Working hours as a fixed length of time had, temporarily at least, ceased to exist. This development played a very important role in eroding managerial authority—a process already well under way in many factories. Managements were quietly dismayed at the sight of workers amusing themselves by playing cards, talking, reading newspapers and even sleeping while sheltering: factories were workplaces. Yet if workers could not work, who could object to their doing as they liked? In many cases, of course, this meant industrial and political discussions on a more or less formal basis in what was a rare opportunity for the political shop stewards. At last their members could be cornered for long periods at work, and new converts to trade-unionism and socialism could be made. It was an opportunity that some stewards seized with both hands, to build links with their members which would later stand them in good stead.

Where the air-raids of the autumn of 1940 struck hardest, the shop stewards played a part in protecting their members' interests despite the general feeling of shock that reigned after big raids. In Coventry, immediately after the terrible raid of 14 November in which sixteen hundred people were killed or injured—some of them at work in the twenty-one factories which were 'severely affected' by fire or direct hits—the problems were prodigious.[123] A large number of workers were made homeless, gas and water supplies were disrupted, food became extremely scarce, and there was a danger of typhoid.[124] In the first week after the raid thirteen thousand were unemployed, and many of those at work were clearing up the debris or were transferred to other factories.[125] Five days later the *Daily Worker* reported that the trades council was to call a meeting of trade unions and shop stewards in order to take over the distribution of supplies. On 22 November Bill Warman, Communist President of the trades council and shop steward at Standard Motors, threatened with action employers who had not yet paid out wages. The next day, after hearing reports from their shop stewards on what had been done to date, meetings in a number of factories called for immediate action on feeding, housing, evacuation and ARP (Air Raid Precautions); on the same day the shop stewards met to make a series of similar demands.[126] The full picture of the shop stewards' role is far from clear, but it is apparent that they were trying to organise help for those in distress, and at the same time criticising the entirely inadequate arrangements which were being belatedly made by the local authorities.[127] The shop stewards had pointed out the dangers, and had seen their warnings amply justified; in the process of picking up the pieces, they refused to let the employers or the local authorities forget their critical presence. In the devastated town of Coventry, the points were well taken by their members: the evidence of their eyes showed how far from alarmist the warnings had been.

Coventry, along with the other heavily bombed areas, provided a high proportion of the delegates to the People's Convention, a body set up by the CP which had succeeded in becoming a movement of some substance by the beginning of 1941. In July 1940, 'People's Vigilance Committees' had been set up, and these formed the basis for the campaign for the People's Convention's first and last big conference in January 1941. The Convention's demands were rather hazy, being for a 'people's peace' and a 'truly representative government', but they reflected popular discontent with the way the war was being run which was not entirely allayed by the formation of the Churchill Coalition government. From September 1940, the People's Vigilance Committees conducted a campaign for the big meeting in the New Year, and harnessed *New Propellor* to their cause.[128]

After its April conference the Aircraft Shop Stewards' National Council and its paper had expanded its notion of those who fell within its terms of reference. Recognising the increasing blurredness of the frontier between the aircraft

112

sector and the rest of engineering, the Council began to make efforts to involve all engineering workers and renamed itself the Engineering and Allied Trades Shop Stewards' National Council (E&ATSSNC). The April conference had been attended by 283 shop stewards from 107 factories, including a respectable proportion from outside aircraft; *New Propellor* continued to claim an expanding sale during the first few months of war.[129] The left influence within a number of important AEU District Committees had also grown, as the War Cabinet Committee on Communism noted with disquiet, fearing that the help that the local officials could give the government would 'correspondingly diminish'.[130] The growth of the CP and E&ATSSNC influence within the workshop and district committee room, together with a small but significant popular movement critical of the Coalition government, was a disturbing development for the Cabinet. When the two movements fused, they would have to be pulled apart again if the growth of a powerful political movement based firmly in industry was to be prevented.

In late 1940 there were some indications that such a fusion was beginning to take place. The November editorial of *New Propellor* stressed the volume of support that the Convention was attracting from shop stewards, while the December issue called on stewards to ensure 'that every factory will not only send delegates to the Convention but will also consult with their members in the respective factories and departments on the six points to be discussed at the Convention'.[131] Some were later to criticise the Convention for the lack of precisely this sort of discussion with the rank and file. Reg Scott, a CP member at Standard Motors in Coventry, recorded in his diary for 11 January 1941: 'Andy, Brindley, Wilcox, Alan. . . Yank going to Convention tomorrow. Give Yank message to hand in on behalf of DW readers (84) here—Pity shop stewards didn't inform men of Convention.'[132] The result of this sort of failure to consult with the rank and file which they were supposed to represent could be hostility on the shop floor, and in some factories claims were made by anti-CP workers that delegates had been specifically repudiated by their members on returning from the Convention.[133]

The difficulty for the shop stewards was, of course, the

political unpopularity of an attitude which could seem to some suspiciously like defeatism; unlike the Popular Front line, the 'imperialist war' position was in general a hindrance to shop stewards trying to keep their members behind them on industrial issues. Although the point that the war was being badly conducted was well taken by many people, the idea of a 'people's peace' was ill defined and open to criticism for being defeatist. Government commentators had been quick to remark that CP shop stewards were usually anxious to restrict their activities to the industrial front when political discussions of this sort were so difficult. As early as July 1940, the Home Office confidently informed the Cabinet: 'Although the CP is opposed to the war, its members are normally careful to refrain at the present time from anti-war propaganda.'[134] The summer of 1940 was hardly a propitious time for making anti-war propaganda, but it would appear that the atmosphere had not changed enough for the shop stewards to risk too overt an association with a potentially damaging point of view, even by the end of the year.

In any event, many of those who spoke at the People's Convention on 12 January 1941 were shop stewards from aircraft factories.[135] It may be that some of them had not heeded *New Propellor*'s exhortations, but their presence was considerable and in itself indicated the possibility that the shop stewards might again be starting to re-emerge as a political force, in a way that had last been seen during the Spanish Civil War. The Cabinet's reaction to the January meeting was to ban the *Daily Worker*; this was an extreme move, but it was only taken after the option of further repressive action against left-wing shop stewards had been rejected.

A week after the Convention had met, the War Cabinet Committee on Communism met to discuss the action to be taken against the CP. On 20 January Herbert Morrison reported to the Committee that the main objection to the *Daily Worker* was that it was identified with the Communist International's line on the war.[136] It had reawakened the old fear that the rulers of the British Empire retained of the 'World Army of Revolution'. But this was not the main reason for suppressing the *Daily Worker*; it was suppressed, it was later recorded by the Committee's chairman, because it 'continually tried to create a state of mind in which people will refrain from co-operating in the war effort and will hinder it'.[137] In other words, the effect on 'morale' was the vital issue. 'Morale' was not considered solely as a political question, but was related to the industrial situation. Bevin, asked whether he was aware of the CP's influence in the aircraft industry, replied that he was, but he made it clear that he was opposed to taking any repressive measures against shop stewards and in particular to detaining more Communist trade-unionists under Regulation 18B. He did not rule out the arrest of left intellectuals, but did not think that arresting workers should even be contemplated in view of the unrest it would cause, as it had done in the First World War.[138] After hearing Bevin's views the Committee decided not to take any action against *New Propellor* which, the Home Secretary said, was 'devoted entirely to the exploitation of industrial grievances and contained no direct references to the war'.[139] The Committee then rejected the option which (as the case of Mason shows) earlier seemed appropriate—the arrest of CP shop stewards—and also decided not to ban *New Propellor*. This decision is important, because while it prevented the development of a political movement with industrial support, it left the E&ATSSNC and its paper intact. The suppression of the E&ATSSNC, which would have had serious effects, was not attempted, no doubt partly because of the vigorous resistance which had already been put up to the sacking of convenors, and so the shop stewards could return to the 'exploitation of industrial grievances' and live to fight another day on the political front.

The problem of 'morale' was not, however, one which could be solved simply by taking action against the extreme left. As we have already seen, the will to defend shop stewards from victimisation was far from limited to the CP. In any case, the most pressing problem related not so much to open industrial conflict as such, but more to workers' growing strength in the labour market in many munitions areas. The result was that employers had to constantly bid against each other for labour; people moved more or less freely between workplaces (causing severe 'discipline' problems); skilled

115

workers deserted their jobs for more lucrative ones irrespective of their value to employers, and so on.

Bevin had in fact framed legislative proposals to deal with these problems by the beginning of 1940, and had played a part in stimulating local agreements such as the Coventry Toolroom Agreement to solve specific shortages of skilled labour.[140] The difficulty, however, was that the AEU in particular was opposed to the introduction of any legislation which restricted the free movement of labour and their members' opportunity to vote with their feet against their employers. It was only, therefore, when the Cabinet had heard that the vital lend-lease arrangements had been pushed through the American Congress, that Bevin's plans for the wholesale compulsory direction of labour were agreed and implemented by the War Cabinet's Production Executive.[141] Strengthened by the American promises, the Cabinet felt confident enough to ignore the AEU's objections, and introduced the Essential Works Order.

The Essential Works Order restricted workers' right to change jobs, and simultaneously strengthened the employer's capacity to take disciplinary measures against his employees. Workers in scheduled establishments were not allowed to leave their employment without giving seven days' notice to both the employer and the National Service Officer, stating their reasons. Also, the employer was not allowed to sack an employee (although he was allowed to suspend him) without going through the same procedure, and unless the employee was guilty of 'serious misconduct'. In this way the Ministry of Labour took up a position behind the employer, and refused to allow the movement of labour save for exceptional reasons, while introducing an element of outside 'fairness' into disciplinary sackings. Sacking remained an inadequate threat in an economy moving towards full employment, however, and the Order therefore specified that an employee might be prosecuted for failing to carry out a 'reasonable order' from his employer. In this case, the employer had to go to the National Service Officer, who would then either dismiss the case or order the employee to carry out the order. If the employee still disagreed, then he could appeal to a

Local Appeal Board (consisting of one trade union official, one employers' representative, and a Ministry chairman). To sugar the pill the Order also specified that employers had to pay a guaranteed week's pay (the plain-time rate in engineering) if there was any stoppage of work through causes outside the workers' control.[142] This last provision was doubtless designed to blunt allegations of managerial inefficiency, which were already occurring. Bevin's biographer, assessing the importance of the Order, points out that it allowed the Minister to introduce improvements in working conditions and in rates of pay where these were below average.[143] Such an interpretation is, however, perverse: as the AEU pointed out, conditions were being improved at a much greater rate by the free play of market forces, previously so beloved of the employers.[144]

Nevertheless, the Essential Works Order did bring a modicum of protection to non-skilled workers who were unable or unwilling to change jobs. It also tended (at least in the minds of many workers) to militate against the employers' unalloyed 'freedom to manage' and, in particular, against the foreman's right to hire and fire. Sackings had to be justified to the National Service Officer, and this stimulated the growth of personnel management, depriving the foreman of the very direct rule over those in his charge which he had previously enjoyed. It became well known on the shop floor that the foreman could not sack you. Moreover, if you wanted your release you had actually to try to get sacked, while at the same time hoping to steer clear of prosecution. The ingenuity required was not beyond some workers (especially younger ones), with disastrous results for discipline.

It was not long before managers began to notice the revival of an old engineers' habit which disturbed them: the practice of doing work for themselves within the factory. In the time spent waiting for materials, engineers had always carried out small pieces of work for themselves, their fellow-engineers and their friends. The large number of names for this practice testifies to its importance: it was variously known as 'doing a foreigner', 'government work', 'secret work', 'contract work' and 'Admiralty work' in different factories. The practice was in any case an old one, but

117

institutionalised job security gave it an additional boost. The materials to hand in aircraft work were often turned to good use: perspex, for example, was apparently useful for cigarette lighters, while the timber used in Mosquitos could be put to various uses. Holes could be drilled in coins to make women's 'jewellery'; silk, occasionally available as a wing covering, made good dress material. The possibilities were endlessly exploited by ingenious engineering workers, despite the fulminations of management. It was another sign of the times that these activities began to thrive once again.

Some insights into the situation in the workshops, and the public reaction to it, can be gained from looking at a report written on Clydeside's 'industrial morale' just after the passage of the Essential Works Order. The report is a uniquely valuable source because it reflects Mass Observation's earnest desire to collect material on popular attitudes and behaviour. Researched and written during March 1941—the result of some fifty researcher-days of intrepid fact-finding—it has nevertheless to be viewed critically. One problem is that despite their 'voluntary' status the Mass Observers were performing an official or at least semi-official function, in collecting material for use by government departments.[145] They therefore tended to focus on problems rather than successes, and might as a result be over-sensitive to popular criticism of government, too ready to find fault, and so on. On the other hand their immersion in a locality could lead them to overstate the particularity of the local situation, and hence to understate the importance of their findings. In this particular report, valuable for its rich and fascinating detail, it would appear (as other evidence shows) that they were not being too highly critical, but tended rather to 'over-localise' their findings. The situation they described, disturbing as it may have been to the readers of their report, was not limited to the Clyde.

The Mass Observation report on Clydeside began by defining 'morale' as 'primarily a matter of hard and persistent work'. By this criterion, they found that the situation in the area might be defined as 'good morale from a revolutionary point of view!'[146] They went on to say that 'Clydeside workers are *also* having a war of their own. . . they cannot forget the numerous battles of the last thirty years, and cannot overcome the bitter memory of industrial insecurity in the past ten years and their distrust of the motives of managers and employers.'[147] There were a number of specific features which confirmed their view, they thought: serious hold-ups in supplies induced cynicism about the 'war effort' (this had apparently been a 'great source of value' to the Communists at Singer's Clydebank factory); workers felt that the employers were not anxious to prosecute the war, as they 'would be just as happy under Hitler'; people felt that they were only being employed for the duration, and that after the war, 'the scrapheap will be higher than ever'.[148] Many of these reflections could have applied to other industrial towns; very similar remarks about post-war unemployment were made in later government surveys of the north-east coast, for example. The Mass Observers felt that Clydeside was different, though. They found 'a scepticism among many of the workers which is more deep and more bitter than anything we have found anywhere else, including even the Merseyside dockers.'[149] The difference here referred to was fundamentally one of quantity and not of quality, however, as the report tacitly allows. Clydeside was 'worse', but its attitudes were often sharply expressed variants of views which could be heard elsewhere in Britain.[150]

The report may well have been on firmer ground in asserting the particularity of Clydeside when it conducted a survey for which we have no equivalent in other areas. It looked at public attitudes to one strike at John Brown's yard and, while too much should not be read into the results, it makes surprising reading. The strike occurred because the few minutes' grace usually given to Brown's workers in the morning were arbitrarily removed 'without really adequate consultation with the men's representatives'.[151] Previously, the system of 'quartering' had been practised, whereby men who arrived after twenty to eight lost a quarter of an hour's pay, but were allowed to start work. Despite the difficulties of transport in a wartime winter, the shipyard management began to lock the yard gates at exactly twenty to eight.[152] The new system was soon abandoned, but the interesting

119

feature of the strike for the Mass Observers was that local opinion was ranged almost exclusively against the company. An informal opinion poll carried out in the area showed that nobody at all actually supported the management, while only six per cent thought that both sides were to blame.[153] Here is a verbatim quotation typical of many (this one from a middle-class man): 'Aye. Oh, it's a terrible thing in wartime. Whoever locked them out deserves to go to gaol, whether it was the head time-keeper or who it was. They don't need conferences or anything else. They should just be told they'll go to gaol if it happens again. They might ha' known the train was late, anyway—the station's just at the side o' Brown's yard.'[154] This climate of opinion was also reflected in the local newspapers, while Dollan, the Lord Provost of Glasgow, made strong sympathetic statements in favour of the men.[155] The survey may have yielded different results in other areas, but the attitude rings generally true. Outmoded disciplinary actions by employers had no place, it was felt, in a desperate fight for national survival.

In perhaps its most important section, the report showed how poor morale was when measured against the criterion of hard work. Investigating this matter in a very direct way, as diligent social observers in a long British tradition, they decided actually to enter a workplace. Since it is quite apparent that these workplaces were unfamiliar to them, their reflections have to be taken with a pinch of salt, but they show a situation which was probably not atypical. The observer assigned the task of visiting a shipyard went round a warship being fitted out in one of the river's big yards. This type of work was difficult to supervise because of the large number of small compartments in warships, but his remarks are nevertheless interesting:

The experience was an astonishing one. There must have been at least one hundred men on board the smallest vessel, of whom not more than ten can really have been working at any one moment. The author came upon a man lying reading a newspaper in a bunk, and watched ten men having a political discussion for twenty minutes. An electrician gazed through a porthole smoking (prohibited) for minutes on end. Whenever a 'bowler hat' came round

there was a slight appearance of activity, but even so most of the
men did not appear to be doing very much. . . the chief supervising
civilian was in a state of nervous despair (extreme nerves), declaring
that now there was no authority over the men, they just did what
they liked. . .[156]

This sort of situation was certainly not confined to Scotland,
especially after the Essential Works Order. In mid-1941 the
Ministry of Aircraft Production's Senior Technical Officer,
S.J. Egerton-Banks, wrote a report on manpower in aircraft
factories in which he recorded a similar state of affairs,
calling it 'this *aircraft works scandal*' (original emphasis). The
scandal that he referred to was in his view epitomised by such
plants as Vickers-Armstrong's Castle Bromwich factory
(where Spitfire airframes were produced), and Armstrong-
Whitworth Aircraft at Baginton. In connection with this last
works, he wrote: 'This shop is the WORST SCANDAL I have
yet come across. Half the men are doing nothing and the
other half are doing women's jobs. . . The shops are in
scandalous disorder—lack of discipline. The management is
obviously weak'.[157]

Similarly outraged tones were adopted by other conservative and managerial voices at this time: in Coventry,
the Conservative *Coventry Standard* printed a letter from a
correspondent which accused men and women in one local
factory of dancing all night to an employees' jazz band. At
Manchester's A.V. Roe factory, Roy Dobson, well known
throughout the district as a works manager with a tendency
to use 'workshop language', apparently ranted and raved at
two men sleeping in the convenient shelter afforded by an
aircraft's nose section; two years earlier they would probably
have been sacked, but in mid-1940 Dobson's conduct was
reported to the AEU District Committee.[158] The sheer
exhaustion of the engineering workers has to be borne in
mind here, especially those on night and shift work: the
body's own demands could drive people to try to get some
sleep at work. But the key reason for the talk of 'scandals'
was the rapid breakdown of the authoritarian workshop
regime of the 1930s, begun by the demand for skilled labour
and institutionalised by the Essential Works Order. A

121

problem which had previously been localised in those areas where labour was in strong demand was generalised by the Order. That such a situation existed on Clydeside is in itself eloquent demonstration of this fact, because it was a district where skilled labour was in relatively plentiful supply during 1940, not an exceptional case like Coventry. The Mass Observers' report was in this respect no more than a rather graphic exposition of the national 'lack of discipline' in the factories.

The report dismissed the suggestion that the crisis of authority in the factories, and strikes in particular, had been caused by Communist influence. Of course, they had arrived on Clydeside just after the banning of the *Daily Worker*, and their view that the left 'work on rich veins with rather clumsy tools' might be disputed in this context.[159] But it was confirmed by a senior manager—in fact, by the managing director of John Brown's shipyard. In a letter to the Admiralty (a government department with a particular tendency to see Communists everywhere), Mr L. Piggott, the managing director of Brown's, confirmed that in the recent dispute over starting times the young journeymen had played a leading part, but took great care to point out that although these young men were of the type popularly known as 'Communistic' they were not actually Communists but rather what he called 'natural agitators'.[160]

The Mass Observers had discovered, largely because of their willingness to ask basic questions from which many others recoiled, that working people were profoundly discontented with the way the war was being run on the home front. The post-Dunkirk realisation that Britain had been brought to the brink of defeat by the Chamberlain government did not suddenly disappear with the formation of the Coalition government. Engineering workers could see that industrial 'mobilisation' was pathetically backward when measured against the tasks that confronted their industry, and were inclined to blame those in political and industrial authority. It was this feeling, which had found expression in the surprisingly large support for the People's Convention, that lay behind the crisis of authority in industry. When there were materials shortages and production hold-ups, blame was being allocated to managements and not to workers. When managers took 'hard lines' with their employees, they were castigated by all concerned and often by the general public for their failure to abandon inappropriate disciplinary threats in the face of the real possibility of a Nazi invasion.

Until February 1941 there had been no indication that industrial discontent was about to become a active force. Strikes had been largely defensive in character. The only form of government action required to deal with popular restiveness had been the suppression of the *Daily Worker* which, as we have seen, was not accompanied by an intensification of action against industrial militants. But early 1941 saw a major industrial conflict which spread across several major manufacturing areas, in the course of which it became apparent that one could not always rely on official trade union procedures to suppress militancy. The apprentices' strikes of 1941 had eventually to be ended by the first use of Order 1305. These prosecutions were not followed by sentences, presumably because to have sentenced adolescents would have made both the Order and the magistrates look ridiculous.

In March 1940 an organising committee of apprentices had asked for delegates from the major Clyde factories and yards to attend a meeting to discuss shared problems. Delegates from thirty-five workplaces attended, and constituted themselves as the Clyde Apprentices' Committee, electing an executive of nine. They agreed on a common programme, which was later adopted by other Scottish apprentices in the interests of unity (since the Edinburgh boys, for example, had drafted their own demands separately). The programme claimed a one hundred per cent increase for all apprentices from the first to the fourth years; the full district rate less five shillings for the first six months of the final year, after which the full rate would apply; a half day's technical training per week in the employer's time; a fuller all-round training in the shops, and no victimisation of the boys elected as delegates.[161] The Clyde Apprentices' Committee organised further meetings when other grievances were aired, among which the long hours worked by many lads in 1940 featured prominently, but the programme worked out in early 1940 was the basis of the 1941 campaign.[162] This campaign was of interest not only to apprentices but to adult workers as well, since it was mainly centred on the issue of pay.

The first year of war had seen a substantial acceleration in the rate of inflation, so that even the out dated Cost of Living Index then used showed a rise of the order of twenty per cent, rising from 155 on 1 September 1939 to 187 on 31 August 1940.[163] Over the next year the index was to rise another thirteen points, and it then remained steady at about the two hundred mark until the end of the war.[164] This rate of inflation put considerable onus on the national pay award; the Scottish Conciliation Officer thought it would have to yield at least five shillings over the plain-time rates to satisfy the local engineers. In fact, however, it only brought three shillings and sixpence.[165] The apprentices received only a proportion of this increase, ranging from tenpence-halfpenny for first-year lads to one shilling and sevenpence for fifth-year apprentices.[166] Meanwhile, trainees were getting the full rate after six months' training, and their elder sisters over twenty-one could get the full skilled rate if they replaced skilled men.[167] These injustices were felt very directly by the boys and were not simply abstract 'comparators'. They worked with trainees and women, whom they were often expected to help; it was stretching their patience too far to expect them, as skilled men in the making, to continue to do this while receiving lower wages. Their pay did not reflect their status in the shops, they felt, and soon after they learned of the increases due to them under the national award they took action as a previous generation of apprentices had done in 1937.

February 1941 brought a number of strikes in different parts of Scotland over various aspects of the apprentices' situation. At the beginning of the month a number of apprentices elected by their workmates to present a set of demands to their employers, Henry Robb's Shipbuilders at Leith, had been sacked as a result. The strike did not last long, but it illustrated that the apprentices resented the allegation that they had been led astray by Communists. Galbraith expected that the local official would be able to secure an immediate resumption of work to allow him to approach the employers and negotiate on the boys' behalf, but he did not, because: '. . . probably due to excessive zeal. . . the official made a very pointed attack on the Chairman of the apprentices' committee and criticised strongly those who were "stupid enough" to be lead [sic] away by the advice of the Communists'.[168] The boys resented these remarks and voted against a resumption of work, although they were soon to start drifting back in any case. The Clyde boys (on whose committee eight of the nine delegates were also members of the YCL) had promised support for the Leith lads, but were overtaken by events when they returned.[169]

Scotland was still bubbling with youthful discontent. In late February a strike of apprentices and journeymen working in the stokehold of a ship in Yarrow's Clydeside yard broke out when a boy was asked to do labourer's work against the advice of his steward.[170] By 25 February, the dispute was settled by a deputation of stewards after an 'unofficial' interview with the Yarrow management.[171] On 28 February apprentices at a Kilmarnock factory stopped work for a wage increase because, the *Kilmarnock Standard* thought, of 'communist elements' exercising a 'subversive influence'.[172] A few days later the Edinburgh apprentices came out in support, and by 15 March there were six thousand Clyde apprentices out.[173] According to Galbraith: 'They had adopted an attitude of refusing to have anything to do with trade unions and of insisting on being allowed to put their. . . own case. . . the reason for this attitude was, as one of them remarked, "disillusionment". They now assert that they can gain more for themselves.'[174] The Apprentices' Committee refused unanimously to accept the local official's offer to negotiate on their behalf.[175] They showed great discipline in insisting that only their representatives should speak for them, and most of the boys were very conscious of the need to maintain this position in the face of the allegations being made against them and the possibility of prosecution. Thus, a Mass Observer was utterly confounded by the solid refusal of the rank and file to speak to him; they 'were intensely suspicious, and although he adopted several methods—such as making a statement to which a denial might be expected—he was unable to extract from them even details of pre-war and present-day wages and information which it is simply perverse to try to conceal, and was consistently referred to the secretary or the press agent of the Clyde Apprentices' Committee'.[176] The representatives of that Committee were 'equally suspicious, but less perverse', providing the observer with some very elementary information. For the first and perhaps the last time, a Mass Observer was effectively stonewalled by a large body of people.

The Clyde Apprentices' Committee maintained that since only some thirty per cent of the boys on strike were members of trade unions, the union officials did not have the right to speak for them. That right belonged solely to the Committee itself. They maintained their independent attitude when Bevin decided to set up a Court of Inquiry—which he later congratulated on achieving its object, 'an early resumption of work'[177]—immediately after the strike spread to the Clyde. The Court asked the Clyde Apprentices' Committee to recommend a return to work if national negotiations between the engineering unions and the employers were immediately set in motion. The Committee initially refused to do this unless they were directly represented in the discussions. The Court eventually persuaded the boys to recommend a return, by promising that they would review the agreed settlement reached by the unions in the light of the apprentices' submissions. In addition, the Court agreed to suggest to the unions that they accept some element of apprentice representation on their negotiating committee.[178] The union officials had always been resolutely opposed to any such suggestions, however, and did not follow the Court's advice. But the boys' committee accepted the Court's undertakings and the Clyde strikers duly returned on Thursday 17 March.[179]

By the time the Court of Inquiry had achieved its objective in getting the Clyde boys back, the strike had already spread into England and Northern Ireland. The Clyde boys had been in touch with their counterparts in Belfast, Barrow, Tyneside and Manchester to discuss shared problems and the possibility of strike action. By 27 March it appeared that the English apprentices were not going to react in any significant way to the Scottish initiative; the Barrow lads had come out, as had the apprentices at Swan Hunter's Tyneside yard, but both groups had returned to work quickly to await the outcome of the national negotiations.[180] Within a fortnight of the first boys coming out on the Clyde a national settlement was agreed, and it was, Galbraith thought, 'on the whole well received'.[181] Wages were to rise with those of the adults, and in a fixed proportion to them, on a 'wage-for-age' basis. Sixteen-year-old apprentices, for example, were to receive twenty-five per cent of the full rate plus national bonus, ranging up to sixty per cent for the twenty-year-olds. For these final-year boys, previously receiving 31s. 3d. per week on the Clyde, the increase amounted to 14s. 9d.[182] But although this was large in percentage terms and showed what could be obtained, it did not satisfy all of the boys. One of the main problems was that the settlement set up further serious anomalies, by virtue of the 'wage-for-age' scale. The Lancashire apprentices in particular took strong exception to the fact that sixteen-year-olds in their district who received twenty-five per cent of the full rate would actually suffer a reduction.[183] The AEU officials had themselves demonstrated what the lads had all along believed: that they were not close enough to apprentices' problems to represent them adequately. This fact brought a further major outbreak of strikes in Lancashire and the direct use of Order 1305 against the boys.

For the government, the Lancashire strike was in some respects more serious than the Scottish stoppages had been, because it occurred in a different context. There was always the chance that the strikes might spread as they had in 1937, while the card of national negotiations had been played and approved by a Court of Inquiry. A local settlement through official channels was an outside possibility, but the local officials would need to be more successful than those at national level if they were to pull this off without further government intervention. Once again, as in 1937, the apprentices' movement started on the fringes of Greater Manchester, in the poorly paid textile machinery trade. Several hundred Rochdale boys sent their representatives to the large concerns in Manchester to 'stir up trouble', as the local Conciliation Officer put it.[184] They were successful in that they recruited the enthusiastic support of the apprentices at A.V. Roe's Newton Heath factory, who stopped work to hold a mass meeting to decide on further action. The A.V. Roe boys decided to try to spread the strike across the Manchester district, and for the rest of the day and the morning of the next the strike committee worked at organising a mass meeting. This meeting was attended by three thousand boys from various factories, who heard Kenneth Warburton, secretary of the strike committee, explain the reasons for the apprentices' movement, urging them to listen to nobody but their own committee. Several other boys spoke, including Fred Withers, who proposed that the employers be given a week to 'think it over', but the meeting rejected his proposal.[185] By that evening there were nine thousand out and the strike was gathering momentum. On the 30th the AEU District Committee, through the local officials, called a mass meeting to ask the boys if they would go back to work to allow them to negotiate with the employers locally. The meeting was reluctant to return without having gained anything; the boys shouted their dissent at the officials from all over the David Lewis Recreation Ground.[186]

Fred Siddall, the AEU District Secretary, an older man and a 'constitutionalist', had not gone down particularly well with the apprentices, and had clearly failed, as the main official involved, to persuade them of his point of view. The Conciliation Officer therefore saw no alternative but to ask the approval of Ministry of Labour headquarters for a prosecution of the 'ringleaders' under Order 1305. That Friday night he had the six members of the strike committee summonsed. The magistrate, informing all concerned that he deprecated delay in such matters, allowed an adjournment until the Tuesday morning to allow a brief to be prepared for defence counsel.[187] The summonsing of the six boys had by that time achieved the desired effect; the strikers began to return to work. Probably because of this, the six members of the executive were bound over.[188] On the following Wednesday, the Engineering Employers' Association agreed to negotiate locally over any apprentices who were

# *The*
# APPRENTICE
# MAG.

**The organ of the**
**CLYDE APPRENTICES COMMITTEE.**

**1d.**

Thursday,
1st May, 1941.

# NEW PROBLEMS

## and the Scottish Conference

The Scottish Apprentice Conference, which will be held in the **Central Halls, Glasgow, on 17th May,** promises to be one of the most important yet held. From it, we will draw up an **immediate programme** of action, around which we can develop the next stage in the fight for better conditions.

It is now evident that apprentices in many parts of Britain are far from satisfied with the wages award. **The increases won, in no way correspond to the big advance in the cost of living during the past months.** Furthermore, resentment is felt by many older apprentices who, after having won wage increases, are now faced with the unhappy prospect of losing as much as **4s. 5d.** weekly tax on a £2 10s. wage.

**Other grievances are reported.**

The freshness of the countryside is denied us because of excessive overtime, and Sunday work. As the summer months approach, our thoughts turn more and more to the need for sunshine and health-giving exercises. **Fatigue and mental weariness are affecting the health of the country's future manhood.**

Letters from apprentices show too that in many factories lads are on the move to improve conditions on the spot! Particularly in relation to canteens, many apprentices have written to us, raising this matter.

**At our conference we want to discuss all these questions.** Only by doing so can we really claim that the C.A.C. and the Scottish Apprentice Committee are leading the young workers of Scotland in the fight to shape a better future life.

In the last issue of "**The Apprentice Mag.**" we said, "The feeling that should be

in all our minds is that the strike has not really been the end of our struggle for better wages."

**That is more than ever true.** The Scottish Conference will prepare the next steps in our fight.

One job we ask you to do. **Make certain that your factory is represented.** Get your delegates elected now. Raise all your grievances **Now,** and come along fully armed to fire the shot and shell that will send us rollicking on the road to round two,—and another victory !

Front page of the *Clyde Apprentice's Mag*

inadequately provided for in the national agreement.[189]

The apprentices' strikes had brought substantial gains: increases of around fifty per cent had been won for many of the boys. Nevertheless, the motive of the dispute remained, in that they continued to resent their position in relation to the women and the trainees who had come only recently into the workshop. Moreover, the 'wage-for-age' scale had set up its own anomalies, as we shall see. The issue was not only financial, though nor was the situation seen by the boys as the fault of the trainees and women; such relative discrepancies were, they thought, morally indefensible, and the blame belonged with the employers and the government for allowing the employers to continue to get away with it. To illustrate this, it is worth looking at what an apprentice wrote to his friend in Canada in a letter intercepted and brought to the attention of the Ministry of Labour by a vigilant censor:

> The apprentices all over the Clyde, Belfast and Edinburgh were out on strike for higher wages. They are bringing in girls who are getting big wages and trainees (boys who serve six months training and then come in and get the man's pay while we have to work—serve—five years at the small rate). To make a long story short we got a rise but not to suit me yet. As you know first year have a standard pay and when you enter your second year you get a little more, etc., etc., for each year until your time is out, well now they are going by your ages—so that a boy who works beside me and has less time served than me is getting 32/6d a week because this boy is eighteen and I am only seventeen. A boy of twenty whether he is just starting or not will get 46/- so don't be saying Canada is the only one who does things wrong.[190]

This apprentice's letter is a lucid individual expression of the strong collective sense of bitterness that the apprentices felt. Yet it was written *after* the award of the very large increases of early 1941. Clearly, the problems remained to be solved, despite the advances which had been made.

The dispute had provided the Young Communist League with the agitational field which many of their older comrades lacked; they thrived in it, and began after the strike to build a national organisation of apprentices to provide some continuous coordination and direction for their activity. On 11 May the first truly national conference of apprentice delegates from the main engineering districts was held. Forty delegates decided to demand a general increase of 3d. per hour, to turn the lively four-page *Clyde Apprentices' Mag* into a national paper, and to meet again on 10 August.[191] This meeting set up an organisation called the Engineering and Allied Trades National Apprentices' and Youth Movement, a title reminiscent of that of the adult shop stewards' body. Its resolutions called for the building of a national youth movement, full trade-unionism, and a threepence per hour increase for all workers under twenty-one. At a second meeting in October 1941, however, the threepence per hour wage demand was dropped in favour of the AEU National Committee's policy of demanding increases which varied with the ages of the boys concerned.[192] The precise reason for the shift in emphasis is at present unclear: it may have been related to the invasion of Russia and the Communists' new line against strikes, or it may have had more to do with the growth of trade-unionism among the boys. Given the importance of the YCL in the apprentices' unofficial organisations, the first explanation appears the more plausible, but we do not know. A history of the apprentices' movements would be immensely valuable for the light it would throw on the historical position of young workers generally, and because of the apprentices' movement's position as an integral part of the trade union movement; many of the apprentices of the thirties and forties served their political time in these disputes.

If the reason for beginning to take a more constitutional line are not entirely clear, the direction of the development is indisputable. The 1941 strikers were truly unofficial in that they were adamant in rejecting offers of official trade union representation. It was therefore an important shift in emphasis when their leaders began to drop their own demands in favour of those of the National Committee of the AEU. The process was to go further in the next few years, although the apprentices were never to be easy for the union to control once they started to act. The AEU itself had begun to realise that it would have to adapt its structure to allow

131

for more active apprentice participation. In 1940 the EC had suggested that District Committees should set up young workers' committees, and these slowly (and with much argument over their scope and functions) began to operate over the next few years.[193] For three years there were to be no major apprentices' strikes. When they did recur they were to prove more susceptible to official union pressures because of the influence of these committees. In any event, the 1941 strikes had taken the edge off the apprentices' wage grievances. By setting up a system whereby the younger workers would automatically receive a proportion of the increases awarded to skilled men, the agreement ensured that it would not be necessary to fight periodic battles to bring youth rates into line with those paid to adults. To some extent, the acute problem associated with the development of an elementary procedure for collective bargaining covering apprentices had begun to be solved.

The apprentices had launched the first large-scale strike of the war, and carried it through with characteristic enthusiasm and panache. Their activity conjured up reminiscences of 1937, and showed that despite the pressures of wartime young workers' combativeness and determination to improve their position had survived. In the end, the strikes were only terminated by the Ministry of Labour's decision to bring prosecutions under Order 1305. The strikes have been awarded some three lines in the official account, and have thereby been pushed to the margins of accepted Establishment history.[194] They may have been unfortunate and isolated events, temporarily interrupting the industrial peace, but they were rooted in the apprentices' daily workshop grievances, and were not simply the result of 'fifth-column' agitation. Moreover, they were offensive strikes in that, unlike those in defence of shop stewards, which were characteristic of 1940, they were not conducted in defence of existing rights, but sought to establish new ones.

More importantly, the apprentices' disputes occurred against a background of declining 'industrial morale'. By mid-1941, the war economy was only just absorbing the last of the unemployed, and was certainly not running at the level of mobilisation or efficiency which working people

132

thought appropriate in the circumstances. Responsibility for this situation could not possibly be laid at the feet of engineering workers, who had worked to the point of exhaustion when called on to do so during the summer of 1940. Most people felt that not enough was being done by those in authority to increase industrial efficiency or to eliminate waste and chaos. 'Fifth-columnists' there might be, but it was not they who were responsible for the fact that long periods were spent in many factories without any work even being made available. Managements could exhort people to 'get on with something', but the something was often no more than a time-filler. Moreover, the threat of the sack was no longer very potent. For the first time in some twenty years, engineering workers did not have to go in fear of losing their jobs to the daily stream of unemployed calling at the office in search of work. It was this fact more than any other which had begun to change the atmosphere in the workshops.

## NOTES

1   A. Calder, op. cit., p. 70.
2   *The Aeroplane*, 5 April 1940.
3   Calder, op. cit., pp. 59–60.
4   P. Inman, op. cit., p. 49.
5   *Oxford Mail*, 3 Oct. 1939.
6   16 Sept. 1939. LAB 10/349.
7   *The Aeroplane*, 8 March 1940, p. 309.
8   W. Hornby, op. cit., chs 4 and 6.
9   *Machinery*, 4 April 1940.
10  *The Aeroplane*, 23 Feb. 1940.
11  Letter from E.C. Gordon England, *The Aeroplane*, 1 March 1940.
12  G.L. Marson, *Coventry: A Study in Urban Geography* (unpublished MA dissertation, Liverpool, 1949), p. 132.
13  P.S. Florence and A. Shenfield, 'Labour for the War Industries: The Experience of Coventry' in *Review of Economic Studies*, vol. 12, 1944-5, p. 43.
14  Ibid., p. 41.
15  Ibid., pp. 38, 41.
16  *Minutes* of the Coventry Engineering Employers' Association, Nov. 1939. The polishing shop had struck for two days in June 1939 (Ibid., July 1939).
17  See, for example, *Minutes* of the Slough Juvenile Employment Committee (Buckinghamshire County Record Office, Aylesbury), 1 Aug.-31 Dec. 1939, in which it is recorded that G.D. Peters Ltd. had increased wages as the result of a strike; this firm had taken young transferees from the depressed areas (especially Wales) during the 1930s, but many of them had run away, been sacked (for 'insubordination' in one case) or had simply stayed at home after the Christmas holidays. (see *Minutes*, Jan.-March 1937, and

South Eastern District, 1 April-31 July 1936).

18  *Annual Report* of the Chief Inspector of Factories, 1940 (Cmd. 6316), p. 19.

19  *Annual Report* of the Chief Inspector of Factories, 1941 (Cmd. 6397), p. 5; *Annual Report,* 1940, p. 6.

20  TGWU *Record,* July 1942.

21  Dorothy Elliott, 'Employment of Women in Wartime', in *Labour Management,* vol. xxii, no. 234, Jan. 1940.

22  Interview with Jock Wallace, 20 May 1980.

23  Interview between Peter Caldwell and Jock Gibson, 7 Nov. 1973.

24  Unpublished manuscript history of the Austin shop stewards' committee by Dick Etheridge, p. 7 (Modern Records Centre, Warwick University).

25  Arthur Exell, 'Morris Motors in the 1940s', *History Workshop,* no. 9, Spring 1980, pp. 92–3.

26  Interview with Harold Taylor, 12 April 1976.

27  TGWU *Record,* Aug. 1944. The union's journal said that three series of lectures had been given in the past twelve months; Jones had been to war workers' hostels as part of an industrial 'brains trust'; a meeting for shop stewards on post-war problems had been held; and ten thousand copies of the District Committee's 'Guide to Engineering Wages and Conditions' had been circulated.

28  23 Dec. 1939. LAB 10/349.

29  *Minutes* of TGWU Finance and General Purposes Committee, no. 884, 1944.

30  *DW,* 22 July 1940, contains an interesting article about problems between the AEU and TGWU in Scotland. *DW,* 13 Sept. 1940, has an article dealing with the Rolls-Royce situation. See also I. Lloyd, *Rolls-Royce: The Merlin at War* (1978), pp. 24–33, on Hillington.

31  26 Oct. 1940. LAB 10/360.

32  TGWU *Record,* Nov. 1942.

33  5 Oct. 1940. LAB 10/360.

34  *Coventry Standard,* 10 Aug. 1940.

35  T. Wright, *Some Habits and Customs of the Working Classes* (1867), pp. 99–100. 'Ringing-in' is also mentioned by A. Williams in his classic *Life in A Railway Factory* (1915), pp. 256–7.

36  See, for example, p. 312.

37  *Factory News* (A.V. Roe), 18 Dec. 1943.

38  2, 9 March 1940. LAB 10/360.

39  *Minutes* of the Coventry Engineering Employers' Association, Feb. 1941.

40  *Minutes* of the Manchester District Committee of the AEU, 29 Dec. 1940.

41  24 Aug. 1940. LAB 10/360.

42  Harold Taylor interview, 12 April 1976.

43  P. Inman, op. cit., pp. 393–4.

44  John Perryman interview with Kim Howells, 11 Jan. 1976.

45  Varying accounts of these events have been given by J. Degras, *The Communist International, 1919-43. Documents,* vol. 3 (Oxford, 1965), p. 441; H. Pelling, *The British Communist Party. An Historical Profile* (1958), pp. 110–213; D. Hyde, *I Believed* (1951), p. 70; R. Palme Dutt disagreed with Hyde's version of events in a review of his book published in the *Daily Worker* on 1 March 1951. Dutt's account stresses the length and sharpness of the discussion. See also J. Mahon, *Harry Pollitt. A Biography* (1976), pp. 249–55.

46  W. Hannington, *Industrial History in Wartime* (1940), is a history of the

shop stewards' movement of the First World War which concludes by making comparisons with the Second World War. The articles by Hannington and Campbell appeared in *Labour Monthly*, Oct. 1940 and Feb. 1941.

47    A. Calder, op. cit., pp. 93–9. Calder cites the views of P. Addison in his argument.

48    *The Times*, 23 May 1940.

49    *Labour Research*, no. 29, p. 82.

50    Ibid., no. 29, p. 101.

51    *DW*, 3, 7, 12, 22 Aug. 1940. *NP*, Nov. 1940.

52    *Labour Research*, no. 40, pp. 4–5.

53    W. Hannington, *The Rights of Engineers* (1944), p. 67.

54    A. Calder, op. cit., p. 133.

55    P. Inman, op. cit., p. 442.

56    28 May 1940. AVIA 22/1030.

57    21 June 1940. AVIA 22/1030.

58    12 Oct., 19 Nov. 1940; 4 Feb. 1941. INF 1/336.

59    I. Lloyd, op. cit., p. 28.

60    Memoirs of M.J. Lipmann, deposited in the Mass Observation Archive, dated 1 June 1978, p. 30.

61    20 April 1940, LAB 10/360. The shipyard in question was John Brown's of Clydeside, well known for its Communist stewards. This may partially account for the detective's presence.

62    *DW*, 3 Aug. 1940; on 7 Aug. the paper's editorial asked Bevin what he was going to do about Mason's internment, and from then on kept up a constant criticism of Bevin for allowing Mason to be interned without trial.

63    *NP*, Nov. 1940.

64    Ibid.

65    Ibid.

66    See J.R. Campbell, in *Labour Monthly*, Oct. 1940 and Wal Hannington in *Labour Monthly*, Feb. 1941.

67    Interview with Jock Wallace, 8 April, 1980.

68    *Minutes* of the Coventry District Committee of the AEU, 16 Jan., 5 March, 30 July, 8 Sept., 13 Oct. 1940. On 22 August the *Daily Worker* also mentioned the case of Ernie Roberts, sacked from Armstrong-Siddeley. Matthews' case is from *Minutes* of a works conference held at the Coventry Gauge and Tool Co., 4 July 1941.

69    *Minutes* of the Coventry District Committee of the AEU, 16 Jan. 1940.

70    *NP*, May 1940.

71    *Minutes* of the Coventry DC, 22 Sept. 1940.

72    5 Oct. 1940. LAB 10/350.

73    *Minutes* of the Coventry DC, 29 Sept. 1940.

74    Ibid.

75    Ibid.

76    10 Oct. 1940. LAB 10/350.

77    Ibid.

78    *DW*, 3 Oct. 1940. *DW*, 5 Oct. 1940. *NP*, Oct. 1940.

79    *DW*, 5 Oct.; *NP*, Oct. 1940.

80    Ibid.

81    *DW*, 9 Oct. 1940.

82    R.E. Dowse, *Left in the Centre* (1966), pp. 194, 201. See also H. McShane with J. Smith, *No Mean Fighter* (1978), p. 236.

83    *The Socialist*, Feb. 1939.

84    7 Oct. 1939; 23 Dec. 1939. LAB 10/360.

85 Those branches who did not send money were prevented from sending it by their Executives, Galbraith stated. 6 Jan. 1940, LAB 10/361.
86 *Daily Herald,* 9 Oct. 1940.
87 Ibid., 9 Oct. 1940.
88 Letter (n.d.) in LAB 10/124.
89 LAB 10/124.
90 26 Sept. 1940. LAB 10/124.
91 Fred Smith to W. Irvine, 28 Sept. 1940. LAB 10/124.
92 Galbraith to HQ, 2 Oct. 1940.
93 Telegram Bevin to Dollan (n.d., copy). LAB 10/124.
94 McAndrew to Bevin, 23 Oct. 1940. LAB 10/124. Emphases original.
95 Leggett to Tanner, 9 Nov. 1940. See also Leggett's marginal note on Galbraith to Leggett, 31 Oct. 1940. LAB 10/124.
96 Galbraith to Leggett, 30 Sept., 8 Oct. 1940. LAB 10/124.
97 Galbraith to Leggett, 8 Oct. 1940. LAB 10/124.
98 'Memo on British Auxiliaries Strike', n.d., LAB 10/126. Galbraith's statement seems to have been accurate; the *Daily Herald* reported men drifting back to work on 6 and 8 November.
99 Loose copy of leaflet in LAB 10/124.
100 *Glasgow Observer and Scottish Catholic Herald,* 15 Nov. 1940.
101 *DW,* 26 Oct. 1940; 'Memo on British Auxiliaries Strike', LAB 10/126.
102 Ibid.
103 15 Nov. 1940. LAB 10/126.
104 Ibid.
105 Leggett to Tanner, 9 Nov. 1940. LAB 10/124.
106 Sillars had certainly been pressurised by the Executive of the AEU in the summer of 1940 to behave in a more constitutional way; together with some other stewards, he had been hauled up to the AEU's offices in Peckham Road, London, on 29 July, for attending the E&ATSSNC's conference (*NP,* Aug. 1940). Memo from Galbraith to HQ, n.d., LAB 10/124.
107 7 Dec. 1940. LAB 10/360.
108 Galbraith to Leggett, 20 Nov. 1940. LAB 10/124.
109 *DW,* 26 Nov. 1940.
110 Galbraith to Leggett, 26 Nov. 1940. LAB 10/124.
111 11, 18 Jan. 1941. LAB 10/362.
112 K. Richardson, *Twentieth-Century Coventry* (1972), p. 77, note 8.
113 S. Orwell and I. Angus, op. cit., p. 370 (Orwell's diary entry for 3 September).
114 Shop stewards used these provisions to open up a wide range of issues with management, including payment during raids and the pay and conditions of spotters (see *NP,* Nov. 1940). On the spotter system, see *Picture Post,* 28 September 1940.
115 *Picture Post,* 12 Oct. 1940.
116 Ibid.
117 *DW,* 22 July 1940.
118 *NP,* Nov. 1940.
119 Ibid.
120 Ibid.
121 *Labour Management,* Nov. 1940, vol. xxii, no. 243, p. 162.
122 *NP,* Nov. 1940.
123 *Coventry Standard,* 30 Nov. 1940. 'Lessons of Recent Heavy Air Raids', Dec. 1940, pp. 3–4. LAB 8/362. A. Calder, op. cit., p. 236. *Sunday Times,*

30 May 1971.

124 *Coventry Standard,* loc. cit.

125 'Lessons of Recent Heavy Air Raids', loc. cit.

126 *DW,* 19, 20, 21, 23 Nov.

127 The role of the local officials (which was apparently minimal in achieving recovery in the town) is scathingly portrayed in Tom Harrison's *Living Through the Blitz* (1976), especially p. 137.

128 *DW,* 1 Sept. 1940.

129 *NP,* Dec. 1939; April 1940.

130 Note by Lord President of the Council: 'CPGB: An Estimate of the Effects of the Present Campaign and Recommendations for Action' (n.d.) CAB 98.18.

131 *NP,* Dec. 1940.

132 Reg Scott's diary; I am grateful to Steve Tolliday for lending me a copy of it.

133 These allegations were made by the Trotskyist *Workers' International News,* February 1941. At Napier's, London, two thousand workers were said to have repudiated their delegates; four hundred were said to have done the same at De Havilland's, Edgware (recalled by Jock Wallace, an ex-Napier's shop steward).

134 Home Office memo of 27 July 1940. CAB 98.18.

135 *NP,* Jan. 1941.

136 'Note by Chairman', 25 Jan. 1941. CAB 98.18.

137 Ibid.

138 Ibid., and 5 Feb. 1941.

139 Memo by Home Secretary, 17 Jan. 1941. CAB 98.18.

140 The Coventry Toolroom Agreement provided for a district average, based on the earnings of skilled piece-workers, to be paid to toolmakers; it was a variant of the National Toolroom Agreement which gave toolmakers a similar average on a plant-by-plant basis. See R. Croucher, op. cit., pp. 203-6.

141 See C.A. Beard, *President Roosevelt and the Coming of War* (New Haven, 1948), p. 68.

142 An excellent description of the working of the EWO was written for shop stewards by Wal Hannington, in his book *The Rights of Engineers* (1944), pp. 67-72.

143 A. Bullock, op. cit., p. 57.

144 AEU *Monthly Journal,* March 1941.

145 Tom Harrisson, op. cit., p. 12.

146 'Glasgow Morale. Preliminary Report', 7 March 1941. File Report 600 (hereinafter cited as MO 600), pp. 1-2.

147 Ibid., p. 3.

148 Ibid., pp. 16, 17, 19.

149 Ibid., p. 17.

150 See, for example, the remarks made in 1943 about this area, in 'Report by Parliamentary Secretary, Raw Materials, Ministry of Supply' (Oct. 1943), in AVIA 9/58. People said that there would be 'little or no hope of employment after the war' in the North-East according to this report.

151 MO 600, pp. 29-30.

152 Ibid.

153 Ibid., p. 31.

154 Ibid.

155 Ibid., pp. 29-30.

156    Ibid., p. 23.
157    'Report on Aircraft Factories and Manpower', S.J. Egerton-Banks, 9 June 1941. LAB 8/374.
158    *Coventry Standard,* 22 March 1941. *Minutes* of the Manchester District Committee of the AEU, 4 July 1940.
159    MO 600, pp. 29–30.
160    L. Pigott to Admiralty, 5 March 1941. LAB 10/138.
161    *Socialist Appeal,* June 1941. These demands were adopted by the Edinburgh apprentices in January 1941 (leaflet issued by the Edinburgh Apprentices' Committee, Jan. 1941, in LAB 10/422).
162    *NP,* Nov. 1940. The question of long hours worked by young people was investigated by the government in 1942. The information gathered indicated that an unknown but undoubtedly very high number of hours had been worked in 1940, and that this was still the case in 1942 (LAB 19/46; R. Croucher, op. cit., pp. 117–9).
163    Cost of Living Index. All Items. Table 89, *British Labour Statistics* (Department of Employment and Productivity, 1971).
164    Ibid.
165    18 Jan. 1941. LAB 10/362.
166    *Socialist Appeal,* June 1941.
167    See J.B. Jefferys, op. cit., pp. 256–7.
168    On the strike, see 7 Feb. 1941 (subject: Messrs Henry Robb, Leith), LAB 10/422.
169    5, 7 Feb. 1941 (subject: Engineering and Shipbuilding Apprentices' Committee), LAB 10/422. 15 Feb. 1941. LAB 10/362.
170    25 Feb. 1941. LAB 10/138.
171    Ibid.
172    *Kilmarnock Standard,* 8 March 1941.
173    15 March 1941. LAB 10/362.
174    15 March 1941. LAB 10/362.
175    Ibid.
176    'The Scottish Shipbuilding and Engineering Apprentices' Strike', 13 March 1941, Mass Observation File Report 604 (MO 604), p. 1.
177    Bevin to Court Chairman, 15 May 1941. LAB 10/138.
178    15, 22 March 1941. LAB 10/362.
179    22 March 1941. LAB 10/362.
180    26, 27 March 1941. LAB 10/140. 22 March, LAB 10/379.
181    22 March 1941. LAB 10/379. The report of the Court was not made available to the Clyde Apprentices' Committee for fear of according them any recognition.
182    P. Inman, op. cit., p. 334, note I. Inman does not distinguish between the two strike waves.
183    Ibid.
184    21 March 1941. LAB 10/379.
185    *Manchester Evening News,* 8 April 1941.
186    Ibid., 4 April 1941; 29 March 1941. LAB 10/379.
187    *Manchester Evening News,* 4 April 1941.
188    12 April 1941. LAB 10/379.
189    Ibid.
190    Extract from Ministry of Information Form: Postal Censorship, Terminal Mails, private branch (LIV 20671), 41, 16 April 1941. LAB 10/138.
191    A copy of no. 1 of the magazine is to be found in the Library of the Working-Class Movement, Manchester. There is a report of the May meeting in

*Socialist Appeal,* June 1941.
192  *Socialist Appeal,* article by the secretary of the Mersey Apprentices'
      Committee, November 1941.
193  J.B. Jefferys, op. cit., p. 263.
194  P. Inman, op. cit., p. 334.

# CHAPTER 3

# THE END OF THE BEGINNING

By the spring of 1941, the threat of imminent invasion had been removed from all but the most pessimistic minds; on the other hand, all but the most optimistic found it very difficult to perceive a likely route to victory. Nobody could detect any light at the end of what looked like a very long tunnel. Indeed, all the indications were that a war of attrition was beginning that might well lead to Britain being starved into submission. It appeared more than possible that the country's vital Atlantic lifelines would be cut as the naval battle in the Atlantic swung sharply in Germany's favour. During early 1941, merchant convoys bringing essential supplies were being sunk by submarine and air attack to a quite alarming extent. In fact, the amount of tonnage lost rose so steeply in the winter of 1940-1 that by April the government decided to stop publishing monthly figures altogether. Clearly, in such a conflict there could only be one real loser. The feelings among the population as a whole were of slow-burning desperation and, despite American help, of isolation. Britain stood alone.

It was therefore with some relief that the British people saw Hitler throw the main weight of Germany's military machine at the Soviet Union at the end of June 1941. Although this meant that the bulk of the Wehrmacht would be fully occupied on the new front for the immediate future, it was by no means clear at the time that the Germans would not crush the apparently incompetent Russians as they had the French. The assault on Britain would then represent only a relatively minor task. Initially, the drive to the East was dramatically successful. Blitzkrieg seemed to be working again. By October German divisions had reached Moscow's outer defences, albeit with tightly stretched supply lines.

Soon afterwards, the entry of Japan into the war created another grave crisis. The Japanese bombed and sunk the British battleships *Prince of Wales* and *Renown*, following up this considerable achievement by destroying much of the American Pacific fleet at Pearl Harbor. The might of America was now harnessed to the same task as Britain and the Dominions, but under a cloud. In Britain, the only immediate result of America's entry into the war was a growing austerity as the U-boats took advantage of their new access to American territorial waters.

All eyes were on Russia. People hoped fervently that the Russians' poor performance in Finland had been no evidence of their capability to defend their own country. Demands for a second front to be opened in Europe to assist the Russians came initially from the Communist Party, but gathered support as time went on and the feeling grew that Britain was not doing her share. The agitation for the opening of a second front was nevertheless resisted by Churchill and the War Cabinet. The government's military strategy as it evolved during this period was centred on the idea of a bombing offensive against Germany as the only way, short of actual invasion, of taking the war to the enemy in his stronghold. Meanwhile, military operations in North Africa were intensified. Up until the autumn of 1942, these strategies had not yielded any very tangible results. Bomber Command was not well equipped to conduct an offensive on the scale required to make any real impact on the Reich's productive capacity, and its raids proved expensive luxuries during 1941 and 1942 in terms both of men and materials. It was more in an attempt to provide some evidence of their seriousness than with any real hope of destroying factories and workshops that the RAF mounted their first thousand-bomber raid against Cologne at the end of May 1942.

Events moved slowly in North Africa after Wavell's rout of Graziani in 1941. With Axis resources largely directed towards the Eastern front where their troops were bogged down in Stalingrad, the British were gradually able to build up a sizeable material superiority over the Afrika Korps, and to take advantage of this in the important battles of El Alamein. Auchinleck's defensive victory at El Alamein in July was

*I Working on Spitfires, 1939*

II    *Painting wing of bomber, 1940*

III    *Making bombs, 1941*

*IV   Women workers at the bench, 1941*

V ... *and in a shell factory*

VI    *Munitions factory*

followed by Montgomery's decisive offensive victory there between 23 October and 4 November. Before long, the Allies were in control of North Africa. At last a perceptible step forward had been taken. For the first time it appeared possible that the war would be won in the not-too-distant future. Britain's self-confidence was largely restored, and a distinct phase of the war had ended; as Churchill said—partly to deflate the over-optimistic—it was the end of the beginning.

Nazi Germany's invasion of the Soviet Union at the end of June 1941 led to a crucial volte-face in the attitude of the influential Communist faction within the engineering union. Having just persuaded the National Committee of the AEU to adopt the demand for a 'people's peace' as their own, the CP themselves abandoned it and adopted instead the line that the war was to be prosecuted with the utmost vigour as a war to defend the socialist motherland. In their view, given the crucial importance of Russia to world communism, the invasion of Russia had changed the whole nature of the war. They thought it unlikely, however, that the British ruling class had suddenly changed its traditional attitude to the Soviet Union, and strongly suspected some of that class's members of hoping that Germany and Russia would exhaust each other to Britain's benefit. They also thought it unlikely that industrialists were really interested in defeating fascism; their only real interest was the pursuit of profit, and production was only useful to the extent that it brought profit. To these ascribed interests the CP opposed their own policies: the opening of a second front in Europe to ease the pressure on Russia, and the intensification of war production by integrating workers more fully and democratically into the war effort. The new industrial policy had implications which could put Communists and fellow-travellers in novel and occasionally difficult positions. Arguing in favour of inten- sified work, enlisting the help of the foreman in the product- ion drive, working against strikes and so on was not always popular on the shop floor when local grievances had accumulated to the point where workers contemplated a stoppage. Stakhanovism did not export well to the British shop floor. Nor, indeed, was the Communist accustomed to playing such a role.

In general, the new line dovetailed neatly into many aspects of the popular view of the war. For many people the CP had re-entered plausible politics, despite the fact that their paper remained banned until September 1942. They had two distinctive assets, in that they advocated radical change in the organisation of industry (which manifestly needed it), while being associated with the Russians and their heroic war effort. From mid-1941 a 'red haze' began to spread across British politics, and the CP benefited greatly. By the end of 1942 it claimed its peak membership since its foundation, with fifty-six thousand members, and despite a rapid turnover this had only dropped to 55,138 (according to party figures) by the end of 1943.[1] This slight decline showed up more markedly in the following year, so that there were only 45,435 in the party by March 1945.[2] The typical party cadre during the war was the AEU member; AEU members formed by far the biggest single industrial bloc at the party congresses held between 1942 and 1945, with approximately one third of the delegates. The TGWU, by contrast, could usually only muster roughly half of the AEU's strength.[3] If the AEU was important to the CP, the reverse was also true. The CP had a considerable amount of industrial pull through the E&ATSSNC and the much-respected *New Propellor*, which went well beyond the limits of its own membership. More and more factory branches were set up to organise the members in the work-shops as the existing members recruited amongst newcomers in the industry. By the beginning of 1943 Coventry, for example, had no less than thirty-three factory branches.[4] So deep and pervasive was their influence, while they were cutting with the grain, that it led a very thorough survey of trade union affairs written in 1944 to reflect that the political differences between shop stewards and union officials were quite faithfully reflected in the differences between the CP and the Labour Party.[5] In many respects these years were the heyday of the Communist engineer. Certainly in terms of numbers, positions held in workplace organisations and political influence with the rank and file, they represented the apex of the Communist Party's achievements from its formation to the present day.

144

The CP's increased influence derived largely from their intimate association with the idea of a radical restructuring of British war industry by sweeping away the obsolete ideas and methods of organisation whose rationale rested mainly on 'red tape', bureaucracy, inefficiency, and the need for a whole stratum of people to service and defend the status quo. The cry, not only of the left but of a wide cross-section of society, was for greater efficiency in industry irrespective of who might lose authority or position. Measured against any notion of full industrial mobilisation, it was indeed true that the industrial reality fell substantially (and some would have said scandalously) short. Until 1943, nobody could reasonably claim that the war industries were working at full stretch.

In mid-1941 it was still possible for a local labour paper to go to press with an item that referred bitterly to the fact that unemployment still stood at a fraction under half a million, while in Germany labour had become so scarce that a million and a half foreign workers had been drafted into the Reich, 'and', the paper added, 'we are supposed to be "fighting" a life and death struggle!'[6] In fact, by the time the paper was published, its figures were already out of date, so rapidly was 'excess' labour being sucked into the factories. In July 1941 unemployment stood at 198,000,[7] and it was not until the late summer of 1941 that the economy had absorbed the immediately available reserve of labour. From this point onwards, expansion of the national labour force became largely a matter of bringing women into the factories as quickly as possible. At the beginning of December 1941, Bevin announced measures for the conscription of women; unmarried women between the ages of twenty and thirty were called up and given the choice of auxiliary service jobs or work in the munitions industry.[8] In engineering this accelerated the dilution of skilled labour. Thus, in general engineering (including marine work), the proportion of women employed rose from 21.6 per cent in mid-1941 to 31.9 per cent in mid-1942.[9] During the period between the summer of 1941 and the end of 1942 skilled labour was diluted up to almost the wartime maximum; by the beginning of 1943 the labour shortage was 'absolute', and the main route to increased productivity lay in reorganising production in ways other than dilution and redistributing existing labour.

Dilution had necessarily to involve massive changes in working methods and the faster introduction of new machines. Initially this meant that there was often a temporary surplus of labour while the changes were made, with the new recruits standing around while their jobs were created. The problems of planning and coordinating orders with component and raw materials supply were superimposed on those set by dilution. In addition, products were constantly evolving and changing, especially in the aircraft industry. During 1940 and early 1941, aircraft production had centred on fighters, but in December 1941 bombers were given priority.[10] Given that before the war the RAF did not have a genuine heavy bomber at all, the product had to be evolved by trial and error. Error usually cost lives, so improvements were constantly being made to the thousands of components that went to make up a heavy bomber.

Moreover, the managerial resources which firms had at their disposal to push these changes through were themselves strictly limited, and they became, as a result, heavily diluted. As the workforce constantly expanded and the calibre of recruits deteriorated (at least from the standpoint of previous experience), the number of foremen and supervisors had to be steadily increased throughout the industry. Many were simply promoted from the shop floor with little or no training.[11] In mid-1941 the Ministry of Labour set up, in co-operation with the Institute of Labour Management, a training programme for welfare supervisors and personnel managers, but it was operated on a relatively small scale and did not penetrate to the foreman level.[12] The net result of this variety of difficulties, the public thought, was an unacceptably poor performance in producing the weapons of war. At worst—and there were some very bad examples in the press—the result was, in a word, chaos.

During 1941-2 there was much concern in the country over industrial inefficiency. It is often difficult to evaluate objectively the validity of any particular allegation, because of the polemical context in which they usually occurred. The point is that a feeling of unease prevailed, and very few were prepared to actually defend the status quo. All were aware of an acute problem, and in a very short time the question became simply what to do about it. Working people's reactions to these troubles were anger and resentment. They were prepared to play their part, yet they felt cheated of the opportunity to do so. These feelings are well illustrated by the diary kept by a woman working at home, the wife of an aircraft shop steward. On 10 September 1941 she wrote:

> There is still no work in the Spitfire shop. The men bring shoe repairing to work. They have made frequent complaints to higher authorities. My husband, as shop steward, has written to the Minister of Labour and to Lord Beaverbrook, but to no avail. When the enemy is at our gates, then the workers will be blamed for low output. The whole system is rotten; my husband is turned forty and past his prime for output, yet he can make double time in every job, and that with a useless woman as a passenger. Someone is profiteering, and one day that someone will have to pay—if it is not too late for anyone to pay for such criminal folly.[13]

An especially interesting aspect of her entry is the role which her husband as shop steward is playing as a messenger of discontent on the shop floor over production difficulties. The following week she wrote that the men themselves considered the position 'disgraceful, to put it mildly', and added that the press published little, while ministers refused to see deputations of workpeople.[14] At the end of October she again stressed the injustice and essential inequality of the situation: 'If a man on a waiting card takes a day off, he is liable to suspension. Hours of time are wasted by tribunals trying his case and when he protests against slackness he is told that it is not the province of his accusers to find the work for him to do.'[15] For the diarist, the position was fairly clearly one of managers and authority in general blaming others for their mistakes and maintaining their status by unfairly disciplining those who reacted against them.

The military trajectory of the war was felt to leave no room for complacency and to be concrete proof that the whole system needed overhauling. Many were convinced that German and Russian industry were more efficiently organised and that drastic moves would have to be made if they were to defeat a system based on ruthless and draconian organisation.[16] In particular, trade-unionists found the possibility of industrialists making fat profits out of the war disgraceful because it called their patriotism and desire to win the war into question. Excess Profits Tax was not widely understood, and the suspicion proliferated that it made no difference. The 'cost-plus' system of awarding contracts to firms was, on the other hand, well known and the subject of much criticism.[17] It was thought that the practice of assuring companies a fixed amount of profit (and indeed a profit that often increased with costs) positively encouraged a thick industrial undergrowth of waste and inefficiency. A good many managers, although rejecting some conclusions of this sort, had at least to concede that industrial planning left much to be desired. In fact, the professional training and collective identity which existed in the higher echelons of management led them, too, to look for solutions. At the end of September 1941, E.C. Gordon England, the chairman of the Engineering Industries Association, told his members that it was 'the unpleasant truth' that war production, measured on an output-per-man-hour basis, had recently declined. He felt that the main reason for this was the lack of a national plan to maximise the use of available capacity.[18]

The growing acceptance and developing momentum of such ideas had important implications for government industrial relations policy, since both the substance and the very existence of the accusations had to be considered inimical to the successful prosecution of the war. It was for this reason that any solution which rested on the reorganisation of ministries, better planning, the training of managers and so on, could only be a partial one, since it would only tackle problems at one level. Not only did inefficiency have to be eliminated wherever possible, but the disaffection of industrial workers had to be reduced and preferably channelled in positive directions. To some extent, then, the requirements of the situation were as much political as technical. The answer, the government came to think, lay in encouraging the development of consultative machinery at workplace level which would provide a route for the identification and solution of production problems. In this way, the discontent could be turned into an advantage, a weapon with which to solve industry's difficulties before they became a source of poor morale and disputes.

Most managers were not generally in favour of any such scheme, as they had shown by their failure in the inter-war period to respond to the progressive managerial institutions' propagandising on behalf of works councils. In fact, they only came to accept it as a 'fact of life' because of the pressures brought to bear on them by government on the one hand and shop stewards on the other. British engineering managements cherished above all else their 'right to manage', which the employers had fought for and won during the national engineering lock-outs of 1898 and 1922. The mentality underpinning this key principle could not be simply wished away overnight. Nor was it. Managers did not trust their workers to cooperate with them, and harboured suspicions that they wanted to encroach on managerial prerogatives. They returned with mirror-like faithfulness the union's suspicion of their motives. The Coventry Engineering Employers' Association told the Ministry of Labour that '. . . this Association did not wish to convey the impression that they were not willing to co-operate with the workers. . . but rather that experience had shown in Coventry that workers are not prepared to co-operate with Managements.'[19] Therein lay the problem.

But certain important employers' representatives were relatively closely in touch with governmental thought on the matter and were willing to break the vicious circle and to take a lead. They understood the lesson preached by journals like *Labour Management* in the inter-war years, that it was good tactics to involve workers in management's problems. Lord McGowan, chairman of ICI, saw this with crystal clarity and told Churchill that he thought production committees would moderate the extremist by giving him 'a place in the sun', and weaken his influence among his fellows by taking him into the management's confidence.[20] The value of drawing on the fund of experience and knowledge which prevailed amongst workers in the industry was also appreciated by at least one crucial employer's representative, General Baylay, the Director of the Midland Regional Board of the Engineering Employers' Federation. Baylay told the Ministry

149

of Aircraft Production that he favoured production committees not because of union pressure (he was no doubt inured to that), but because he thought they would help to improve and coordinate the activities of the industry in the Midlands.[21] The attitudes of these men were of more than passing interest. McGowan played a part in persuading his friend Churchill of the value of production committees. Baylay too was a pivotal figure as the top representative of managerial opinion in the vital Midlands. His view was one of the essential prerequisites of setting up experimental Joint Production Committees in the Midlands at the beginning of 1942.

A vital factor at the other end of the political spectrum was the position of the Communists, whose opposition would have doomed any such organisation to failure in the large munitions factories where they had some influence. When Bevin had suggested setting up very similar bodies in December 1940, the *Daily Worker* had roundly denounced the idea, comparing it to the Nazi system of factory organisation,[22] and the proposition was shelved. The effect of their new line on the war from June 1941 was to make the CP agitate strongly for JPCs. In fact the CP went much further than is sometimes thought in making the policy work, because it pushed both trade union officialdom and management in the right directions, creating space where previously there had been none.

When the idea was revived, trade union executives had initially been suspicious of the proposed committees for their own reasons. It may have been true, as the official historian has remarked, that Charles Dukes and Jack Tanner (of the NUGMW and AEU respectively) had spoken in favour of joint committees in a general sense before the invasion of Russia, but their views were not reflections of union policy.[23] The government was well aware of this. In August 1941 the Midlands Chief Conciliation Officer of the Ministry of Labour reported to headquarters that the unions were in fact restraining demands for production consultation;[24] at the end of September, a Ministry of Aircraft Production memorandum to the Cabinet's Production Executive remarked that the unions did not want JPCs because they were being sponsored

'No! George refuses to have a Production Committee and sit together with ignorant work people!'

by the CP and the 'National Shop Stewards' Movement'.[25]

It was not long before the unions had to revise their official position in the light of the highly effective and impressive campaign for JPCs run by the E&ATSSNC. Had they not done so, they would have run the risk of allowing a devolution of power within their own organisation towards the left, which was precisely what they had been trying to avoid. *New Propellor* and the E&ATSSNC pulled out all the stops to mobilise all available support for a large-scale conference of workers' representatives to be held at the Stoll Theatre in London on 19 October. The meeting was repudiated by the unions officially, but the E&ATSSNC nonetheless claimed no less than 1,237 delegates from over three hundred war factories.[26] They were given ample opportunity to put their points of view, with only a relatively short introduction and summing-up by Walter Swanson. Swanson was well fitted to his task as chairman: a highly-skilled engineer with sea-going experience, capable of both skilled fitting and the demanding requirements of jig-boring, he combined technical expertise with union position, as AEU convenor at Napier's important Acton aero-engine factory. An excellent speaker and Marxist theoretician, he was well to the fore in the CP and E&ATSSNC's campaigns around the production issue.[27] Twenty-five delegates' speeches were summarised in the official conference report, almost all of them elaborating on the theme of inefficiency and providing example after example of managerial incompetence; predictably enough, many of them recommended JPCs as the answer. Finally, the conference was asked to pass resolutions calling for increased production, the opening of the second front, the lifting of the ban on the *Daily Worker,* and so on. Interestingly, the meeting was not actually asked to pass a resolution dealing with JPCs directly, but instead agreed a summary of no less than twenty-two points *en bloc* as the basis for a submission to the Select Committee on Public Expenditure.[28] The conference conveyed, overall, an impression of remarkable strength and unity of feeling. It was well publicised in the press and made a considerable impact nationally; to many, it seemed quite apparent that some form of joint consultation would have to come.

Some trade-unionists present at the conference, including Rachel Ryan, a shop steward from West London, criticised the orientation of the CP at this point as fundamentally wrong on the grounds that it was collaborationist.[29] Others were later to develop reservations from a more pragmatic point of view. But both criticisms were certainly in the minority during late 1941. The E&ATSSNC's conference of October 1941 was its biggest to date and arguably its most successful ever in terms of political impact. The majority of trade-unionists at the time did not regard the JPC demand as collaborationist, for two important reasons: first, because the existing low level of independent trade union organisation across the industry as a whole made JPCs appear attractive. It is important here to see the JPC campaign in its relationship to the existing state of trade-unionism. Secondly, and importantly, engineering workers saw managements opposing the idea and vigorously defending their 'right to manage'. The committees were only obtained after real struggles in the course of which large numbers of workers saw for the first time that it was possible to force their managements into taking unpalatable decisions.

By the beginning of 1941 the AEU had told the Ministry of Aircraft Production that it would drop the objections it had previously made to Bevin about participating in works committees with non-craft unions, if it was a question of war production committees.[30] Now that the AEU's official attitude was becoming clearer, the MAP thought that the Midland Regional Board should be allowed to proceed to implement JPCs on an experimental basis.[31] Later in the month the AEU appeared to have been totally convinced of the need for JPCs: it circulated a report on production based on replies to a questionnaire devised at headquarters and answered by lay officers of the union, which ended by recommending the establishment of joint committees.[32]

While the Midlands experiment was being carried on, the Ministry of Supply somewhat forced the hands of private employers by making an agreement with the trade unions within the Royal Ordnance Factories to set up JPCs.[33] In March the employers accepted the inevitable. The Engineering Employers Federation signed an agreement with the

153

engineering unions providing for the establishment of JPCs. They were to exist for the duration of the war only, and wage problems were specifically excluded from discussion. Committees could be set up in factories employing one hundred and fifty or more where satisfactory alternative arrangements did not already exist, and were to be elected by the entire workforce, although only trade-unionists could stand for election.[34]

The establishment of the committees in each particular workplace had nevertheless to be secured by agreement between the employers and the unions. The national agreement merely legitimated the setting-up of committees and laid down certain guidelines for their work. Nor was the government prepared to force JPCs on employers. Shop stewards therefore often found themselves spending a good deal of time and energy in trying to pressure their employers to set them up. At the Rover No. 2 shadow factory in Birmingham the convenor had been highly critical of the management, and was sacked at the end of October 1941 along with another steward, allegedly for starting a strike. The AEU District Committee took the matter up, and the episode gave a sharp edge to the battle for a production committee in the factory.[35] In both of the Rover shadow factories in Birmingham, works councils existed, and the company felt that these could act as JPCs. The shop stewards disagreed and the management decided that elections for a JPC would be held, with the old works council standing as candidates. The stewards carried on a 'terrific' campaign at Rover No. 2 for workers to vote for their candidates rather than those of the works council; they organised mass meetings and debates, and issued leaflets. On the morning of the poll, the stewards issued seven thousand poll cards with the names of their nominees on them. After the cards were distributed, work was held up while a demonstration went round the factory en route to the various polling stations. The result, not surprisingly, was a 'crushing defeat' for the works council.[36]

In the larger factories like Rover No. 2, JPCs often functioned fairly effectively, but the question of how general this experience was, in how many factories the committees really worked as intended, is an important one. Reliable statistical information is difficult to find. The figures which are often quoted are those derived from the AEU's surveys carried out amongst lay officers, which should be treated with some caution since they originated in a campaigning context, and the respondents could reasonably be expected to be those with a fair amount of interest in the committees. It is clear, however, that the majority of factories had set up some sort of committee by the end of the war. Government figures for June 1944 stated that there were 4,565 in existence at that time.[37] Even this assertion should be treated with some caution, however. All types of consultative committees were encompassed by these figures (including works councils), and a committee did not have to have met more than once to qualify for inclusion. The official history itself admitted that one third of the MAP's contractors had adapted existing machinery to fulfill the JPC function.[38] Some such committees were farcical: one even consisted exclusively of supervisory staff.[39] In two Coventry factories there were no stewards on the JPCs, and trade-unionists had dubbed them 'the Gaffer's Committee'.[40] Given that many of the JPCs only met once and then effectively ceased to operate, it appears that country-wide coverage may well have been achieved during 1942 rather than later in the war when many committees only existed on paper. The AEU survey at the end of 1942 showed that 6 per cent were set up before January 1942, 15 per cent were set up between January and March, 50 per cent between April and June, 24 per cent between July and October; the rest gave no date of foundation.[41] Of those which actually met, in Coventry for instance only fifteen out of forty-four met regularly. Overall, the picture which emerges from the evidence available was correctly drawn in a detailed report prepared in 1944 for Mass Observation, which identified the months between January and September 1942 as not only the period of the JPCs' initial growth, but also the plateau of their activity.[42] Initial enthusiasm on both sides provided an impetus which was in many cases never regained.

According to the agreement of March 1942, the JPCs were intended to 'consult and advise on matters of production. . .

in order that maximum output may be obtained from the factory'.[43] In general, they did perform precisely this function for most of the time. Yet it was usual for committees to discuss matters other than production.[44] Perhaps the reason for this was a feeling on the part of the members of the JPC that they should discuss not only what the management wanted on the agenda but also matters of direct interest to themselves. An attempt at a very precise estimate of how much time was spent by JPCs on different areas of concern was attempted by the MAP at the end of 1942. Through detailed observation, the MAP inquiry found that 63.5 per cent of the committees' time was taken up by technical and production questions, while 27.4 per cent was taken up by welfare matters.[45] In another report, prepared for Mass Observation in 1944, the percentages of JPCs discussing different *types* of welfare matters were: canteens, 57 per cent; sanitation, 38 per cent; ventilation, 36 per cent; transport, 33 per cent; lighting, 26 per cent; heating, 22 per cent. Although the original objectives of the JPCs were being modified by formal discussion of topics other than production, managements appear to have accepted it as a price they had to pay.

The figures do not reveal very much more than the framework within which JPCs were operating. The actual content and texture of relationships within the framework were elusive even to knowledgeable contemporary commentators. The guarded comments made about the relevance or otherwise of the committees tended to be characterised by uncertainty and ambivalence. All of them laid some emphasis on the difficulties experienced in involving people on the shop floor, however. The detailed report drawn up for Mass Observation in 1944 concluded that the committees had been 'beset by difficulties' which flowed from the suspicions on both sides. At the same time, the author of the report felt that the committees could have a therapeutic effect in that they could draw out grievances and allow them to be discussed before they reached the point of open conflict. They could, at their most effective, give workers 'a real sense of participation' which sometimes brought 'a democratic feeling and a sense that the unit of production is a co-operative group with many similar objects', but the report stressed that it was unrealistic to expect the committees to dispel entirely the suspicions which they had been largely founded to allay.[46] In March 1944 *The Economist* reviewed the progress made by the committees and concluded that the majority were 'indifferent', that there might not be any real cooperation between the representatives on their two sides, and that they had experienced 'no great success in enlisting the interest or support of the factory workers as a whole'.[47] Only a few months earlier, a Ministry of Aircraft Production report on industrial morale in the North-East reported that a 'typical' statement from a shop steward was that 'no real information reaches the workers through the JPC. No bulletins are ever issued in the workshops'.[48] Perhaps it was this type of situation which engendered the plaintive remark of an official from the Midland region in the summer of 1944, that: 'Workers generally do not appreciate that the existence of a JPC does give to them a real measure of responsibility in running the factory.'[49] Perhaps the real problem was that the JPC was *not* giving them a real measure of responsibility in running the workplace, and they had simply assessed the situation correctly.

As early as the October 1941 E&ATSSNC conference, the possibility had been recognised that JPCs might draw some shop stewards into the discussion of problems that were properly management's, thereby depriving stewards of independent initiative and making them lose sight of their main objective, which was representing their members. There were those shop stewards even within the CP itself who later considered that this had in fact happened amongst some of their fellows. Without documentary evidence it is difficult to evaluate these claims, but it is clear that it was not until they had been functioning for some time that the JPCs caused any debate on this issue within the CP. Jock Wallace alleged that when he was convenor at Napier's Liverpool factory, he and some others began to draw up an indictment of the management's performance within the works, but were criticised for doing so within the CP. According to his account, Walter Swanson (who was both convenor at Napier's Acton plant and chairman of the E&ATSSNC) and five or six leading CP members travelled from London to Liverpool to insist on their dropping all their criticisms of management. The precise nature of the disagreement is unclear, but it is apparent that Wallace at least felt that the leadership of the Napier's shop stewards had adopted the slogan of 'Peace with the management'.[50]

In any event, the fear that JPCs would put some shop stewards in an ambiguous position vis-à-vis their managements proved not to be entirely unfounded, although in most cases the skilled rank and file saw to it that they retained some control over their representatives. The adoption of the production argument by the shop stewards could provide management and government alike with opportunities that they would otherwise have found hard to create. An example of this is the negotiations to reduce exceptionally high piece-work earnings in some Midlands factories, initiated by the Ministry of Aircraft Production in 1942. The MAP and other government departments had considered very high earnings in some Midlands factories to be a problem since 1940, but did not lend their support to managerial attempts to reduce them until 1942. During 1940, fixing piece rates on new work had proved very difficult for rate-fixers: when 'loose' rates were fixed, operators could make exceptionally high earnings. This was especially the case in Coventry, where labour was very much in demand and the cost of the product much less important than its production. But high piece-work earnings could also lead to a loss in production, as workers could make sufficient money on only a few hours' work per day. Fear of 'breaking' the rate by earning inordinate amounts led engineering workers to limit their earnings and thereby restrict production. Encouraged by government support, management put this argument to the shop stewards in Coventry factories, but they replied that high piece-work earnings provided an incentive rather than a disincentive to work, that prices once fixed should not be reduced as a matter of principle, and that earnings levels had to be maintained. At the Standard Motor Co. in Coventry, the highest-earning factory in the town, the company did achieve limited reductions on piece-work earnings in the Bristol engine shop. This case is mentioned as a success by the official historian, as reductions of fifty per cent in piece-work prices were negotiated after the company went right through procedure in 1942.[51] Opposition on the shop floor had been strong, however, and in several other cases prevented agreements. An attempt to force a reduction on one section in the same firm in 1944 led to a motion being carried at a section meeting to discontinue negotiations with the management.[52] Indeed, just after the Standard agreement, a meeting of all shop stewards in Coventry passed a motion against 'the attack on piece-work prices' and stressed the 'drastic' effects that this would have on production.[53]

In general, as the official historian recognises, attempts to reduce piece-work earnings in the Midlands met with the resistance that could have been expected at any time. Although wage discussions were not intended to be carried on in JPC meetings, the fear that a general ethos of collaboration would insinuate itself only proved justified within well defined limits. The shop stewards' position (which was also that of the E&ATSSNC), and above all the clear reluctance of the working engineers to accept reductions on established rates, made managements reticent about pushing the matter too hard. At the end of the day, strike action could not be ruled out confidently enough for managements to pursue the issue across a broad front.

The verdict which emerged from contemporary discussions after a couple of years' experience of the effects of JPCs was that they could succeed in involving the workforce as a whole, but usually did not. The delegates themselves usually became involved, but there was little evidence to suggest that they had become integrated into their management's perspectives to any great extent. But the biggest stumbling block, all agreed, was the suspicious approach of the rank and file to the committees. One manager commented that any steward on the JPC was 'apt to get accused of backing up management', while another thought that if he agreed too much with the management without adequate explanation, he was branded a 'management man'.[54] The official historian's views on the value of the committees are slightly more optimistic overall than those of the wartime commentators. As usual, she is careful not to overstate the case, but she does tend to a more positive evaluation than her predecessors of their

159

usefulness in increasing worker-management cooperation.[55] The roots of her optimism lie not only in the ingrained tendency for official historians to end on an optimistic note, but also in the author's method. The relations between the committees and workers in the factories were not systematically examined and therefore, looking from above, the two looked to amount to approximately the same thing. More interesting than the question of how many committees functioned and how many did not is perhaps the question of who was influenced by them and who was not. It was quite possible for convenors and senior shop stewards to be wholly behind the idea of joint consultation while sections of the membership might be unrepresented, apathetic or even downright hostile. Engineering workers' attitudes, positions and sentiments at this time have to be reconsidered.

To some the case for the JPCs's usefulness as made out by Mrs Inman rested on the fact that they had avoided a number of strikes. The committees undoubtedly played a role in this but, as she says, they were one of a number of trends which acted in a similar direction. The promising progress of the war and the strong opposition of trade union executives were two of the more important additional reasons which might be cited, but the official historian plays down another important one: the opposition of the Communist Party and the E&ATSSNC to strikes.

The trend in disputes in the early part of 1941 had not been encouraging from the government's point of view, in that despite the suppression of the *Daily Worker* the apprentices' strikes had caused serious disturbance to production. Furthermore, Order 1305 had to be used against strikers for the first time. After the invasion of the Soviet Union, the whole industrial situation changed because of the CP's change of line. For the first time this century, the number of trade-unionists prepared to advocate industrial action on political grounds was reduced almost to vanishing point. The members and their fellow-travellers in the E&ATSSNC had established themselves in a position of industrial influence out of all proportion to their numbers, by gaining leading positions in the shop stewards' movement and through their paper

*New Propellor.* The direct influence of these stewards in maintaining industrial peace should therefore not be under-estimated. There can be little doubt that if the CP had continued with its earlier line the discontent which persisted amongst apprentices would have been exploited, at the very least. As it was, in so far as major industrial action was involved, the apprentices' movement was practically at an end.

The terrific growth of the CP during 1942, which tailed off as the war progressed, was related to their leadership of a popular anti-managerial current of some depth. This feeling, which one can sense in the diary of the shop steward's wife quoted earlier, did not inevitably lead in the direction of a campaign for setting up JPCs. There were still plenty of shop stewards who saw the problems and the solutions in more traditional terms; the left had to argue for their views and push even the E&ATSSNC in the direction of the JPC solution.

Before examining the terms of this discussion within the shop stewards' movement, it is relevant to evaluate the overall significance of the JPC campaign. Many historians of the period have pointed to the voluntary nature of the joint production machinery, and this was indeed a vital feature of the JPCs when established: they certainly had not been forced on the workforce, but in many cases management had been very reluctant. The political space required had been created by the E&ATSSNC. Bevin had been forced to drop his earlier plans when he sensed the mood of the unions and the shop stewards, but in the new situation it was the shop stewards themselves who were implementing them. No legislation was required, and a major victory for Bevin's cherished principle of 'voluntaryism' had been registered. The JPC campaign also represented a victory for a certain strand within trade-unionist thought which could be crudely summarised in the phrase 'extending collective bargaining'. Shop stewards had been struggling for several years, as we have seen, to open up new areas for collective bargaining which managements had previously fenced round with their 'managerial prerogative'. But JPCs now opened up for dis-cussion with management matters such as production itself and welfare. Admittedly, there was no scope for 'failing to agree' as in the Machinery for the Avoidance of Disputes, but managements now had at least to talk to their workers' representatives about important issues previously closed to them. The CP and E&ATSSNC, while not arguing that the machinery was anywhere near ideal, presented it as a major step towards democracy in industry.

Viewed from another standpoint, and with the advantage of historical hindsight, the JPC campaign and later the JPCs themselves represented a 'gain' of very doubtful value to the engineering workers on the shop floor. The engineers were beset by many serious material problems, not the least of which was an antiquated and unsatisfactory wage structure. When these issues were raised on the shop floor there were always those who advocated the use of some form of industrial action. Such action was opposed by the E&ATSSNC shop stewards. But it could not, of course, simply be opposed and left at that. The use of the negotiating procedure and lobbies of Parliament were two of the main alternatives offered. Both options gained considerable weight from the fact that the new period in industrial relations which was supposedly beginning was one of joint regulation of workplace affairs under government supervision. In reality, where workers' material conditions and industrial discipline were concerned, no such new beginning was apparent. Yet the JPC drive provided a considerable 'legitimating' argument in that direction. In a sense, the very existence of JPCs ensured that the view that 'managements only understood one thing', industrial action, raised to a political level by those who argued for the independence of the trade unions, only gained a limited amount of ground during the war.

The expansion of these arguments can be seen in a thorough and confidential report of a meeting of shop stewards in Coventry written by an unknown Mass Observer who appears to have been able to get into the meeting because he or she was with Richard Crossman, Labour parliamentary candidate for a Coventry constituency. The meeting was one of several during January 1942 called by various trade union bodies. One was called by the shop stewards' committee at Cornercroft Ltd. (a small firm of precision and sheet metal working engineers of Parkside, Coventry), another by the TGWU District Committee, and another by the Area Shop Stewards' Council (affiliated to the E&ATSSNC).[56] The meeting in question appears to have been that called by the latter body to report back from a delegation to the relevant ministries in London to protest at the poor production situation in the town, and in particular to complain about the dispute which had arisen at Corner-croft. Headed by the well known Communist Joe Steele, an AEU shop steward at Armstrong-Whitworth Aircraft, the delegation explained that some workers there, when refused permission to leave work one hour early on Christmas Eve in order to do some shopping, had been sacked (for, as the Ministry of Labour Disputes books recorded it, 'deficient timekeeping').[57] One hundred and seventy-two workers were in fact dismissed, including one hundred and eight highly-skilled sheet metal workers. Their forty-two remaining colleagues went on strike on Boxing Day 1941 until 5 January 1942, to secure their reinstatement.[58] An appeal to the Local Appeal Board led to the National Service Officer directing the strikers to return to work and the company to accept them. However, when they returned to the factory on 6 January, they were astonished to find that all the jigs, tools and fixtures had been removed to another Cornercroft factory, in Manchester, and that they were dismissed as 'redundant'.[59] In a private letter George Hodgkinson, local Labour Party activist, called this, with some accuracy, a 'scorched-earth policy' by the firm's owner, Captain W.F. Strickland.[60] Whether Hodgkinson was justified in his judgment or not, it certainly reflected the feeling of outrage among the Coventry shop stewards, as our unknown observer found. The document, valuable for its wealth of detail, is presented in full:

*Shop Stewards' Meeting. Coventry. Jan. 18th 1942.*

11 o'c on Sunday morning: held in comfortable lounge of Pub. Chairman was age about 30—dark, intellectual looking Scot a worker at the Daimler (?) factory. Secretary age about 35. Present about 50 brothers and one sister. (Throughout meeting members addressed each other as 'brother'). They were an extraordinarily well-dressed,

well set up and nice looking lot of men.

Obs. accompanied by Parliamentary candidate, a German worker and an Austrian woman worker entered to find Chairman addressing the meeting. He was explaining that the meeting had been convened to find a method of dealing with the serious situation in Coventry of underproduction and unemployment of skilled men. This was tacked on to a lot of talk about the workers understanding the meaning of the fight that was now being waged against Fascism whereas the Managements didn't mind so very much who won. There were Municheers still in the Government and there were Municheers still running business.

The meeting was open to discussion. First speaker another Scot aged about 40 who read out a letter which appeared in Saturday's *Midland Daily Telegraph*. This letter was taken very seriously as it was written by a Works Manager. It was a detailed account of muddle, mismanagement and injustice in his factory. Next speaker was a very powerful chap aged about 40—a first-class speaker who said that it was no good any more continuing with letters, telegrams, delegations, demonstrations. They had tried all that and no notice was taken. There was only one thing left which might bring a public inquiry and that was action and this meeting must decide what that action should be. He said that the monstrous lock-out at Cornercroft's was the last straw which showed which way the wind was blowing and it wouldn't be long before other works followed suit and where now there had been a dozen or so men put off, there would soon be hundreds. Then a dark anxious looking man aged about 25 who said he was from Cornercroft's gave a long account of the patient negotiations the men had attempted and how everything had failed. It seemed to be no-one's business. He advocated an immediate strike.

Other speakers followed making various suggestions but always stressing the dilemma of striking when they wanted to increase production. It was suggested that any time lost should be made up by working overtime. There was a suggestion that there should be a sit-down strike starting with one hour the first day, two hours the second day, three the third and so on: a suggestion that all factories should refuse to work any overtime at all until things were put right: that the Hippodrome should be taken for a Mass meeting and a demonstration. (There have already been two processions round the town, one with police permission and one without): a suggestion that some of them should go to Parliament and make a scene.

Two much older men spoke about the rise of the Shop Stewards' Movement in the last war and how though they realised that the issues in this war were quite different from last because it was no longer a capitalist war, they had found then that the workers had to use the only weapon they have got which is the power to strike and they were sure it was the same in this war. Another older man pointed out the unpopularity of the Shop Stewards' Movement with the T.U.s and the friction between the different T.U.s whose organisers were more interested in their jobs than in the rights of their members. He also cautioned the meeting that they must not take action unless they were convinced that they had sufficient backing in the shops.

Brother Crossman was called on to say a few words and he said that it was like breathing real air again to get back to real political struggle because though this seemed as if it was in some cases for wages and hours, it really was political and they must never forget it. His job was propaganda to the enemy and he saw that with only tanks and guns as our weapons the war would last for ten years at least. One of the best weapons would be propaganda for equality and freedom which he could only put across if he were talking for a free and equal country and not a plutocracy. He told of the state of mind of workers in Germany and the experience of workers from other countries who had just got out. In all the factories of the Reich the workers were anti-Fascist and were waiting the day until they saw the workers of other countries ready to help them in their struggle etc. etc. He wondered if they would like to hear a German brother engaged in the struggle to free Europe from Fascism. They immediately clapped and Brother Naumann spoke very movingly saying that he felt more at home in this last hour than he had done since he attended exactly similar meetings in Germany etc. etc.

The meeting then returned to discussing action. Everyone was given a copy of a cyclostyled leaflet and the meeting voted on its adoption as a basis unanimously. Someone demanded that five brothers should be selected to go to Parliament and make a shindy and that in fourteen days' time the Hippodrome should be taken for a mass meeting. This was carried but various men expressed dissatisfaction at the wait of fourteen days. One man asked for help for some of the 130 men locked out at Cornercroft's and it was decided that a collection should be taken in the factories.

The meeting closed at 1.15.

*Addenda.* Several times in the speeches the visit of the Soviet Trade delegation was mentioned and the fact that they had expressed disappointment and surprise at idle machines and empty floor space.

7 brothers were nominated and adopted to go to London. One of them had been thrown out of the House before.[61]

The 'cyclostyled leaflet' is quoted below:

*Points for a policy for the Shop Stewards' Movement*

1) We recognise that increased production is the key to victory—the only means whereby we can sustain our Russian allies, our own fighting men in Libya and Malaya and help to speed victory over Hitler. We therefore declare our readiness to do everything on our side to make this increase possible, and accept whatever sacrifices are necessary in the interests of increased production.

2) To achieve increased production and total mobilisation of the man and woman power resources of the country are necessary, organised and directed to the points where it can be most efficiently used. We call for a single plan for the direction of Labour and for a single control in the organisation of our productive war effort.

3) To assist total mobilisation it will be necessary to secure the entry of women into industry in far larger numbers. We call for adequate training of female labour, their organisation in Trades Unions, and the payment of the rate for the job in all cases where women are doing the work of men.

4) Transference of Labour to points where it can be more efficiently utilised is an essential step to increasing production. We declare that such transference will be facilitated by the rigid application of the Government Order regarding prior consultation with the men's representatives in all cases. Furthermore, since hardship for those transferred often arises owing to different wage rates, and thus acts as a deterrent on transference, we call for deferment of income tax charges, or abolition of income tax on overtime, or a review of all cases where transference involves financial loss with the aim of modifying the burden of income tax.

5) We declare that one of the most fruitful means for securing increased production is the immediate establishment of Production Committees in all factories representative of Managements and men.

Such Committees to have power to make recommendations to the Regional Production Boards which bodies should be invested immediately with plenary powers to operate recommendations directed to securing improved output.

6) In view of the chaos and disorganisation of production in Coventry, we call for an immediate Government Inquiry.

The report shows in quite a concrete way the political influences at work amongst those stewards linked at a local level to the E&ATSSNC, from outside in the shape of Labour Party candidates and even, on this occasion, in the shape of a German émigré intellectual. Within the body of stewards present, perhaps the most interesting role was played by the two older workers, who interpreted the experience of the shop stewards' movement of the First World War to their colleagues. The message of the two older stewards taken together seems to have been that despite the differences between the Second World War and the First, the strike was common to both as the only weapon at workers' disposal. The third older man mentioned also spoke in a way that came recognisably from a very similar tradition, when he talked about the attitude of the union at the official level and the need for workshop support before taking action. The contributions of these men stemmed firmly from within one of the shop-steward traditions of the ASE and AEU, in that they defended the right to take strike action when the members wanted to do so, irrespective of the political or military situation or the views of the officials (who were seen as servants of the membership in this regard).[62] Nevertheless, this tradition was clearly far from being the only influence at work within the meeting. It is interesting to see that despite the fact that no less than four speakers advocated some form of industrial action, the vote went unanimously in favour of adopting the proposals of the leaflet presented to the meeting. This may have been partly due to skilful chairmanship, but is more likely to have been due to the appeal to support the Russian and British servicemen, combined with the proposals of certain political alternatives to industrial action. Specifically, these amounted to the demand for a single plan for the direction of labour and the war effort, the formation of JPCs and an immediate government inquiry into war production in Coventry. These arguments obviously weighed heavily with the stewards, especially with the Labour Party candidate present emphasising the political aspects. The question at the back of people's minds must have been whether the delegation would actually bring results. On its return the delegation argued that it had played an important political role, in that coming as it did on the eve of the confidence debate in the House of Commons (which began on 27 January), it had tipped the scales in favour of the appointment of a Minister of Production.[63] Whether this entirely convinced or satisfied the shop stewards in the Area Council is unknown, but the problem at Cornercroft remained unsolved and, given some of their earlier speeches, there seem to be grounds for doubting that it did.

In towns like Coventry, where the CP had developed considerable strength during 1941-2 and the craft mentality amongst engineering workers as a whole was much less predominant than in the northern towns, it is perhaps not altogether surprising that the 'ASE view' did not become the major problem for the CP. When strikes occurred in the Midland towns they were usually short, sharp affairs over piece rates.[64] In other areas, however, and especially in Scotland and the North-East, the 'ASE mentality' was much more important. Behind this mentality, and buttressing it at many points, was the skilled engineers' view of the function of a craftsmen's union and their place within it. They viewed the AEU as their organisation in so far as it should reflect their needs and status as skilled men by involving them fully in the decisions that affected their workshop interests. They very often had the feeling—and this was not a new feeling, but had existed since at least 1898—that their Executive was infringing their rights of democratic participation, and as a result was following policies which did not accord with the needs of the engineers. Many members, particularly in the strongholds of craftism in Scotland, thought that their organisation was missing the boat. Their view was that it might well be true, for example, that production was chaotic, and that the fault lay with management: as skilled men they were often quick to point it out. They simply drew different conclusions from those drawn by the union officials and many of their stewards. If management was inefficient, then it should be overhauled or removed, possibly by the government. The legitimate task of the AEU (which many persisted in calling 'the Society') was not to do management's job for them, but to improve wages and conditions by ensuring that management was deterred from telling them how to do their jobs. It seemed as if the area of control which they had always fought to retain, the legendary circle around the turner's lathe over which the foreman was advised not to step, was now threatened not only by the traditional enemy but by a disturbing tendency within their own unions to advocate joining with management in committees set up for the express purpose of invading that area of control. To the left, the attitude appeared 'old-fashioned' and 'backward', because it was taken to imply that skilled engineers were incapable of improving on management's performance. From their standpoint, the craftsman's pride in the independence of his union was admirable, but his insistence on carrying it to the point at which he was opposed to playing a part in the company he often invested a working life in, represented an unfortunate narrowness of view which blinkered him to the possibilities inherent in the People's War. Nevertheless, a stratum of engineers abided by it.

The 'ASE mentality' may have been transmitted by the older members of the workshop community, but their experience was readily accepted by many of the younger shop stewards. The majority of trade-unionists were young, inexperienced and enthusiastic, and so the advice of the older men carried some weight with them. At a typical London war factory in January 1943, organised by all three main engineering unions, no less than forty-nine of the fifty-four shop stewards were under forty. Thirty-seven had been elected during 1942.[65] Such a relatively youthful body of stewards was common in large engineering works in the London area, and was bound to listen attentively to older craftsmen's representatives. Like the shop stewards' movement of the First World War, shop floor organisation in the Second drew much of its vigour from the youth of the activists. They very often had political affiliations on the left and constituted a formidable ginger group within existing organisations. In Glasgow, for example, the Scottish Conciliation Officer reported in March 1942 that there was an anti-JPC faction on the AEU District Committee, and that its members were 'most of them young and far to the left'.[66] Later in the war, *Labour Management* blamed the rising strike rate on the large number of new stewards, 'elected from among the younger and more vociferous elements'.[67]

The so-called ASE mentality was not entirely untypical even of some of those engineers on the left who advocated the establishment of JPCs. The Manchester District Committee of the AEU, for example, set up a sub-committee to prepare a report on the desirability or otherwise of JPCs. It came down in favour, but was 'fully aware of the complications involved'. The report detailed the complications:

> On the one hand we are working under a capitalist system, more highly organised for exploitation, even than in peace time. Every advantage that the employers can secure from collaboration and relaxation will be, and is being, ruthlessly acquired throughout the industry. No sacrifices are being made by the employers. No fraction of managerial power is being surrendered. Instead of sacrifice, the employers have actually strengthened their position in relation to the sub-division of labour, while their profits are guaranteed. For the workers it is truly a war on two fronts, or, if you like, back and front.[68]

The report went on to conclude that the tragic consequences of a Nazi victory were too readily apparent for the correctness of a policy of increased production through JPCs to be questioned. The analysis is distinctively Marxist, and may well have been written by one of the leftists prominent on the Manchester District Committee. At the same time it reflects the experience of the engineering workers in its emphasis on the employers securing advantages from relaxation and collaboration. Indeed, most of the report as recorded in the Manchester AEU District Committee Minutes dwelt on these problems. The fact that these advocates of JPCs at least were well aware of the problems involved is important when set beside some of the cruder statements of policy made by those leftists who did not work in the industry.

At the same time, the sensitivity of some sections of the left to the problems involved in JPCs did not deter a stratum of engineers from disagreeing with them quite sharply. In March 1942 the *Catholic Worker* published a letter from a plumber in a Clyde shipyard. The paper's editorials were favourable to JPCs, but the plumber showed that, in his yard at least, the point of view received short shrift. Reporting back on a London production conference, the man was 'howled down'. He explained why: 'Since production to the workers was always management's duty, they detested any union official speaking in favour of it. What the workers wanted was wages.'[69] This feeling of hostility to the Stakhanovite partisans of increased production was not uncommon, especially on the Clyde. In October 1941 the Scottish Deputy Chief Industrial Commissioner, Mr Galbraith, reported to London:

> A considerable body of the rank and file in the workshops seem to resent the invocation to do more from the very men who, not so long ago, were advocating a policy of indifference as increased production was dangerous to the workers. Many of the rank and file cannot understand how it is no longer dangerous and are asking embarrassing questions. The answer normally given is to say that the organised power of the workers can provide the necessary safeguards. But this explanation existed previously and is not very convincing. Accordingly, the workers who previously were all out for production are resentful and inclined to be perverse, whilst those who lent an ear to the Left-Wing propaganda in the past are now unsettled. This seems to be one of the factors in creating the present difficult mood of so many of the workers in this area.[70]

Given this context, it is hardly surprising to find that on the Clyde, as in some other districts, the introduction of Joint Production Committees created some friction within the unions. In March 1942 Galbraith remarked that 'a considerable number' of the Glasgow District Committee of the AEU were opposed to the introduction of JPCs, because they believed that they would enable the employers to intensify exploitation when peace returned. The opponents were often young, and 'most of them far to the Left'.[71] The Communist Party began to lose some of its old supporters because it began to take a rather rigid line on the production front:

> They [the Communists] are now emphatic in their insistence upon uninterrupted work at the highest standard of intensity. For this reason they are rather suspect and have lost any influence which they had; in fact, they have stirred up a considerable measure of suspicion amongst those who were previously willing to follow their leadership, although far from being converted to their doctrines. This is particularly noticeable in the case of those trade unionists—and there are many of them—who have associations with the ILP.[72]

Evidently some fellow-travellers had begun to move away from the Communists in their attitudes to industrial affairs.

It was not long before Galbraith started to expand on his earlier statement as to where the opposition was coming from. At the end of July he noted that Beardmore's Parkhead Forge had recently belied its reputation as a centre of industrial trouble, but added that there was still some strike activity there despite the new attitude of those he called the 'previous agitators'.[73] He went on to say that these erstwhile agitators 'are being described by the rank and file as dictators because they simply insist that whatever happens work must be continued'.[74] The location of the discontent at Beardmore's is significant, because it gives rise to the suspicion that this feeling sprang from the skilled men's view of the nature of trade-unionism. Galbraith confirmed this suspicion in his next report to headquarters. Reference was made to the 'frictions' that were occurring, and he continued:

> It is quite evident that there is a considerable body of opinion in these [frictions] which rather resents the present tendency towards intensified co-operation between employer and workers. They belong to the old school for the most part—the school who thought it the duty of the Trade Unions to extract as much as possible from the employers, and they take the view that even in wartime this should be the policy of the organisations. They are taking the place of the Communists in leading any group which has a grievance and in encouraging this to take action normally apart from the trade unions, to get it removed.[75]

The strike leaders then, tended to be the type whom he credited on a later occasion (and in a similar connection) with an 'ASE attitude'.[76]

One important consequence of the 'ASE attitude', Galbraith reported in February 1943, was 'the somewhat curious fact', as he put it, 'that the militant shop stewards have not won for themselves any reputation on JPCs but this may be due to the fact that their philosophy does not allow them to think in terms of joint action'.[77] Indeed, in some factories and districts JPCs had been quite strongly resisted both before and after their establishment. In London one District Committee had a large faction of delegates who were against JPCs, and the committee as a whole came close to rejecting the idea altogether.[78] The shop stewards at Enfield Royal Ordnance Factory refused to set one up at all, while at the Leeds ROF a JPC was resisted until 1945.[79] When they were set up, it was not always with the wholehearted approval of the stewards. At Vickers-Armstrong, Manchester, where there was a Communist 'Factory Brigade', interviews carried on by the local CP secretariat revealed that the shop stewards were 'definitely opposed' to the JPC which was operating there.[80] At Beardmore's Parkhead Forge it appears that although one was set up, it was not without some spirited discussion, as a result of which some of the stewards who argued for it were voted out of office.[81] Outright resistance to JPCs may have been more widespread than has been admitted by many historians, but judgment should perhaps be reserved, pending further research. Resistance on a more passive level, however, was almost certainly quite widespread. It was far from uncommon for workers to harbour suspicions of their delegates, once elected. The trade union report prepared for Mass Observation in 1944, for example, simply reflected the mainstream of conventional thought when it concluded on the strength of interviews with managers that stewards were 'apt to get accused of backing up management'.[82] Stewards could be accused of this at any time, but it seems to have been very common criticism of JPC delegates.

Engineering trade-unionists as a whole were not, of course, carrying on the sort of sustained and demanding battle that could be required to resist the setting up of a JPC. They were primarily concerned with their own immediate problems. For those workers outside of the skilled men's traditions of craft trade-unionism, members of the general unions, the JPCs appeared to inspire less active opposition. The level of trade union organisation amongst the semi- and unskilled was certainly lower, and they were therefore less concerned about what they might have to lose and rather more optimistic about what they had to gain from a regular meeting with management. Even for many of those within the AEU there seemed no particular harm in the committees, very few saw them as something to be resisted at all costs.

It was only on the fringes of shop stewards' organisation, amongst the tiny groups of the extra-CP extreme left, that a policy of consistent opposition to JPCs was advocated. Their arguments often appeared in an extremely abstract and abstruse form, but there was sufficient overlap between their policies and the views of some stewards for them to achieve some limited influence amongst stewards in a few factories. In the examples given earlier of factories which had opposed the establishment of JPCs, those within the Royal Ordnance Factories can be linked with the influence which the extreme left exerted within an unofficial committee of shop stewards operating within the ROFs.[83] Their influence, such as it was, rested on the fact that they held a coherent point of view which they were often well able to put across; this allowed them to take over some small part of the role that CP stewards had once filled as the leaders of militant anti-management battles. In the ROFs, just a few stewards scattered amongst the shop stewards' committees of the country's munitions factories were able, given the grievances of the skilled men within them, to fight a sustained rearguard action against JPCs and the ethos of collaboration which went, they thought, with them.

It is not proposed here to delve too deeply into the micro-history of these groups, but since no historian has yet attempted to come to terms with their small but significant role amongst shop stewards it might be useful to do so here, giving at the same time some relevant political background to a number of disputes which took place from about the

*VII   Turner, 1940*

VIII  *Tank factory, 1939*

*IX*  *Engineering & Allied Trades Shop Stewards' National Council Conference, October 1941*

X  *Cable works, making flex*

*XI   Soviet delegates in war factory, 1942*

XII  *Joint Production Committee in session, 1942?*

Autumn of 1942.

All of the Trotskyist groups were tiny, numbering only dozens during the 1930s; by September 1939 the two largest groups, the Workers' International League and the Revolutionary Socialist League, had only thirty and eighty members respectively. Nevertheless, the group which most interests us because of its development during wartime into the more important of the two is the WIL. The WIL published a duplicated agitational paper entitled *Youth for Socialism* at irregular intervals from September 1938 onwards, as well as its already established theoretical journal, *Workers' International News.* These papers were published without any help from Trotsky's Fourth International, which the WIL refused to join.[84] The RSL was the British section of the Fourth International, and factional squabbles rapidly reduced it to an even tinier group than before. Up until the invasion of the Soviet Union, both groups were in a difficult position because of their insistence on a 'revolutionary defeatist' line on the war. However, the WIL was already laying important foundations for its later industrial work by sending its members out of London with instructions to find work in provincial munitions factories and to win stewards' cards as quickly as possible. In Scotland, where the group already had a small base, WIL workers were encouraged to stay on.[85]

The WIL started to make some headway from June 1941. Their twice-monthly paper changed name and format, becoming *Socialist Appeal,* a much more attractive and professional offering with good industrial coverage. *Socialist Appeal* claimed an average paid sale of eighteen to twenty thousand in 1943, and although this may be an exaggerated claim it seems likely that the Trotskyist paper did gain from the absence of the *Daily Worker.* By that year membership was at around two hundred and fifty. The overwhelming majority of these members, an internal document of late 1942 revealed, were trade-unionists, and most of these were members of the AEU.[86] Distribution was localised, with a good deal of both membership and support being concentrated in Scotland. The organisation was quite well placed to intervene in industrial affairs, because WIL workers were organised in factory groups wherever possible, as a result of an internal decision of late 1942.[87] All in all, the WIL's prospects, in so far as they were ever good, were relatively good during the two years from late 1942. This was because of the quite specifically favourable conditions which then existed, especially in Scotland. The strike rate was rising, there was full employment and the extreme left had a clear attitude to militancy which the Communist Party rank and file did not always have. The WIL's line on the war was that Russia had to be defended, but that the ruling class would have to be forced to do this even partially. The only satisfactory way of defending British or Soviet workers from Nazism was by a Socialist Britain, based on workers' control in the factories, making a 'Socialist appeal' to workers throughout Europe to rise against the Nazis. The appropriate method of achieving Socialism was, they thought, to build an entirely independent revolutionary party. They supported strikes, opposed Joint Production Committees as class-collaborationist, and demanded instead 'workers' control of production to end chaos'.[88] The Trotskyists, in common with some other workers, thought that trade unions should retain their independence of the employers and the state during the war. In practice this meant that they agitated for strike action to defend workers' interests, a demand that did not always go entirely unheeded. Moreover, they were able to call on some support in their agitation from the ILP, another organisation which was to some extent revived by the peculiar conditions of wartime.

The Independent Labour Party was a much more amorphous organisation than either of the Trotskyist groups. The *New Leader* did not propose any particular line on the nature of the war, although it did carry articles that were opposed to war from a generally pacifist point of view. It was also frequently critical of the Communist Party, and tended to become increasingly so as the war dragged on. The ILP did not suffer from its lack of anything like a clear approach to political questions, however. Indeed, it seems to have benefited from its independent, non-sectarian stance, as it has been estimated that it grew to about two thousand members by the end of 1943.[89] It began seriously to interest itself as an organisation in the shop stewards after the Communists' change of line on the war. The ILP's industrial committee held a number of meetings on workers' control in Bradford and Birmingham in the autumn of 1941, which were followed by similar discussions in Glasgow and Motherwell in December 1942.[90] These meetings were not specifically aimed at shop stewards in the munitions industries, but after October 1942, as a result of the general upturn in the level of militancy in munitions, the ILP began to publish a series of cheap, interesting and lively pamphlets which were intended for this audience.[91] The first of these pamphlets, *Engineers in Action,* leaves one in little doubt that the ILP was at that time developing close links with the Trotskyists, since much of the information is remarkably similar to that contained in *Socialist Appeal.* Be that as it may, the pamphlets were part of an important development in the history of militancy in the industry, in that they reflected an increasing interest, within the small organisations of the revolutionary left, in the shop stewards.

These groups of the extreme left, together with the Anarchists and their papers *War Commentary* and *Freedom,* experienced some growth in numbers and influence during the second half of the war, in an atmosphere of intense political discussion. They remained tiny, but their influence in industrial matters cannot be immediately written off. Even the official historian mentions the Trotskyist involvement in two disputes, which in itself suggests that the subject should be more closely examined.[92] But the whole question, both then and now, is fraught with ideological dangers because of the inconceivably bitter polemics fought out between the left-wing groupings from the late 1930s to the present. During the war the Trotskyists, the ILP and the Anarchists vilified all to their right, but reserved their most savage attacks for the Communist Party. The CP was 'His Majesty's Communist Party', the 'Stalinists' whose craven capitulation to the interests of the ruling class knew no bounds. The attitude of the CP to the extreme left was similarly slanderous. In a series of outlines for tutors of CP educational meetings published in 1943, the subject of Trotskyism was dealt with thus: 'How must they be treated? (Expose them to the workers as Nazi agents; no toleration of them in working-class organisations, still less as representatives; no debates or other forms of association or treatment as fellow workers).[93] To the extreme left, the 'Stalinists' were class traitors; to the CP, the Trotskyists and ILP were 'Nazi agents'. A tone had been introduced into discussions on the left which had probably not been heard since the CP had attacked the Labour Party in similar terms in the late 1920s. But despite the difficulties involved in unearthing the historical realities behind the polemics, the task cannot be dodged. We have to distinguish between the internal wranglings of the left and the relationship of the left to working-class activity.

All these groups were to play a small role in and around some important strikes in the second half of the war through their AEU members, while their papers constitute a useful if highly polemical source for the history of the shop stewards during the war. Needless to say, they remained essentially on the edges of the trade union movement despite occasional temporary and localised points of purchase. The real motive force behind the discontent amongst the munitions workers had nothing to do with such 'agitators' and their persistent but generally fruitless attempts to influence working people through their bizarre politics. Much more material was the strongly held conviction of the skilled men in their strongholds on the northern shipbuilding rivers that they were underpaid. As our Catholic plumber from Clydeside quoted earlier had said, what they wanted was wages.

The problem of low wages was exacerbated by the widely held view fostered by some newspapers that to be a war worker of any description meant holding a particularly well paid sinecure. The high earnings of the West Midlands, selectively quoted from the highest-paying factories, were often the basis for this opinion. Specific features such as the concentration of war industry in the area, the Coventry Toolroom Agreement of 1941 (which provided local shop stewards with a mutually agreed monthly statement of skilled piece-workers' earnings in the district, the average of which was taken as the basis for calculating a district rate for toolmakers)[94] and a number of other local factors were responsible, but this was rarely pointed out. Some of the

historians quoting earnings have followed this tradition in
their search for the spectacular example; Angus Calder, for
example, mentions factories paying £4. 10s. per day.[95] Yet
the highest-paying factory in Coventry (and quite possibly
therefore the highest-paying in Britain) paid an average of
5.34 shillings per hour to its skilled piece-workers between
September 1940 and September 1944, giving them weekly
pre-tax earnings, for forty-seven hours, of £12. 11s.[96] If
higher earnings were achieved in reality, then it was through
overtime. The Coventry workers were well paid in terms of
piece-work bonuses. In other areas, bonuses were not so high.
In May 1941 the *Manchester Evening News* enraged a local
engineer who signed himself 'WP' with the information that
the Select Committee on National Expenditure had found
the average earnings, including overtime, of the most highly
paid men in an aero-engine factory to be £7 per week. 'WP'
wrote in protesting that it was 'all piffle', and speculated that
the committee had estimated so high a figure because they
had examined the managerial staffs' salaries by mistake.
Where he worked, skilled men earned between £3. 19s. and
£5. 4s. for a forty-seven hour week, including bonus, and
'where the £7 to £14 per week comes from I personally—
along with thousands more—would be delighted to know'.[97]
The gap between WP's figures and those of the National
Committee on Public Expenditure arose partly, of course,
from the fact that they were quoting from different individual
factories, probably within different sectors of the industry.
In the aircraft industry, earnings tended to be consistently
higher than in metal, engineering and shipbuilding. (By
January 1943 average earnings in metal, engineering and
shipbuilding were officially given as £6. 11s. 6d., while in
aircraft, motor vehicles and cycles the equivalent figure was
£7. 8s. 7d.; by January 1944, the wartime earnings peak,
they stood at £7. 1s. 10d. and £8. 6s. 1d. respectively.[98] )

An important group falling well below the average were
those workers who had little or no opportunity to increase
their earnings through piece-work. A high proportion of the
skilled men working in the northern shipbuilding and marine
engineering works were paid on plain-time rates. Piece-workers
could increase their earnings by increasing their effort or by

renegotiating rates when the means or methods of production were changed, but plain-time workers could only work longer hours. The impact which overtime could make on earnings was also minimised by the employers' insistence that the national awards made in wartime were kept out of the basic rates on which overtime pay was calculated. At the beginning of 1942, skilled marine fitters and turners on the Clyde earned £3. 17s. 8d. for a forty-seven hour week, while their Tyneside equivalents received just £3. 16s. 6d.[99] The contrast between myth and reality was acute.

Low wages constituted the main reason for the relatively high strike rate in the shipyards and engineering shops of the Clyde. The Tyne had tended to be rather less strike-prone, but in both areas discontent simmered just below the surface of industrial relations. Up until the autumn of 1942, however, strikes in all areas were limited to individual factories, and showed very little sign of spreading beyond the workplaces in which they originated. The Tyneside 'Total Time' strike of October 1942 was the first stoppage since March 1941 to spread across a whole district, and from that time on there was an increasing tendency for shop stewards to threaten to extend action in this way. Such threats were taken seriously by the Conciliation Officers in the Midlands and North-West on four occasions in 1943 and early 1944.[100] This discernible shift in the extent to which strikes were generalised is quite important, but it is glossed over by the official history with the remark that the great majority of strikes were limited to 'individual firms or localities'.[101] It was hardly a matter of indifference to the ministries concerned, however, whether some engineers at Vickers' Elswick works alone stopped work, or whether their colleagues at other Tyneside yards and 'inside' departments had joined them, as a cursory glance at Conciliation Officers' reports will show. Quite apart from the loss of production entailed, any such development raised serious doubts about the state of 'industrial morale', with all the usual fears about less than full cooperation from industrial workers in general. The district-wide 'Total Time' strike therefore marked a crucial watershed in the history of wartime industrial relations.

The 'Total Time', or 'Lying-On Time' dispute on Tyneside showed that the industrial situation was rather more volatile than had been previously thought. It arose out of an apparently trivial issue, which did not in itself fundamentally affect the material interests of the local engineers, but which amounted to the final straw which broke their collective back. A pattern of long spells of relative passivity followed by large and determined strikes characterised the Tyne workers' history. In each generation—in 1871 during the Nine Hours strike, in 1907 in the long strike against a wage reduction, and again in 1942—a particular sort of strike ethic was shown to have implanted itself locally, whereby after long periods of quiescence the strikers showed an unimpaired ability to develop unofficial organisations to run the dispute and defend it against its various opponents, together with a particularly strong feeling against blacklegs.

On 5 September 1942 Jack Bowman, the Tyne District Secretary of the AEU (whose first experience of trade-unionism had been as an apprentice in the 1907 strike) sent a letter to all shop stewards in shipbuilding and ship-repairing explaining that the employers had suggested a new way of calculating a week's pay, to which the AEU and CSEU had agreed. The new method, Bowman explained, had been proposed because of the depletion of clerical staff in relation to the amount of office work which had to be done. Staff could not continue to pay out on Friday, and the employers suggested 12 noon on Saturday as the best time both for paying and as the basis for calculating a week's pay. The union had persuaded the employers that midnight on Sunday would be preferable as the basis for calculation, as men would not then lose pay for a Sunday worked when they were paid the next Friday. The change involved a 'short' week when it was first made, as men would be paid from the previous Sunday to the next Friday, instead of from Friday to Friday. To get around the problem, the employers agreed to make an advance on future earnings to bring the first week's earnings up to average; the debt incurred by the workers would be repaid by deductions from wages in instalments to be spread over five weeks. The whole issue was essentially minor, one might have thought,

181

but the arrangement brought a flood of protests from the members.[102]

On the night of 5 September Brother Moody, the secretary of AEU Jarrow No. 3 branch, read Bowman's letter to the branch meeting. The next day he wrote to Bowman, conveying his branch's 'strong disapproval of those officials who have signed. . . and wish to state that in any future Matter of this character that the decision of the Rank and File be First considered'.[103] By the beginning of October Bowman had received at least eight such motions from branches, and four from shop stewards and convenors.[104] Some were especially indignant at their officials' behaviour: South Shields No. 6 branch voted a censure on the District Committee, and called for the instant dismissal of J.W. Mitchell, the Divisional Organiser,[105] while a shop steward at Armstrong-Whitworth wrote:

> Whilst it was not denied by the members that the EMPLOYERS [original emphasis] had made out a good case for the adoption of this proposal of the extension of lying-on time, they failed to see that the District Committee had explained their omission in not consulting the ordinary working member before adopting such an alteration of working conditions.[106]

Two motions were passed unanimously by the shop meeting, one stating that the District Committee had 'over-reached their powers by signing away a part of their members' wages', breaking the Truck Acts by so doing, and the other strongly recommending them to make no agreements in future without the knowledge and consent of the members concerned.[107] The message was coming over loud and clear that the members resented the officials' and the District Committee's agreeing to the arrangement, and on 10 September a deputation went to see the CSEU officials.[108] Possibly as a result of this meeting, the employers soon afterwards made an offer allowing the repayment of their initial 'sub' to be spread over twelve weeks, but this did nothing to appease the Tyne shipbuilding and repair workers, whose blood was clearly up. On 5 October a number of yards refused to start work.[109]

The Communist Party was faced with the first serious strike since the lifting of the ban on the *Daily Worker* had allowed the paper to reappear on 7 September 1942. The first issues of the rehabilitated paper had to demonstrate the CP's determination to oppose such action in no uncertain terms. In its leading article of 6 October the editorial board made its position crystal clear: the strike was 'a disgrace to all concerned', and the matter in dispute was 'not worth a day's stoppage in peacetime, let alone in the most critical period of the war'.[110] The *Daily Worker* vigorously denied the suggestion made by the *Catholic Herald* that there had ever been any equivocation amongst the local CP members in their attitude to stopping work. Paul McArdle, a prominent Catholic Actionist and member of the CSEU District Committee, had been quoted by the Catholic paper as saying that the Communists had only argued against the strike in the later stages of the agitation. The next day, the *Daily Worker* protested strongly. After the strike, McArdle wrote to the *Catholic Herald* and denied having commented on the Communists' attitude, while a Catholic shipwright wrote indignantly: 'The Communists had nothing to do with the strike, they were not even on strike.' The editor of the *Catholic Herald*, who was not a particular friend of the CP, completely withdrew his earlier suggestion.[111] Even their enemies had to admit then that they had publicly set their faces against the strike. In fact, all the evidence suggests that they had pulled out all the stops to restrict the scope of the strike once it had started, whether local CP shipyard workers had earlier nursed reservations or not. Several facts point in this direction. Harry Pollitt, restored to the leadership of the CP after his earlier disagreement in 1939 over the nature of the war, and himself an ex-boilermaker with extensive contacts in the Boilermakers' Society and other unions (the Boilermakers' headquarters were in Elland Place, Newcastle), apparently travelled up to Tyneside and contacted every shop steward in or around the CP there to ask them to work energetically towards a quick end to the stoppage.[112] On 7 October the Tyneside District Committee of the CP issued a leaflet calling for a return to work; the E&ATSSNC issued their own leaflet condemning the strike, while fifty shop stewards opposed to the strike distributed a circular complaining that, as opponents of the strike, they were not allowed to attend the meetings of the stewards running the dispute.[113] Indeed, by this stage at least the Communists had made their views as well known as they possibly could.

The mood of the strikers was not especially militant in terms of the vehemence against employers which often accompanies disputes, directed as the stoppage was as much towards pressurising the local officials into renegotiating the agreement with the employers as against the employers themselves. Every day the men gathered between the yard gates and the rows of steep terraced houses sloping down towards the river to hear from the stewards whether the system had been withdrawn, only to disperse again when they heard that it had not. Nor was the stoppage entirely solid: on Wednesday 11 October the *Newcastle Journal and North Mail* described it as 'unorganised', with in some places just a few workers turning up for work and elsewhere whole establishments continuing to operate.[114] Indeed, on 9 October it seemed likely that everyone would soon be back, because at a meeting in North Shields it was agreed to return if an independent inquiry was instituted and if the rest of the yards accepted this solution.[115] But the other yards met and rejected the idea of an inquiry as insufficient, and by the weekend there were eighteen thousand out, according to the hostile *Newcastle Journal.*[116]

The strikers were not the only ones opposed to the idea of an independent inquiry. So too, but for rather different reasons, were the trade union officials and District Committees. They took the view that they had been well within their rights when they had negotiated the agreement because, as J.W. Mitchell put it to a meeting of members in Jarrow during September, it was the District Committees' business to come to decisions every week. The AEU District Committee had two shipbuilding and repair representatives sitting on it, and so they as members had 'indirectly' been consulted.[117] Mitchell's argument had been radically challenged by the South Shields No. 6 branch, which contended that notices of the change had been posted in the yards and shops before the District Committee meeting.[118] Whether this was actually so is unknown, but the feeling of the rank and file against the conduct of the officials was strong: between 5 and 16 October at least seven more branches sent in motions criticising them or the District Committee, or both.[119] The officials were clearly stung by such rigorous and sustained criticism, and reacted by adopting an aggressive attitude towards the strikers. On 10 October J.G. Morgan, the chairman of the CSEU District Committee, said that stewards were 'wasting their time' coming to see him about it, and the CSEU District Committee rejected the idea of an inquiry as 'outside interference' and refused to renegotiate the agreement with the employers.[120] When the AEU District Committee also opposed the strike, Bowman wrote to stewards asking them to convene meetings to make its attitude known.[121] With the District Committees, the officials, and the E&ATSSNC all arguing actively for an end to the strike, its life was bound to be strictly limited. On 12 October the Central Strike Committee met at Wallsend Town Hall and voted by seventy-five to twenty-two to recommend a return to work, while at an open meeting of the strike committee at South Shields a meeting of over two thousand expressed their agreement with the actions of their committee to date, and demanded an impartial inquiry.[122] On 13 October the few remaining strikers read in the *Newcastle Journal* that a Ministry of Labour official had promised that an inquiry would be held into whether the new system was really necessary, and although no details were given concerning the terms of reference of the committee or its composition, the strike was spent.[123] By 14 October it was over.[124]

The end of the strike did not see the end of the feeling against either those who had made the agreement or those who had opposed or worked through it. Bowman's letter asking the stewards to organise meetings to make the District Committee's views plain provoked angry responses from some stewards. One steward wrote to Bowman rejecting his request, while two gate meetings decided unanimously not to return until the other yards also decided to do so.[125] Brother Herdman, the AEU convenor at Smith's Dock, replied to Bowman's letter: 'I don't intend to ask our Members for to

185

return to work. They blame our District Committee and our Delegate for all what has happened. To my opinion they have made all this trouble, it's up to them to get us out of it.'[126] With acrimonious criticism flying from rank and file to officials and back again from officials to strike committee, while the CP and E&ATSSNC censured all of them, the strike committee saw fit to take an unusual step. It decided that all of its members should resign as shop stewards, and it called on the stewards who were opposed to the strike to do the same. The strike committee was apparently entirely re-elected, but some of the non-striking shop stewards lost their cards as a result, much to the disgust of the *Daily Worker.*[127] According to the extreme-left *Socialist Appeal*, 'a strong bloc' left the CP as a result of the experience, while the influence of the remainder was 'almost wholly shattered'.[128] Even when allowance is made for the almost obligatory use of political hyperbole by the Trotskyists, their evidence cannot be entirely dismissed. It is known that the WIL had two members sitting on the strike committee and so they were probably at least well informed.[129] Moreover, the circumstantial evidence from other witnesses (including the *Daily Worker*) suggested that the strikers did not take kindly to being condemned and told to return to work. It would not have been entirely out of the question for some CP members to have left the party under the circumstances, though it is unlikely that the influence of the CP in the area was almost entirely destroyed.

The Total Time strike was significant in the history of war-time industrial relations for a number of reasons. From the point of view of the generalisation of strikes, it marked a watershed. Since the apprentices' strikes of 1941, strikes had been localised and fragmented; the Tyne shipyard and repair workers had shown that this pattern was beginning to give way to one in which disputes spread to other factories in the same district or company. Rather more significantly, the strike had shown up strong discontent with the behaviour of the local officials and District Committees. Previous strikes had not been directed against the officials to the same extent; they may have been *un*official, but they were not in any sense *anti*-official, like the Total Time strike. Later experience was to show that the anti-official strike was not to be a common phenomenon. Nevertheless, this stoppage did signal a small but noteworthy trend amongst the skilled workers of the North to show their active disapproval when their representatives at any level from shop steward upwards refused to assist them during strikes. Finally, it also brought about a reassessment of the overall situation on the left. The extreme left sought, of course, to make capital out of the CP's difficulties during the dispute and to point to it as an example of the rank and file sweeping them out of the way when they opposed them; such was the message of *Engineers in Action,* the first of the ILP's penny pamphlets for shop stewards. It also appears likely that the CP itself drew some lessons from the dispute in terms of how to approach a serious strike. They were still learning the unfamiliar skills involved in opposing stoppages, but this episode on the Tyne probably led the party to tone down their stridently anti-striker message when faced with later strikes. Only access to CP archives could confirm whether such a judgment is correct, however, and the question must therefore remain open.

Soon after the Total Time strike it became apparent that on the Clyde, too, strong disagreements were beginning to come to the fore between the skilled engineers and their representatives at every level. In a dispute at the North British Locomotive Co.'s Queen's Park works in October 1941, the senior stewards on the shop stewards' committee, described as 'ex-Communist' by Galbraith, only agreed to take strike action to obtain a guaranteed piece-work bonus when they had been 'stiffened by the attacks upon them by the rank and file'.[130] Having been the initiators of the strike, the stewards found themselves involved in 'a clear-cut battle between the official and unofficial elements' amounting to what Galbraith picturesquely called 'a vendetta'.[131] The strike ended after the union officials and Galbraith himself intervened at a mass meeting.[132] The 'vendetta' was resumed in another dispute which took place at the same factory soon afterwards. This one concerned some boiler-makers who objected to the introduction of new methods for paying bonuses, and sat in the factory on strike.[133] The boilermakers displayed their usual stubborn solidarity and resisted all attempts to get them to start work again, as did the AEU men out with them, with whom the Communist-influenced District Committee 'took a strong line'.[134] Eventually, prosecutions were initiated against the one hundred or so strikers, bringing the dispute to an end.[135]

This last strike had ended just three days before Christmas, not long before the AEU shop stewards' first quarterly meeting of the new year. A group of shop stewards and convenors, disappointed by the role of their District Committee in the recent dispute, had produced a circular leaflet condemning the Communists' opposition to the strikes and calling for a good turnout at the quarterly meeting, which was to re-elect two of the four shop stewards' delegates to the District Committee.[136] It was signed by three district committeemen: J. Gray (a Labour Party activist who, it will be recalled, was earlier involved in the meeting with Galbraith over the British Auxiliaries strike in 1940 and was also a convenor), Doherty (an ex-convenor and at that time senior shop steward at Beardmore's Parkhead Forge) and Menzies (about whom we know nothing other than his membership of the District Committee).[137] This circular enraged the Communists, who proposed a motion on the District Committee that the three men should be suspended from holding all union office for twelve months; the motion was passed by thirteen votes to eleven.[138] According to *Socialist Appeal*, a deputation of shop stewards attended the next meeting of the District Committee to protest at being deprived of the services of their convenors, and some Communist shop stewards even took public issue with their comrade Tommy Sillars.[139]

The Communists on the Clyde were soon faced by a small but determined opposition comprising an assortment of stewards, who could occasionally reach an audience wider than their co-workers. While many people were prepared in a general political way to accept many of their arguments concerning the prosecution of the war, there were some who felt that by consistently opposing strikes the Communists were not behaving in a proper trade-unionist manner. This was particularly true when the skilled engineering and ship-building trade-unionists were the strikers in question: these engineers had a strong tradition of defending their interests as they saw them, come what may, war or no war. They had shown a similar tendency during the First World War, and it was to this historical tradition that a small group of stewards returned at the beginning of February 1943.

On 10 February of that year a letter appeared in *Socialist Appeal* saying that a meeting had been held in the Clyde district, called by the shop stewards' committee at the North British Locomotive Co., to discuss the fining of the boiler-makers who had participated in the strike there. Delegates from seventeen factories attended the meeting, and the representative from the Boilermakers who was present suggested that there was a 'strong possibility' that the men would refuse to pay the fines if they thought that support would be forthcoming from other factories. He was not reported as having specified whether he had in mind financial support or some sort of collective action, but it seems that the meeting felt that it had to acquire some systematic idea of the situation in different plants before anything could be done. A further gathering was called for the following Sunday (which was meeting-day during wartime) to hear reports from other workplaces in the district. In the general discussion about the problems within the district, a definite need was expressed by some delegates for a militant organisation like the Clyde Workers' Committee of the First World War, to provide a lead.[140] By the early summer of 1943 this need found expression in a district organisation of political militants which claimed the mantle of the Clyde Workers' Committee.

The shift away from small domestic strikes and towards disputes of a more district-wide complexion was not yet an all-pervading movement involving the mass of the engineering workers. It was so far evident in only one or two specific cases, and was never to affect more than a minority. A whole range of constraints, from strikers' liability to prosecution to the opposition of the whole of the official and much of the lay trade union machinery, helped to ensure this throughout the war. But the shape and content of strikes was changing in significant ways. In the northern centres of war production,

189

the wave of enthusiasm for JPCs had often been qualified by strong criticisms from some quarters that what was required was not so much militant demands for a share in management as direct-action campaigns to improve wages. Indeed, on the Clyde engineers were beginning to show active discontent with the conduct not only of their officials but also of their CP shop floor representatives when they tried to introduce politics into trade union matters. There were even the beginnings, albeit modest, of an alternative left-wing semi-syndicalist organisation, the revived Clyde Workers' Committee, in the West of Scotland.

After three years of war, a certain section of engineers was growing impatient and felt that insufficient advantage had been derived from their crucial position in war production. The demand to sweep away inefficient managements, while attracting a good deal of support from many engineering workers, was not really the point as far as others were concerned. Their low wages were now impelling them towards stoppages that were directed almost as much against their own representatives as against the employers. In these disputes the tempo of activity and discussion increased dramatically, sometimes giving a toehold to some extreme-left political agitators. It was at this point too early to speak, as some of these agitators did, of a 'second front at home'. Their industrial millenarianism was out of place; but the end of 1942 undoubtedly marked 'the end of the beginning' in more senses than the phrase's originator intended.

## NOTES

1 H. Pelling, op. cit., p. 192.
2 CP, *The CP On The Way To Win* (May 1942); *Victory, Peace, Security* (Oct. 1944); *Communist Policy for Britain* (Nov. 1945). Details of delegates.
3 Ibid.
4 Jack Cohen, 'Coventry's A.G.M.', in *Party Organisation—Weapon for Victory* (1943), pp. 8–9.
5 *Trade Union Report,* 1944 (anon.). Industry Raw Materials, Mass Observation Archive, p. 24.
6 *Gloucester Labour News,* July 1941.
7 P. Inman, op. cit., p. 49.
8 A. Calder, op. cit., p. 309.

9   P. Inman, op. cit., p. 80.
10  W. Hornby, op. cit., p. 209.
11  AVIA 15/2567, 'Personnel Management, Midland Region', 10 July 1943.
12  L. Urwick and E.F.L. Brech, *The Making of Scientific Management* (1946), p. 210. Later in the war the Training Within Industry scheme did begin to train a large number of foremen to cope with both technical and human problems, but it had not yet had any impact.
13  WAL Diary, 10 Sept. 1941. Industry Raw Materials. MO Archive.
14  17 Sept.
15  27 Oct.
16  J.H. Millington to T. Harrisson, 28 Jan. 1942, Industry Raw Materials MO Archive.
17  See the letters from E.H. Gilpin and G. Scott Atkinson to *The Times*, 8 Jan. 1942.
18  *The Times*, 25 Sept. 1941.
19  *Minutes* of the Coventry Engineering Employers' Association, Nov. 1941.
20  A. Calder, op. cit., pp. 458–9.
21  'Notes on JPCs', 17 Feb. 1942, AVIA 15/2539.
22  The *Daily Worker* of 28 December 1940 said: *'This proposal, closely resembling the Nazi system of factory organisation, is the most dangerous of the Fascist methods of industrial organisation yet introduced by Mr. Bevin'*. (original emphasis).
23  P. Inman, op. cit., p. 377. J.T. Murphy also complained that the AEU Executive and the London District Committee of the AEU had not helped to set up JPCs (see *Victory Production!* (1942), p. 98).
24  30 Aug. 1941. LAB 10/351.
25  MAP to Production Executive, PE 41152, 27 Sept. 1941. AVIA 15/2539.
26  E&ATSSNC, *Arms and the Man*, full report of the E&ATSSNC conference, 1941.
27  This was the judgment of Swanson's ex-colleague and fellow Communist at Napier's, Jock Wallace, who later fell out with him (interview of 8 April 1980).
28  E&ATSSNC, *Arms and the Men*, full report of the E&ATSSNC conference, 1941.
29  Ibid.
30  Memo of 1 Nov. 1941. AVIA 15/2539.
31  Ibid.
32  J.B. Jefferys, op. cit., pp. 253–4.
33  P. Inman, op. cit., p. 378.
34  Ibid., pp. 380–3.
35  Message to the members, headed: 'AEU, Birmingham District' (n.d.).
36  Bert Williams, 'Trade Unionism in Birmingham', in *The Birmingham Journal*, vol. vii, June 1953, pp. 10–11.
37  *Trade Union Report* (1944), MO Archive, p. 106.
38  P. Inman, op. cit., p. 380.
39  *Trade Union Report*, MO Archive, p. 106.
40  Ibid., p. 112.
41  Ibid., pp. 106–7.
42  Ibid., p. 106.
43  P. Inman, op. cit., p. 383.
44  Ibid., pp. 382–3.
45  'Report on JPCs', 7 Jan. 1943. AVIA 9/57.
46  *Trade Union Report*, MO Archive, p. 14A.

47  *The Economist,* 11 March 1944.
48  'Report on North-Eastern Morale' (n.d., probably late 1943), AVIA 9/58.
49  Midland Deputy Regional Controller to MAP, 30 June 1944. AVIA 15/2539.
50  Interview with Jock Wallace, 8 April, 1980.
51  P. Inman, op. cit., p. 326.
52  *Minutes* of a works conference held at Standard no. 2, 21 Jan. 1944.
53  *Minutes* of the Coventry District Committee of the AEU, 11 Aug. 1942.
54  *Trade Union Report,* 1944, p. 109 (MO Archive).
55  P. Inman, op. cit., p. 389. Her claim was that JPCs had brought greater worker-management cooperation than had existed for fifty years.
56  *Minutes* of the Coventry District Committee of the AEU, 6, 27 Jan. 1942. 7 Feb. 1942, LAB 10/352.
57  *Report* of Coventry shop stewards' delegation, 22 Jan. 1942, p. 4. MO Archive. LAB 34/56.
58  LAB 34/56.
59  *Report* of Coventry shop stewards' delegation, p. 4.
60  Letter from George Hodgkinson to Tom Harrisson (n.d.), enclosing an unpublished letter to the *Coventry Evening Telegraph.* Hodgkinson thought that his letter had not been published because Strickland was 'under the patronage' of Lord Iliffe, the paper's owner (MO Archive).
61  The chairman of the meeting was probably Jock Gibson, TGWU steward and CP member, who worked at Daimler. The secretary was probably Joe Steele (see Coventry AEU District Committee *Minutes,* 2 Dec. 1941, in which a steward from Armstrong-Whitworth Aircraft is referred to as having signed a letter convening a meeting of the Area Shop Stewards' Council). The 'German brother engaged in the struggle to free Europe from Fascism' may well have been Karl Anders, alias Kurt Naumann. Naumann was an intellectual who had fled Germany for Czechoslovakia in 1933 and came to England in 1939, returning to Germany in 1948. He wrote a book called *Der Strafvollzug im Dritten Reich (Justice in the Third Reich),* see W. Sternfeld and E. Tiedemann *Deutsche Exil-Literatur, 1933–45* (Heidelberg, 1970), p. 24.
62  This evidence must surely call into doubt Angus Calder's claim that the 'syndicalist feeling' so apparent during the First World War had 'withered' (op. cit., p. 459).
63  7 Feb. 1942. LAB 10/352.
64  See R. Croucher, op. cit., pp. 212–14.
65  *Trade Union Report,* 1944, p. 96. Industry Raw Materials, MO Archive.
66  28 March 1942. LAB 10/363.
67  *Labour Management,* vol. xxvi, no. 272, Feb.-March 1944, p. 11.
68  *Minutes* of the Manchester District Committee of the AEU, shop stewards' sub-committee, 8 Jan. 1942.
69  *Catholic Worker,* March 1942.
70  25 Oct. 1941. LAB 10/362.
71  28 March 1942. LAB 10/363.
72  2 May 1942. LAB 10/363.
73  25 July 1942. LAB 10/363.
74  25 July 1942. LAB 10/363.
75  1 Aug. 1942. LAB 10/363.
76  22 Aug. 1942. LAB 10/363.
77  20 Feb. 1943. LAB 10/364.
78  4 April 1942. LAB 10/358.

79  P. Inman, op. cit., p. 392.
80  'Manchester Sub-District Proposals', 19 June 1943: Interim Report of the Factory Brigade.
81  *Socialist Appeal*, June 1942.
82  *Trade Union Report*, 1944. (MO Archive), p. 109.
83  See, for example, *Socialist Appeal* on the Enfield ROF situation, and WIL *Industrial Bulletin* (May 1943), Tarbuck Collection, Warwick University, on the Trotskyists in the ROFs. CP, Report of Conference of Party Comrades in the Metal Industry (n.d., probably 1942), p. 2, reflects the concern of the CP at this development and affirms their determination to eliminate the Trotskyist influence. Mrs Inman, in the official history, also refers to the extreme left in footnotes on pp. 334, 336. Her references to the ROFs show clear signs of Trotskyist influence (pp. 392, 416).
84  'On Unification of the British Section', Founding Conference of the Fourth International, in *Documents of the Fourth International*, ed. W. Reisner, New York, 1973, pp. 268–70. J. Higgins, the author of 'Ten Years For the Locust, British Trotskyism 1938-48', in *International Socialism*, 14, Autumn 1963, reprinted by Swansea International Socialists, n.d.), in his haste to publish the sectarianism of this period of British Trotskyism, is guilty of slight distortion in saying that the founding Congress 'dismissed' the WIL as 'a nationalist grouping in essence reactionary'. In fact, 'On Unification of the British Section' says: 'It is possible for a national group to maintain a constant revolutionary course only if it is firmly connected in one organisation with co-thinkers throughout the world and maintains a constant political and theoretical collaboration with them. The Fourth International alone is such an organisation. All purely national groupings, all those who reject international organisation, control, and discipline, are in their essence reactionary.' The Conference then invited the 'Lee group', as they dubbed them, to 'reconsider their decisions' and to join the new International (W. Reisner, op. cit.). In his attempt to define the International Socialism group against an earlier tradition, Higgins may be wrong in characterising the Fourth International's stance as being more hostile than it actually was.
85  Interview with Jack Williams, 3 Nov. 1972. J. Higgins, op. cit., note 5. A Scottish organisation called the Revolutionary Socialist League had earlier joined the Fourth International as a part of the British section (W. Reisner, op. cit., p. 269).
86  J. Higgins, op. cit., p. 4. 'Organisational Report of the Control Committee', Nov. 1942 (Modern Records Centre, University of Warwick).
87  Industrial Committee, 'Building Factory Groups' (sub-titled 'Directive to all Locals', n.d., but probably late 1942), Modern Records Centre, University of Warwick.
88  *Socialist Appeal*, Oct. 1941.
89  This estimate was given to me by Peter Thwaites of the London School of Economics, who derived it from an at present unavailable internal ILP document.
90  *New Leader*, 13 Sept. 1941; 26 Dec. 1942.
91  These pamphlets cost one penny each.
92  P. Inman, op. cit., pp. 334 (note), 366 (note).
93  CP, 'The CP: Its Theory and Practice', March 1943, second edition, Maitland-Sara collection, University of Warwick.
94  For a detailed discussion of the agreement, see R. Croucher, op. cit., ch. 6.
95  A. Calder, op. cit., p. 523.

96   Coventry Toolroom Agreement *Minutes.*
97   *Manchester Evening News,* 30 May 1941.
98   Department of Employment and Productivity, *British Labour Statistics. Historical Abstract,* table 40.
99   P. Kerrigan, in *Labour Monthly,* Jan. 1942.
100  6, 20 Aug. 1943. LAB 10/380; 5, 12, 19, 26 June 1943. LAB 10/353; 31 March, 7 April 1944. LAB 10/444.
101  P. Inman, op. cit., p. 394.
102  J. Bowman to AEU shop stewards, 'Shipbuilding and Ship-Repairing— Extension of Lying-On Time', 5 Sept. 1942.
103  G.J. Moody to J. Bowman, 6 Sept. 1942.
104  Letters from Jarrow, no. 1JE, 7 Sept.; Armstrong-Whitworth, 7 Sept.; Wallsend, no. 1, 7 Sept.; S. Shields, no. 6, 14 Sept. (two letters); S. Shields, no. 3, 16 Sept.; H. Charlton, 10 Sept.; Wallsend, no. 5, 14 Sept.; Middle Dock Co. steward, 1 Oct.; Walker, no. 8WE, 14 Sept.
105  S. Shields, no. 6: both letters dated 14 Sept., from John Hardwick.
106  William W. Knox to Bowman, 7 Sept. 1942.
107  Ibid.
108  Untitled document in Bowman's writing.
109  Ibid.
110  *DW,* 6 Oct. 1942.
111  *DW,* 10 Oct.; *Catholic Herald,* 2, 9, 16, 23 Oct.
112  *Socialist Appeal,* Oct. 1942. The biography of Harry Pollitt by John Mahon is useful for his background, but does not mention the strike.
113  *DW,* 7 Oct.; *NP,* Nov. 1942. WIL (internal), 'Political Statement of the Central Committee', Nov. 1942.
114  *Newcastle Journal and North Mail,* 8 Oct. 1942.
115  Ibid., 10 Oct.; *DW,* 9 Oct.
116  Ibid., 12 Oct. 1942.
117  Bowman's notes of meeting at Jarrow, 21 Sept. 1942.
118  S. Shields 6 to Bowman, 12 Oct. 1942.
119  Wallsend 5, 5 Oct.; Wallsend 1, 5 Oct.; N. Shields 3, 10 Oct., N. Shields 38, 17 Oct., Walker 3, 10 Oct.; S. Shields 6, 12 Oct.; Newcastle 14, 12 Oct.; Wallsend 7, 13 Oct.; Whitley Bay, 20 Oct.
120  *Newcastle Journal,* 10 Oct.; *DW,* 8, 10 Oct.
121  Bowman to stewards, 'Alteration of Lying-On Time', 8 Oct. 1942.
122  *Newcastle Journal,* 12 Oct.
123  Ibid., 13 Oct.
124  Ibid., 13, 14 Oct.
125  Hawthorne Leslie Brass shop steward to Bowman, 10 Oct.; Bringham and Cowan shop steward to Bowman, 11 Oct.; G. Davison to Bowman, 12 Oct. 1942.
126  R. Herdman to Bowman, 9 Oct. 1942.
127  *DW,* 15 Oct. 1942.
128  *Socialist Appeal,* Oct. 1942.
129  WIL, 'Political Statement of the Central Committee', Nov. 1942.
130  31 Oct. 1942. LAB 10/363.
131  31 Oct., 14 Nov. 1942. LAB 10/363.
132  Ibid.
133  2 Jan. 1943. LAB 10/364.
134  19 Dec. 1942. LAB 10/363.
135  2 Jan. 1943. LAB 10/364. LAB 34/58.
136  WIL, Industrial Bulletin, May 1943. Modern Records Centre, University of

Warwick.
137  AEU *Journal,* March 1942. See also R. Croucher, op. cit., p. 432, for
     further information on Gray.
138  *Socialist Appeal,* Jan. 1943.
139  Ibid., Jan., Feb. 1943.
140  Ibid., Jan., Feb. 1943.

# CHAPTER 4

# IRRESPONSIBLE ELEMENTS

From the beginning of 1943 the tide began to flow with increasing force in the Allies' favour. The entry of the United States into the war after Pearl Harbour brought enormous productive resources into play which virtually guaranteed success in the long run. As Churchill said, 'All the rest was merely the proper application of overwhelming force'.[1] But if American industry was ultimately an important factor, it was the Red Army that was beginning to bleed the invading forces white in 1943. The battle of Stalingrad represented the key military victory of the war, ensuring that the Wehrmacht's drive to the East would not succeed. At the end of January 1943 General von Paulus surrendered with his entire army, and Hitler, who had raised the stakes in that prolonged and terrible battle, had gambled and lost. By the summer of 1943 the Soviet Union's forces had the advantage over the Germans in both men and materials, an advantage of paramount importance as the invaders were pushed back. Enormous quantities of Axis equipment fell into Russian hands while some two and a half million Germans were killed or wounded. By January 1944 the Red Army was pushing westwards towards its frontiers, and had already reached the Polish border. Meanwhile, the North African campaign was brought to a close, making possible the invasion of Sicily, while in the Atlantic the U-boat threat was greatly diminished by the summer of 1943. Within Europe, the growth of resistance movements also began to play a significant part in sapping the power of the Reich, with strikes, sabotage and passive resistance becoming increasingly common in France and Italy in particular.

But it was still being argued by some that overwhelming force was not being properly applied. Britain's direct attacks on Germany still consisted almost exclusively of the strategic bomber offensive, and bombing was both costly of men and machines and dubious in its effects on German war production. The development of the highly effective Lancaster with its large bomb load at least improved the terms on which the offensive was conducted, but until 1945 the air battle over Germany was strongly contested by the Luftwaffe. Losses of bombers were often of the order of five per cent per raid, and in some raids very much higher. Churchill thought the air war of prime importance; in the absence of a second front it almost had to assume such primacy. The second front, when it eventually arrived, had been long awaited. As the war swung visibly in the Allies' favour, people's thoughts turned to post-war Britain and what it was they were fighting for. Ideas on radically reconstructing society from top to bottom became current and, as Paul Addison has shown, a whole new political consensus emerged. In the workshops, engineers wondered whether post-war Britain would bring another long period of unemployment. The feeling that a new Britain was not merely a luxury but an absolute necessity was very general throughout the country, often irrespective of people's political affiliation. A fairer, more egalitarian society, almost everybody agreed, would have to be built at the end of the war.

It was, then, with enormous interest that the Beveridge Report was received by the public at the beginning of December 1942. It is unlikely that an official publication has ever aroused such wide and lively discussion. The detailed report aimed at the elimination of poverty through a comprehensive system of contributory social insurance covering unemployment, sickness and disability, maternity and death. It made a number of assumptions and raised a whole number of further issues, such as the nature of a future national health system, the prospects of employment, and so on. In short, it posed fundamental questions about Britain after the war. Within a week of its publication, nineteen people out of twenty had apparently heard of the report, and nine out of ten believed that its proposals should be adopted.[2] Yet the government reacted to the plan only slowly and partially; Churchill and Bevin alike constantly stressed the importance of winning the war first. For some three months the government remained silent, thereby fostering suspicions that they were not as wholeheartedly in favour of its proposals as was the population at large.[3] In fact, Churchill was known to be opposed to it, and was adamant that if its recommendations were to be implemented at all, then it would not be before the end of the war.[4] Eventually he felt constrained to adjust his view slightly in response to popular pressure, and some of its suggestions were accepted in principle by the government.[5] But there was a feeling, especially within the Labour Party, that a greater element of social justice should be immediately introduced, and the Labour members of the Coalition government came under strong criticism from the left, led by Bevan and Laski, for insisting on so little in return for their loyal support.[6] There can be little doubt that they reflected popular opinion on this point more faithfully than the Cabinet. Many people regarded the Cabinet's procrastination and initial refusal to implement the recommendations of the report as grounds for anxiety. They found little encouragement for their hopes that Britain would be a better place to live and work in after the war than it had been in the Depression. As one worker had written to *Picture Post* in December 1942: 'If Sir William Beveridge's recommendations are not given the consideration they deserve, it will make the majority of us wonder what we are fighting for. . . In my opinion, this scheme of 'Social Security' is the first step in post-war planning and the Powers-that-be will inspire confidence or not, by the way they deal with it.'[7] In the event, many felt that the treatment given the report was less than satisfactory. Workers could not look to the future with any real sense of security; if one found oneself at the labour exchange at the end of the war, as at the end of the First World War, no guarantees had been made even as to the terms of one's unemployment. At the back of many workers' minds lay the feeling that if this was to be the case, then it was important to make hay while the sun shone.[8]

The growth of a strong belief that the whole system needed overhauling had important repercussions for the way that many people conceived of strikes. During 1940 and early 1941, strikers (except possibly in Scotland) faced popular hostility: strikes were sabotage as far as most people were concerned. In the second half of the war the matter became more complex and a shift in opinion is discernible. Many people continued to think that strikes were wrong, but were at the same time sympathetic to those who felt the need to stop work. Thus, the public face turned towards strikers could be rather more tolerant than the same public face turned towards the government. It was quite common for Ministry of Information surveys of public opinion to record that there was sympathy for strikers. while also recording that the government was being criticised for not taking decisive action.[9] The blame for strikes was not always laid at the feet of those who stopped work. The Ministry of Information's survey of November 1943 showed that in some areas people thought that strikes were incited by industrialists. One reason given was that they thought industrialists were raking off too much to want the war to end yet, another that they wanted to be able to say after the war that workers sabotaged the war effort, and a third that they wanted to slow down aid to Russia.[10] It was not always employers who provoked strikes, of course, and during the apprentices' strike of early 1944 many adults—while hesitating to blame the government—were prepared to say that it was quite understandable if boys learning a trade did not want to go down the pits. In this case, the apprentices benefited once again from the sympathy of their elders, as well as from their appreciation of the arduous jobs that they were being asked to do.[11]

From the government's point of view, prolonged strikes and go-slows represented an important loss of production and, more importantly, a setback for its industrial policy. In terms of production, industrial action in such highly integrated industries as aircraft building could have serious military repercussions. A Ministry of Aircraft Production survey of the effects of strikes and industrial action on aircraft production showed that from 1 January to 30 September 1943, such action caused the loss of some sixty bombers and fifteen fighters. Particularly serious was a go-slow at Rootes Speke works, making Halifax bombers, which was still continuing at the time of the survey and in which about fifty bombers had been lost. In the other factories production had tended to increase after the strikes; the MAP found that much of the lost ground had been made up as workers pushed on harder.[12] Nevertheless, such production losses could be ill afforded with a bomber offensive providing the main thrust of the British war effort. They would affect Bomber Command's ability to continue the air war in the face of heavy losses: indeed, the summer and autumn of 1943 saw a slackening in the air offensive and this was partly due to labour problems in firms producing Lancasters.[13]

Strikes could give rise to relatively large losses of production partly because technological efficiency and the division of labour had so far advanced that less and less time was required to build a bomber. By 1943 roughly thirty thousand man-hours were required to produce a bomber, but assembly itself was being achieved in only three thousand man-hours.[14] During 1943 as maximum mobilisation was reached, productive efficiency probably reached its peak. The extent of this mobilisation was prodigious and exceeded, in terms of man- and woman-power, that of any other combatant nation. All of the ministries involved in war production now had to accept cuts in the number of new workers they had requested as their share of the manpower budget. The MAP, for example, which as usual received the lion's share, had to be satisfied with an extra 503,000 workers as opposed to the 603,000 it thought necessary to fulfil its production targets.[15] The total employed in the engineering and metal, explosives, chemicals and shipbuilding industries rose to its peak figure of 4,847,800 in the summer of 1943, of whom roughly one third were women.[16] It was possible to expand the labour force in some unusual ways, by calling on labour from Ireland or by using more part-time women workers, and both of these resources were used to great effect. Some thirty thousand Irish workers came to Britain from Eire to work in the munitions industries, and part-time women workers numbered about two hundred thousand by the end of 1943.[17] With the influx of less skilled labour, piece-work spread as the characteristic method of paying semi-skilled workers, so that in 1945 it was estimated that about ninety per cent of women in engineering were paid by the piece.[18]

A restricted labour supply and a general trend for strikes and absenteeism to increase meant that both the Ministry of Aircraft Production and the Ministry of Labour began to take an increasing interest in the quality of management at all levels, with important results for shop floor trade-unionists. When Cripps (an ex-munitions manager of First World War vintage himself) took over at the Ministry of Aircraft Production, he continued to encourage the establishment of JPCs, but he also began to deal directly with inefficient managements. The most famous case of direct action by the MAP against a management occurred at Short's, an established aircraft firm with factories at Bedford and Rochester. In this case Cripps appointed a new chairman and an authorised controller, while vesting all of the company's shares in MAP's nominees.[19] Soon afterwards Cripps took wider powers to deal with inefficient managements under Defence Regulation 54CA, under which the Minister was entitled to appoint directors after establishing whether the government had made a 'substantial' contribution to the firm's finances.[20]

The Short's case created a considerable stir. The general impression was that in some cases the government had decided to 'take the gloves off', and the result was to further strengthen those trade-unionists who had argued that many managements were incompetent and should be removed. As Maurice Edelman, active in Coventry, put it in 1943: 'If a dozen fighter pilots had been court-martialled for dereliction of duty, the shock to the public mind could hardly be greater.'[21] Against this background the old cry of the engineering employers that they had 'the right to manage' sounded like the swansong of a dying breed. New Propellor did not hesitate to extract maximum political advantage from the affair, and working people as a whole saw Cripps' move as one in the eye for management.[22]

The general direction of even the austere Cripps' policy towards managements was not punitive, however. Both he and Bevin thought it important to try to improve and reform management practice. In the summer of 1943 the MAP ran its first course for managers, with a nine-week university-industry-university sandwich course, and followed this up by producing a set of leaflets on personnel management.[23] At foreman level, the Training Within Industry scheme began to tackle the problem of training through its 'job relations' project, through which nearly fifty thousand foremen passed between 1943 and 1945.[24] This was accompanied by a drive to appoint more and more welfare and personnel managers in firms, under the Essential Works Order. By 1944 the Ministry of Information claimed that over ninety per cent of munitions factories had some form of welfare supervision.[25] These changes undoubtedly altered the framework within which stewards operated, and may even—as the official history suggests in the face of its own unequivocal evidence to the contrary—have had an effect on the rate of absenteeism in the factories. And now that production was somewhat less problematic and managements were undergoing changes in the way they related to their workforce (in formal terms at least), how did stewards and workers see the new developments? The answer is important because it provides the background to many later strikes.

Trade-unionists viewed both personnel and welfare managers with a good deal of suspicion, it appears. During 1945 there was a discussion in *Labour Management* on this question. One article drew on interviews which the author conducted with shop stewards to try to find out what their members felt. She argued that workers drew a distinction between personnel and welfare managers, in that they were opposed to the first but 'greatly in favour' of the second. One steward in particular was emphatic that both he and his fellow workers objected to personnel managers: 'The Personnel Manager asks us questions about our home life and takes an interest in us, not for our own good, but in order to get the best out of us for the firm, and, subsequently, the pockets of the shareholders.'[26] A later article argued that although trade-unionists were initially hostile to personnel managers, they could be persuaded to change their views. At a conference of trade-unionists and managers which she had attended, the former were 'definitely hostile', and used words like 'Gestapo', 'stooge of the management', and 'stumbling block to the trade union movement'.[27] A commonly held view was that personnel managers should be appointed by the government rather than by companies themselves.[28] Nor does the evidence from other witnesses exempt welfare officers from similar strictures.[29] They were criticised not necessarily because of their lack of training or ability, or even their backgrounds, but largely because of their position in the management structure. They were often regarded by production managers as a luxury, and consequently had ill defined roles and little power to change things. Seeing this problem, trade-unionists sometimes argued for state-appointed officers who would compel the rest of management to recognise trade-unionism and improve conditions. They saw the improvements that were taking place as deriving basically from the insistence of the Ministry of Labour on demanding certain minimum standards of factory occupiers, under the Essential Works Order and the Factories Act. They felt that managements had to be forced to make improvements by the government, and their attitude to personnel and welfare officers was simply an extension of that logic. At the same time the extension of personnel management to large numbers of engineering firms very often assisted the unionisation process. There is no doubt that personnel officers, who had in many cases been trained by the Ministry of Labour, were well aware of the advantages to companies that could derive from the extension of collective representation. The reduction of absenteeism, perhaps their prime objective, could usually be best achieved with the cooperation of the shop stewards. Their view of the legitimate functions of trade unions differed from those of most shop stewards, but they were generally prepared to accept and even encourage union membership.

Trade union organisation was constantly improving both quantitatively and qualitatively at the peak of the war effort, despite some friction between the engineering unions. According to Sheila Lewenhak's estimates, 1943 brought a large increase in membership, and trade union density in her over-wide definition of the industry increased to forty-eight per cent.[30] In many cases this meant that efforts to secure closed shops were under way. Managements, on the other hand, were strongly opposed to making any agreements on the matter, and supported the right of individuals not to join the union if they so wished.

The drive towards the closed shop was an important feature of the later war years. In some cases it led to serious disputes of national importance, such as that at Swan Hunter's Neptune works on Tyneside in early 1943. Stewards had been elected there in mid-1942 and pushed ahead vigorously with trade union organisation, so that by 1943 they had all except five people in the union. These five repeatedly refused to join, and were approached for the last time on 21 January 1943, when they reiterated their refusal. On Monday 25 January everyone presented themselves for work, but refused to go in when they heard that the five still refused to join and that the management would take no action. At noon they were joined on strike by the 'outside' department. According to the strike committee, the men told the outside steward after the strike began that they were members of the NUGMW, but their statement was not accepted.[31] At least one of the men concerned was a lapsed member of the AEU, who told Jack Bowman, the AEU District Secretary, that he had been involved in the 1922 lockout without any benefit and had been forced to sell his piano; he added that he thought that 'the general unions should organise all labour'.[32] Bowman himself felt that the men had made a sacrifice by taking dilutees 'into their shops', and that the dilutees' own patriotism could be challenged if they were prepared to allow a strike to take place on their account.[33]

The strikers printed appeals for financial aid and moral support and distributed them all over the country, and they received support from collections taken in the local workplaces.[34] Indeed, it was feared by the Chief Conciliation Officer that the strike might spread; but on 5 March, when the men had decided to pay their arrears or apply for membership of the AEU,[35] the local shop stewards called a meeting to bring the strike to an end. The management made a 'gentleman's agreement' with Bowman that the works was now a closed shop, although precisely what they understood by this is not clear.[36] The Neptune strike was a determined battle, stretching out over some six weeks, to enforce

# Neptune Strike Committee

NEPTUNE HOTEL.
NEWCASTLE-ON-TYNE 6.
22nd February, 1943.

# AN APPEAL TO ALL TRADE UNIONISTS

**F**OR any Trade Unionist to stand aside from this conflict, and to let the Employers ride roughshod, would be a betrayal of everything our forebears have fought to achieve in the course of long years of struggle.

Whatever the motive is of the management, and the action taken by them, it is not only helping Fascism but is actually, for the time being, challenging the whole of the Trade Union Movement.

The men in dispute treat the management's plan seriously, and it is possible that there are men in the governing circles of the Masters' Federation who are contemplating the breaking of the Closed Shop Agreements. The last few weeks of this dispute have rendered this perfectly plain, and it is only because the management has attempted to destroy our rights (undisturbed) that we have answered their challenge by this stoppage of work.

We strikers are at war with Hitler and all that he stands for. The management are being shameful in their attitude to our cause, and if they are allowed to impose their conditions and we are forced to accept them, it will be infinitely WORSE than anything we have yet suffered.

We ask all Trade Unionists not to exile themselves but to come forward and strengthen our CAUSE.

We ask for your moral and financial support to help us. Not for a VICTORY for ourselves, but for the whole of the Trade Union Movement.

Sec.: Wm. Bryden,  Yours fraternally,
42, Hexham Avenue,  pp. WM. BRYDEN,
Walker, Newcastle-on-Tyne.  Strike Committee.

Appeal issued during the struggle for a closed shop at the Neptune works full membership in an important firm's works. Its successful conclusion was of more than local significance.

Shop steward organisation improved markedly in the second half of the war and especially in 1943, in terms of the number of stewards operating, the links between them, and the relationships between themselves and those they represented. The number of stewards recognised in Coventry suggests a considerable increase even when some turnover is allowed for, with 1943 as the peak year:

> 1941 : 426
> 1942 : 319
> 1943 : 441
> 1944 : 336
> 1945 : 236[37]

In Manchester, where the District Committee did not record every steward appointed in the same way as their Coventry counterparts, the records of attendance at shop stewards' quarterly meetings showed a similar upward tendency in 1943:

> 1940 : 54
> 1941 : not known
> 1942 : 72
> 1943 : 154
> 1944 : 141
> 1945 : 145[38]

The shop stewards' quarterlies were valuable in providing a forum for exchanging information, for evolving tactics on problems of general interest in the district, and for coordinating action. These meetings were allowed for in the AEU rule book, but stewards started to organise similar joint meetings, which were not sanctioned by rule, of stewards from the different plants owned by large companies. One such committee at A.V. Roe's, already mentioned, had on one occasion seventy-nine delegates from the various factories in attendance.[39] This committee was a very early example of a 'combine committee', which had originated in the 1930s; from 1943 a number of others grew up, as at the Daimler, Dunlop and Vickers-Armstrong factories.[40] If an urgent need arose, as at the Humber Co.'s Stoke (Coventry) works in

1945, stewards could establish contact quickly and informally. In early 1945, some stewards 'commandeered' a staff
car (they were made there) to drive up to Ryton, just outside
Coventry, to see the stewards at Rootes Securities No. 2
factory on a matter of mutual interest.[41]

The links between stewards and their members grew
stronger as the war continued, as they had constantly to
tackle a wide range of personal and social problems. Fire-
watching rotas had to be drawn up, hostels for transferred
workers changed when unsuitable, transport to and from
factories arranged with both bus companies and management, a watch kept to see that petrol was fairly distributed,
and so on. At one factory, matters brought to the steward
included not only such industrial issues as a girl's application
for increased pay at the end of her probationary period and a
request for more wash basins, but also domestic matters such
as a request for help in dealing with a defaulting contractor
at home and another for intervention against a landlord.[42]
Pay As You Earn Income Tax was another wartime innovation which stewards had to master. At one Liverpool factory,
the problem of high payments because of late assessment
was overcome by the company investing a certain amount to
cover repayment of the tax, and then deducting a fixed
amount each week from everyone's pay packet.[43] Stewards
were usually involved in developing these schemes, as companies were very cautious in making such changes to pay
packets.[44] In November 1943 two stewards at A.V. Roe's
produced a PAYE ready-reckoner which enabled people to
calculate how much tax they should pay.[45] This was
important to workers, because knowing how much tax one
should pay each week not only helped to check one's total
pay but also allowed a greater degree of planning in the
domestic economy. The wide range of individual and social
problems thrown up by the 'total war' both inside and outside the factories offered considerable opportunities for the
active shop steward. For many workers the shop steward
held a position of respect, and was someone to whom they
could turn for advice and assistance on any problem. Many
shop stewards were not only workplace representatives, in
any case; they were very often also local councillors,

208

# TO ALL OPERATORS IN THE MACHINE SHOP

This leaflet has been produced by the Trade Unions in the Factory to assist you in obtaining all you are entitled to under national and local Trade Union Agreements. Keep this by you for reference—when in doubt see the nearest shop steward.

1. All prices on jobs must be fixed by mutual agreement between you and the Ratefixer, therefore, be sure you have some idea of what you think the job is worth BEFORE accepting the price.

2. When being timed set a pace that you can keep up for a full day. When the ratefixer tells you the time you have taken see that it coincides approximately with the time you think the job is worth.

3. When you have mutually agreed to the time taken which must cover all things you do when working normally, such as using all your gauges, clocking on and off, etc., you will receive a bonus allowance which will vary according to the type of job you are doing.

4. Should you have a job where there is an infrequent flow of work you should ask for a plus price for small batches.

5. Should you be unable to carry on with your work for any reason you are entitled to a waiting-ticket, for which you are paid waiting time. This covers all waiting time—waiting for work, waiting for toolsetter, tool trouble, machine breakdown, etc.

It is important that you fully understand all you are entitled to, if any problem arises which is not covered by this leaflet, don't keep it to yourself but contact your nearest shop steward and remember, the Trade Unions exist to look after your interests —THEREFORE, JOIN THE UNION.

Issued by The Austin Motor Shop Stewards Committee.

An example of shop stewards' activities in the Austin Motor Co., Birmingham

*For the future struggles that
lie ahead....*

●

# SUPPORT THE
# SHOP STEWARDS'
# FIGHTING FUND

●

Our activities create expenses, do your
bit and give what you can.

No Shop Stewards receive any remuneration for lost time.

*Unite to provide a decent wage for
the boys returning home after the war.*

COMMERCIAL PRINTING CO. (BIRMINGHAM) LTD.

Issued by the Austin Motor Shop Stewards' Committee, 1944

secretaries of sports clubs, officers of tenants' associations, and so on. The importance of what might be termed this industrial social work that the stewards performed can hardly be overestimated in evaluating the nature of the relationships which stewards developed with their members during the war.

A picture of a strong shop stewards' committee in operation during the second half of the war was given in a pamphlet written in 1945 by a man who knew the shop stewards at Woolwich Arsenal well. As a body with a history that stretched back to before the First World War, they were perhaps not typical of shop floor organisation in these years, but they nevertheless reflect some of its strengths and weaknesses. In 1943 there were one hundred and sixteen skilled shop stewards at the Arsenal, members of seventeen trade unions. Together they constituted the Skilled Shop Stewards' Committee, which had four officers (president, vice-president, secretary and treasurer), and an Executive Committee of five. The secretary was reported as working at his trade, but the other members of the EC alternated between work and representing members. Trade union membership stood at ninety per cent. The Executive met once a week and filled all the posts on the factory safety committee, the canteen advisory committee, the JPC, the apprenticeship and training committee, and other bodies. The full committee met once a month, and attendance during 1943 averaged 71.3 stewards over thirteen meetings. Most shops had a regular report-back from their stewards, and a monthly duplicated report was circulated for notice boards. Sixpence per month was collected from every member affiliated to the committee, which gave the stewards £650 in hand by the end of 1943. The committee operated according to a set of standing orders which were strictly adhered to, and its status was 'extremely high' (Charles Job). Members had the right to go to any shop on union business, but dilutees were not allowed to become shop stewards or members of the skilled committee unless they were coopted for a special issue. Women shop stewards were allowed to attend the monthly meetings with full speaking and voting rights on the basis of one for each area of the Arsenal; the rest could attend only as visitors.

The committee published its own annual report and had its own library. It was affiliated to the Woolwich Labour Party, as were the other shop stewards' committees. The Woolwich Arsenal also had a Joint Shop Stewards' Committee which represented the semi- and unskilled, and its organisation was similar to that of its skilled counterpart. There were eighty shop stewards on this committee. Both committees met together periodically on the Combined Shop Stewards' Committee, with the secretary of the skilled committee as chairman and the secretary of the non-skilled as secretary.[46] The Arsenal shop stewards, with their strong craft-consciousness, were not typical in their institutionalising of the barriers which existed between the engineering craftsmen and others. By this time the overwhelming majority of shop stewards' committees were joint committees on which representatives sat irrespective of their craft status or their union. Nevertheless, in their highly articulated and even sophisticated formal organisation, the Arsenal stewards did reflect a growing preference for organisational structures which enabled trade-unionists to deal with their problems collectively, on a factory-wide basis rather than in more piecemeal, sectional ways.

Gradually, shop stewards began to win the sort of facilities required to make the job of representing their members easier. Time off with pay while taking questions up with management was perhaps the most important facility of all. Some firms began to pay the basic rate to shop stewards involved in negotiations, but in most cases the shop steward could still expect to lose money when representing members. Sometimes stewards claimed a certain amount back from shop stewards' funds, but they generally accepted that they would be unable to make any 'killings' on piece-work.[47] Another important facility was being able to hold shop stewards' committee meetings in works time. Working hours in wartime were particularly long, and stewards could find it difficult to attend meetings held after work. At the Standard Motor Co., Coventry, the shop stewards' committee met once a week for the last hour of the day, and carried on after working hours once momentum had been established.[48] In general, however, shop stewards' committees still had to

212

meet outside of working hours. The matter of where to meet was also important. Companies were often willing to allow stewards to use canteens for their meetings; at Austin Longbridge, however, the shop stewards' committee began to realise that information from their sessions was getting back to management. Some thought it was even possible that the canteen was bugged, and so they sought permission to build their own union hut in the factory precincts, where they could meet in private. The hut, once built, came to be thought of as the place where one went to get union help; it was the physical expression of the union's presence at the Longbridge complex.[49] But this was unusual. Parallels would probably only be found in other very large groups of factories. The overall impression is of a trade union organisation with only minimal facilities to carry out its business, despite the advances which had undoubtedly been made. Many managers were reluctant to allow the shop floor union organisation to put down roots, for fear that they would continue to sustain the shop stewards in the less favourable conditions of peacetime. This reluctance made the stewards' lives difficult in many ways, but it also ensured the health of workplace trade-unionism. It was in particular a guarantee that working engineers would regard their representatives with a certain minimum of respect. When someone took on the shop steward's job, they could hardly be doing so out of motives of personal gain. And it was unlikely that they would lose touch with the shop floor, because the constant round of procedural meetings which some stewards had to attend from the 1960s onwards were not yet a feature for most of their number.

Shop stewards during the later war years often used the shop meeting both as a way of keeping in touch with their members and as a method of raising collective understanding of workshop issues. Report-back meetings enabled stewards to keep their fingers on the pulse of opinion in the factory, and also helped them to approach managements fully confident of support amongst their fellow-workers. The relevance of the meeting as a key weapon of organisation was fully grasped by the left-wing stewards in particular, who knew how to exert pressure while avoiding strike action.

Perhaps the best illustration of this comes from Bill Warman, Communist steward at the Standard Motor Co., Coventry, in these years:

> During the war a lot of us had the hammer and sickle badge in our lapels because we were either Communists or near-Communists (I was a member of the CP—still am as a matter of fact) and as shop steward I had one of these badges on my apron. Anyway I had some trouble with my throat, went to see the doctor and sat down in front of him. And the first thing he said to me: 'You don't think I'm going to treat you with that badge on?' I said 'Oh'. He said: 'Your people have been denounced anyway by Mr. Bevin.' So I said: 'That's very nice—you're not going to treat me then? Right, I'll get up and go.' So I got up and walked out. He tried to call me back but I walked out. So I went back to the factory and called together the shop committee. I reported to them what had happened and they immediately said: 'Right, we'll have a shop meeting', so we had a shop meeting that dinner time. So it was reported to the shop and a resolution was immediately moved that we demand an apology from Dr. Elton and that resolution was sent to the shop stewards' committee. The Joint Shop Stewards' Committee turned the resolution down, said it wasn't strong enough and demanded the expulsion of the doctor. We took that resolution to Sir John Black, and in the meantime walked round the factory with the convenor, talking to various shops, how it was going, they were having their meetings, all endorsing the decision: 'This bloke's got to go'—so after a couple of hours we were sent for by Sir John Black, and the convenor and myself went up to his office. (This bloke, he fancied himself, but we made use of this), he stood up when we came in, tall fellow, well dressed, fifty guinea suits in those days, he walked towards us and said: 'Well, Warman, I've sent for you in order to tell you that I've dismissed Dr. So and So. Yes, as far as I'm concerned you're entitled to your politics as long as you don't allow them to interfere in this factory'.[50]

Perhaps there was already some feeling in the factory against the doctor (factory doctors were in a position to make themselves unpopular), but the real point is that opinion was fully mobilised to great effect.

Both managements and government consistently referred to the fact that factory meetings in 'protected places' were illegal under the defence regulations if they were concerned with political rather than industrial matters. But Bill Warman's case illustrates the extreme difficulties involved in enforcing this legal proscription: was the case a political one or not? We can be sure that the issue was seen, in part at least, as political by those involved, even if Sir John Black tried to emphasise the steward's right to his politics 'as long as they were kept out of the factory'. In general, shop stewards defended their right to hold industrial and political meetings. They usually succeeded, because they were seen to be the defenders of the right of free speech and democracy. The atmosphere in the workshops was no longer that of the 1930s, when workers could describe themselves as 'coolies', without any rights. People considered themselves to be engaged in a 'people's war' in which they had the right to be actively and democratically involved. Those who spied on meetings and reported them were treated with contempt: several ex-stewards reported how they had offered to speak louder and slower for the note-taker!

The management at Beardmore's Parkhead Forge submitted a detailed report to the Ministry of Labour in 1944 showing how they had been completely unable, despite all their efforts, to have stewards disciplined by their union, the National Service Officer, or the police. Mr Henderson, the machine shop superintendent, based his report on both his own experience and the evidence submitted to him by a foreman. The dossier complained of meetings held in the machine shop during March and April 1944 and contained quite detailed information about what was said in them. The meetings were held despite a constant stream of threats that they were illegal, that the stewards would be prosecuted, and so on. These threats received short shrift. On 4 April, for example, the toolroom decided to hold a shop meeting at 7.45. The shop stewards were told that a written application for a meeting would have to be made, giving particulars of the agenda. No application was submitted, and the men held their meeting in the toolroom's top gallery. The manager and foreman reported that they summoned the shop stewards just before the meeting began and warned them that it was illegal to hold a meeting and that the men should be told this. The stewards replied that no application would be made, but they would tell the men and were prepared to abide by their decision. The convenor addressed the meeting first and said that they could meet inside the factory or outside; the men could decide, but the stewards recommended inside. The motion was carried unanimously. The meeting went on to discuss five items, carefully itemised by the foreman, and went on for just over an hour. None of the items were explicitly political, but unfavourable references were made to the manager and foreman. At meeting after meeting, the dossier complained, similar warnings had been defied so that the management felt powerless: 'We have had no backing, with the result that the men will not recognise any regulation whatsoever, and in all cases take the law into their own hands, and we cannot see any peace until they are forced to recognise procedure.'[51] In this and many other cases shop stewards were able to build on their members' consciousness of the importance of free speech and democratic discussion to re-establish an historic right of the workshop community.

The increasing strength and confidence of trade union organisation on the shop floor tended to encourage members to raise an increasing volume of grievances with their employers. It was not that a permanent minimum of grievances existed in any given workforce and that these emerged willy-nilly; whether objective problems were translated into active grievances depended, and depends, to a very considerable extent on the means available for solving them. This aspect of the growth of union membership has been ignored by some Marxist historians, who have painted a rather one-sided picture of the situation by arguing that joining a union simply made workers take up grievances through 'legitimate' channels which institutionalised and restricted conflict.[52] This argument is valid, especially in wartime, but it is inadequate because at the same time unionisation brought many engineering workers for the first time into active, rather than passive, conflict with managements. Recently unionised workers were no less confident about taking up matters with management than long standing members. Indeed, the reverse is true. In December 1943 the Midlands Chief Conciliation Officer commented that 'indiscipline' among the rank and file was becoming more common, and this was, he thought, because people of little or no industrial and trade union experience were joining unions. He went on to report that these new members 'look to their new alliance with organised labour as a means for promoting quickly their ends regardless often of the merits of their demands or of the provisions of Order 1305'.[53] Having joined a union, they expected results.

The growing stream of grievances which resulted in industrial action of one sort or another set up tensions within the trade unions themselves which could increasingly only be resolved by the intervention of the state. At Fairey Aviation, Manchester, for example, one hundred women strikers refused to return to work despite the fact that the local TGWU official had obtained a works conference, because they felt that they would gain too little from it. The advice of both the Ministry of Labour's Conciliation Officer and the trade union official was again offered, that they should go back, but they refused and only returned when prosecution was threatened.[54] In this apparently insignificant dispute the problem was encapsulated: women and new trade-unionists generally were becoming more persistent in strikes and were rejecting the advice of their officials, leaving the Ministry of Labour little alternative but to threaten prosecution. The problem was that prosecution had to be used with great discretion. The Betteshanger colliery strike of January 1942 had shown that it was impracticable to prosecute large groups of determined workers and tended only to bring the law into disrepute. Even the prosecution of one or two 'ringleaders' had to be approached cautiously, because if prosecution failed strikers could consider their action justified, and the last card had been played. On 5 June 1943 Galbraith wrote to London saying that employers were becoming increasingly reluctant to rely on prosecution to bring strikes to an end, because of the consequences of failure.[55] Similar doubts about the prosecution weapon were expressed in a major memorandum by Bevin himself only a few days later. On the whole, Bevin thought that the trade unions had been strengthened by Order 1305 in dealing with sporadic troubles, but that the penal clauses of the Order could put Executives in a difficult position: when they pointed out to strikers the legal consequences of their action, they could be seen as threatening them with imprisonment. Bevin suggested that this could lead to 'a weakening of trade union executive authority and control'.[56] In general it was felt that the exercise of trade union discipline through the trade union officials was the way to deal with strikes, but when these disputes became more persistent and frequent then recourse to prosecution or the threat of prosecution could subvert the very authority it was intended to support.

In the autumn of 1943 a major strike occurred in Barrow which brought the authority of the AEU Executive into question. The Total Time strike had merely put the local officials and District Committees under pressure; in this dispute, on the other hand, both the District Committee and the local official supported the strike. In addition, the Barrow strike had an important national dimension that was missing from its predecessors, in that it was directed quite directly against the state's central means of wage regulation, that is against a decision of the National Arbitration Tribunal itself. Its outcome was therefore a matter of interest to all trade union members up and down the country, since they were all affected by NAT decisions. The Barrow strike also marked a turning point in the history of wartime industrial relations, in that it was the first truly offensive strike since June 1941 and the left's change of line.

Barrow then, even more than today, was an isolated town with a strong sense of community. Almost the only employer in the town was Vickers-Armstrong, who also owned many of the houses. The Vickers shipyard and engineering works was an enormous concern stretching along the coast; even today its giant cranes tower over the town, an ever-present symbol of the importance of the shipyard. Practically all the men, and many of the women, worked at Vickers for Lord Craven, and those who did not were dependent on Vickers or its workers for custom. Ever since 1902 the Vickers workers had been paid by a system of payment by results known as the premium bonus system, which had been strongly opposed by the Amalgamated Society of Engineers wherever it operated. Under this system, a man was allocated a time for a job, as

218

under normal piece-work. However, his bonus was limited by the ingenious device of paying him a maximum of one half of his basic rate for the time 'saved' on the job (if any). The problem from the workers' point of view is readily seen, because the system set a ceiling on piece-work earnings while making anything over a fifty per cent bonus extremely difficult to attain, as the time 'saved' rapidly approached the total amount of time allocated to the job. By this simple method piece-work earnings were kept relatively low.

The national engineering pay claim which led to the NAT award No. 326 introduced a new complication into this existing local problem. The AEU at the Executive level had been concerned to improve basic pay by consolidating part of the existing national bonus into the basic rate, which could not easily be withdrawn at the end of the war in the event of a depression.[57] The NAT award accepted that £1 should be consolidated, but a difficulty arose for piece-workers. The NAT decision specified that the new basic rate would be 66s., and that piece-work times should be fixed so that workers 'of average ability' could earn 27½ per cent over the basic rate. The employers initially took this to mean that the £1 was not to be consolidated for the purpose of fixing piece-work times (which was clearly not the intention of the award), but later took the view that piece-work times would have to be adjusted downwards to yield 27½ per cent over the new base rate of 66s. In other words, if someone earned 46s. on the basic rate, plus 60 per cent on piece-work, he would earn 107s. 1d., but if he earned 66s. on the new base rate plus only 27½ per cent on piece-work he would suffer a sizeable wage cut, as he would earn only 97s. 8d.[58] The employers had been allowed sufficient room by the NAT's decision to make such an interpretation, but it was one which intensely annoyed low-paid engineers like those at Barrow, because they saw the possibility of wage cuts.

The dispute had a long history that had its roots in the engineers' hatred of the premium bonus system, but its immediate origins lay in a local conference held during May 1943, when the Vickers representatives made no concessions to the men's demand that time-saved earnings should be paid in the proportion of 85 per cent to the worker and fifteen per cent to the company. As a result, at a second works conference the men became 'more bitter' according to Ford, the AEU's Divisional Organiser, and asked that the whole award be referred back to the Executive. At this time there were eight or nine districts in this division alone asking Ford for clarification of the award. After starting and then abandoning a go-slow to force the issue, the District Committee called a mass meeting on 24 August recommending that twenty-one days' notice of strike action be given, and demanding all bonuses to be paid on the new 66s. base rate.[59] The recommendation was adopted by all but six of the five thousand present. After nine days the Executive informed the Ministry of Labour that they had withdrawn the strike notice, and instructed the Barrow District Committee to inform the members accordingly.[60] The District Committee replied immediately that they disagreed with the EC's action.[61] As a result, the EC instructed the District Committee that they were to hold a mass meeting on 16 September to make the EC's views clear, and required the District Committee and District Secretary to sign undertakings that they would then and at all future times abide by the rules of the AEU and the decisions of the EC.[62] The District Committee refused to sign the declaration and surrendered control of the strike to the shop stewards, who proceeded with the mass meeting. The meeting decided unanimously to take strike action, and stopped work the same day. In fact, many of the engineers had already greased their tools and put them away in anticipation of the decision.[63]

On 22 September the District Committee was suspended and the Secretary, sixty-four-year-old Bill Heron, was sacked, although he was in fact paid by district levy.[64] The dispute was conducted by a strike committee elected from amongst the stewards; it had thirteen AEU and six ETU members, and was chaired by Thomas Trewartha of the AEU.[65] Until the beginning of the strike, Trewartha had confined himself to political activity, having been a Labour councillor in Barrow for five and a half years. He now took a leading part in running the stoppage, and consistently advocated keeping politics out of the dispute; although clearly immersed in local politics, he considered that they played no part in industrial affairs. At the Special Conference of the AEU held to discuss the problems within the union in November 1943, he still held this view, and remarked that the EC was in the grip of 'a political and industrial creed' and that political influence was 'damning the organisation. The AEU should be run for industrial purposes solely'.[66] His view was to be important in terms of the political direction that the strike took. The Communist Party received short shrift from the start of the stoppage. Very soon after its formation, the strike committee expelled two CP members from its meetings for attempting to make the strike a political issue.[67] When George Crane, the Communist National Organiser for the AEU, arrived on 22 September, he claimed that he was allowed only three minutes to speak to the strike committee and that he was threatened with being thrown down the stairs.[68]

Trewartha's attitude to the CP during this dispute epitomises the view taken by strikers of attempts by the CP to intervene in stoppages in the second half of the war. Indeed, it represented an enduring and deeply rooted aversion within the British trade union movement to the introduction of politics into trade union affairs. Despite the fact that Trewartha himself was very active in the local Labour Party, he and the strike committee rejected the CP's attempts to bring the strike to an end and expelled them from the committee when they publicly spoke out against the stoppage. Political activity was one thing, to be carried out in Parliament and local councils; trade union activity was quite another, to be carried out in the workplace and the trade unions. Although shop stewards were very often prepared to link the two (by encouraging payment of the political levy, for example) when they were not in open conflict with their employers, they were not prepared to have political reasoning used against them when they were on strike. The important thing, they thought, was the fight with their employers, and the criterion which they applied to political activity was whether or not it furthered their dispute. In this case, it clearly did not.

The strike committee lost no time in organising an active

strike which sought to extend the dispute within Vickers, to look for support outside the district, and to involve as many of the engineers as they possibly could. Appeals were sent out all over the country asking for financial support, and by the end of the strike over £3,000 had been subscribed, including £450 collected at Vickers Crayford (London) factory in the space of just two days.[69] On 23 September the District Committee received support from an unexpected quarter, when the Huddersfield District Committee (on which ILP members were influential) resigned in protest at the EC's suspension of their Barrow colleagues.[70] While the strike was receiving more support and attracting more interest externally, it was also spreading within Barrow: by 25 September the women workers and apprentices had joined the men outside the Vickers gates, bringing the proportion of employees out to almost one hundred per cent.[71] Nevertheless, there were still one or two people working, and the picketing which had been going on 'developed on more robust lines' at mid-day on Thursday 24 September, when between fifteen hundred and two thousand people accompanied an AEU member all the way to his house in Island Road. The man was escorted by the police and 'subjected to a lot of booing and called many uncomplimentary names' all the way home and back again.[72] Meanwhile, the strike committee's social subcommittee arranged entertainments including a social at the town hall and a 'needle' football match between the AEU and ETU teams, while the Irish Nationalist and St Mary's Clubs were thrown open for the use of all during the stoppage.[73]

By 30 September, when the NAT met to hear the submissions of the unions and the EEF on the interpretation of Award 326, the strike had been on for almost a fortnight. On 28 September the NAT confirmed that their only requirements were that the consolidated pound should not force a reduction on anyone, and that piece-work should yeild 27½ per cent on the new basic rate.[74] Vickers stated that they had always been prepared to pay the new basic rate, but only subject to the terms of the award, which provided for a 'maximum' 27½ per cent.[75] The main objective of the strike had not been achieved, and accordingly the strike committee recommended no return; when Trewartha suggested to a mass meeting held at Hilker Street football ground that they return to work under protest while continuing to try to get the award overturned, his proposal was 'overwhelmingly rejected'. A motion was passed instead calling for the strike to continue until satisfaction was gained on the bonus issue, calling on the Ministry of Labour to intervene, and condemning the EC of the AEU for suspending the District Committee and requesting their reinstatement.[76]

For the Ministry of Labour to have intervened would have been to break the Ministry's policy. Bevin had always preferred to leave officials to deal with disputes; to intervene directly would serve only to undermine their authority. This particular case was unusual in that the District Committee and District Secretary were unwilling to exercise any influence to obtain a return (and were in any case suspended), but Bevin brought the 'strongest possible pressure' to bear on the union leadership while reminding the rank and file that the NAT's decision was both final and binding, that the strike was illegal and that they should go back to work.[77] The EC of the AEU was in any case taking exceptionally strong steps to end the dispute, which were condemned as 'Hitler tactics' by the Barrow shop stewards.[78] George Crane, the National Organiser, had been instructed to go to Barrow on 22 September, where he joined his counterpart and CP comrade Frank Foulkes, National Organiser for the ETU.[79] Wal Hannington, the well known CP member and AEU National Organiser, had been sent to Huddersfield to look into the resignation of the District Committee there. Crane worked hard to try to end the strike, negotiating with Vickers and then speaking to the strike committee, constantly shuttling back and forth between them. His task was made easier after the NAT's clarification of its position, since the strike committee had hoped that the NAT would support its interpretation; when it did not, the committee had come round to thinking that the strike should be ended.[80] But the rank and file, despite the constant calls from the EC to return, had yet to be convinced.

It took until 5 October for Crane to negotiate an acceptable settlement with Vickers. A new system of payment was agreed upon. The premium bonus system was abolished and another more closely resembling normal piece-work was established. Premium bonus times were not to be reduced by 13.3 per cent as the company had originally wished, but only by 10 per cent. For jobs which had a piece-work time already, times were to be reduced by one sixth.[81] At the last mass meeting of the strike six thousand people, 'including a good proportion of women', decided to return to work on this basis.[82]

The Barrow strike had ended in a compromise with the company that left the NAT Award 326 unscathed; in other words, although the award had at least been clarified on its margins to ensure that nobody actually received a reduction, the problem of the low basic rate and of low-earning piece-workers had not been even partially solved. Locally, the compromise proved quite beneficial to the Vickers workers, if the optimistic statements of outsiders can be believed. By the middle of January 1944 it was estimated that the average increase among the skilled men since the strike amounted to 17½ per cent—over £1 a week.[83] Outstanding cases of women's pay under the Relaxation Agreement had been settled, bringing a number of women back-pay at Christmas ranging from £10 to £60.[84] Yet the strike left behind it a residue of bitterness against the EC and also against the Communist Party, whose most important officials had played such a leading role. The bitterness against the Executive spread amongst a thin layer of district activists throughout the union nationally. The Barrow District Committee was not reinstated after the strike had ended, and the Barrow shop stewards circulated other districts with their inter-pretation of the affair.

It was in order to try to clear the air amongst these activists that the AEU Executive decided to call a Special National Conference, the first since June 1922. The conference was to discuss affairs in the AEU generally, but was in fact largely taken up with discussing what had happened at Barrow. Two or three delegates from all districts attended, together with all Divisional and National Organisers.[85] It had originally been intended that no delegates should attend from Barrow but, according to the Barrow stewards, 'CP snoopers' urged the EC to allow some delegates to attend so that Barrow would not be discussed behind their backs and the EC thereby shown in an unfavourable light.[86] Crane was therefore instructed to hold a meeting of shop stewards to elect two delegates; the members of the District Committee were left to demonstrate with placards outside the Holborn Hall.[87] Many of the delegates, including several of the CP members, thought that the District Committee should be reinstated. Some criticised the EC bitterly: Gray of Glasgow accused it of suspending the Committee at the instigation of the EEF, and said that the EC was tied to the war machine (to which Tanner replied that he 'wanted to make it quite plain that the Union was part of the war machine'), while Beale of Huddersfield stated that the District Committee there had resigned because of its dealings with the EC generally and not just because of the Barrow affair.[88] Several speakers agreed with Billy Stokes that seventy-five to eighty per cent of the members had been in sympathy with the strikers; Stokes went on to argue that they needed support and called for the lifting of the suspensions.[89] In reply, Joe Scott of the EC (and CP) stressed that there were those in the employing class who were not concerned about beating fascism, and who had encouraged the EC to attack Barrow. Scott said that he would not attack Barrow, and called at the same time for 'more trust and loyalty'.[90] Tanner ended the second day of the conference—which he had begun by reminding all present that they had no power as a meeting to take formal decisions—by saying that there were elements 'prepared to gang up against the EC' and that the Executive was prepared to fight them. If the suspension of the District Committee was lifted, he said, then *Socialist Appeal* and other such papers would say that the EC had backed down. He hoped that the conference had cleared relations between the membership and the EC.[91]

The conference had not, however, entirely managed this. When it was over, the Barrow shop stewards circularised districts with a leaflet entitled *Facts v. Filth,* asking the questions 'Where are we going?', and 'Of *whom* is our EC the servants?' Attacking the arguments used by the EC at the conference and commenting on the role of the CP,

225

the leaflet ended by asking:

> Fellow members—Where *are* we going? We the Barrow shop stewards say, to pawn us in 1922, if we allow the present lack-a-daisical methods of our E.C. to continue, of *whom* is our E.C. the servants? *Ours* if we fight and deserve it, the Communist's Party *[sic]* if we do not.
>
> On November 19th, Bro. Tanner and Bro. Gardner met the Employers in Manchester to discuss ways and means to smash unofficial strikes.[92]

The Barrow stewards had made a classic statement of the traditions of local democratic control which are so central to the history of the AEU; it was clear that these traditions were very much alive at the end of 1943. It is interesting to note how the Barrow stewards had included the CP in their tirade against the Executive. As the CP had had more and more trade union officials elected to office in the late 1930s and even more during the war, they were becoming more closely identified with the union machinery; from time to time after mid-1941, the price they had to pay was unpopularity amongst some of the activists in the union. It is important, therefore, to approach with care statements made later by George Crane about the situation in Barrow. Crane claimed in May 1944, writing in the AEU's *Monthly Journal,* that 'substantial benefits' had materialised from Award 326, that membership had increased, and that the reinstated District Committee 'is a contrast to the old methods of working; it is more constructive and understands the responsibility of leadership'.[93] Although Crane was probably right when he spoke of the changed atmosphere on the District Committee, Award 326 could not basically solve the problem of the relatively low basic rate being paid nationally, because it did not add any new cash but merely consolidated part of the 'national bonus' into the basic rate. Although the local discontents lapsed into quiescence, a good deal of the material basis for them remained.

It is at the same time important to point out that the Barrow strike, in so far as it had a national dimension, had failed. The NAT Award 326 remained essentially intact

*New Propellor*, March 1943

despite the attempts of the local engineers to have it revised. Barrow had been a test case which had been watched closely by engineers throughout Britain, because it involved an important issue. Even though the Vickers strikers had not established any principle of national application, there were still to be important disputes over the award: at A.V. Roe's Woodford works the members twice overturned deals on the implementation of the award negotiated in 1944, during a strike which threatened to spread to the whole A.V. Roe group.[94] There can be little doubt that if the Barrow engineers had won, there would have been a national movement for similar advances throughout the industry. This was precisely the reason for the NAT's refusal to change its original decision, of course, and their ability to hold the line ensured the preservation of the tribunal's authority.

During the Barrow strike there had been hints that the Workers' International League was taking some interest, and these hints were to harden into reliable evidence in some later disputes. Roy Tearse, the Industrial Organiser of the WIL, had been to Barrow, and *Socialist Appeal* had published detailed reports of the strike, but a spokesman for the strike committee publicly denied suggestions that anyone on the committee was attached to any such organisation.[95] The determination of Trewartha and the committee to keep politics out of the dispute certainly suggests that the spokesman was right and that he was not simply being defensive when speaking to reporters from the local paper. It seems unlikely that the WIL played any real part in the strike, but it may have made some contact with activists there, since a representative or representatives had been present at the first meeting of the Militant Workers' Federation before the strike, in early June 1943 in Glasgow.[96] The WIL and the ILP had set up this organisation at a meeting in the ILP rooms in Dundas Street, Glasgow, on 4 and 5 June 1943 to coordinate militant activity in industry and, as the ILP shop stewards' pamphlet put it, to work 'for a national link-up of stewards'.[97]

The Militant Workers' Federation had its first meeting in Glasgow—which was no coincidence, as it had been at a meeting in Glasgow that the Clyde Workers' Committee had 'proclaimed itself revived' in May 1943. Like the CWC of the First World War, delegates did not have to represent anybody except themselves, although many of them were stewards and the eventual aim was the affiliation of shop stewards' committees. The committee's precarious claim to be descended from the original CWC derived merely from the fact that two of the old committee's members attended its meetings.[98] The other members of the committee are not all known, but seem to have included three shop stewards at the North British Locomotive Co.'s Queen's Park works, Doherty, the ex-departmental convenor at Beardmore's Parkhead Forge (until he was suspended from office for twelve months for criticising the District Committee) and two or three shop stewards from Rolls-Royce Hillington.[99] Roy Tearse was elected secretary. He was the WIL's Industrial Organiser and an ex-shop steward from De Havilland Edgware who was excused military service for medical reasons.[100] It is almost certain that this is not an exhaustive list, but some tentative conclusions may be drawn from the members that we know. Despite the fact that the committee only existed on the fringes of shop steward organisation, it had collectively a good deal of experience available to it and was in a position to know what went on in the most important local factories.

The Clyde Workers' Committee was regarded as a model organisation by the WIL, and the Militant Workers' Federation was conceived of as a federation of similar bodies throughout Britain. Such overblown hopes were never to materialise, the MWF remaining a tiny body organised amongst a very narrow group of shop stewards on a very general 'militant' basis. The MWF's programme, adopted at its first meeting, could perhaps be accurately described as syndicalist. Indeed, most of its programmes, if not all, could be accepted by members of the CP. The programme comprised of:

1. The coordination of all militant trade union activity
2. The annulment of all anti-working-class legislation
3. Every shop a closed shop
4. Workers' control of transfers
5. a) A higher standard of life for all workers
   b) A better standard of wages and allowances for workers

in the forces

6. A national confederation of workers' committees

7. Workers' control of industry.[101]

Neither the CWC nor the MWF ever publicly issued any other programme. It was not perhaps surprising, then, that the MWF was able to extend its contacts within the engineering unions on such a general basis. By about the end of 1943 an internal WIL document stated that the MWF had some support on eight AEU District Committees, and that forty shop stewards' committees had also declared their support for it.[102] All such claims, even when made internally, must, of course, be treated with a degree of scepticism; inflated estimates of support within left-wing organisations could be used by the leadership to encourage a small beleaguered membership to believe that their efforts were meeting with some success. Whatever the reality, the Ministry of Labour, possibly over-anxiously, was quite concerned by the early growth of the MWF in industrial disputes. In November 1943 Galbraith wrote directly to Bevin asking for support of an unspecified kind in dealing with it. In substantiation of his request, he wrote: '[The MWF] seems to be acquiring increasing influence, and because of this to be able more readily to undermine official trade union authority.'[103] It was to be some months before Bevin took any action to deal with the problems which Galbraith had brought to his attention. When he did he was to take a major legislative initiative designed to deal not only with the MWF but also with a much wider stratum of trade-unionists.

Bevin was forced into amending the defence regulations because of a resurgence of apprentice militancy caused by the proposal to draft one in ten apprentices into the coal mines. A momentary crisis occurred while Britain prepared for the invasion of continental Europe in the summer of 1944. The manpower options open to the government in its attempts to boost coal and munitions production while expanding the armed forces were very restricted. All of the available labour was already mobilised, so that any labour required by one particular sector had to be taken directly from another. Yet the Cabinet considered it had no option but to draft apprentices into the mines. Many workers felt that there was another option: returning the miners scattered throughout other industries and the services to the pits, but this appears to have been ruled out.[104]

The coal industry was the sector most fundamental to the war economy, and at the same time the most problematic in terms of its contribution. Production in the mines had fallen steadily from 1942 (204 million tons of deep-mined coal) to 1944 (184 million tons), and was to fall further in 1945.[105] One of the reasons for this was the increasing average age of the miners. Another was the high strike rate—the highest in all of British industry. But whatever the reasons, coal was the foundation on which the economy rested, and its position had to be guaranteed if the opening of the second front was to be a success. On 2 December 1943 Bevin announced a scheme to select young men to go into the pits rather than into the services. The scheme was to be carried out by ballot, and about one in ten were to be selected. Young workers from the engineering and shipbuilding industries who had either reached the age of twenty or had already finished their apprenticeships, were to be included. If chosen, either the lads themselves or their employers could apply for exemption, but it was made perfectly clear that very few exemptions would be granted.[106]

The scheme is admitted by Bevin's biographer to have been 'highly unpopular'.[107] Neither parents nor their sons relished the idea of the boys being sent down pits, where the work was arduous and accidents common. The apprentices of the North-East and Scotland objected particularly strongly; they felt that they had real skills to offer in the engineering and shipbuilding industries, and wanted to complete their apprenticeships to their trades. It is important to stress here the position of the apprentices in the marine engineering shops. In 1941 the employers in the North-East had explained to the Ministry of Labour that it was impossible to employ either transferred machinists or women on a number of skilled machining jobs, because they considered that they lacked either the particular skills or the manual strength required. The only answer they could think of was to use existing apprentices, who had some idea of the methods involved. The Ministry of Labour therefore recommended that they follow a determined policy of 'dilution' with the apprentices, because the number of skilled men required was considerably below that needed in Scotland, where such a scheme was impracticable. The only drawback the employers could see was that the apprentices were 'disgruntled'; it was 'not a bit of use taking a job to them with the old price, they just turn their back on the lathe'.[108] In the North-East in particular, the apprentices could see their own importance in the marine engineering shops. Moreover, youths in marine engineering secured relatively large rises during 1943: between January and July 1943 they increased their earnings from 112.2 per cent over the October 1938 level to 147 per cent above it, compared to 60.3 per cent and 77 per cent respectively in the case of adult male workers.[109] In other words, just as things were starting to get rather better for young workers in this sector of engineering, they had to face the prospect of being sent down a pit.

The apprentices' strikes of 1944 occurred in a rather different trade union context from former boys' strikes in that, formally at least, if slowly and at times clumsily, the AEU was evolving a structure that recognised the separate needs of young workers. In 1940 the Executive had recommended the establishment of junior workers' committees, but in 1941 it became clear in the case of Manchester—where a 'Central Junior Male Workers' Committee' had been envisaged in April 1941 with its own constitution—that the EC intended to exercise strong control over the form that these committees took.[110] It did not approve of the Manchester committee's constitution, which it called 'very far-reaching', and instructed the District Committee that no such body was to be set up.[111] In 1942 when a model constitution had been prepared, the Manchester District Committee was unable to persuade a single apprentice member to attend.[112] At the end of 1943, with the threat of the 'Bevin boy' scheme in the background, a general meeting of apprentices in the Manchester district rejected the EC's proposed constitution and called for shop steward representation of apprentices.[113] The number of apprentice members in the district moved slowly upwards between January 1943 (4,775) and June

232

1944 (5,104), as interest in union affairs developed with the first suggestion of the ballot scheme in the summer of 1943 and the concern aroused by its application in the spring of 1944.[114] By the end of 1943 the AEU nationally had a total membership of 100,701 boys and youths.[115] On Tyneside, however, there was no Junior Workers' Committee until the end of March 1944 (at least according to the local Ministry of Labour).[116] If there was one before that date it must have had a shadowy existence indeed, as the union officials were reported at that time as having to do 'everything possible' to set one up.[117] Nevertheless, despite the fact that the Junior Workers' Committees did not really function until after the apprentices' strikes had actually begun, the idea had gained momentum since 1941 and union officials and District Committee members were much more aware of union policy on the matter than they had been only a few years earlier. This was to be an important factor in the course of the 1944 strikes.

A few days before Christmas 1943, at the inaugural meeting of the unofficial Tyneside Apprentices' Guild in the Socialist Hall, Newcastle, a campaign began on Tyneside against the Bevin scheme, probably in concert with some apprentices on the Clyde.[118] The meeting elected three officers: C. Hepplewhite, an apprentice fitter from the North-East Marine Engineering Co. (chairman), J.C. Brown, an apprentice plater from the Middle Docks and Engineering Co., South Shields, and J.W. Davy, from the Wallsend Slipway Co. (secretary).[119] The local Ministry of Labour officials had excellent information on these apprentice leaders, and sent it to London. That on the first two boys described them as having 'no political inclinations', but Bill Davy was rather different: '[He] has strong political views—fluent speaker—strong personality—has had Communist views since age 14—recently expelled from the Communist Party on account of his activities in connection with the Apprentices' Guild.'[120] Bill Davy was in fact in close touch with Roy Tearse at this time.[121]

The first lad to be called up for mining duties was an apprentice called Martin, who worked for an electrical contractor. The reaction of the Tyneside Apprentices'

Guild was organised very quickly; members called at all the labour exchanges along the Tyne and informed the managers that unless Martin's call-up was cancelled there would be a strike on 14 March. Similar notices were received by factory and yard staff.[122] The problem was that Martin's case was not a very clear one; the Ministry of Labour had already ascertained that he might be eligible for deferment, but at the same time were anxious not to give the impression that they were climbing down.[123] The boys had decided to lobby their MPs, but received no information from them. At least one of the MPs (Ritson) had in any case already asked the Ministry of Labour what he was to say to the boys. He was told to tell them: ' "Go home and go back to work. The right way to handle this is to take it up through your union officials. . ." [it was] emphasised that above all things the Minister would want to avoid any appearance that these apprentices were being given any recognition whatsoever. Mr. Ritson took the point very cordially.'[124] The result of the lobby was disappointment for the boys, but on 11 March it appeared that victory was theirs, since Martin received notice of his call-up being cancelled. Martin's call-up was later withdrawn (although precisely when is unknown), but it appears that a certain amount of confusion had been created amongst the apprentices and 14 March came and went without incident.[125]

The TAG had held their first 'mass meeting' on 11 March, but (possibly because Martin's call-up had been deferred) was something of a flop, as only about two hundred boys turned up. The committee issued their first bulletin in which they called for speakers, workers and couriers to help run the dispute.[126] On 12 March they took up the cases of three eighteen-year-old apprentices who had been called up; they contacted the Clydeside apprentices, and on 13 March notice was simultaneously served on the Tyne and the Clyde that if these boys' call-up to the pits was not cancelled there would be a strike on 28 March.[127] The TAG then, had chosen to take up an anomaly whereby lads under twenty could be conscripted, and in fact had already written a letter to Bevin demanding that the anomaly be rectified.[128] This letter, it appears, was written not by Davy but by Jock Haston of the

Revolutionary Communist Party (as the WIL had renamed itself after merging with the even tinier Revolutionary Socialist League in early March 1944), and typed by Ann Keen of the same organisation.[129] At the same time, the trade union officials were trying to breathe life into the Junior Workers' Committee. One of the problems they faced was the fact that only a small proportion of the apprentices were members of the AEU, and could not therefore be reached by the JWC. Nevertheless, the secretary of the JWC since its foundation, nineteen-year-old William Kennedy (an apprentice fitter at the Wallsend Slipway Co.), began to argue forcefully against the strike.[130] It was now that Davy decided, before the strike began, to leave the TAG and join the JWC in order to oppose Kennedy from within his own organisation.[131]

On 27 March the apprentices lobbied Parliament again, but failing to gain any more satisfaction than on their previous visit there, they struck simultaneously on Monday 28 March on the Clyde and Tyne and in Huddersfield.[132] The first day of the strike saw about six thousand apprentices out on the Tyne, of whom 3,473 were in shipbuilding and 2,560 in engineering; this left a considerable number still at work, but on the Tuesday another twelve hundred came out.[133] On the Wednesday seven thousand apprentices were reported as having struck on the Clyde, although in two instances the boys had returned after only a few hours.[134] Galbraith suggested that the strike was not all solid in the West of Scotland; on the Tyne, however, even the *Newcastle Journal and North Mail* had to admit on the 28th that the majority of the Tyne apprentices were out.[135] By 30 March only 4,800 apprentices were out on the Clyde (about thirty-five per cent of the total).[136] By 30 March the local union officials were beginning to have some success in challenging the TAG for leadership of the Tyne strike. On that day they addressed a 'rather stormy' meeting at Swan Hunter's recreation ground in Wallsend. The TAG had a picket on the entrance, and refused admission to the press and to apprentices who were known to be opposed to the strike. The officials offered to meet representatives of the strikers, but not members of the TAG, with whom they refused to deal. They claimed that recruitment into the mines 'should not affect' the boys. The problem was that the meeting wanted the TAG to represent them—the TAG was, as one of them later put it, 'government of the apprentices, by the apprentices, for the apprentices'.[137] The union officials closed the meeting but later, after a meeting of a section of the strikers, they were asked to see a deputation, which they agreed to do providing that they were not TAG representatives.[138]

Kennedy of the JWC was also working hard to prevent the strike from beginning. He had been touring the yards and engineering shops, urging the lads to stay at work and to allow the local officials to take the matter up, and telling them that they and their employers could apply for deferment. At Vickers Armstrong, the most important engineering factory on the Tyne, Kennedy succeeded in persuading the large number of boys who worked in No. 22 shop to stay at work, despite the fact that about half the boys in the factory as a whole had stopped work. His success was publicised on the front page of the *Journal and North Mail*'s issue of 3 April, together with the information that he had been similarly effective at C.A. Parsons.[139] On the Clyde the District Committees and officials had solidly opposed the strike from the start, and it seems to have started to disintegrate rather more quickly than on the Tyne. A mass meeting on Glasgow Green on 31 March was reported by Galbraith to have been 'a flop', while John Brown's yard had decided to return to work by 1 April.[140] Three days later, only 3,087 apprentices were on strike on the Clyde, and the dispute would have ended had it not been for the victimisation of some lads at John Brown's.[141] In both areas the Ministry of Labour itself was putting considerable pressure on the strikers, calling up boys selected for the pits for medical examination prior to conscription into the services.[142] The choice was thus made clear to the boys: it was either the services or the mines; but the Ministry of Labour regarded those selected as conscripted, and if they did not want to go into the coal industry they could go into the services instead. By the end of the week the Tyneside boys were isolated, as their Clydeside and Huddersfield support had completely disappeared. During April the press was suggesting forcefully that the Trotskyists were involved in the dispute, which became something of an embarrassment to the apprentices. Lurid reports detailed their exploits (often with a wealth of factual error), stressed their extremism and their recent readmission to the Fourth International, and misspelt their names.[143] Under these pressures the strike began to crumble on Tyneside, and by 12 April the last of the strikers had straggled back to work.

On earlier occasions there had been whispers of Trotskyist and ILP involvement in disputes, but these apprentices' strikes drew a much louder reiteration of the allegations. The role that they had played in the strike was, however, small; indeed, it had been if anything slightly greater in previous strikes. During the Rolls-Royce strike in 1943 the extreme left had been thought responsible for tipping the balance in favour of stopping work not only at Hillington (see p. 289) but also at the other plants affected. Inter-district cooperation had been a feature of previous apprentices' strikes as well as the present one. The extension to Huddersfield may well have been tied in with the ILP influence there, but it constituted in any case a small and unstable addition to the ranks of the strikers. The Trotskyists had produced forty-eight thousand copies of three different leaflets, the main one being *Fight The Pit Compulsion Plot,* which was apparently distributed amongst miners as well as the apprentices.[144] They had also persuaded the boys' own battle nor was it a demand limited exclusively to the RCP. A certain amount of clerical help had been provided, but on the whole the RCP's influence had been marginal RCP. A certain amount of clerical help had been provided, but on the whole the RCP's influence had been marginal to the course of the dispute. The ILP, which had also supported the boys with a leaflet (entitled *Why The ILP Supports the Apprentices*), had also demanded the nationalisation of the mines under workers' control, and asked workers for full support for the boys and an end to the industrial truce.[145] Their actual impact on the strike (with the possible exception of the extension to Huddersfield) seems to have been limited to the gratitude expressed by some boys in the *New Leader* for the support they received.[146] As for the Clyde Workers' Committee, Harry

McShane .(a member of the original CWC) put his finger on their weakness with great accuracy when he wrote of them on the day the strike broke out: 'Despite bombastic promises they have never led a successful strike.'[147] According to McShane, who covered the apprentices' strikes for the *Daily Worker*, the CWC's main activity was spreading rumours about the effect of the ballot scheme.[148] McShane's evidence might be considered somewhat dubious, as he was not well disposed towards the 'so-called' CWC, but Galbraith's reports tend to support the general impression that the CWC had not been very prominent amongst the boys' supporters.[149] The support which he pinpointed came from a group of ex-CP members, now members of the Workers' Open Forum, who ran a 'solidarity press' and printed the apprentices' leaflets for them free of charge.[150]

Although the *Daily Worker* had not given a great deal of coverage to earlier strikes (indeed, it ignored some sizeable disputes altogether), it had joined in the general chorus of condemnation of the RCP and ILP. The line taken (in the absence of any employers to condemn for causing the dispute) was to stress the political influence of these groups to the point of gross hyperbole. Thus, an article in the *Daily Worker* of 4 April was entitled 'Lads Duped to Aid Trotskyist and ILP Anti-War Campaign', and four days later another article claimed that the ILP had fomented the strike on the Clyde and in Huddersfield.[151] The very real feelings of discontent and fear which reigned amongst the apprentices were not mentioned and rather than attack the boys for their action the paper attacked the extreme left for 'rumour-mongering'.

Bevin had been well aware of the role of the extreme left in the disturbances in the engineering industry in the summer and autumn of 1943, through the reports which he had received from local officials, and he had drawn attention to the Trotskyists' activities at that time.[152] When the apprentices' strikes loomed on the horizon, therefore, the Ministry and the press alike were already sensitised to the question. At the end of February, Leggett, Deputy Secretary at the Ministry, after examining reports from the districts, wrote a note in which he remarked: 'I think it is extremely clear from this that the militant socialist movement is playing an exceedingly active part not only in the apprentices' agitation but also in the mine workers' troubles. . . it is likely that the Minister will be asked to take steps to intern these agitators.'[153] In March, Low, from Headquarters, wrote to Emmerson in Newcastle: '. . . it appears that it would be extremely useful to find out exactly who is at the back of the Clydeside Apprentices' Committee and the Tyneside Apprentices' Committee. One gets the impression that there must be an adult mind here, and it seems to me that your means of investigation might be able to get to the bottom of the matter.'[154] Four days later Emmerson began filing reports from J.L. Wilcock, local officer of the Ministry of Information.[155] On 5 April the police Special Branch raided the RCP's North-East headquarters (a house in Walker-on-Tyne), Davy's house in Wallsend and the RCP's headquarters in Harrow Road, London, to gather information.[156] These raids led to charges being brought against Jock Haston (Organising Secretary), Roy Tearse (Industrial Organiser), Heaton Lee (North-East Area Organiser) and Ann Keen. The charges, under the 1875 Conspiracy and Protection of Property Act and the 1927 Trades Disputes Act, were of conspiracy to cause an illegal dispute, inciting such a dispute and furthering it.[157] The four RCP members were found guilty of furthering the dispute but innocent of the other charges. Tearse and Lee were sentenced to twelve months each, Haston to six and Keen to thirteen days (which meant her immediate release).[158] In September the Court of Appeal quashed the sentences on the grounds that the prosecution had not shown that the four had furthered the strike after it had begun, and one could not 'further' a strike that had not begun.[159] Needless to say, the result of the appeal was hailed as 'a victory for Labour' (as the RCP leaflet put it), a victory that they felt was clearly forced by the agitation of the Anti-Labour Laws Victims' Defence Committee set up to campaign for the release of the three in prison.[160]

Bevin's biographer, Alan Bullock, wrote of the Minister's earlier public statements on Trotskyist activities that the grounds for them were 'a mystery'. The Trotskyists' role on Tyneside was 'hardly on a scale to justify Bevin's belief that political motives played a significant part in industrial discontent'. The only explanation which Bullock could offer was that the 'wartime strain' was beginning to tell on Bevin.[161] In fact, however, Bevin acted, in 1944 at least, on the information available to him in the reports of the local officials of both his own and other ministries. Much of this information is still not available to researchers under the fifty- and hundred-year rules imposed on parts of the public records, but quite enough is now available to make the grounds for his allegations quite clear. And it certainly was not always Bevin who took the lead in instigating witch-hunts for Trotskyists, as shown by Leggett's note stating that it was likely that the Minister would be asked to take steps to intern the agitators. He could have interned the Trotskyists under the defence regulations, but he chose not to. He decided instead to initiate a prosecution under longstanding legislation, and at the same time to initiate a new and draconian regulation (Regulation 1AA) directed at a much wider stratum of activists within the trade union movement who might under certain circumstances consider strike action as an option.

Bevin dealt with the situation in this way because he was faced with a crisis in industrial relations which went far beyond the problem caused by a handful of extremists. He was too experienced a trade union leader to think that the Trotskyists 'caused' strikes, but he did realise that such groups could play a significant role when the trade union movement was balanced on a knife-edge.[162] Between 24 January and 11 April, when preparations for the invasion of the continent were at an advanced stage, there were strikes that accounted for no less than 1,850,000 working days lost in the mining industry, while apart from the apprentices' strikes, thirty thousand engineers and shipyard workers were out in Belfast because of the imprisonment of five shop stewards by the Northern Ireland government.[163] This constituted the largest conglomeration of stoppages in the two industries since the beginning of the war. Moreover, while the miners' strikes were caused by the 'Porter' pay award, and were therefore wage grievances, the apprentices' disputes had an important political dimension. As many commentators both within and outside the Ministry of

Labour pointed out, the boys' strike constituted a direct challenge to the government's right to direct labour where it saw fit. Such a challenge was not only not to be tolerated, but could not be allowed to recur.

The apprentices' strikes have to be seen as part of a process of which these strikes marked the apex: a process, though uneven and irregular, that was nevertheless quite perceptible to those who had the Ministry of Labour's files open to them. It involved a number of closely interrelated tendencies: strikes were causing an increasing number of working days to be lost, were drawing in workers other than those involved in the original dispute, and were becoming harder for the trade union executives to solve. More importantly, from strikes to defend trade union rights they had developed into offensive strikes against employers, strikes against decisions of the National Arbitration Tribunal, and now a strike against a government decision. Such a process could clearly not be arrested merely by trying or interning a few Trotskyists: much more fundamental measures were required.

The day before the last apprentices returned to work (11 April), Bevin presented a draft of the new regulation, 1AA, before the Trade Union Consultative Committee. A Ministry of Labour memorandum made its purpose plain: '[The Regulation] should strengthen the hands of Trade Unions in dealing with irresponsible elements.'[164] In its original form, as shown to the TUC at the Consultative Committee, the regulation provided for the prosecution of any person who declared, instigated, made anyone take part in, or otherwise acted in furtherance of a strike amongst workers engaged in essential services. This included any strike which was otherwise legal under Order 1305. The penalties laid down were five years penal servitude, a fine of £500, or both. 'Essential services' was to mean any workplace scheduled under the Essential Works Order. In short, it provided stiff penalties for anyone instigating or trying to extend a strike in a scheduled workplace, under any circumstances. It therefore made picketing illegal.[165]

The TUC made several suggestions, one of which caused some discussion at the meeting of the Consultative Committee. Dukes of the TUC pointed out that a trade union

241

official could be prosecuted if he inadvertently said something at a meeting which could be taken out of context and construed as instigating a strike.[166] Bevin replied that the regulation would not normally affect union officials, as a local official trying to act in accordance with the arbitration order would not incite a strike. On the other hand, '. . . some members of unions did instigate strikes against the advice of the responsible Executives, and such persons would be prosecuted under the new regulation.'[167] Bevin thereby tried to sidestep an amendment exempting speakers at meetings called in accordance with trade union rules. However, the amendment was accepted (Bevin left the room during the meeting), and it was later realised by the Ministry that under this particular clause shop stewards had also been allowed to slip through the net, since they were allowed, under AEU rules, to call a shop meeting for any purpose.[168] But it was not generally realised at the time that the regulation had such a loophole, and the new law caused a parliamentary furore. A minority of the left of the Labour Party, led by Aneurin Bevan, proposed a prayer in the House of Commons to annul the regulation. Bevan argued that it did not defend the unions as such, but the official 'who had arterio-sclerosis and cannot readjust himself to his membership'.[169] Bevin replied that his old opponent was advocating an unfettered right to strike, and was objecting to Order 1305 rather than to Regulation 1AA. Many of the Labour members decided, however, to abstain on the vote, so that although the prayer was defeated by the overwhelming majority of three hundred and fourteen to twenty-three, only fifty-six Labour members voted in favour, while one hundred and nine abstained.[170] Meanwhile outside Parliament, the CP and the E&ATSSNC carried on a campaign against the regulation.[171]

The regulation was never actually used against anyone, and this may have been because of its loophole, because of the opposition within the Labour Party, or because its enactment was sufficient. It seems reasonable to suggest that it was, in fact, effective in so far as legal regulations could be, in restricting the volume and scope of strikes; the details of the statutory instruments were not where the significance of Bevin's initiative lay. The point was that the regulation was successful in isolating potential strike leaders (and especially the extreme left), thereby stabilising industrial relations until military victory was secured.

Historians of wartime labour policy have consistently failed to come to grips in their accounts with the role of Regulation 1AA. The official historian simply ignored it, thereby leaving her later colleagues in some interpretative difficulty. As we have seen, Bullock felt that it was a 'mystery', while Michael Foot was almost as baffled by it.[172] A more recent historian asserted that it was intended to deal with the CP.[173] All these historians' difficulties arise from the fact that they have given accounts which could be called 'history with the shop floor politics left out'. According to them, Bevin, for all his vaunted abilities as Minister of Labour, suddenly over-reacted. Ironically, they underestimate the man. Bevin was well aware of the relationship between political agitation and industrial discontent in all its subtleties, and realised that when Trotskyists and ILP members were having even marginal influence in disputes they were only doing so because they were cutting very much with the grain.

Regulation 1AA ended a period of developing industrial unrest which had begun in the autumn of 1942 with the Total Time dispute. The evolution of the scope of these strikes was a matter of some concern to the state. There was a corresponding increase in governmental and police interest in industrial militants, which had seemed to have relaxed somewhat after the Soviet Union had entered the war. The Trotskyists were brought to trial under the Trades Disputes Act of 1927, and Bevin had considerable powers under the defence regulations to intern 'agitators'. Yet he chose to promulgate a new regulation because it was apparent that what was needed was a political announcement of the government's intention to come down hard on industrial militancy in general.

By taking this action, Bevin astutely exposed the limitations of the militancy which had arisen, which had its roots in the enormous economic strength of the engineers at the height of wartime mobilisation. Until the apprentices' strike of 1944, action had been directed almost exclusively at the employer. When the pre-invasion labour shortage necessitated directing one of the most combative groups—the apprentices—the boys had risen to the challenge. But this was exceptional and momentary. Bevin's intervention rested on the certainty that the political leadership of the shop stewards' movement would not seriously campaign against the regulation to the extent of defying it. Unlike the shop stewards' movement of the First World War, the E&ATSSNC was opposed to strike action and in favour of the vigorous prosecution of the war effort. The Trotskyists (who were in any case at this time mainly occupied with their own defence) were in no position to present themselves as an alternative leadership. Indeed, during a war against fascism which was supported almost unanimously by the British working class, there would be those who would deprecate the regulation, but nobody was willing openly and politically to defy it.

The tight labour market which had constituted the background to the disputes of the middle of the war was in any case beginning to ease. In the last year of war a gradual run-down of the war economy very much restored the industrial initiative to government and managements.

## NOTES

1   A. Calder, op. cit., p. 305.
2   Ibid., p. 609.
3   A. Bullock, op. cit., p. 225.
4   Ibid., pp. 225, 228.
5   Ibid., p. 229.
6   M. Foot, *Aneurin Bevan* (1963), pp. 109, 112.
7   F. Justice, Sheffield, in *Picture Post*, 12 Dec. 1942.
8   See, for example, replies to MO Directive, Nov. 1943: R. Beck (1935), F. Bosomworth (2975), W. Challis (3307).
9   25 Nov. 1943. INF 1/282.
10  Ibid.
11  MO Directive replies: E.J. Ausden (1048) and others (MO Archive). 14 April 1944. INF 1/282.
12  These figures of the Director General of Aircraft Production were slightly higher than those determined by his researchers, with whom he took issue. (Chief Exec. (Director General, Aircraft Production) memo, in AVIA 15/2548).
13  A. Verrier, *The Bomber Offensive* (1968), p. 188.
14  Chief Exec. memos, AVIA 15/2548.
15  P. Inman, op. cit., pp. 5, 191.
16  Ibid., p. 5.
17  Ibid., pp. 173, 177.
18  *Report* of the Royal Commission on Equal Pay (1946), p. 47 (note).

19 *The Economist,* 3, 17 April, 27 March, 1943.
20 'Appointment of Directors to Firms' (23 Dec. 1942): P. Seef to Sir Archibald Rowlands, 15 April 1943, AVIA 15/3780.
21 *Picture Post,* 17 April 1943.
22 *NP,* April 1943.
23 12 Aug. 1943, 30 Oct. 1944. AVIA 15/2567, and Inman, op. cit., p. 262.
24 Ministry of Labour *Report* of Conference on Joint Consultation, Training Within Industry, Works Information and Personnel Management (1948), pp. 18–20.
25 A. Calder, op. cit., p. 452.
26 E. Gray, 'The Trade Union Attitude to Welfare and Personnel Management Today', in *Labour Management,* vol. xxvii, no. 278, Feb.-March 1945, p. 9.
27 *Labour Management,* vol. xxvii, no. 280, June-July 1945, p. 64.
28 Ibid.
29 'Welfare in Industry', 13 Feb. 1942, MO Archive, Industry Raw Materials.
30 S.T. Lewenhak, 'Trade Union Membership among Women and Girls in the United Kingdom' (PhD thesis, University of London, 1971), table 5.
31 'Neptune Strike Committee' (leaflet), 10 Feb. 1943.
32 Bowman's pencil notes, March 1943.
33 Ibid.
34 See *Daily Mirror,* 25 Feb., which claimed the men received £5 a week from collections; Bowman thought they received on average 38s. per week (notes, n.d.).
35 Bowman, 'Ministry of Labour', *Newcastle Journal and North Mail,* 5 and 6 March, 1943.
36 Bowman's notes on the back of a resolution from Walker No. 8 branch dated 1 Feb. 1943.
37 Coventry AEU District Committee *Minutes.*
38 Manchester AEU District Committee *Minutes.*
39 *Factory News,* 3 Oct. 1944.
40 Manchester AEU District Committee *Minutes,* 16 Nov. 1944; 7 July 1944. LAB 10/444; *Coventry Evening Telegraph,* 8 Jan. 1946.
41 *Minutes* of a local conference, 1 Feb. 1945.
42 Trade Union *Report* (Industry Raw Materials, MO Archive).
43 ETU Executive Committee *Minutes,* 15-16 March 1942, pp. 14–15.
44 *News Chronicle* has a report of the stewards' comments on a similar scheme, 5 Feb. 1942.
45 S. Phelan, op. cit., p. 50.
46 Charles Job, *London's Arsenal* (1945), p. 35, ff. (Maitland-Sara collection, University of Warwick).
47 Interview with Jock Wallace, 20 May 1980.
48 Interview with Bill Warman, 1973.
49 Letter from W.R. Lord to Hindmarsh (convenor), 28 Oct. 1944. Manuscript history of Austin Longbridge shop stewards by Dick Etheridge, p. 7. (Modern Records Centre).
50 Interview with Bill Warman (by Peter Caldwell), 1973.
51 The dossier is attached to a report from Mr A. Henderson, supervisor, machine shop, Beardmore's Parkhead Forge, to Mr A. Williamson, managing director (dated 2 May 1944). The meeting referred to specifically took place on 4 April 1944. The items on the agenda were: 1) levy on workers to assist apprentices on strike; 2) explanation of PAYE income tax; 3) embargo on overtime by millwrights and attitude of toolroom to their work; 4) refusal of heavy machine shop to work piece-work. Effect of this

on toolroom bonus; 5) General. Subs for workers off sick; alternative members for production committee. These papers are in LAB 10/463.

52 See, for example, Penny Summerfield's article, 'Women Workers in the Second World War', offprint from an article in *Capital and Class*, no. 1, March 1977, p. 19.
53 10 Dec. 1943. LAB 10/353.
54 17, 24 Sept. 1943. LAB 10/380.
55 5 June 1943. LAB 10/364.
56 'Minister's Proposals', 8 June 1943. LAB 10/248.
57 *Report* of the Special National Conference of the AEU, London, 4 and 5 Nov. 1943 (published March 1944), p. 3, 60, hereinafter cited as SNC.
58 *North-West Evening Mail*, 30 Sept. 1943.
59 SNC, p. 8.
60 Barrow District Shop Stewards, 'Barrow District and the Interpretation of NAT Award 326' (circular), hereinafter cited as BDSS.
61 Ibid.
62 Ibid.
63 *Barrow Guardian*, 18 Sept. 1943. BDSS; SNC, p. 7.
64 BDSS.
65 SNC, p. 7.
66 Ibid., p. 7.
67 *Barrow Guardian*, 2 Oct. 1943. *North West Evening Mail*, 21 Sept. 1943.
68 SNC, p. 8.
69 Ibid., pp. 18, 19.
70 Ibid., p. 17, 24-5.
71 *Barrow Guardian*, 25 Sept. 1943.
72 Ibid.
73 *North-West Evening Mail*, 20 Sept. 1943.
74 *Daily Herald*, 30 Sept.
75 *Barrow Guardian*, 2 Oct.
76 *Daily Express*, 30 Sept., *Barrow Guardian*, 2 Oct. 1943.
77 A. Bullock, op. cit., p. 268. *Daily Herald*, 2 Oct. 1943.
78 BDSS.
79 *Barrow Guardian*, 25 Sept.; SNC, p. 8.
80 For Hannington's views on Huddersfield, see SNC, pp. 24/25. For the strike committee's position, see *Daily Express*, 30 Sept., and *Barrow Guardian*, 2 Oct. 1943.
81 *Barrow Guardian*, 9 Oct. 1943.
82 Ibid.
83 Ibid.
84 *Daily Herald*, 14 Jan. 1944.
85 SNC, p. 1.
86 Barrow Shop Stewards, 'Facts v Filth'.
87 Ibid.
88 SNC, pp. 15, 35.
89 Ibid., p. 21-2.
90 Ibid., pp. 31-3.
91 Ibid., pp. 33-5.
92 'Facts v Filth'.
93 AEU Monthly Journal,May 1944.
94 9 Nov. 1944. LAB 10/493. See also S. Phelan, 'The Avro Conspiracy' (Labour Studies dissertation, Ruskin College, Oxford, 1979), pp. 41-2, 71.

95 *Socialist Appeal,* mid-Oct., Nov. 1943. *Barrow Guardian,* 2 Oct. 1943.
96 *Socialist Appeal,* mid-June 1943.
97 ILP Shop Stewards' pamphlet no. 4, entitled 'For a National Link-Up of Stewards'.
98 *Socialist Appeal,* mid-June 1943.
99 WIL Industrial Bulletin, May 1943; on Doherty, see *Socialist Appeal,* Jan., Feb. 1943; *NP,* Nov. 1943. The formation of the committee seems to have attracted the attention of the CP nationally, and to have made Jack Owen (the Communist engineer and councillor from Manchester who was a member of the *Daily Worker*'s editorial board and wrote a regular column for some years entitled 'Workshop Notes') travel to Clydeside as soon as the revival of the committee was mooted there. At least, this was the opinion of the Anarchist *War Commentary,* which was far from being an unequivocal supporter of the CWC (*War Commentary,* April 1943). That their opinion was not far-fetched is illustrated by one of Owen's subsequent reflections on the Clyde workers: 'The Clyde workers are heroic fighters for their class, possessing a vitality invaluable to us, if we can guide it into the correct channels. . . in such soil the fungoid growth of Anarchism, ILPism and all such theories of the mentally inert grow.' (*DW,* 17 March 1943.)
100 *Daily Herald,* 3 May 1944, *DW,* 6 May 1944.
101 *Socialist Appeal,* mid-June 1943.
102 WIL, 'National Industrial Report Made to Central Committee' (n.d., but probably late 1943 or early 1944).
103 Galbraith to Bevin, 10 Nov. 1943. LAB 10/281.
104 *Minutes* of the Coventry District Committee of the AEU, 8, 15 Feb. 1944. The District Manpower Officer of the Ministry of Labour reported to the Coventry District Committee that there were no miners physically capable of mining work employed in the engineering industry.
105 A. Calder, op. cit., p. 503.
106 H.M.D. Parker, *Manpower* (1957), p. 465.
107 A. Bullock, op. cit., p. 260.
108 *Minutes* of a meeting between North-East Coast Marine Engine Builders and Ship Repairers and Ministry of Labour officials, 17 May 1941. LAB 8/405.
109 *Ministry of Labour Gazette,* Feb., Aug. 1943.
110 J.B. Jefferys, op. cit., p. 263; *Minutes* of the Manchester District Committee of the AEU, 29 May 1941.
111 Ibid.
112 Ibid., 5 March 1942. The branches had to be circularised to form a new committee.
113 Ibid., 16 Sept. 1943.
114 Ibid., 26 Nov. 1944.
115 Ibid.
116 27 March (note, signed 'WB'). LAB 10/451.
117 Ibid.
118 *Evening Chronicle,* 31 March 1944.
119 After six weeks in existence, the TAG produced an 'Appeal to the Apprentices at Vickers-Armstrong's', signed by Davy, which said that only one shop had elected delegates to the TAG and called on the apprentices to elect two delegates from each shop, who were to contact C. Brider (136 shop) or Davy on the night of Wednesday 9 Febrauary at the NUGMW Rooms, Sycamore Street, Wallsend. This leaflet is one of a number of

documents kindly lent me by Ray Challinor of Newcastle Polytechnic.
120 Emerson to HQ, 14 Feb. 1944. LAB 10/451.
121 *Evening Chronicle,* 31 March 1944.
122 9 March 1944. LAB 10/451.
123 17 March 1944. LAB 10/451.
124 11 March 1944. LAB 10/451.
125 17 March 1944. LAB 10/451.
126 27 March 1944. Note signed 'WB'. LAB 10/451.
127 Ibid., and 28, 29 March 1944. LAB 10/451.
128 *Socialist Appeal,* July 1944.
129 J. Higgins, 'Ten Years for the Locust', reprinted from *International Socialism* 14 (1963) by Swansea International Socialists, n.d., p. 5.
130 *Newcastle Journal and North Mail,* 8 April 1944.
131 27 March 1944. LAB 10/451.
132 28 March 1944. LAB 10/451. *Newcastle Journal and North Mail,* 28, 30 March 1944.
133 28 March 1944; 29 March 1944. LAB 10/451.
134 Galbraith to HQ, 29 March 1944. LAB 10/451.
135 *Newcastle Journal and North Mail,* 28 March 1944. LAB 10/451.
136 28, 29 March (Galbraith to HQ). LAB 10/451.
137 *Sunday Sun,* 9 April 1944.
138 *Evening Chronicle,* 31 March 1944.
139 *Newcastle Journal and North Mail,* 3 April 1944.
140 11 April 1944. LAB 10/451.
141 Ibid., 4, 5, 10 April 1944. LAB 10/451.
142 1 April 1944. LAB 10/451.
143 See, for example, *Newcastle Journal and North Mail,* 1 April; *Sunday Express,* 2 April; *Daily Mail,* 6 April; *Daily Dispatch,* 6 April; *Morning Advertiser,* 8 April. None of these reports added anything of real interest to the story of the strike itself.
144 *Newcastle Journal and North Mail,* report of trial of Trotskyists, 19 May. See also 'Fight the Pit Compulsion Plot', in Tarbuck papers, Modern Records Centre, University of Warwick.
145 'Why the ILP Supports the Apprentices', this document was kindly lent to me by Ray Challinor.
146 *DW,* 4 April 1944.
147 Ibid., 28 March 1944.
148 Ibid., 1 April 1944.
149 The phrase is Harry McShane's, writing in the *Daily Worker,* 4 April 1944.
150 30 March 1944. LAB 10/451.
151 *DW,* 4 April 1944; Ibid., 8 April 1944.
152 A. Bullock, op. cit., pp. 269–70.
153 Note dated 22 Feb. 1944. LAB 10/451.
154 Low to Emmerson, 16 March 1944. LAB 10/451.
155 20 March 1944. LAB 10/451.
156 *Newcastle Journal and North Mail,* 6 April. Haston remarked: 'If the Government imagine that by closing us down or suppressing our publications they are going to stop the wave of strikes they are mad.' (Ibid.).
157 *Socialist Appeal,* mid-July 1944.
158 Ibid.
159 Ibid.
160 The Anti-Labour Laws Victims' Defence Committees, according to *Socialist Appeal* at least, had some success in mobilising support, however. Jimmy

248

Maxton, Aneurin Bevan and other sympathetic left-wingers were involved. Just after sentence had been pronounced, Ann Keen spoke in Newcastle with Bill Davy and Jimmy Maxton. Len Harrison of the ILP chaired the meeting, attended by four hundred trade-unionists. (*Socialist Appeal*, mid-July 1944).
161   A. Bullock, op. cit., p. 270.
162   A. Bullock, ibid. As Bevin said in the quotation from Bullock (above), his analysis of the situation was based on a review of the 'contributory causes' of disputes as revealed by the inquiries of the Ministry of Labour.
163   LAB 34/59.
164   Industrial Relations Dept., 'General Memo: Defence Regulation 1AA: Scope of the Regulation' (n.d.), p. 5. LAB 10/467.
165   Ibid.
166   *Minutes* of the Forty-Second Meeting of the Consultative Committee held at the Ministry of Labour, 11 April 1944. LAB 10/467, p. 2.
167   Ibid.
168   Industrial Relations Dept., op. cit., p. 3.
169   M. Foot, op. cit., p. 453.
170   Ibid., pp. 453–5.
171   *NP*, April 1944.
172   M. Foot, op. cit., ch. 13.
173   Keith Middlemas, *Politics in Industrial Society. The Experience of the British System Since 1911* (1979), p. 300.

# CHAPTER 5

# WOMEN AT WAR

The history of women's relationship to the groundswell of shop floor trade union activity, and in particular to the steadily increasing industrial and political ferment of the later war years, deserves separate and close attention. This is not because we consider the history of women in the trade union movement as separate, or as somehow occurring outside of the men's history, but because the subject has generally, until recently, been ignored. On those rare occasions when it has been dealt with, it has received a treatment by historians which has tended almost to obliterate some of its major features. If we err in the opposite direction, then, it is because of our historiographical starting-point.

Many historians have accepted the unspoken assumptions of society about industrial workers. The very term 'engineer' is and was laden with certain connotations and overtones. To most people in the industry and probably all outside of it, the word meant '*man* working in engineering'. It conjured up visions of gigantic lathes, grease, oil and swarf, hard physical work in dirty conditions which was only suitable for the supposedly tough, brutish make-up of men. Engineers simply were not women; the two terms did not go together. The First World War, and the widespread employment of women in the engineering shops and munitions factories, had not destroyed this widely held assumption. Neither had the extensive employment of women before the war in some branches of the engineering industry. It was a view of women's place which existed to some extent independently of the practicalities of the shop floor because it was buttressed by men's deep-seated fears for their jobs, for their position in the family and in society as a whole.

It is within this context that the skilled men's attitude to women engineers has to be considered. It is also within this context that women's attitudes to working in the engineering shops have to be seen. They did not usually think of themselves as engineers, but as temporary helpers with an important but strictly transient contribution to make towards winning the war. Primarily they thought of themselves as women, and frequently expressed their grievances in the language of femininity, stressing their different needs and requirements from the men working in the industry. The women used this currency to defend themselves in the factories and to assert their rights, but they also began to develop some trade union organisation, which had hitherto been the almost exclusive preserve of the men.

Historians have often pointed out that whatever problems accompanied the mobilisation of women, it represented a remarkable administrative and political success when measured against the achievements of other combatant nations. At the peak of the war effort one in three engineering workers was a woman, and many sections and workshops in engineering factories were 'manned' almost exclusively by women.[1] The new entrants to engineering improved production in many sectors, and unquestionably gave the drive for arms production a much needed boost. For many historians this has been quite unproblematic: the reasoning has been that this mobilisation was necessary and that women were willing to 'do their bit'. But it was not quite as simple as that. When this reserve army of labour was mobilised, it had largely to be conscripted because attempts to encourage women to register voluntarily for war work in January 1941 were a substantial flop: and once there, women were not as malleable a part of the workforce as had been hoped. Mass Observation, employed by the government to report on the reasons behind the early-1941 drive's failure, adopted the criticism offered by Bevin's own eight-woman Consultative Committee that the matter had been approached wrongly, giving the women the impression that they were being *ordered* to register. Bevin should have appealed to the women, went the argument. The Mass Observers offered another criticism: that the women did not know what they would earn. Every woman they watched registering asked what she would be paid, and was simply given a leaflet that pointed out that 'a lot depends on whether the firm employing you pays union rates. If it does, then the minimum will be thirty-five shillings'. This uncertainty, they argued, was quite a considerable deterrent to the women, and was typical of the government's approach.[2] Presumably those responsible for the leaflet would have argued in reply that they were simply telling the truth: the situation was uncertain.

The failure of the January 1941 campaign to recruit enough women volunteers into the industry led the War Cabinet not to appeal to the women as Mass Observation recommended, but to conscript them (despite the objections of Conservative MPs concerned with the effects on the family). From December 1941, women were progressively conscripted into industry or the services. The women were divided into two categories: 'mobile' (without family responsibilities) and 'immobile' (with family responsibilities). The distinction was important in terms of where rather than whether they worked: if they were classified as 'mobile', then they were generally sent to areas of labour shortage such as the West Midlands or North-West. If not, then they worked nearer home. But mobile or immobile, they had to register for national service. Thus the government, which was not unaware of the differences between volunteer and conscript labour, was compelled to opt for the latter in the absence of the former.

Many of the women working in the factories, whether or not they had been conscripted, were anything but strangers to work: in the metal industries as a whole, a quarter of them had been in similar work before, half had come from another job and only a quarter from home or school, a government survey of 1943 revealed.[3] In some areas, of course, there was an established tradition of women working whether they were married or single. This was especially true of Lancashire, where they had long worked in textiles and had a history of factory work, albeit under quite different conditions. But many factories had sprung up in unlikely rural settings, and in these plants many of the women had much less experience of waged labour. These differences can, however, be exaggerated. Most women came into factories

253

that were new to them and, irrespective of their experience in other types of work, had now to establish themselves in a new workplace with all that implied.

In general, women's work in engineering factories was repetitious and boring, usually carried on under a system of payment by results. Typically, their jobs were broken down into short operations which could be mastered in a very short time simply by watching the toolsetter perform the work. On machining, jigs were generally used which meant that work was located on the jig and the tool brought onto the work, very often in very short cycles within which the whole operation might take a maximum of ten seconds. The most difficult (and therefore the more interesting) parts of this type of work were usually done by men. Setting up capstan lathes, milling machines, grinders and power presses (all of which they often worked) could be the only relief on repetition work, but it was frequently done by skilled male toolsetters. The simpler aspects of riveting, sub-assembly and 'viewing' could offer more opportunity to at least move from the machine, but were similarly boring. All sophisticated aircraft inspection, for example, was done by the MAP's Aircraft Inspection Department (AID), which seems to have consisted almost entirely of men. There were, of course, exceptions, and women proved that they were quite capable of toolroom machining, welding and tank assembly.[4] But widespread underestimation of women's capabilities, combined with the advanced state of the division of labour and trade union attitudes to women, conspired to ensure that they generally had only the most tedious jobs to fill their hours at work.[5] This background is crucial to the contemporary comments made about women's desire for sustained effort, as it is to their militancy. The relationship between work and militancy is a complex and important one, and deserves more attention than it has received.

A Mass Observation publication of 1942, *People In Production*, reported that in general women were happier with their jobs than men. They did not publish any comparable statistics for men's attitudes, but men must have been discontented indeed. In their survey of a group of factory workers, they found that 39 per cent of the women 'really liked' their jobs, 36 per cent were 'satisfied without being very enthusiastic', 11 per cent were 'unenthusiastic, ranging through to definitely hostile', while 4 per cent 'condemned their jobs emphatically'.[6] These responses cannot be taken at face value for at least two reasons. First, they were obtained relatively early in the war, when many of the women had only just come into the factories. In time, the cumulative effects of tedium would probably have significantly changed the proportions giving these answers. Second, the responses have to be set firmly within the context of the real ways in which women related to their work in the factories. The actual content of their working day has to be examined if we are to evaluate their responses to abstract questions in questionnaires.

One report on a 'typical day' in a factory written for Mass Observation in February 1942 suggested that the proportion of non-working time during the day was fairly high. The report stated that the younger girls started late, 'chattering in the cloakroom', although the older women started on time. During the afternoon a number of girls again retreated to the cloakroom, for periods of up to half an hour. Others simply stopped work while at their machines: 'In the shop, too, most of the girls are talking a large part of the time—one working rather languidly at her machine while the other leans on the bench and talks to her.'[7] Another Mass Observation report, this time published as *War Factory* (1943), drew attention to the considerable amount of 'clock-watching' which went on:

It is at a little before eleven that the first signs of slacking off begin to appear. People start going out to the cloakroom and hanging about there for long periods, doing their hair, talking, eating the cakes they have bought for dinner and tea. The subject of what time it is (which by four in the afternoon, as we shall see, has become almost an obsession) begins to appear in conversations:

'It's five past eleven.'

'That clock's gone slow again. It's nearly ten past. Jack, don't you make it nearly ten past?'

'Eh?'

'It's ten past eleven, isn't it? Isn't that clock slow?'

'That's not slow. That's right.'

255

'What, is it only five past?'

'That's right.'

'Oh.' Groans from both girls. 'Only five past.'

The official time for dinner is one o'clock and the official time for getting ready for it is five minutes to; actually preparations start a long while before that. Between half past twelve and five to one the cloakrooms are locked (the idea of this is to prevent people getting ready before the appointed time) but what happens as a result of this is that from 12.20 a crowd of girls is to be found in the cloakroom washing their hands, preparatory to going back to the bench and doing nothing whatever for half an hour, so as not to get their hands dirty again before dinner.'[8]

In practice, then, the women made their attitude to work quite clear. As a woman from another factory said: 'The work [is] so monotonous. . . boredom is our worst enemy.'[9]

Penny Summerfield has argued in an impressive article that single women were less susceptible to financial incentives to increase productivity largely because the changes brought about by the war decreased financial pressures on them. The most persuasive reasons that she gives are the lack of consumer goods for purchase and the relative infrequency of long-term relationships which would stimulate saving. She has also pointed out that single women and women from Eire were especially resistant to industrial work discipline.[10] But it is important to add that Irish women (as we shall see) also wanted urgently to send money home, and were therefore often far from satisfied with their earnings. More generally, many women did not wish to work intensively all day, and this attitude was not necessarily incompatible with a desire to increase their earnings, since they viewed the engineering wages structure as fundamentally unfair. Also, as some women were to argue, low wages provided no incentive to work hard.

Women's relationship to their work did not, of course, exist in a social vacuum. The skilled men could often resent and even resist the introduction of women to work which they traditionally regarded as theirs. Dilution was more or less completely resisted in sheet metal shops by the determined opposition of the sheet metal workers' unions throughout the war, despite many attempts to force them to allow women on to their work.[11] Shop stewards in the northern and Scottish engineering factories could also on occasion show considerable reluctance to allow women to do certain jobs. At the North British Locomotive Co.'s Queen's Park works we even find a Communist shop steward in the summer of 1943 threatening strike action in the tank-erecting shop if women were brought on to assembly work. He maintained they were 'unsuitable' (no doubt deploying the usual physical arguments), but the evidence of other factories proved him wrong.[12] J.T. Murphy also reported how reluctant skilled men were in his London factory to show women how to do engineering work. Murphy went on, however, to say that the men found it difficult to adopt a hard line, because of the 'sex factor': the men found it was 'not easy to maintain a hard attitude of unhelpfulness to good-looking and

*Factory News*, 31 July 1944

well-built girls and women'.[13] This 'sex factor' could provide an important defence for the women. As Penny Summerfield has shown, men toolsetters confronted with women workers in difficulties with their work reacted with amused tolerance, particularly when the women affected helplessness. She quotes a Mass Observer's report on the 'carefree atmosphere' in a machine shop:

> The chargehands in the machine shop are all men, in their twenties and early thirties. One and all they all pay much more attention to the mechanical side of their job—setting up and looking after apparatus and machinery—than to their other task of discipline and leadership among the girls on their bench. They almost all adopt the same attitude to the girls—one of amused tolerance; nothing a girl can do will bring her a reprimand from a chargehand; the worst she has to fear is a piece of good-humoured sarcasm. The girls themselves revel in the situation. If the chargehands choose to look on them with amused masculine superiority as scatterbrained little nitwits who can't do anything right, then what could be easier than to accept this role. . .[14]

This sort of attitude, prevalent among chargehands and setters, was much less common amongst foremen or supervisors, whose roles were more clearly managerial. Even in a very patriotic and romantic novel published in 1944 by a woman who had herself worked in a war factory, Rosie, one of the two young heroines, is doing her bit in a munitions factory when she encounters a distinctly unsympathetic foreman:

> She was slowly and carefully turning out yet another nut when a man's voice said behind her: 'And how do you think you're going to like your contribution to the war effort?' It was a queer voice, with a note in it which made her feel quite suddenly rather unhappy and discouraged. She turned round, and saw a tall man with dark, greyish hair, a dark trim moustache and a pale face. He wore a grey overall and grey flannel trousers and she thought how like one of the long grey machines in the room he looked. She thought also: 'How miserable he looks. I wonder who he is?' Aloud she said: 'Very much, I think, thank you. I'm not getting on very fast at present, I'm afraid.'
> 'So I see', said the melancholy speaker, sounding now quite

unreasonably sarcastic. Rosie looked confused. 'I—well, I've only just begun', she said. He lit a cigarette and remarked, 'I'm quite aware of that'. This annoyed Rosie because it seemed both rude and unkind, and to her own surprise she said quite briskly, 'I don't see how you can go fast at first'. The melancholy man puffed at his cigarette. 'Sentiments of that kind nearly lost us the war in its first couple of years', he observed. 'Would it be asking too much that you should contrive to produce nuts instead of standing doing nothing?' Rosie felt this was beyond the limit. 'I should like to know what right you have to speak to me like that', she exclaimed, losing her head completely. He raised his eyebrows. 'Quite a hot-tempered young woman, aren't you?' he mocked. 'It happens that I am your foreman. My name is Spender.'[15]

Spender's sarcasm causes Rosie to break a tool, and she is only consoled by Micky the toolsetter: 'Old Spender? Don't let him upset you. He's got a nasty manner, but his bark's worse than his bite.'[16] She is also soothed by Rene, an older woman who shouts over: 'We don't take any notice of him.'[17] After a while, Spender induces in Rosie what she calls 'The factory habit of "answering back", and finishing with a grievance, instead of brooding over it politely in silence.'[18] Ultimately, Spender's humanity is only establish-ed by his courtship of Rosie's aunt; his conduct in the factory remains unaffected, but Rosie comes to accept him. Foremen of the Spender type did not exist only in novels; the Scottish Conciliation Officer, for example, thought air-craft managements to be of this sort, 'with just a tendency to military brusqueness'.[19] Women could also come across the sort of management who saw themselves as the guardians of the girls' morality in the midst of the workshop's moral laxity. In an article written for a factory paper at one of A.V. Roe's plants in the North-West, entitled 'Prunes and Prisms', a correspondent wrote:

It may seem rather far-fetched, but if tales we hear of the rules and regulations there in force are true, we would not be wrong in like-ning the Process Dept. to a Young Ladies' Academy. . . someone there seems to have a Victorian attitude on the female sex. For the female staff are not allowed to smoke, nor to infringe the dress regulations by, for instance, wearing slacks at work. The men, on the

259

other hand, may wear trousers and smoke all day. It is the men we pity rather than the girls: they must feel that their moral welfare is being neglected. They may do as they like and go to hell in their own way, while the girls are sheltered carefully from the wiles of My Lady Nicotine, and from the steep and slippery path which the trousered girl must tread.[20]

The article continued that although the point might seem trivial major inequalities derived from small ones, and it ended by encouraging the girls to break the rules. It was just such petty restrictions that annoyed women workers and tended to make them resent management's attitude.

Women supervisors, who became more common from the middle of the war, could offer a solution to the problems which male foremen often experienced with women workers. Yet the appointment of women to these positions did little to help the situation. Chargehands were often appointed from amongst the women themselves, but higher supervisory and welfare staff were generally brought in from outside and frequently had less knowledge of the industry than those they were supposed to supervise.[21] A Mass Observer reported on the welfare officers in two local firms:

> There are elderly women welfare officers in P and A who are ridiculed, especially by the younger women as being merely 'narks' who are put there to keep an eye on them and are not really concerned with their welfare. Many workers do not seem to know what the welfare is supposed to consist of or what the Welfare Officer's job is unless it is concerned with his or her own welfare and that of the management and employers.[22]

Since many working women had more experience of industrial work than the women who by virtue of their class or education were appointed to managerial positions, they frequently reacted against their supervisors.

Defining themselves as against management, and adopting the 'factory habit of answering back', were important stages in the development of women's trade union consciousness. Almost as important was the business of developing a critical attitude towards their working environment. During the war, criticism of conditions became increasingly common. Perhaps the main reason for this was the fact that more and more women whose domestic experience and standards of cleanliness were very different from those in industry were being compelled to come into the factories. A woman crane-driver of forty-five earned the approval of her workmates when she complained of her job in a Birmingham war factory:

> It's the ventilation that's so awful, and it's worse when you're up on the crane. You get all the fumes up there and the heat's terrible. We used to get milk to drink up there, then they stopped that with the shortage and we got a cold drink. It wasn't so good, but it helped. Then they stopped that—they reckoned up the cost, and found it came to more than the milk—so now we don't get anything. You need the milk, it's healthier to get that, it sort of gets rid of the germs. I don't know why they want to go spending a lot of money on lavatories for the men when they've done without for forty years—it would be more sense to spend it on ventilation—have sliding roofs for the blackout like they do in some other factories. All the crane drivers in the next shop to me have died of consumption.[23]

The blackout frequently posed such problems with ventilation, and this type of complaint was quite common. Another typical set of problems related to aircraft work, and these are described by Doris White, who worked on aircraft repair:

> Up the wooden steps and into the aircraft. What a strange world of cat-walks, rivets, and wires, like strands of spaghetti running along each 'wall'. Bomb doors and gun turrets. . . Our main concern was not to fall out of the darn thing, through standing in its doorway. . . It was obviously very cold inside this 'tin box', all the more so when we were told we had to do 'nights'. So we arrived at eight at night and worked until eight in the morning. Our breath would come out as vapour as if it was a frosty morning, feet and hands so cold, as were our hands holding metal rivet guns. . . One thing we had no control over was the urge to drop off to sleep, which was always worse when not having a job. . . With a rat-tat-tat, drills whirring, men whistling. . . disappeared in the distance as oblivion took over, lifting one's head, repeated over again. It was much better to have something to do although in the dinner hour I would snatch a snooze on the chargehand's desk, the hard wood unnoticeable as I curled up, like a cat.[24]

Women shop stewards sometimes raised similar complaints, but went rather further and drew conclusions about trade union organisation. A woman shop steward from Scotland ('intelligent, pleasant, sympathetic and feminine', as she was described by a woman Mass Observer) gave a graphic description of the conditions in her factory:

> To reach the factory we have to wade through a park, and then have to stand all day with wet feet. There are one thousand women on three shifts with three lavatories and no water. There are cisterns but no water. Two towels every three weeks. Two wash bowls but no soap. We have an hour for lunch. The canteen is five minutes from the factory and we have to stand in a queue for twenty. Our dinner hour is nearly up before we get seated; and we have to eat our dinner with dirty and greasy hands. We don't mind doing men's work but we are women and don't want to be treated as if we were animals. . . what we want are better trade union facilities for women. Let women have a committee of their own.[25]

The conditions in their factories offended the sexual identities of the women quoted above: they felt that men might not mind such conditions, but they were definitely not suitable for women. The Scottish shop steward obviously thought that the male stewards were not concerned enough about the problem, and that a women's committee would be more effective. But although a few women's shop stewards' committees were set up, they were not the predominant vehicle for women's trade-unionism. Women participated in the Joint Shop Stewards' Committee in most factories.

There can be little doubt that women's considerable contribution to the wider shop floor movement was largely in the field of health, safety and welfare. Here their influence was felt long after the majority of women had left the engineering industry, because while wage increases could be eroded by inflation and short-time working, improved washing and eating facilities and similar structural alterations remained. Women were more prepared to take action on their conditions of work than the men they worked with. The women at the Bifurcated and Tubular Rivet Co. in Aylesbury, for example, were reported by a man working there to 'work well, but are not willing to put up with much'. During a recent cold snap, they had gone home 'in a body' because the works were too cold, causing the management to try to improve the heating.[26]

One of the main problems faced by women was the perennial one of having two occupations, one in the home and one in the factory. The dimensions of the problem are indicated by a brief description in the *Wolverton Express* at the beginning of 1943 of forty-eight-year-old Mrs Agnes Etheridge's day. Mrs Etheridge got up at half past five in the morning, prepared breakfast for her family, at ten to seven left for work in the town's railway factory where she worked all day on a grinding machine, returned home at six, prepared a meal, cleaned the house, washed and mended clothes and went to bed at eleven o'clock.[27] Many other women, especially in the isolated Royal Ordnance Factories, had to add a good deal of travelling time to their working day.[28] Married women therefore tended to cut down on their sleep, especially when working nights, when they were 'free' during the day and found sleep difficult.[29] As the war continued, the strains began to tell. In March 1944 a woman of forty-three said:

> The two jobs of home and work are getting me down. I'm tired. . . the longer hours here, and the long time it takes to do the shopping, and rushing home to get your hubby a good meal, and I do all my own washing and I don't have a bit of help—well, what I feel is that when the war is over I'll want a good long rest. A real holiday.[30]

These examples were typical, and go part of the way towards explaining why many women had initially been reluctant to enter the factories.

Partial remedies to these problems lay in the field of institutionalised welfare facilities such as nurseries and canteens, as Bevin fully realised. Of the two, nurseries were probably the most pressing need, at least for parents. Children, after all, had to be cared for every day of the week. Nurseries were only provided by employers in a very few cases (almost exclusively where they had already existed before the war). Although the influential Lady Reading advocated factory nurseries, the TUC opposed any such development.[31] Bevin, as we have seen, played an important role in supporting the Ministry of Health's application to the Treasury for money to help equip nurseries, on the grounds that the intention was to facilitate the labour supply. For as long as it reasonably could, the Ministry of Health resisted the suggestion that nurseries were essential, maintaining that there was little real demand for them.[32] But demonstrations and petitions from local groups of women, together with the increased demand for women's labour, forced it by the end of 1941 to abandon this attitude. In December 1941 Bevin wrote to lord mayors asking them to increase nursery provision, and a joint circular from the Ministry of Health and the Board of Education entitled *The Care of Young Children of Women War-Workers. A Vital Need* went out to all local education child welfare authorities.[33] By September 1944 there were 1,450 nurseries,[34] which had grown up in a piecemeal way, simply in response to 'demand' as perceived by the Ministry of Labour and local authorities. They had not been designed for the use of all working people, but were rather a makeshift measure to facilitate the labour supply in a number of key areas. This is reflected in the fact that only a small minority of children of working mothers ever had access to a nursery in wartime; the 1,450 nurseries had to provide facilities for the five and a half million working women in Britain. Moreover, the basis on which the nurseries had been established was essentially a temporary one: by urging local authorities to set them up with central funding, the government laid the foundations for phasing them out later. By March 1945 the *Daily Worker* believed there were 'strong grounds' for thinking that the nurseries were merely being tolerated preparatory to their closing down. At the end of the war, despite the Education Act of 1944 acknowledging local authorities' responsibilities in this area, the Treasury withdrew funding, thus ensuring that only a small minority of authorities would continue to bear the expense of nursery provision of any kind.[35]

Finding time to buy the necessities of life in sadly depleted shops constituted another persistent problem for women with family responsibilities. This worry built up frustrations which went deeper than the difficulties of providing for their families, by disturbing a habit which provided an element of creativity and relaxation for women working in industry.[36] The need for women to have time off for shopping was only seriously tackled in the summer of 1942—when absenteeism also was being tackled by the Ministry of Labour in a systematic way—but there remained many areas without any satisfactory arrangements: Coventry was singled out by Mass Observation as being particularly bad in this respect, despite its relatively strong trade union organisation.[37] The problem was recognised by the Welfare Department of the Ministry of Labour, who organised local conferences with employers, unions and shop owners, which led to a variety of solutions. Sometimes women were given time off to do their shopping (clearly the best answer from their point of view); elsewhere shopkeepers gave factory women priority cards, and some factories employed professional shoppers to take women's orders, and so on.[38] Nevertheless, the whole question remained a vexed one until the end of the war.

A partial solution to the shopping problem was achieved by providing factory canteens. Before the war, workers in many factories had been less than enthusiastic about the canteens provided by their employers, because their low earnings created a need to practise the strictest domestic economy.[39] However, by 1941 munitions workers were beginning actually to demand them because of the imposition of tighter rationing, the employment of women and their own increased earnings. Bevin fully realised the need for adequate canteens, and pushed very firmly towards his goal of a canteen for every sizeable factory. By March 1943 there were seven and a half thousand works canteens, a number which was to increase before the end of the war.[40] But it should not therefore be assumed that the canteens were used by a majority of those eligible to do so.[41] At A.V. Roe's Chadderton works, Manchester, only four hundred dinners were sold to over two thousand people, and there was talk of organising a boycott.[42] The operation of canteens was widely criticised in many factories. At a conference held by the Labour Research Department in March 1943, insufficient helpings, high charges and inadequate service on the night shift were amongst the main charges made.[43] From quite an early stage in the war, stewards began to try to improve the situation. Heavy manual workers were entitled to extra supplies which were normally delivered to the factory by the local Food Control Officer, but stewards often took steps to exert some control over the food themselves: at one London firm, the shop stewards threatened a strike when the management proposed to institute tea trolleys instead of issuing dry tea and sugar directly, while in Barrow the stewards at Vickers gained permission from the Food Control Officer to buy and distribute the food themselves from the local Co-op.[44] Canteen boycotts were not uncommon, in an effort to improve standards, and in some factories workers took over the running of the canteen themselves.[45] Occasionally, even, strikes broke out either for the provision of canteens or for their improvement, as at Kelvin, Bottomley and Laird (Hillington) and Hawthorn Leslie (Hebburn).[46] To many workers it appeared, as it did to *The Economist,* that the management regarded good food in the same light as other aspects of welfare—as impositions.[47] As the war continued, trade unions took up increasingly significant positions on the welfare issues which concerned women. Almost all the activity was at the level of national and regional officials responding to initiatives by the Ministry of Labour, however. Shop stewards' committees remained overwhelmingly male organisations throughout the war, and matters of specific interest to women were rarely discussed. It was not until 1943 that the AEU and TGWU organised their first women's conferences. At both of these the questions of shopping, more nurseries, the eligibility of part-time workers to send their children to nurseries, clinics and communal feeding centres were discussed, and positions adopted on all of them.[48] The difficulty was in implementing those positions and in negotiating the detailed application of welfare schemes to the needs of trade-unionists. It was this that appears to have been so rare.

It was not so much trade union pressure at the shop floor level as widespread individual action by the women which brought about such changes as did occur. Absenteeism was a major problem among women working in war industry: across industry as a whole it was about twice as high among women as among men, and higher among married than among single women. It was, moreover, a persistent problem, in that rates of absenteeism did not decline as the war went on but remained at a relatively constant level of around 12-15 per cent of hours worked.[49] This serious under-utilisation of human resources was common to all combatant countries, including Germany.[50] In Britain, the policy aimed mainly at improving welfare facilities and appointing welfare and personnel officers rather than resorting to disciplinary measures. But in some cases managements did seek to exert disciplinary pressure on absentees through the trade unions and JPCs. Unable to improve the attendance records of some women workers, they could turn to the shop stewards from outside of the work group and confronting the traditional defences thrown up against management, discipline could come from within the work group itself, leaving the absentee isolated. This strategy was sometimes successful. Perhaps the clearest example has been given by Arthur Exell, shop steward, talking about his experiences at Morris, Cowley, during the war. On the difficulties which girls had with soldering work and their tendency to kick against it by staying away, he recalls that the works manager sent for him and asked what he was going to do about it. Exell answered that the girls were not in the union, and that there was therefore nothing he could do. But the JPC made a difference, because the union promised to see that people came to work provided they were in the union. The management then gave Exell full permission to recruit all of the women. The women joining brought Radiators up to one hundred per cent membership, and according to this account the union kept their side of the bargain, 'although, it gave us problems as we had to come down a bit hard on some of these females'. The women were threatened with suspension and imprisonment (under the Essential Works Order and the defence regulations), but some girls 'were still very bad'.[51] There is no evidence from the women themselves to set beside this ex-shop steward's testimony, but it would seem likely that they might have had quite a different perspective on the matter. Their trade union membership was, after all, being used to discipline them in an unequivocal way.

Not all trade-unionists were willing to fulfil the management's expectations that union membership would lead to shop steward or JPC discipline. Jock Wallace, for example, gave a similar example to Arthur Exell's, but recalls that his attitude was rather different:

> We even had a situation where people, who were in key positions in the factory being absent, meaning that the whole line was idle. The management were so confident that they were getting our support to run a chap in open court, they sent for me. They really expected me to go into the box against them at that time, which was wrong, I wouldn't do that anyway. But that was the attitude and we falsely let them believe that would be done.[52]

Even in this case, however, it may be significant that the person involved was a man; in any event, no defence of the individual concerned was mentioned. But in other cases trade-unionists reacted strongly when imprisonment was inflicted on women absentees. In Coventry, for example, the District Committee of the AEU called before them two out-of-trade members who sat on the local bench, Sidney Stringer and George Hodgkinson (both Labour Party activists), to explain their actions in the case of two young women known as 'the two Jeans' who were imprisoned in early 1942 for absenteeism.[53] Imprisonment, as Arthur Exell points out, was sometimes threatened but rarely carried out; trade-unionists regarded it as quite inappropriate as a remedy to the real problem.[54]

Managements hoped that social pressures would be adequate to deal with absenteeism among women, and therefore in some cases encouraged their unionisation. So the general unions often had at least tacit managerial approval in their determined drive to recruit women in munitions. The TGWU in particular made an effort to do so, paying some attention to the needs of the increasing number of part-time women who were employed from the beginning of 1942 onwards (reaching two hundred thousand by the end of 1943).[55] In June 1942 the TGWU asked for a conference with the engineering employers to put forward a claim for part-time workers, who had received no wage increase under the national settlement.[56] In later national negotiations (when the AEU had begun to admit women) all engineering unions raised the issue, but as in so many matters affecting women the TGWU had started the ball rolling.

Up until 1943 when the AEU started to recruit women, the proportion of women in trade unions was very low. Various estimates of the extent of women's membership during the war years have been attempted, but they are highly unreliable because of the problems created for primitive trade union statistical and office facilities by the pressures of war. Such statistics as there are suggest that women's membership almost certainly never stood at above one third of the possible total at any time during the war years, reaching a peak at the end of 1943.[57] Nevertheless, it is important to point out that much of the aircraft industry was housed in very small sub-contracting units which were probably almost all non-union, and this tends to obscure the existence of relatively high levels of membership in many of the major factories. Until 1943 the field was largely left open to the general unions, but in some areas where they might have expected it, the AEU did not always allow them to recruit as they wished amongst women. In Scotland, for example, the general unions were often cleverly excluded by the use of informal arrangements. It was common practice, for example, for AEU convenors to represent women for a penny a week 'subscription'.[58] This sort of arrangement had the 'advantage' of keeping women out of the general unions. At the same time it meant that the women themselves remained the passive recipients of help, without their own stewards and the rights of union membership. Even within the Midland factories where the Workers' Union had long ago established a tradition of women's trade-unionism in engineering, men did not really feel that trade-unionism was appropriate to women. A Scottish women's delegation from the STUC to the Midlands which visited plants in Birmingham, Stoke, Rugby and Coventry during October 1942 found, especially in the newer factories, that: 'The girls did not naturally turn to their trade unions for any needed advice or assistance. . . we were told of girls who had made enquiries of male operatives working alongside of them, but apparently with poor encouragement to proceed further with the matter.'[59] If, despite this sort of discouragement, women persisted and became active within their union, they often found that their male brothers were inclined to give their problems a low priority. A woman steward of the TGWU employed at Harland and Wolff's Clydeside works, who claimed that she had recruited the women there into the union, said she had been 'up against victimisation from the management', but she did not find her union very supportive because 'they are always engaged on a men's strike at Hillington and don't care what happens to women workers'.[60] Women had to be very determined to press on in the face of the attitude that, even if it was preferable that they should be members, trade-unionism was really none of their business. Negotiations, it appears, were usually carried on by men throughout the war, despite increasing union organisation among women. Even at the lowest levels of recorded procedural negotiation, women stewards were a rare sight indeed. In the Coventry district, for example, women shop stewards made a total of only eleven appearances at works conferences between June 1940 and June 1943, while men stewards made four hundred and four.[61] From mid-1943, however, women stewards began to participate more fully at this level: between the summer of 1943 and the summer of 1944, thirty women stewards were involved in negotiations, compared to 334 men stewards.[62] This period was the wartime peak of women's trade union organisation in engineering, and women stewards were rather more active in every way than in 1941 and 1942.

The weakness of women's trade-unionism at this time also had a bearing on the relevance of JPCs for the solution of their smaller problems. Only trade-unionists were allowed to stand for election, and as often as not shop stewards were elected. Moreover, under the March 1942 agreement on JPCs (though this rule did not apply in the Royal Ordnance Factories), workers had to have two years' continuous service in the workplace to stand, thereby immediately ruling out many women. In some factories, the continuous-service clause was watered down by negotiation to one year or, as in the ROFs, to six months.[63] In its survey of 1943 the AEU found that in forty-eight factories surveyed, only nineteen had any women at all on the committee, while in those nineteen there were only thirty-seven women to two hundred and fourteen men.[64] It was hardly surprising, then, that only six per cent of the committees discussed women's questions at all. Women sometimes had informal links with the JPCs, as they did with unions; the Ministry of Supply found women asking men to raise issues for them in the ROFs, for example.[65] Yet these unbeaten tracks in many ways served to underline the inadequacy of the established routes. There is little doubt that, to the extent that JPCs were an alternative to the trade union for raising workplace problems, they functioned even less effectively for women than for men. Welfare questions were often a bone of contention for women, and could be discussed on the JPC. But inadequate women's representation placed a severe limit on the extent to which such discussions took account of the women's own views and feelings.

The reasons for women's relatively poor position in terms of both trade union organisation and consultative machinery are quite complex. The factor most often mentioned by men trying to recruit women was their attitude to trade-unionism. A man working at English Electric, Bradford, remarked of the ex-mill girls working with him: 'They are absolutely disinterested in any form of organisation or Unionism. They would never bother to consult a shop steward over any of their difficulties or dissatisfactions, although the AEU and shop stewards are willing to assist them.'[66] It is dangerous to take this sort of statement at face value, because it is made by a man and may well reveal more about his own mentality than that of the women he purported to observe. Similar remarks were often made by those who tried to recruit semi- and unskilled men. The key to the problem lay in trying to make trade-unionism relevant to their needs as engineering workers. J.T. Murphy, who as the theoretician of the shop stewards' movement of the First World War had more than an average understanding of these questions, did not attempt to organise the women in his London factory directly. He spoke to a likely woman and then encouraged her to undertake the task herself, which she apparently did.[67] She was no doubt able to present the union as having something to offer her colleagues in a way that a male steward could not. The method of approach was all-important. The man from English Electric quoted above was trying to make out a case for works committees as being the most appropriate channel for women to raise their grievances, and cited their enthusiasm for the committee as proof:

> They will really vote for a delegate, and really delegate their representative to ask for specific things. The matter nearest their hearts is a question of hours, and through the Works Committee a demand that overtime should be spread over weekday evenings rather than Saturday afternoons was forcibly made and granted to the satisfaction of the girls, who really felt that their Works Committee functions.[68]

One of the differences between the works committee and the union seems to have been that while on the former they had a delegate, in the union they had no direct representation. Their delegate was able, with the strong backing of her fellow-workers, to win the support of the works committee and establish, in this case at least, its relevance to their needs. Thus the conclusion that could be drawn from the writer's interesting evidence might be quite different from his contention that women related better to works committees than to unions. It could be concluded that the AEU stewards had not been sufficiently sensitive to the women's problems and had been too distant even if 'willing to help', and perhaps this was why the women reacted positively to the works committee. Being willing to help was not enough; the women wanted to feel that their representative really represented them, and men were not always able to inspire this degree of confidence. Women were not generally anti-union and pro-works committees; in fact, the general drift of the evidence suggests the reverse.

The reason why so many women were not members of trade unions is given by Doris White; as far as she and her workmates were concerned:

> One thing that really annoyed the men in our shop, especially
> Mr. King the shop steward, was the fact that us girls did not belong
> to a Union, we could see no reason as we were described as being in
> temporary employment, at least that is what our cards stated, what
> the men stated was. . . 'Ye'll have the rises though won't yer?'. And
> so Mr. King, a lay preacher and union boss, with his hands resting on
> his rotund stomach covered by a white tie-round apron, would lean
> back telling us the folly of our ways, sometimes I think he meant
> our gay attitude, going dancing, meeting uniformed boys. Amy, as
> charming as only she knew how, would put an arm round his neck
> and chide him 'Aw, cummon' and taunt him into a smile, all his
> religious teaching forgotten and being a man he shyly and coyly
> grinned, 'Ooooh, go away', his normally red florid face turning
> several shades redder, contrasting with his virgin white detachable
> celluloid collar.[69]

In this case the women had argued that the temporary nature
of their employment (insisted upon, of course, by the AEU)
meant that there was no reason for them to join. In most
cases the stewards argued that it was precisely because the
women were the 'guardians' of men's positions while they
were away that they should join. In fact, many of the women
at this works joined as the war went on.

The association of trade-unionism with the shop steward's
Methodism was also clearly important in the above case. The
whole ethos of trade-unionism in the small railway town of
Wolverton was regarded as intolerably severe and puritan by
the girls conscripted up from London. Nationally, however,
the main reason for women being very poorly unionised up
until 1943 lay in one simple fact: the AEU would not recruit
them. The engineering union's traditions of craft exclusiveness proved so durable that they led it to lose considerable
ground to the general unions before the policy was reversed
in January 1943. The opening of AEU membership to
women marked the beginning of a distinct new phase in the
history of women in the munitions industries.

The AEU Rules Revision Committee had decided in 1942,
following a vote by the membership in favour to admit

women to membership of the AEU for the first time in its history. With this decision, the last main pillar of the craft union's 'exclusiveness' crumbled, opening up the possibility of the widespread unionisation of women in the engineering industry. The Communists had been pressing for this move for some time, but the decision had to be taken because the AEU was coming under increasing pressure as a result of the successful recruitment of women by the general unions. In the Midland and Scottish factories the TGWU had established important bases of support, ensuring that the AEU's old claim to be the only legitimate engineering trade union could never realistically be made again. But the tremendous dilution of the old engineering skills made such a move well overdue. It would have been impossible for the AEU to retain any significant measure of control within engineering in the long run if it had not taken this decision. Yet in a sense it was already too late: from being in a position to sweep the board in the mid-1930s, it had adapted too slowly to the changing conditions and had become no more than first amongst equals by 1943.[70] By the end of the year 138,717 women had joined the AEU, many of them paying the political levy.[71] The ETU also joined in the scramble, with the creation of a Special Women's Section at the end of 1943: by the beginning of 1944 they had recruited 9,077 women.[72] The TGWU by the end of 1943 had 306,707 women members, while the NUGMW had 45,000 by the end of 1945.[73] In the general unions much of the membership worked outside of the engineering industry, however. The AEU's decision to admit women was of key importance, because it was by far the most important engineering union: during 1943 alone, the AEU recruited women members equivalent to roughly seventy per cent of the TGWU's entire membership in the industry.[74] By the end of 1944 the total membership of the AEU had climbed to well over nine hundred thousand.[75] It was hardly surprising, then, that during 1943 in the core of the engineering industry proper (general and marine engineering and aircraft) women's membership had risen to well above ten per cent, while in many of the bigger factories with large and active shop stewards' committees, one hundred per cent was being approached.[76] Two facts emerge quite clearly from the inadequate statistics that are available: the first is that membership, and especially women's membership, expanded very rapidly in 1943; the second is that only a small minority of women were in unions even at the peak of the war effort. In 1944, the figures began to fall again as women started to leave the industry.[77]

Within this relatively small body of women trade-unionists began a development which the old 'craft' AEU men would have thought impossible only a few years earlier. The women started to throw up effective activists from within their own ranks. This was extremely important, because it meant that battles which had previously been fought *for* them became to an increasing extent fought *by* them. Only one or two examples can be given here, but there are many impressive ones from which to choose. Mrs Sillett, who was twenty-nine in 1942, had trained as a mechanic, and when she went into a garage on war work she organised everyone there into the TGWU. She then organised several local building sites into a new branch of the union, of which she became the first branch secretary. As the local TGWU official remarked, not only was she an accomplished recruiter, but she had the added advantage of being less likely than a man to be called up for military service.[78] We know nothing further about this woman's background, but we do know that some women stewards had gained experience in the labour movement outside the trade unions, and had been prepared for stewardship in this way. The first AEU woman steward on the Tyne was fifty-year-old Mrs R.A. Dixon, a veteran of the women's section of the National Unemployed Workers' Movement and a Labour Party member. Mrs Dixon was confident enough to address a mass meeting at her Tyneside marine engineering works immediately after her recognition as a steward.[79] Indeed, it may have required a woman of Mrs Dixon's age, experience and marital status not only to stand up to the management but also to establish herself in the northern works, in which women remained a small minority.[80]

Despite the fact that women trade-unionists were very much in the minority in engineering as a whole, women's shop steward organisation could be quite well developed in some large factories. Before the end of 1944 women shop stewards of the TGWU had started to elect convenors from amongst their number; this happened at the GEC factories in Coventry, at Rolls-Royce, Hillington, and at G. & J. Weir's, Glasgow.[81] At this last factory the stewards enlivened wartime social life and the union itself by entertaining fifty-five overseas servicemen on Christmas Eve 1942.[82] Such events could also play an important role in boosting the union in the factory. Nevertheless, women's battle for recognition within the AEU had only just begun. The AEU did not appoint any women officials (unlike the general unions, who had officials of great experience like the TGWU's National Women's Officer, Florence Hancock),[83] and although annual women's conferences were organised from which six delegates were elected to the National Committee, these delegates could not vote and could only advise the committee on women's questions.[84] Women stewards had to be at least twenty-one or, if there was no alternative, nineteen, because, the Executive wrote, they had to 'have regard to the dignity of negotiations within the industry'.[85] In the ETU the situation was similar: members of the Special Women's Section were allowed to be stewards only for members of their own section, and were only allowed to vote on matters concerning women at the branch.[86] The National Union of Foundry Workers continued to refuse to allow women into membership at all throughout the war.[87]

Stewards active in the general unions often questioned the motives of the AEU in recruiting women because of the restrictions they imposed on women's rights. Many of the old rivalries between the craft and general unions were fuelled as competition for members sharpened. In February 1943 a shop steward of the NUGMW called Campbell approached Widdows, an AEU steward at Mather and Platt's in Manchester, about the AEU recruiting women. Widdows reported to the AEU District Committee that Campbell had said to him: 'the AEU had only just awakened to the fact that women wanted organising; that they had rendered no service in the past to women workers and would throw them out at the end of the war'.[88] Campbell's feelings were echoed by many other stewards at this time. It was in an effort to overcome these problems that the AEU, TGWU, NUGMW and Iron and Steel Trades Confederation signed an agreement in July 1943 pledging themselves to assist one another in achieving full trade-unionism throughout the industry.[89] Nevertheless, some friction continued.

The criticisms levelled at the AEU and the craft unions in general by the general unions are of more than passing interest, and should be examined more closely. The question which they raised concerning the way the AEU saw women's role in the industry and in their union is of fundamental importance to understanding the relationships between the skilled men and the dilutees which were to be important in later women's strikes. The craft unions were suspected of organising the women to ensure that they did not constitute an economic threat to their own members by being under-paid for operations previously performed by skilled men, and it was thought that they would attempt to get rid of the women at the end of the war. There were strong grounds for believing this—amply demonstrated by the first clause of the Extended Employment of Women Agreement of 1940, which stated that dilutees were to be regarded as temporarily employed.[90] In contrast to Arthur Deakin of the TGWU, Jack Tanner did not stress the theme that women were 'here to stay'. At the Third Annual Women's Conference, held in May 1945, Tanner reflected the fears of the rank and file when he said that there would not be enough jobs for men, let alone women, at the end of the war.[91] Union leaders were often guarded in their statements, conscious as they were of relations with other Executives, but on the shop floor views were expressed rather more forcefully and the general unions were left in no doubt that the AEU shop stewards intended to apply the letter of the 1940 Agreement. In fact, even Communist shop stewards made it clear that they would, too. At A.V. Roe's Chadderton factory the CP's factory paper, *Factory News,* was written and produced by a team of skilled men of whom the most active was Stan Grundy, an AEU toolsetter.[92] The paper constantly pushed the theme of equal pay, directing its remarks mainly to the men, but at the same time made it quite clear that the 1940 Agreement should be rigidly applied and that dilutees were to be removed at the end of the war. In the autumn of 1944 a large meeting of delegates from throughout the A.V. Roe group met to discuss redundancy. The paper noted 'a marked cleavage of opinion' between the outlook of the skilled men and that of the recent entrants to the industry. The view was expressed at the meeting that as soon as a dilutee was made redundant (s)he should be immediately removed from the factory. The paper went on to express its disgust with the position at one factory in the group, 'in which AEU members have grown so indifferent that the M&GW and the T&GW can take over the leadership of an engineering factory'.[93]

The most extreme expression of this attitude was to be found in the National Union of Foundry Workers, which continued to refuse to organise women despite the AEU's decision. Their attitude was made crystal-clear to the other craft unions when they met in mid-1943 to discuss women in the engineering industry. Mr McLearie attended for the NUFW, and gave a detailed report to his Executive, in which he said he had told the meeting that the NUFW was not in favour of women having come into the industry. They saw great danger, moreover, in even negotiating and laying down standards for their employment, as this might seem to countenance their presence and stabilise their position, 'because all the time we were hopeful at the close of hostilities they would leave the foundries'. Up to then they had only been allowed to enter as dilutees (with registration being insisted upon), 'that having been made perfectly clear', apart from at certain foundries where they had always done certain classes of work. McLearie was opposed to special women's rates, and advocated the rate for the job, irrespective of the worker who performed it.[94] This report showed in a brutally direct way the policy of his union. The key requirement was to protect the interests of the skilled men: from this flowed both the demand for the rate for the job and an insistence that women were only to be tolerated in the industry for the duration of the war.

Yet the craft trade-unionists' attitude to women was double-edged. Although on the one hand it emphasised that the men would not tolerate women in skilled work at the end of the war, on the other it stressed that women should not be used by the employers to undercut skilled rates. The women, in their view, were guardians of men's jobs while they were away in the Forces, and all concerned had to fight to ensure that their jobs had not been either taken over or degraded by the presence of women. This attitude was crucial because it opened up the possibility of many individual and some collective battles for the rate for the job for women. Although on issues such as nurseries the craft-unionists had not used their position of strength within the industry to help the women to any great extent, the same was not true of the rate for the job. Their insistence on the wages question often coincided with the women's own feeling, and generated a growing trend towards wages militancy on the part of the women workers themselves.

Women's grievances about their pay deserve detailed examination in terms of their objective position, and also of the way that both they and the men who worked with them saw the issue. There was no doubt that women were at the bottom of the industry's pay ladder. The national women's rates were always lower than those of male labourers, just as their hourly earnings generally were. In July 1943 women's hourly earnings averaged 1s. 6d. per hour, compared to men's 2s. 7d. Women's earnings in the metal, engineering and shipbuilding industries expressed as a proportion of men's had risen during the war: in October 1938 they stood at 47.4 per cent, in July 1943 they were 58.1 per cent, and in July 1945, 62.5 per cent. Many stewards felt that the differential was partly due to the employers' failure to implement the Extended Employment of Women Agreement of 1940; in 1945 the E&ATSSNC surveyed 30,643 women in fifty-eight factories, and claimed to have found 6,010 women replacing men and 6,475 on the same work as men, but only 2,050 actually receiving the full man's rate.[95]

In public, the engineering employers protested their innocence of the charge made by the unions that they interpreted the 1940 Agreement with utter rigidity. Probably the biggest employer of them all, the government, was at the same time privately conceding that this was so. At the beginning of 1944 the official section of the Engineering

Trades Joint Industrial Council for Government Industrial Establishments considered a memorandum submitted by the Air Ministry, which stated that the department had taken the view that a woman applying for the man's rate would have to prove that she could do the whole of a mechanic's job without any more supervision than he would require, even where this was not required by the job in hand. It continued: 'Hitherto the 100% of the male rate has only been sanctioned in very few cases, where it is clear beyond all shadow of doubt.'[96] Women machinists applying for the full male rate had to be prepared to demonstrate their ability to carry out difficult tasks on different machines on their own in front of a battery of skilled assessors (something not required of any male apprentice). The Air Ministry excused this attitude by admitting that they had thought when they had made the agreement that 'the 100% provision would in all probability not in fact be operative'.[97] But the number of applications for the full male rate was increasing in the winter of 1943-4;

'Don't say "gimme" Felice. It makes Daddy think of the plant.'

*New Propellor*, 1945

in fact, by May Sir Charles McLaren, chairman of the council, advised a more liberal interpretation of the 1940 Agreement in order to stave off claims for new agreements.[98]

It was little wonder, then, that young women transferred to strange towns often found themselves in a difficult financial position. Many were asked to send money home, needed money for occasional visits home, and often had to pay over the odds for food, accommodation and travel. Numerous cases of transferred girls in financial straits were quoted in factory papers in 1943 and 1944. A typical case was that of a transferred girl in a north-western aircraft factory in early 1944, who earned 37s. 9d. and had to pay 30s. for her digs alone.[99] This girl was earning less than average, but earnings based on piece-work were always insecure and many girls could find themselves in a similar position if they had a 'bad week'. The averages concealed daily and weekly fluctuations from which no piece-worker was immune. Irish women in particular, brought in from Eire with promises of high earnings in British war factories, were often very disappointed with their actual take-home pay.[100] Shop stewards were not slow to stress the moral dangers of having young girls, away from home, wandering the streets of big towns with little money, and tried to appeal to managements on this ground.

A detailed investigation carried out for Mass Observation in the late summer of 1942 among the women in a Birmingham arms factory showed considerable discontent with their wages for a number of reasons.[101] All the concrete comparisons that the women made with other workers' earnings were unfavourable. Both men and women complained that their particular firm paid badly in comparison with others on similar work in the same area, although the investigators thought that this was not actually true. Samples of the women's comments included: 'There's girls at Hercules earning £7 a week. What don't speak can't lie, and I've seen her wage sheets.' 'Tubes isn't a good paying firm.' 'There's others pay better,'[102] and so on. Most women did not understand the complicated engineering wages structure.[103] None of them were able to say how their actual pay packets were made up in terms of basic pay, bonus and overtime pay. On the whole they seemed to rely on the men they were working with or the foremen to tell them how much they were entitled to.[104] Usually complaints were made to other women about the pay, but sometimes the discrepancy between what a woman expected and what she actually received was so great that she insisted on having it checked. A woman of thirty, finding £3. 19s. in her pay packet, said:

> I'm going to ask them about it. They told me that once you reach £4:10/-, on piece-work, you never drop below it. I've sweated my inside out this week, and get under £4 for it. I can't work for this. I could stay at home and take things easy. I'm out of pocket working for this—I've got to pay out to have the babs minded. I'll ask for my bleeding cards back, and be glad to have them.[105]

The report thought the women otherwise 'fairly well satisfied with their usual wages', but much of their evidence flew in the face of such a comment.[106] Frustration developed when women found apparently inexplicable differences in the pay of women doing similar work. 'Maisie got more than anyone. She got £2:8:11d., and she's only 21, and I'm 23. There's something funny about it, because we both work in the same place.'[107] Another added: 'There's girls doing the same amount of hours, and they've all got different pay.'[108] Angry comparisons were also made with the men when the girls were not paid at overtime rates for working bank holiday week. A girl who had been on holiday and so was not affected roundly berated the others:

> The *men* get overtime for Bank Holiday week—it's your own bleeding fault for letting them do it. Why don't you have the pluck to go and make a fuss about it? They wouldn't give *me* £2 for a week's work. Oh, what are you all grumbling about? You've got 2½d. when you've paid your lodgings and fares, ain't you? You girls make me sick—you ought to go up about it. If they see you managing on a little bit, they'll bring all the wages down.[109]

At the end of August 1942 changes were made in the rates of pay, both basic and bonus, but the women's attitude was still 'highly critical', and they took to returning their pay packets to ask how they were made up. The report concluded that wage grievances among women were caused by discrepancies between pay that were not understood by them, rather than by the absolute level of wages, and that the reasons for these differences should be made clear.[110] Although the Mass Observation conclusion in this respect contained an element of truth, in that the women were concerned with what they earned compared to what those around them earned rather than compared to other groups in society, this was not the whole story. The pressure of trying to balance their domestic economies could also lie behind these comparisons, could indeed have given rise to them in the first place. Nevertheless, the Mass Observation conclusion can be accepted in so far as the comparisons they could make at the factory level were seen as unfair and inexplicable. Against this background it is easy to see the appeal of grading schemes which specified a particular basic rate on particular machines and operations, and even easier to see the appeal of the demand for equal pay for equal work.

The question of equal pay for equal work was not only raised by the Extended Employment of Women Agreement, but was being actively debated in a wider social context as the feeling grew that equal work *deserved* equal pay. The trade unions had played a part in stimulating this debate by advocating equal pay from the start of the war, but their agitation became a part of a broader consensus in the second half of the war. Both the Labour and Communist Parties raised the question more and more frequently. In August 1942 Jennie Lee wrote an article in *Picture Post* entitled 'A New Life Opens Out For Women', in which she emphasised the need for equal pay as the first item in a programme for women's emancipation.[111] In 1944 the same popular magazine was exploring the domestic aspects of the topic, with an article by Edward Hulton called 'Wages For Wives?', where Hulton discussed the merits of Dr Summerskill's petition to the House of Commons calling for women to be entitled to an equal share of the home and its income.[112] Hulton was not entirely in favour of the petition, but thought that 'changes are undoubtedly required'.[113] Through this sort of popular medium the question of women's economic position in society in the post-suffrage era was being raised. Nor were such ideas solely the obsession of a few writers for the leftward-leaning *Picture Post*. In early 1944 the largely Conservative House of Commons voted in favour of amending the Education Bill to give women teachers equal pay, and only the direct challenge of a vote of confidence persuaded them to reverse their decision.[114] It was this current of opinion, combined with the industrial agitation, that caused the government to establish the Royal Commission on Equal Pay in 1944. Asked what their evidence to the Commission would be if they were to be asked for it, Mass Observers responded by giving their opinion on the matter; amongst the men respondents to the question, eighty-two were in favour and eleven against, with twenty-four giving no opinion.[115] Amongst the women, opinions were even more clearly in favour. Both men and women often emphasised as a corollary the importance of paying family allowances, while women frequently recalled the fight for women's suffrage, seeing the fight for economic equality as the next step.[116]

The specific form taken by women's agitation for pay increases derived not only from from these general trends of thought, nor even from the interaction between these trends and the women engineering workers' particular grievances, but also from the policies of the various unions. The AEU had always argued for the full application of the Extended Employment of Women Agreement, but the general unions evolved another, quite different policy. They had no interest in preserving the position of the skilled men, and from the beginning of 1943 were in direct competition with the AEU for women members. The general unions often tried to get the 1940 agreement applied (although they were not in fact party to it), but they followed a policy at national level of trying to negotiate with the engineering employers a national grading agreement for women. Determining whether a particular type of work had been 'commonly performed' by women in the industry before the war therefore became irrelevant. Types of work were simply graded, and the particular rate for that work paid accordingly. A national agreement between the general unions and the EEF was signed in December 1942, but the EEF refused to implement the section dealing with grading unless the AEU signed it, on the argument that otherwise the AEU would continue to press for the full men's rate for women.[117] The general unions were more interested, on the other hand, in delivering wage increases through grading which had already been agreed with the employers. They complained that large numbers of women workers were being underpaid because of the AEU's insistence that they already had an agreement on women's pay, and would not sign the December 1942 agreement.[118]

The AEU's position was supported by the E&ATSSNC, whose Acting Committee, meeting with delegates from a number of important districts in March 1943, expressed satisfaction that the AEU had rejected the agreement.[119] In general the E&ATSSNC (which reflected the influence of the AEU within the CP) felt that the December 1942 agreement represented a retreat from the campaign to force the employers to honour the 1940 agreement. The answer, they felt, lay in the effective deployment of shop steward organisation to ensure that the rate was paid when women replaced men. The TGWU and NUGMW, on the other hand, felt that such views were impractical because it was not always possible to argue that when women replaced men the work in question had not been 'commonly performed' by women before the war. Some women, they felt, could be regraded upwards despite the fact that they could not obtain the full men's rate. The position in 1943 and 1944 was unstable, with two different policies being pursued, both at national and shop floor level, and the unions were concerned that a domestic agreement which crossed their policy might encourage others, thereby overturning the whole applecart.[120]

It was in this context that the most important wartime strike on women's pay occurred at Rolls-Royce's Hillington factory near Glasgow in November 1943. The factory was built to the highest standards of mass production, and a steadily increasing programme of dilution followed its opening in 1940. By the time of the strike, of the twenty thousand who worked there 39 per cent were women, while only 4½ per cent were skilled men.[121] Most of the workers travelled from Glasgow out to the Hillington industrial estate, because the

Penilee Estate built near it was slow to develop and the rents were initially considered too high.[122] As in many of the new factories the workforce had been recruited exclusively under 'boom' conditions, there was no existing body of long-serving workers to form a stable core around which new workers could be assimilated, and from the start the factory seethed with trade union and political activity. The Rolls-Royce management, unprepared for such problems, was taken aback: all their experience was with a skilled and stable workforce imbued with an unusual pride in their superlative products. One manager complained that the district 'is seething with communists and strikes and threats of strikes occur the whole time', while another said: 'The Clydeside workers are the most difficult people in the world to handle. The fact that Hillington is a government factory they consider gives them the right to criticise it from all angles.'[123] The CP was undoubtedly strong in the factory, and we have already seen that the Clyde Workers' Committee had a few stewards working there, but both of these organisations had to contend with a third: the Catholic Workers' Guild. The left had often had to face criticism from Catholics in Scotland, and the CP had felt the need to issue an appeal for Catholics to unite with them to secure increased production, which was distributed *en masse* in Scotland and reproduced in the *Daily Worker* in early 1943.[124] The Catholic Workers' Guild rejected this approach in favour of a policy of industrial militancy and continued to criticise the CP's policy at Hillington, their Scottish stronghold. The Catholic workers had a regular weekly meeting on Friday evenings, and ran a book club in the works (one of the most popular books being Belloc's *The Servile State.*)[125] During the dispute they gave consistent support to the strikers, constantly attacking the CP.

The factory contained a number of clearly defined political attitudes, but it was the organised Catholic presence which was the most distinctive. Catholic trade-unionism had a long tradition in Scotland, but it was unusual for Catholics to advocate industrial action when the Communists were opposing it. One of the reasons for this peculiar situation was, of course, the unusual industrial-political position which the

CP found itself in, but this does not entirely explain the Catholics' vigorous industrial policy. Another important factor in the relative positions of the two groups was the introduction of large numbers of women from Eire into Britain. We have already touched on these women's grievances as far as earnings were concerned, but this was only the tip of an iceberg of problems. The Eire workers came from a neutral country, and had a reputation for not being amenable to factory work discipline. At Fords and Briggs' Bodies, Dagenham, which also employed a high proportion of Irish labour, the immigrants had played a vital role in the battles to organise these two important plants, as the Ministry of Labour, *Catholic Worker* and the Connolly Association agreed.[126]

Because the Hillington factory had a high and steadily increasing proportion of semi-skilled labour and much of the machinery was new, there had been great difficulty in determining the appropriate rates to be paid to men and to women. The question was whether the work had 'customarily' been performed by women before the war, and the arguments could become extremely obscure, as a result of the impact of advanced technology on traditional skills. The AEU had taken up the question of women's rates forcefully in May 1942 because the firm was not, the union claimed, observing the Extended Employment of Women Agreement. Negotiations went on up to Central Conference level until July 1943 without agreement being reached, while frustration gradually built up within the factory because of the delay.[127] Meanwhile, the TGWU stewards (with more than three thousand members in the factory)[128] had been negotiating with the management for implementation of the national grading scheme.[129] In July a strike broke out because of the reduction of the piece-work rate on one particular job. The prominent Communist convenor, McElroy, put a motion to the shop stewards' committee that a limited strike of a thousand workers should be financially supported by the rest of the factory, but this was defeated and he was reported as having resigned from the CP. There is little reliable information on the dispute, but according to *Socialist Appeal* the whole factory decided to come out on strike against the recommendation of the shop stewards' committee, but soon returned. Craigie Hill, the departmental convenor, apparently denounced the stewards' recommendation and called on the members to replace the CP members on the committee. As a result, *Socialist Appeal* claimed, five CP stewards lost their cards.[130] Whatever the truth of the matter, there had clearly been some strong feelings expressed on the shop floor, despite the fact that Bevin had already agreed to the request of the AEU Executive that a Court of Inquiry should be set up to look into the problems in the factory.[131]

The inquiry, under Lord Wark, was held in private in Glasgow and Hillington between the end of July and the end of August; it found that the company had in fact broken parts of the 1940 agreement, but recommended a negotiated settlement based on grading.[132] The stewards began to negotiate on this basis with the management, and on 30 October an agreement was signed providing for four grades of women workers in the factory (as in the December 1942 agreement).[133] The TGWU stewards had always been in favour of such a solution, but the AEU stewards had not; nonetheless they finally agreed to accept the scheme after some pressure from sections of the membership.[134] A problem arose when strong rumours circulated that the actual implementation of the proposed scheme would mean that those receiving the full men's rate would be very few. *Socialist Appeal* claimed that eighty per cent of the women would be entitled to a rate of no more than 25s., which was the national women's rate.[135] The E&ATSSNC later took issue with this and contended that roughly one thousand women would get the men's rate (grade 1); one thousand would get grade 2; two thousand would get grade 3; and three thousand would get grade 4 (29s. at the time of negotiation).[136] Whatever the reality, the workforce was confused and concerned. Strike action was urged on their members by the stewards of the CWC, and section by section, block by block, men and women alike left work until some sixteen thousand were out.[137] The shop stewards seem to have been divided by the strike: some stood by the agreement on the grounds that if the union tore this one up, the management would tear up the next one, but the majority of the negotiating stewards seem to have been swayed by the arguments against the agreement, and supported the strike.[138]

The strikers demanded that everyone in the bottom grade (4) should receive 34s. instead of the 29s. which a subdivision of grade 4 was to receive. Wal Hannington, who had travelled to Glasgow to deal with the strike, and Andrew Dalgleish, the National Secretary of the TGWU's Metal, Engineering and Chemicals Group, recommended that the demand be remitted to the unions' national Executives, and work be resumed.[139] But at a mass meeting held soon after the strike began, described by Galbraith as 'a complete failure', only three hundred of the five thousand or so present voted for a return to work.[140] The strikers were circularised by the Catholic Workers' Guild with a leaflet entitled *The Crux of the Strike,* which blamed the firm for not moving even part of the way towards meeting the terms of the 1940 agreement. The leaflet ended by saying: '. . . provocation has been caused by the management. It is said that the workers have no right to take advantage of war-time conditions, but. . . the employers have taken advantage of war-time conditions by paying unfair wages to women workers.'[141] This was the first time that anything approaching a Catholic Workers' Guild statement of policy had been widely distributed in Scotland, and James Darragh, its local secretary, claimed that many congratulations on the leaflets were received from Catholics and non-Catholics alike.[142] Meanwhile, the CWC stewards were also intervening. According to *New Propellor,* the CWC stewards, having attacked the union officials and the majority of the shop stewards for passively accepting the agreement, attempted to hold their own mass meeting with their members to set up a separate strike committee.[143] Whether they had in fact tried to do this, and what came of their committee, is not known, but no further evidence of such an attempt has so far come to light.

Galbraith's reports do allow us, however, to pinpoint the CWC's attempts to spread the strike into a general battle for a higher basic rate. An extension of the strike had briefly occurred just after the Rolls strike had begun, when women at the nearby Aeroplastics factory on the Hillington industrial estate came out on 2 and 3 November for equal pay.[144] On 9 November Galbraith reported in a special letter to London that women at the Coventry Gauge and Tool's factory in Yoker had come out on strike, and that those at Barr and Stroud's and the North British Locomotive Co. had also voted to do so, in response to the CWC's leaflet *A Message To All Clydeside Workers.*[145] Clearly, the strike was taking on more than a domestic character, and Galbraith became concerned as to how to end it.

The strikers were being attacked by the newspapers both locally and nationally for their action: P.J. Dollan, the Lord Provost of Glasgow, berated the women for taking the law into their own hands in the *Clydebank Press,* while the *Sunday Dispatch*'s leader-writer condemned them as 'traitors' and 'footpads'.[146] The *Daily Worker* did not publish anything on this occasion that could be construed as an attack on the strikers, leaving *New Propellor* to criticise the CWC after the strike had ended.[147] Hannington and some shop stewards were nevertheless working hard to secure a resumption of work. A number of stewards had contacted Galbraith with a view to enlisting his cooperation in getting the company to re-open negotiations and presenting this to the strikers as the basis for a return. At first it was not clear whether Rolls-Royce were in fact prepared to resume negotiations, but these stewards wanted to hold a secret ballot with this information clearly displayed. Galbraith was reluctant to release the ballot papers until it was certain that the company did agree; when this was established the stewards organised their secret ballot. In a poll of some twenty-five to thirty per cent of the strikers, 3,522 voted to return and 967 to stay out, on the basis that negotiations would be resumed in seven days.[148] The threat of the dispute spreading had been avoided for the time being at least. By the beginning of December the dispute had been to arbitration and was settled by a complex formula which named each machine in the factory and laid down a rate for it.[149] The settlement which was eventually made thus had relevance only to the Rolls-Royce factories. This was not entirely the end of the matter, as the women at the Rolls-Royce Thornliebank and Alexandra

Parade factories were still not satisfied with the grading arrangements, and stopped work for ten days. There were attempts to stimulate sympathetic action in the Hillington plant, but only one section of one hundred stopped work for a short time.[150]

The Rolls-Royce strike had been described by Galbraith as 'a most serious interruption of work', which had aroused 'acute interest' in the whole question of women's wages and which had at one point seemed capable of spreading to England.[151] It was quite apparent that the issue of women's pay was hot enough to make stoppages spread beyond their factory of origin; this was why the tiny spark provided by the Clyde Workers' Committee's stewards had been enough to start and to extend the strike. The support of an equal number of men and women strikers had been particularly significant; it had shown that the problem of women's wages was not one which the men regarded with indifference. One of the most important results of the strike was the adoption by all the unions of a more radical position. The AEU rejected altogether the idea of work designated as women's work, and at the end of 1943 the AEU and ETU, together with the general unions, submitted a claim for work to be graded irrespective of the sex of the operator.[152] The employers refused to concede this, presumably because they had hoped for the AEU's acceptance of the 1942 agreement and at the same time the abrogation of the 1940 agreement, which would not have been the corollary of a non-discriminatory grading scheme. In any case, the energies of the AEU and its stewards remained exclusively directed towards implementing the 1940 agreement. The dispute had been of national significance but it had not spread much beyond Rolls-Royce for very long, despite the fears expressed by Galbraith. Nor had it been as solid at its core as the Barrow strike had been; several thousand were still working despite the fact that the great majority had stopped. Nevertheless, it was the first large-scale wartime strike by men and women on women's wages, and caused a stiffening of the official trade union attitude to grading schemes.

The Rolls-Royce strike and the cluster of disputes which surrounded it were soon resolved by the arbitration award, and the number of working days lost through strikes at Rolls was to drop drastically during 1944. But the strike and its settlement had aroused great interest in the Clyde district. Another strike followed hard on the heels of the Rolls-Royce settlement, at Barr and Stroud's Anniesland and Kirkintilloch factories. However, this unsuccessful action nipped in the bud the movement for higher women's wages which seemed to have begun on the Clyde.

The women at Barr and Stroud's were only about one quarter trade-unionised, and they needed twelve shillings on the basic rate to bring them up to the national minimum of 26s. The company offered them eight shillings for time-workers and seven for piece-workers, but the union rejected the offer; on 13 December 1943 two thousand women struck at the Anniesland factory, and one hundred and twenty at the Kirkintilloch works. The shop stewards' committee at Anniesland was split right down the middle on whether or not to give the women their support. The Divisional Organiser, Allan, apparently insisted that the shop stewards' committee should have a two-thirds majority before it could take strike action, and that since the committee was split a strike decision was impossible.[153] From the beginning, the strike was a battle royal between some stewards on the one hand and the union officials on the other. The men at Anniesland had initially come out in support of the women, but had been persuaded by the officials that the strike decision was incorrectly taken.[154] Some of the stewards, according to Galbraith, had 'openly encouraged the strike' and had consistently tried to keep the union officials out of their mass meetings, and when the TGWU official managed to gain admission to one he was given no support by the stewards.[155] As a result, on 6 January 1944 four hundred men stopped work, but one thousand men who had not attended the meeting remained at work.[156] It soon became apparent that this extension of the strike had not benefited the strikers in the long run, because the section of the men in favour of supporting the women had been isolated from the rest. Initially it seemed possible that the strike would spread, and this was certainly the intention of the group of stewards led by Charlie Menzies, the AEU convenor.

One steward spoke of 'emptying the river', and attempts were made to start a wider national strike, according to Galbraith, although it is hard to see on what basis.[157] It would have been difficult to conceive of a broader campaign to bring women up to the national women's minimum as most women already earned this, but it is possible that Galbraith had in mind an extension to other Barr and Stroud factories. In any case, the only support that actually material-ised was financial; collections at Albion Motors, Beardmore's Parkhead Forge and Vickers Barrow brought £48, £58 and £100 respectively.[158] The real problem, however, was that despite repeated efforts on the part of some shop stewards the strike had not spread to the majority of the men at Barr and Stroud's itself. Although Galbraith thought the strikers were prepared for a 'fight to the finish', the workforce was clearly divided, and 'shop stewards' circles' were calling for a secret ballot as at Rolls-Royce.[159] In the end the strike com-mittee, under pressure from the men on strike, recommended a return to work, despite the fact that the company had only offered negotiations within forty-eight hours of a return.[160] Menzies regretfully recommended the strikers to return at a final mass meeting held after almost a month out, saying it was 'one of the rottenest jobs I have ever had to do' but that they had to take into account that they had not had the support of the men as a whole, nor of the workers on the Clyde.[161] In the end, the women obtained only an extra shilling on their piece-work rates.[162]

The failure of the Barr and Stroud strike was recorded by Galbraith with satisfaction in his report to London. The strike had been defeated despite, as he put it, the concentra-tion of all of the 'unofficial elements in the area, from Barrow and elsewhere'.[163] He predicted (with a degree of accuracy) that the issue of women's wages would not come up again after this second defeat.[164] Just as in the Rolls-Royce strike, the problem had been that only a section of the shop stewards were prepared to participate actively in a strike on women's wages; some were influenced by the argument that women's pay should not be allowed to undercut men's to the extent of making them willing to strike to ensure it, but these were only a part of the movement. Others, although they might agree that women were too low paid—indeed, the CP and the E&ATSSNC pushed the argument quite hard—could not see their way clear to supporting strike action during wartime. At the other end of the ideological spectrum, of course, there were always those who felt that women's pay was not too low. Be that as it may, the fact was that amongst the rank and file in the workshops only a certain proportion of the men would support the women. At Rolls it had been rather more than at Barr and Stroud's, but this fact imposed a limit on the strikes, both internal and external. Neither the Ministry of Labour nor managements saw any overwhelming arguments in favour of giving in to a partial strike when such concessions could have important repercussions within the industry nationally. Nor did stewards from other firms see why they should press for sympathetic action in a dispute that was far from unanimously supported by the men at Barr and Stroud's. Moreover, it was much more difficult for the women themselves to organise support for their action when they were mostly cut off from trade union contacts and channels of communication. The informal lines of communication between stewards and branch secretaries were controlled for the most part either by 'constitutional' trade-unionists or by the E&ATSSNC; when even the E&ATSSNC 'unofficial' movement was against them, only such tiny organisations as the CWC and MWF could help, and these disputes showed the pathetically small contribution that they could make.

H.A. Emmerson, Bevin's right-hand man at the Ministry of Labour, had written in an important memorandum on the causes of industrial unrest at the beginning of November 1943 that disputes relating to women's wages were 'proportionately more prone to result in strike action than where men are concerned'.[165] If the defeat of the Barr and Stroud strike represented a setback for the movement to improve women's pay, it certainly did not mark its end. At the E&ATSSNC's meeting of 12 March, Miss Violet Coulthard from Hawker Aircraft was 'heartily cheered' when she said that it was not easy to 'put the right spirit' into girls when they were paid such 'miserable' rates, that these rates were a danger to men's position in the industry, and that women should get the rate for the job.[166] In May a factory paper reported that there was 'a great deal of feeling on the point' on the Manchester District Committee of the AEU, and in the same month *Labour's Northern Voice* reported that the Essex Federation of Trades Councils had passed a resolution in favour of equal pay, together with another which said that 'the present economic situation lends itself to a successful prosecution of a campaign for the rate for the job'.[167] Soon afterwards the same paper announced that the Manchester and Salford trades council had convened a special conference to discuss the question of equal pay.[168] There were already signs that this general mood would again be translated into industrial action: in April the Ministry of Labour's London Conciliation Officer reported that 'women generally feel strongly about the matter', and thought that 'a determined effort' would soon be made to achieve equal pay.[169]

The movement tailed off during the last year of war, however, when one of the principal reasons for a lack of industrial action was the existence of the Royal Commission on Equal Pay. A Royal Commission had been mooted as a possibility during 1943, but it was not announced in the House of Commons until May 1944.[170] The Commission first met on 17 October after what was described in the Commons as a 'staggering' delay.[171] Despite further urgings from some MPs, Attlee refused to require the Commission to report within any particular period of time. Eventually, after considering one hundred and ninety-five written submissions and hearing oral evidence for fifteen days, it reported in October 1946.[172] By this time the industrial situation had changed completely, and women had been moved out of war industry and were mostly back in the home. The Commission's report was of no more than academic interest to the majority of women.

A good deal of attention was paid by trade-unionists to the existence of the Commission, but few realised that it had very restricted terms of reference. It was instructed: 'to examine the existing relationship between the remuneration of men and women in the public services, in industry and in other fields of employment, to consider the social, economic and financial implications of the claim of equal pay for equal work, and to report.'[173] A number of the civil servants who reported to the Commission, including the statistician E.C. Ramsbottom, had also reported to the disappointingly conservative Atkis Committee on women in industry which was set up in 1918.[174] All of the official witnesses from the Treasury and the Ministry of Labour were warned that their evidence would have to cover some of the nation-wide effects of equal pay (such as pressure for more and better family allowances, tax relief, and so on) and that statements on these questions would certainly need to be covered by ministerial authority.[175] When Bevin publicly stated that women in industry had been as productive as men, Gould (a senior civil servant in the Ministry of Labour) was quick to draw the attention of his colleagues to the fact that Bevin had used the phrase 'with the help of the production engineer', lest they might infer that their Minister was in favour of equal pay.[176] With all these pressures at work before the official witnesses even testified, it was perhaps hardly surprising that the Royal Commission produced a majority report which suggested that the effects of introducing equal pay would be negative. A memorandum of dissent was appended by three of the four women members of the Commission (Dame Anne Loughlin, Dr Janet Vaughan and Miss L.F. Nettlefold), who disagreed with the majority's view that women's lower pay was caused by their lower efficiency and argued that it was the result of weaker trade union organisation. They concluded that the requirements of individual justice and the development of national productivity 'pointed in the same direction' (presumably towards equal pay, although they did not actually say so).[177] Even the equal pay minority was not prepared, then, to recommend equal pay in so many words.

There were some within the trade union movement who had anticipated such an outcome even before the Commission had met. Miss Samuels of the Manchester and Salford trades council, for example, had drawn an explicit parallel with the role that the Sankey Commission had played in defusing the miners' demand for nationalising the mines at the end of the First World War. The working class, she said, had 'bitter memories' of Royal Commissions.[178] Yet these voices were in the minority. On the whole, trade-unionists cooperated with the Commission: the three main unions all gave evidence despite their reservations about its composition and terms of reference. By the time the Royal Commission had reported, industrial demobilisation was in any case complete. Women's temporary industrial power had been removed by their return to the home, and the movement for equal pay returned to the sphere of abstract philosophical debate.

The industrial demobilisation of women was in general achieved with very little disturbance or objection from the women involved. There were some protests from Lancashire women directed out of the munitions industries and into cotton. In May 1945 four hundred women from a Ferranti factory in the North-West were directed back into the mills. They made 'strong protests' because they stood to lose in terms of wages, conditions (which were much worse in the mills than in munitions) and seniority (job allocation was strictly according to seniority, and returning women could not expect the best spinning jobs irrespective of their experience on the work).[179] This sort of problem was not, however, typical, and arose from the particular situation in Lancashire.

The ease with which the demobilisation of women was achieved related partly to the wishes of the women themselves. Their individual attitudes to working in industry at the end of the war were the subject of a number of surveys, and although these have to be handled very cautiously they do appear to show that most women were not set on staying. A Mass Observation survey produced in 1944 showed that less than twenty-five per cent of women working in factories wanted to continue in their present job. Most of those who did were either part-time workers or had worked for an above-average length of time.[180] There was no doubt that part-time work was very attractive to many women: over two hundred thousand had worked part-time during the war, most of them in the aircraft industry, and they had found the arrangement by and large suited them.[181] The majority of women took a different attitude, tending to regard wartime work as a necessary evil, a temporary interlude. As one girl interviewed by Mass Observation said: 'You can't look on anything you do during the war as what you really mean to do, it's just filling in time till you can live your own life again.'[182] Many others expressed similar sentiments, especially young women who had been conscripted into industry. They had no choice, and it is not difficult to surmise the way in which they interpreted the official term 'release' from war work. Even amongst those women who wanted to stay, there was often a feeling that they would like to use the opportunity presented by the end of the war to have a break from work. It is difficult, on the basis of the data available from the none-too-sophisticated surveys of women's views on these matters, to make very definite assertions, but it does seem that women were very far from united in their desire to work after the war. Without a greater degree of consensus among them, it was difficult for the minority to press their case in a collective way.

As we have already mentioned, such facilities as there were for working mothers had been provided in a way that left little doubt as to their temporary nature. This was yet another factor that deterred women from carrying on at work after the war. Yet it might still have been possible to envisage a campaign to retain women's jobs into peacetime had it not been for one overriding consideration: the attitude of the Amalgamated Engineering Union.

The AEU had always taken pains to stress to engineering employers and government alike that it regarded its agreement on the extended employment of women as a temporary one, only to last as long as the war itself. They had only agreed to relax their traditional insistence that certain types of work were skilled and carried the full skilled rate because of the national emergency. This principle was enshrined within the 1940 Extended Employment of Women Agreement. As we have also seen, the AEU regarded the agreement as its safeguard against the introduction of cheap labour. In other words, their principal motive in 1940 had been to guarantee the position of the skilled men, and they therefore insisted that dilutees should be registered as the temporary custodians of their jobs. So the dilutees were given special white AEU union cards when recruited, and section V (Temporary Relaxation Agreement) membership. Arguing for the rate for the job for these workers had always been intimately tied up, in the AEU shop stewards' minds, with the idea that if the rate was not secured then women could undercut skilled men in the post-war labour market. It was this same viewpoint which ensured that dilutees, and women in particular, were told by the AEU stewards that they were only in the industry temporarily and that if there were redundancies they would have to leave. The fact that the rate for the job had not generally been secured tended to increase the desire of the skilled stewards to insist that the letter of the 1940 Agreement be applied. Here, then, was the other side of the 'rate for the job' movement: the formidable strength of the AEU shop stewards, hitherto deployed to lead all engineering workers together towards the more general application of the skilled rates, was now turned towards making sure that dilutees did not stay in engineering.

It was to be expected that the general unions would protest against this attitude, but their protests were to little avail. The AEU remained the main engineering union not just in terms of numbers but, even more importantly, by its virtual monopoly of the key shop stewards' positions. At Renold Chain's Manchester factory the General and Municipal Workers' Union protested that it had no agreement with the employer that women dilutees should be removed before men, but the AEU stewards recruited the support of their District Committee in insisting that the company stick to the 1940 Agreement.[183] There was little that the general unions could do. Occasionally disputes arose about which women were to go first, since many women were members of the AEU. In some cases (as in Glasgow) the unions objected to the normal procedure of the 'most mobile' women being released before the others, because many of the 'most mobile' were union members, and 'nons' were therefore being kept on in preference.[184] Even in this case, however, the shop stewards were merely insisting on a certain order of redundancy amongst different groups of women. The general principle of women first was not in question.

The drive towards women's unionisation, the individual

and collective battles to secure the rate for the job and the wartime industrial agitation of the engineering shop stewards were significant factors in the history of British working women. The main motive of the AEU remained throughout the protection of its male, and especially its skilled, membership, at the expense of women workers. Nor did the left succeed in diverting the AEU from this policy. In the end the objections of the smaller general unions to AEU policies appeared far from groundless; engineering had become once more an overwhelmingly male industry.

But the balance sheet cannot be left at that. There was a credit side to the wartime experience. As after the First World War, a rather higher proportion of women stayed behind in the factories than had been there in 1939, to keep the tradition of women's trade-unionism alive until women began to stream back into the industry in the 1950s and 1960s. Many of the women entrants of the Second World War had been exposed to the 'rate for the job' argument and made it their own; in due course, the Equal Pay Act and the attendant upturn in equal pay agitation would be the result. But there were wider implications. Even if only briefly, many women had experienced trade-unionism in a highly political form. A very high proportion of the new trade union members of the war were persuaded to pay the political levy; many experienced the primitive democracy of workplace meetings; others read and discussed factory newspapers. There can be little doubt that these and other encounters with factory politics lay behind the largest ever women's vote for the Labour Party in 1945.[185]

## NOTES

1  A. Calder, op. cit., p. 383.
2  'A Pretty Typical Government Campaign', 20 March 1941. File Report 615. MO Archive.
3  A. Calder, op. cit., p. 383.
4  V. Douie, *Daughters of Britain* (1949), pp. 97-100.
5  *Coventry Standard*, 13 June 1942.
6  Mass Observation, *People in Production* (1942), p. 117.
7  'Typical Day in a Factory', 11 Feb. 1942. MO Archive.
8  Mass Observation, *War Factory* (1943), pp. 26-7.
9  Quoted by R. Adam, *A Woman's Place, 1910-1975* (1975), p. 146.
10 Penny Summerfield, 'Women Workers in the Second World War' (in *Capital*

*and Class,* no. 1, March 1977).
11  See P. Inman, op. cit., pp. 60–2.
12  25 July 1943. LAB 10/363.
13  J.T. Murphy, *Victory Production* (1942), p. 52.
14  P. Summerfield, op. cit., p. 18.
15  Lorna Lewis, *Feud in the Factory* (1944), p. 59.
16  Ibid., pp. 59–61.
17  Ibid., p. 61.
18  Ibid., p. 71.
19  7 Sept. 1940. LAB 10/360. The importance of tolerance towards women workers was mentioned by a machine shop superintendent of an aircraft factory in an interesting article in the *Coventry Standard* of 13 June 1942.
20  Undated copy of *Factory News* (A.V. Roe), probably Feb. 1945.
21  G. Williams, *Women and Work* (1945), p. 35.
22  Mass Observation, Industry Raw Materials: *Welfare in Industry,* 13 Feb. 1942. This report noted that the sports club and social facilities provided in many of the factories surveyed were not widely known about and were little used.
23  *Tubes Report,* p. 43. Industry Raw Materials, MO Archive.
24  Doris White, *No Name on the Signpost.* I am grateful to the author and publisher for permission to quote from this manuscript (to be published in 1981).
25  AK Diary, 25 Jan. 1942, p. 114. Industry Raw Materials, MO Archive.
26  Special Report from A.K. Smith, Buckland Wharf, Aylesbury, Jan. 1942. Industry Raw Materials, MO Archive.
27  *Wolverton Express,* 15 Jan. 1943.
28  P. Inman, op. cit., p. 364. See also H. Emmerson, 'Causes of Industrial Unrest', 3 Nov. 1943. LAB 10/281.
29  *Wolverton Express,* 26 June 1942.
30  File Report 2059. 8 March 1944. MO Archive.
31  Lady Reading's motive was probably to try to ensure that the nurseries were retained after the war. Note of 4 Nov. 1940, MH 55/695.
32  See, for example, Z.L. Puxley to Miss Smieton (Ministry of Labour), 24 Aug. 1940, MH 55/695.
33  See, for example, a demonstration of Hampstead mothers, *Picture Post,* June 1942. 5, 9 Dec. 1941, MH 55/884.
34  Ferguson and Fitzgerald, p. 190.
35  *DW,* 14 March, 1945.
36  See *Further Notes on Woman Power,* 1 April 1941. File Report 625. MO Archive.
37  Mass Observation, *People in Production* (1942), p. 183.
38  J.B. Priestley, op. cit., pp. 37–8.
39  *Annual Report* of the Chief Inspector of Factories, 1941. Cmd. 6397, pp. 1, 27.
40  *The Economist,* 13 March 1943.
41  Ibid.
42  *Factory News* (A.V. Roe), 16 Jan 1945. See also 18 Jan. 1944, which reports a boycott at A.V. Roe's Ivy Mill works.
43  *The Economist,* 13 March 1943.
44  28 Feb. 1942. LAB 10/358. *Socialist Appeal,* June 1941.
45  *The Economist,* 13 March 1943.
46  The first strike was on 23-4 April 1942 and involved 337 workers, and the

second on 16 March 1943 involved 560 (LAB 34/57; LAB 34/58).

47   *The Economist,* 20 March 1943.
48   The AEU's conference was reported in the *Manchester Guardian,* 21 May 1943; the TGWU's in the TGWU *Record*, Nov. 1943.
49   P. Inman, op. cit., pp. 277–8.
50   This is documented in an unpublished paper kindly lent me by Stefan Karner of the Historisches Institut, Graz (Austria), entitled 'Arbeitsvertragsbrüchige im Dritten Reich'. Apparently the management of the Flumo aero-engine works in Untersteirmark called women 'soft currency' because of their high rate of absenteeism (p. 23).
51   Arthur Exell, 'Morris Motors in the 1940s', in *History Workshop Journal,* no. 9, spring 1980, pp. 94–5.
52   Interview with Jock Wallace, 8 April 1980.
53   *Minutes* of the Coventry District Committee of the AEU, 14 July 1942.
54   A. Exell, loc. cit., p. 95.
55   P. Inman, op. cit., p. 177.
56   TGWU *Record*, June 1942.
57   See S.T. Lewenhak, op. cit., p. 31; R. Croucher, op. cit., pp. 133–7.
58   12 July 1941. LAB 10/362.
59   *Report* to the General Council of the Scottish TUC and the Organisation of Women Committee by the Scottish Trade Union Delegation to the Midlands (1942) TUC, p. 18.
60   AK Diary, 25 Jan. 1942, p. 113. MO Archive.
61   R. Croucher, Survey of Works and Local Conference *Minutes* for Coventry.
62   Ibid.
63   E&ATSSNC, 'How to get the best results from the agreement for JPCs and advisory committees' (E&ATSSNC Bulletin, 23 May 1942).
64   *Manchester Guardian,* 21 May 1943.
65   V. Douie, *Daughters of Britain* (1949), p. 117.
66   Tirrell Report, p. 6. Industry Raw Materials, MO Archive.
67   J.T. Murphy, *Victory Production!* (1942), p. 67.
68   Tirrell Report, loc. cit.
69   Doris White, op. cit.
70   A. Calder gives the best summary of the AEU's position vis-à-vis women, op. cit., p. 465.
71   J.B. Jefferys, op. cit., p. 260.
72   *Electrical Trades Journal,* Jan. 1944; on the history of the ETU's debates on its auxiliary, industrial and women's sections, see ETU EC *Minutes* 5 and 6, 5 June 1942, and *Minute* 4, 11, 12 April 1943.
73   International Labour Organisation, *The War and Women's Employment* (Montreal, 1946), p. 90; B. Drake, *Women in Trade Unions* in G.D.H. Cole (ed.) *Trade Unionism Today* (1945), p. 249.
74   TGWU Home Study Course: *The Background of the Union* (1962), appendix 3, p. 22.
75   J.B. Jefferys, op. cit., p. 260.
76   S.T. Lewenhak, op. cit., table 5, estimates 11.2% for her wider definition of the industry.
77   Ibid.
78   TGWU *Record*, Aug. 1942.
79   *Newcastle Journal and North Mail,* 10 Feb. 1943.
80   The level of dilution in marine work reached its maximum of 15.8% in 1944 (25 July, LAB 10/363; Inman, op. cit., p. 80).
81   *Minutes* of a works conference held at GEC, 20 Dec. 1944; TGWU *Record*,

Feb., Nov. 1943.
82  TGWU *Record,* Feb. 1943.
83  Florence Hancock joined the Workers' Union in 1913 and became the District Officer in Wiltshire in 1917; she was on the General Council of the TUC from 1935 and became the TGWU National Women's Officer in 1942 (TGWU *Record,* Dec. 1942).
84  S.T. Lewenhak, op. cit., p. 146.
85  EC letter: 'Women Shop Stewards' (17 Feb. 1943) in Manchester District Committee *Minutes* (AEU), 4 March 1943.
86  ETU Executive Committee *Minute* 4, 11, 12 April 1943.
87  NUFW EC *Minutes.*
88  AEU Manchester District Committee *Minutes,* 18 Feb. 1943.
89  J.B. Jefferys, op. cit., p. 260.
90  P. Inman, op. cit., p. 441.
91  Deakin, 'We Demand Fair Pay For Women Workers', TGWU *Record,* Oct. 1942; *Report* of Proceedings of the Third Annual Women's Conference, 1, 2 May 1945, Blackpool, p. 12 (TUC Library).
92  Grundy was a self-taught linguist and 'a man of very great ability'. See S. Phelan, op. cit., p. 50, and *passim.*
93  Ibid., p. 55. *Factory News,* 3 Oct. 1944.
94  NUFW EC *Minutes,* 7 June 1943.
95  *The Economist,* 12 May 1945.
96  'Skilled Engineering Women' (memo by Air Ministry), 8 Feb. 1944, p. 3. LAB 10/475.
97  Ibid., p. 2.
98  Engineering Trades Joint Industrial Council for Government Industrial Establishments, official side meeting, 4 May 1944. LAB 10/475.
99  *Factory News* (A.V. Roe), 24 Jan. 1944. See also *Labour Research,* no. 30, p. 93, for a similar case from Coventry.
100  *Tubes Report* (Industry Raw Materials, MO Archive), p. 44.
101  The women from Ireland surveyed by Mass Observation said that they were told in Ireland that they would earn £4 a week, but not that they would have to work overtime for it. One girl felt that employers thought they earned so little in Ireland that they would be satisfied with anything. (*Tubes Report,* pp. 44, 45.)
102  *Tubes Report,* p. 42.
103  See J.B. Jefferys, op. cit., p. 256.
104  *Tubes Report,* p. 42.
105  Ibid., p. 43.
106  Ibid.
107  Ibid., p. 45.
108  Ibid.
109  Ibid., p. 46.
110  Ibid., p. 47.
111  *Picture Post,* 1 Aug. 1942.
112  Ibid., 5 Feb. 1944.
113  Ibid.
114  A. Calder, op. cit., p. 466. Calder interprets this as evidence that women's inequality was taken for granted, but the episode does not actually support this view.
115  The survey is based on the Directive replies for May 1944 (MO Archive).
116  See, for example, the comment of Hastings (3574, MO Archive).
117  TGWU Finance and General Purposes Committee *Minute* 320, 1943.

118 Ibid.; NUGMW Biennial Congress *Report*, June 1945, p. 87.
119 E&ATSSNC, Report of National Meeting Held Sunday 7 March 1943 at the Conway Hall, London.
120 See TGWU GEC *Minute* 998, 1943.
121 *Report by a Court of Inquiry into a Dispute at an Engineering Undertaking in Scotland* (Cmd. 6474, Oct. 1943), pp. 5–6.
122 I. Lloyd, op. cit., pp. 26–7.
123 Ibid., pp. 32–3.
124 *Catholic Worker*, Feb. 1943, commented: 'The CP as a whole appears to have been inflicted *[sic]* with amnesia. Fortunately Catholics have good memories and are not likely to be deceived by this Trojan horse strategy. One of the many things Catholics do remember is that, for twenty-two months, Catholic men and boys worked, and fought, *and died* for that liberty which permitted these same Communists, in those same twenty-two months, to sabotage actively the war effort in which they now profess themselves to be so interested.'
125 Other popular books were Werfel's *Song of Bernadette*, Lunn's *Now I See*, and O. Dudley's *Pageant of Life* (*Catholic Worker*, Feb. 1943).
126 5 May 1944. LAB 10/443. *Catholic Worker*, Aug. 1944; Connolly Association: *The Irish in Britain* (n.d.), Sara-Maitland collection, University of Warwick. The role of the Irish workers in the foundry emerges quite clearly from these sources, but no mention is made of it in the Lovell papers at the Marx Memorial Library, nor in the *Daily Worker* article written by Bob Lovell, the Communist District Secretary, which appeared on 15 November 1968.
127 P. Inman, op. cit., pp. 364–5.
128 TGWU *Record*, Sept. 1943.
129 P. Inman, loc. cit.
130 *Socialist Appeal*, mid-Aug., Oct. 1943. A CP shop steward wrote to the paper and denied that the CP were, as *Socialist Appeal* had put it, 'on the retreat' in the factory, but he did not deny the claim that five CP shop stewards had lost their cards (ibid., mid-Aug. 1943).
131 P. Inman, op. cit., p. 365.
132 Cmd. 6474 (1943), p. 10.
133 P. Inman, loc. cit.
134 *Catholic Worker*, Feb. 1944.
135 *Socialist Appeal*, Nov. 1943.
136 E&ATSSNC, 'Rolls-Royce Scotland. Application of May 1940 Relaxation Agreement' (Bulletin, 18 Nov. 1943).
137 LAB 34/58.
138 *Catholic Worker*, Feb. 1944. Mrs. Inman writes on p. 364 that the stewards supported the strike—a statement probably based on Galbraith's report of 5 November 1943 (LAB 10/364). The real situation appears to have been rather confused.
139 5 Nov. 1943 (LAB 10/364); Dalgleish joined the Workers' Union in 1907. In 1916 he became a member of the union's organising staff, and later assistant to the National Industrial Officer. He was National Secretary of the Metal, Engineering and Chemicals Group from 1931 until his retirement in 1945 (TGWU *Record*, April 1945).
140 5 Nov. 1943. LAB 10/364.
141 *Catholic Worker*, Feb. 1944.
142 Ibid.
143 *NP*, Dec. 1943.

144   5 Nov. 1943. LAB 10/364.
145   Galbraith to Gould, 9 Nov. 1943. LAB 10/281.
146   *Clydebank Press,* 5 Nov. 1943; *Sunday Dispatch,* 7 Nov. 1943.
147   *NP,* Dec. 1943. The *Catholic Worker,* Feb. 1944, agreed that the CWC, 'which is what is called a Trotsky movement', had urged strike action on the Hillington workers, but did not condemn the CWC for it, unlike *New Propellor.*
148   12 Nov. 1943. LAB 10/364.
149   P. Inman, op. cit., p. 366.
150   12 Nov. 1943. LAB 10/364.
151   12 Nov. 1943. LAB 10/364. Galbraith to Gould, 9 Nov. 1943. LAB 10/281.
152   P. Inman, op. cit., p. 366.
153   *War Commentary,* Jan. 1944.
154   17 Dec. 1943. LAB 10/364. 7 Jan. 1944. LAB 10/445.
155   7 Jan. 1944. LAB 10/445.
156   Ibid.
157   *War Commentary,* mid-Jan. 1944; 14 Jan. 1944. LAB 10/445.
158   Ibid., mid-Jan. 1944.
159   31 Dec. 1943, LAB 10/364. 7 Jan. 1944, LAB 10/445.
160   *War Commentary,* Feb. 1944.
161   Ibid.
162   28 Jan. 1944. LAB 10/445.
163   14, 28 Jan. 1944. LAB 10/445.
164   28 Jan. 1944. LAB 10/445.
165   H.A. Emmerson, 'Causes of Industrial Unrest', 3 Nov. 1943. LAB 10/281.
166   *Gateshead Herald,* April 1944.
167   *Factory News* (A.V. Roe), 29 May 1944; *Labour's Northern Voice,* May 1944.
168   *Labour's Northern Voice,* Sept. 1944.
169   7 April 1944. LAB 10/443.
170   Hansard Parliamentary Debates, V series, vol. 399, col. 1709, 9 May 1944.
171   The word was used by Mr W.J. Brown. Churchill was also asked by Mrs Cazalet Keir why the government did not simply accept the recommendations of the Atkis Committee of 1919 (Hansard, vol. 403, cols. 27–9).
172   *Report* of the Royal Commission on Equal Pay, 1944-6 (Cmd. 6937), title page.
173   Ibid., p. 3.
174   R.M. Gould to E.C. Ramsbottom, 27 Dec. 1944, LAB 10/523. On the Atkis Committee, see Arthur Marwick, *Women at War, 1914-18* (1977), pp. 151–2.
175   'Evidence by Official Witnesses', unsigned memo in LAB 10/253.
176   Bevin's speech was delivered on 21 November 1944, and reported in the *Daily Mirror,* 22 November 1944. Gould to Ramsbottom, 27 Dec. 1944. LAB 10/253.
177   *Report* of the Royal Commission on Equal Pay, 1944-6, p. 196.
178   *Labour's Northern Voice,* July 1944.
179   *Oldham Chronicle,* 12 May 1945.
180   'Will the Factory Girls Want to Stay Put or Go Home?' File Report 2059, 8 March 1944, MO Archive. Broadly similar attitudes were revealed in G. Thomas, *Women at Work. The Attitudes of Working Women towards Post-War Employment and Related Problems* (Wartime Social Survey, June 1944). A good deal of statistical material is provided in this survey,

but it has to be handled with care because of the way that questions are put.
181 P. Inman, op. cit., p. 177. J.B. Priestley, op. cit., pp. 57-9.
182 'Will the Factory Girls Want to Stay Put or Go Home?', p. 6.
183 *Minutes* of the Manchester District Committee of the AEU, 26 Oct. 1944.
184 26 Jan. 1945. LAB 10/354.
185 *Gallup Political Index,* Jan. 1964.

# CHAPTER 6

# WINNING THE PEACE

' We regret to inform you that, owing to the termination of Government contracts, your services have become redundant as from. . .'[1]
*(Standard notification issued to redundant engineering workers in 1945)*

The spate of strikes and disturbances which had reached a peak in the early months of 1944 had been related to the frustration which preceded the opening of the second front in Europe. Many workers, and especially the left-wing shop stewards, felt that the Anglo-American forces had left the 'Strike in the West' as late as they possibly could so that German morale and resources could be worn down in the East. Paradoxically, despite the Communists' opposition to anything that slowed down production, the 'second front' agitation may have helped to build up tensions which were partly released in strikes. This is speculation, but there is no doubt that the invasion of continental Europe by Allied forces on 6 June 1944 clearly marked the beginning of the war's final phase not only in a military but also in an industrial relations sense. It was widely recognised that the opening of a second front in the West, provided that it could be successfully consolidated, meant that it was only a matter of time until the main war aim, unconditional surrender, was achieved. All eyes were therefore turned on the Normandy coast in early June, and the capture of Rome on 4 June was hardly noticed, despite the bitter fighting which had preceded it. Now that the initial danger period of the landings was over, although the Allied command was restricted to a limited beach-head it was able to build up its armies until Caen was taken at the beginning of July. By the end of that month the American armies had made a decisive break-through, and large tracts of France and Belgium were liberated during August and September. In the East, also, the Wehrmacht was being driven inexorably back, as the Red Armies drove into Poland and Bulgaria. Although remarkably resilient, the German war machine was being pounded by intensified bombing, and supplies of all industrial materials were running low. But in September the Western front was stabilised, and the 'Bulge' salient was not pinched off until January 1945. By February the Russians had advanced to within forty miles of Berlin, and with almost total freedom to attack with impunity over German industrial towns the British and American air forces wrought terrible havoc. In mid-April the bomber offensive was officially brought to a close under the cloud of Dresden; there was no need to go further. Germany surrendered on 7 May, and 8 May saw scenes of tremendous jubilation as factories closed down to give everyone the opportunity to celebrate VE Day. The war against Japan remained, of course. It was generally thought that it would take six months or a year finally to win the war in the Far East. The Japanese were conducting a desperate defensive campaign in the Pacific and it appeared likely that eventual victory, though assured, would be extremely costly in terms of lives. But on 6 August an atomic bomb was dropped on Hiroshima, and three days later a second bomb was dropped on Nagasaki. The Soviet Union declared war on Japan, and the Japanese had no choice but to surrender. The world war was finally over.

The strike wave of early 1944 receded during April as the miners and apprentices returned to work. Although 1944 saw the peak wartime total of working days lost through strikes (1,048,000), most of this aggregate had accrued in the stormy first three months of the year. March had been an especially difficult month for the government, with both coal and munitions production disrupted by stoppages which had important political implications. But Regulation 1AA had the desired effect, and the rest of 1944 saw a diminution of the strike rate, which continued into 1945 with only just over half a million days lost through strikes.[2]

Regulation 1AA was perhaps the most important of a number of factors which tended to dampen down the militancy which had flared up in the winter of 1943-4. In engineering, the most important disputes during these months had involved large numbers of women and apprentices, many of them non-unionised (although certainly not un-organised). It seems that fear of prosecution under the new legislation did have the general deterrent effect of subduing these groups. The outcry against the regulation had been most apparent amongst trade union activists, and it was amongst these workers that defiance of the legislation was most likely still to be found. The campaign against Bevin's measures had been quite widespread within the AEU: the E&ATSSNC complained that it was unnecessary, and many District Committees passed motions which showed their agreement.[3] Eventually Jack Tanner himself had to admit that he wished he had opposed the regulation from the outset.[4] Given this climate within the AEU, it is not perhaps surprising that some militant engineers were prepared to defy the new legislation. At Beardmore's Parkhead Forge, Glasgow, the most strike-prone factory on the Clyde, a stoppage occurred in the heavy-machine shop in April 1944.[5] With the new statute fresh in the public mind, the Scottish Lord Advocate warned the offenders that they would in future be prosecuted under 1AA, but in September when a similar stoppage lasting one week occurred in the same shop no prosecutions were in fact brought.[6] Nonetheless the harsh new penalties brought in with 1AA must have deterred many less determinedly anti-employer engineers from stopping work when they might previously have done so.

There were other reasons for the downturn in the strike rate. Some engineering workers were concerned at the possible insecurity that might accompany the return of peacetime employment conditions, and did not want to lose any work time as a result. But, more importantly, the employers too anticipated the return of a free labour market and the restoration in the post-war period of what they regarded as 'normal' labour relations. The growth of the shop steward organisation in their factories and the increasingly militant stance taken by many groups on the shop floor they thought of as unfortunate wartime developments. While the winter of 1943-4 saw an increase in the strike rate, it also saw a significant series of victimisations of leading shop stewards. This was the beginning of what can only be called a counter-offensive that continued into 1946. The employers felt that their 'frontier of control' would have to be strengthened against the engineering workers as peacetime loomed on the horizon. In particular, they warned that the high rates of earnings established on 'cost-plus' work would not be permissible if private contracts were to be won in the post-war years. They saw the closing phase of the war as the time to restore their position in the workshops, and a determined attack on workshop organisation was the result.

In wartime it was often difficult to discriminate between victimisation by an employer and victimisation through the operation of wartime labour controls exercised by the Ministries of Labour and Manpower. When labour was declared 'redundant' at one factory and made available for production reasons for transfer to another, the discussions between managements and government officials preliminary to certain individuals or sections being declared redundant may well have included the question of union activity. Contemporary trade-unionists certainly subscribed to such a theory, but many such discussions left no records, and others are closed to the researcher. Managements certainly did take the advice of Ministry of Labour officials when they wished to discipline or sack trade-unionists: this occurred, for example, when Reg Birch was sacked from Landis and Gyr in 1944.[7]

At the E&ATSSNC's conference held in March 1944 much emphasis was placed by the speakers on the 'urgent need for action' to 'stop the victimisation of shop stewards through transfers and redundancy', and it was pointed out that the declaration of 'surpluses' of skilled labour under the Essential Works Order was increasing. The conference heard of the sacking through redundancy of Bill Abbott, the Communist convenor at Metro-Vickers in Manchester and well known local militant, only two days after travelling to London to tell MPs about the unsatisfactory state of affairs at his factory. The four thousand five hundred workers in the East shop appeared likely to strike, but the management refused to take Abbott back and would not even let him into the works to collect his tools.[8] Nine months earlier Jack Owen, the ex-Labour councillor who had his own column in the *Daily Worker*, had been declared redundant by the same employer.[9] Bill Abbott recalled in 1979 that stewards like Bill Blackwell who might have been expected to fight these

310

redundancies had left by the time he himself was pushed out.[10] These dismissals might have been thought of as deriving simply from the particular situation at the factory, but the E&ATSSNC conference feeling was that, following hard on the heels of the sacking of Len Hine, convenor at Lincoln Cars, London, and a number of other dismissals, it was part of a more general trend. There is some evidence to support their impression. The *Daily Worker*'s files show that no less than thirty shop stewards and convenors were sacked in the four months from October 1943 to February 1944.[11] In the spring, eight Northern Irish shop stewards were imprisoned under the defence regulations, causing a large strike, and the summer saw the sacking of Sweetman, the TGWU convenor at Fords Dagenham foundry, and Lynch, an AEU shop steward at the neighbouring Briggs' Bodies.[12] When the many shop stewards and activists who had attended the E&ATSSNC's conference read this news they must have felt the views expressed there were confirmed.

The victimisation of shop stewards and their removal from factories in which they had established themselves with their workmates led necessarily to a feeling on the part of shop stewards generally that it was not wise to 'stick your neck out'. This fear seems to have afflicted the shop floor movement throughout 1944. The question was, of course, what could be done about it? The E&ATSSNC had long been campaigning for the legal recognition of shop stewards and the statutory definition of their rights and functions (something which was not to happen until the 1970s), but for the time being they recommended the use of the appeals machinery laid down by the Essential Works Order.[13] They remained, of course, totally opposed to strike action to defend the shop stewards, because of the adverse effect this would have on production. Sometimes the EWO machinery could work, as in the case of Lynch, the Briggs' Bodies steward, who was reinstated by the tribunal and went on to play an important part in organising the factory.[14] But the general trend was in the opposite direction, as most contemporary commentators agreed. F.H. Happold, the industrial correspondent of *Financial News,* who could be expected to take a less than sympathetic attitude to the problems faced by trade union activists, drew attention to what he described as the 'widespread problem' of employers refusing to reinstate workers found to have been unfairly dismissed under the Essential Works Order.[15] The initial persuasive effect of the EWO on employers was wearing off, and they were becoming increasingly inclined to ignore Appeal Tribunal instructions to reinstate workers.

The sacking of an important scattering of leading shop stewards at the beginning of 1944 had a generally intimidating effect which was in some ways even more damaging than Regulation 1AA. Whether planned or not, the removal of leading trade-unionists from key positions weakened the position of all shop stewards. The effects were magnified by the fact that, as already noted, the trade union movement as a whole, including the E&ATSSNC, was resolutely opposed to striking to secure the reinstatement of victimised representatives. The CP, in sharp contrast to its attitude of 1940, insisted that the way to deal with such cases was by appeals through the machinery of the Essential Works Order, lobbying relevant government departments, building up the strength of the E&ATSSNC and exerting pressure on managements by methods short of industrial action. These methods could be successful: the London and South-East officer of the Ministry of Labour reported that two militant stewards at the Park Royal Coachworks had led a demonstration through the factory to the managing director's office to demand a production bonus for indirect workers, and that the company had only refrained from taking action against them because this incident occurred just before the E&ATSSNC's meeting at the Stoll Theatre, and they did not want to give the conference more ammunition on the victimisation issue. When prevailed upon by Claude Berridge, the AEU official, to stop their demonstrations, the shop stewards initiated a campaign of banging on benches and making a commotion twice a day.[16] This action appears to have been successful, but where managements were determined to remove a shop steward and to reassert their authority such methods were generally ineffective. This was one of the reasons for the relative quiescence on the shop floor in the summer of 1944. Similar action to that at Park

Royal was taken at Lincoln Cars to try to obtain the reinstatement of Len Hines, but failed.[17] Before long, however, even more serious problems presented themselves in the form of redundancies across the whole engineering industry. Sensing that they could seize the opportunity to restore some of their lost control on the shop floor, employers were not slow to take advantage of the new climate.

The only organisation with a plausible claim to be able to lead a successful industrial-political campaign against mass redundancies was of course the E&ATSSNC. Although the Militant Workers' Federation had been able to involve itself on the fringes of industrial militancy in the very particular circumstances of late 1943-early 1944, the situation was rapidly exposing the limitations of such tiny organisations. The RCP and its leadership appreciated this, and the editorial of its first *Industrial Bulletin,* circulated in November 1944, pointed out that redundancy was 'the most important question our industrial comrades have to face up to at the present time', but that it had to recognise the small size and resources of the organisation.[18] In a period of full employment, with the whole economy stretched almost to breaking point, a rather artificially friendly environment had been created for politically-motivated industrial agitators. When isolated strikes occurred, the strength of the tiny MWF could be brought to bear to organise sympathetic meetings and collections, and to give propaganda help—in other words, it could perform a servicing role. The situation in late 1944-5 was entirely different. Large-scale redundancies meant that only a body with much wider-reaching roots in the factories could even aspire to lead an unofficial movement to campaign against mass redundancies. In order to have any prospect of success, a widespread general movement on a national scale was needed. Individual factories could not hope to soldier on indefinitely in isolation. Between the apprentices' strike and the end of the war, the Ministry of Labour's records do not reveal much concern for the machinations of the MWF or the Clyde Workers Committee. Although they continued to exist, they had been overtaken by events. The E&ATSSNC, on the other hand, was a much stronger organisation. Some idea of its influence is necessary as the essential backdrop to those battles that did take place on the redundancy issue.

On the face of it, the E&ATSSNC had never been so strong. The left shop stewards had led resistance to the victimisation. During the winter of 1943-4, deputation after deputation called on the various government departments to protest at the attacks on shop stewards and to complain of their managements' shortcomings on the productive front. The stewards followed the E&ATSSNC's strategy of obtaining the maximum press publicity for their visits, although they had always to contend with the War Cabinet's counter-strategy of restricting such publicity.[19] The government's policy had been decided on in October 1941 and was to be implemented by the Ministry of Information, but it remained difficult for the readers of *New Propellor* to avoid the impression that the ministers were becoming like Mexican presidents, constantly besieged by supplicant deputations from different areas. One particular factory, Desoutter's of London, was the focus of a campaign which became quite widely known. Desoutter's had refused to recognise trade unions and had sacked a shop steward whom they refused to reinstate despite the ruling of a tribunal under the Essential Works Order. The E&ATSSNC outcry probably played a role in leading to the 'de-scheduling' of the company under the Essential Works Order by Bevin, but the shop steward was not reinstated.[20]

The E&ATSSNC had not held a national conference since October 1941, although it had organised one for shipbuilding workers in April 1942. These conferences required a major organisational effort, which was magnified by the decline in CP membership from the peak of 1942, and the last one of the war was not held until March 1944. All the stops—too many, some felt—were pulled out for this meeting. Immediately before the conference a printed open letter headed *Scottish Shop Stewards* and addressed to the government and shipbuilding employers called on them to 'settle the wages issue before the offensive opens'. It carried a large advertisement on the back for the 12 March meeting, and was signed by three hundred and sixty stewards from thirty shipbuilding, engineering and aircraft works. But the document may not have been compiled in an entirely scrupulous way. According to the Ministry of Labour's local official, the stewards concerned had been unaware that they were signing a letter that would be published. Even if they had been fully conscious of what they were signing, the relationship between the pamphlet's claims and the reality was not justified. The pamphlet began, 'We, the Shipyard and Engineering Shop Stewards of Scotland', yet many large and important factories were not included in the workplaces of the signatories.[21] Nevertheless, the conference was an impressive one: 1,824 people came from four hundred and ninety-seven factories, purporting to represent over one million arms workers.[22] The conference was conceived on the grand scale, and the pamphlet produced as its report was entitled *Millions Like Us. New Propellor* announced in ringing tones: '[The Conference was] surpassing in scope and influence any previous gathering of its kind. . . [it] marked a turning point in the history of the British working class.'[23]

The conference was certainly the largest ever held by the E&ATSSNC, and reflected a very considerable range of influence. Yet it lacked the anti-capitalist rhetoric of the October 1941 conference, and its timing just before the invasion of occupied Europe suggested a greater concern with winning the war than with the vital problems that were to affect engineering workers after the landings. The talk was far more of production than of grievances. This shift away from the sensitivity to workers' problems at the point of production which had marked the E&ATSSNC of the earlier war years can be seen in *New Propellor*. Forced constantly to shrink in size because of the need to increase circulation despite the paper shortage, the E&ATSSNC's paper contained far fewer articles from the shop floor and had certainly lost its sense of humour and liveliness. Shortly after the war it renamed itself *Metalworker*, which underlined its decline, since no British worker of the time thought of himself as a 'metalworker' unless he was a sheet metal worker.[24] The title was more reminiscent of the terms used in Europe and by the early Communist International, than of British shop floor parlance.

The activity of Communists in the factories remained as powerful an influence as it ever had been however. The left continued to play the important role it had always played in the battle to spread and strengthen trade union organisation. Perhaps the most notable set-piece battle was the fight at Fords to unionise the factory, which had been going on ever since the Ford plant had been built at Dagenham. Here the Communist District Secretary Bob Lovell, who had long devoted himself to this task, was at the centre of the struggle to organise the factory in the face of determined opposition from an employer whose hostility to trade-unionism both in America and Britain was legendary. Amongst the beleaguered shop stewards, said Vic Feather of the TUC, there were five or six people 'inspired by political motives' which they shared with Lovell, and this led Feather to agree with Fords that the accreditation of shop stewards should not be carried out locally even if stewards were to be recognised.[25] These stewards (who were not recognised by Fords) had occupied the works manager's office in January 1944 and had managed to force the issue to the extent that the TUC and Fords reopened talks that had begun in the late 1930s. The Fords issue was not settled for many years, but an important first step was taken with the conclusion of an agreement signed in the summer of 1944, which recognised the trade union officer's right (though, crucially, *not* that of the shop steward) to represent his members.[26] Many were very disappointed at the outcome, but an important and symbolic breakthrough had been achieved against this rigid employer. The role of the Irish Catholics in the foundry, who struck to defend their TGWU shop steward Sweetman and who had become pillars of the union at Fords, has to be acknowledged, but it was the CP stewards and above all Lovell himself who were to be identified with the gains that had been made.[27]

Left-wing shop stewards had also become prominent as editors and contributors to the many shop stewards' newspapers which sprang up in the second half of the war, and especially in 1944-5. These newspapers were an important feature of factory life in these years. Along with the large numbers of political pamphlets produced by the CP and other left groups, they enriched political life within the factories by stimulating discussion across a wide range of topics amongst workers who had usually never had access to such literature. At their best (and some were very profession- ally produced), these papers could open up dialogues between their editors and the ordinary workers which represented real extensions of democratic discussion on the issues of the day and have only rarely been paralleled since. Letters from readers were usually given ample space, thereby allowing the full range of humorous, sporting, personal and social talking- points debated in any factory to take their place along with wider, political matters. Such papers were thus often workers' papers in the best sense of the phrase.

During the latter war years there was a new wave of these factory papers, the first on a national scale since the CP had produced its much more limited and sectarian factory papers in the Third Period between 1929 and 1932. The previous wave had been smaller, less impressive and less informative because the papers had largely been written from outside the factories and were directed at workers who were often afraid to contribute for fear of losing their jobs. But both waves had in common the fact that CP members were often prominent as editors and contributors. Many have not survived and we know all too little about the circumstances of their production, but it is clear that they did not all have the same relationship to trade union organisation in the factories. Some, such as *Factory News* (later re-titled *Yousedit, A.C.D.C.* and *Current News*) produced at Vickers- Armstrong, Manchester, *Spot-On* (Napier's, Liverpool) and *Humber Bulletin* which became *Humber Clarion,* Coventry, were adopted as the official papers of the shop stewards' committee.[28] Others, such as *Gun,* from Vickers-Armstrong, Elswick, were issued by the Communist Party. Still others, like *Factory News* from A.V. Roe's Chadderton factory, were issued by the CP but specifically repudiated by the shop stewards' committee. The left seems to have been active in almost all of them: Frank Allaun edited *Factory News* (Vickers-Armstrong), Jock Wallace of the CP edited the Napier's paper, while a cursory glance at *Humber Clarion* makes the left-wing affiliations of the editors clear.[29]

A recent detailed study of *Factory News* (A.V. Roe's, Chadderton, Manchester) offers a number of insights into the

317

way this particular paper was produced, the composition of the editorial group and its relationship with its readers. The paper may not have been entirely typical of its kind, since it was an openly CP product, but it is useful in that it allows us to test the reactions of readers to CP politics. It also provides the best consecutive run of any factory paper yet unearthed, from which to generalise. The paper seems to have first appeared despite the paper shortage at some time in early 1943, and was therefore probably amongst the earliest of its kind. Extant copies run until just after the end of the war. *Factory News* was written and produced by members of the A.V. Roe CP group, not by the local Blakely branch of the CP (later to become the North Manchester branch), of which there was a good deal of mistrust within the factory group. Many of the Blakely branch members were scientists from ICI's local factory, who were apparently known to the A.V. Roe group as 'those bloody Blakely scientists'. The editorial committee consisted of a number of remarkable men (there do not appear to have been any women involved in turning the paper out). The driving force was Stan Grundy, a skilled toolsetter, a member of the shop stewards' committee and a self-taught and accomplished linguist. According to another member of the editorial committee, Sam Street, Grundy was 'a man of very great ability', who provided much of the paper's extremely well written content. Sam Street was in his twenties, a Classics graduate who had got a job as a fitter in the factory and a CP member married to a woman from a family with a long left-wing tradition. *Factory News* was duplicated in his house, a mile and a half away from the Chadderton works. Other members of the editorial committee recalled by Sam Street included Walter Long, 'a very superior sort of man', Ellis Pott, a toolroom worker and Jim Haigh, another toolroom worker and member of the works committee. The group was clearly more than a little distinctive, not only by virtue of CP membership but also because of its prodigious collective talents and activities. All of those mentioned as active in the paper's production were fully skilled men, except for Sam Street. The group was therefore not representative of the mass of people within the factory, the majority of whom were unskilled and women. The need

318

for a circumspect and sensitive approach to the problems confronted by the majority was thus more difficult to satisfy than it might have been if the group had had any representatives of the majority working with them to voice their interests.[30] *Factory News* appeared at weekly intervals except for occasional weeks missed, usually on a Monday, and its two hundred copies were sold for a penny each during working hours. A considerable writing, production and organising effort must have been required to bring the paper out on such a regular basis since, Sam Street recalls, there were 'never enough active workshop correspondents'[31]; this problem may to some extent have been reflected in the paper's ambiguous relationship to its readership.

On the one hand, the paper's content obviously appealed to the minority of workers who bought it. Its humorous assessments of Avro food ('A fitter found a small nail in his dinner, but not until it was in his mouth did he detect it. He wasn't so pleased about it. . . even when someone told him it was a new way of distributing iron rations')[32], its thorough coverage of factory entertainments and sporting fixtures and its cartoons, all helped to make the paper lively and probably to attract a readership well above the two hundred buyers. On the other hand, many aspects of the paper's commentary on factory and trade union affairs attracted explicit criticism in the letters column. A letter from three men written in reply to an article in the paper entitled 'Every Minute Counts' accused the editorial group of hypocrisy because it had justified the penalty of five hours' suspension imposed on several people late back from the dinner break after missing their bus; in October 1943 a group of women wrote in to complain of a cartoon which had implied their incompetence the previous week; in January 1944 the editor admitted that 'more and more objections to our line of thought are coming in lately'; in March the committee asked for more contributors, adding: 'We don't need to ask for criticism—we get plenty of that.'[33] These complaints created a climate of hostility to the paper which ultimately led to the works committee mounting a serious attack on it. In March 1944 the committee went so far as to write to Herbert Morrison to ask for the paper's suppression, so far had the hostility developed.[34] The precise reason for this move is not clear, but since it contained very little explicit criticism of the shop stewards themselves in its columns, it was probably to do with the fact that *Factory News*'s positions on factory affairs had upset people in the workshops. In any event, the shop stewards' request was evidently not acted upon as the paper continued to appear.

The difficulties experienced by *Factory News* were not unrelated to those experienced more widely by the CP in the engineering industry. There was a growing tendency for some left-wing shop stewards to emphasise the paramount need for increasing production rather than the day-to-day problems that confronted their members on the shop floor. As early as 1943 the CP's leadership had told Party members in their pre-Congress discussion: 'Experience has shown that the carrying out of the Party's policy requires that more attention be given to grievances. . . How can this work be strengthened?'[35] By 1944 these problems had grown more acute. In September 1944 it was apparently being said in Scotland, for example, that the CP stewards were too busy recruiting to the CP to be bothered with inspecting union cards.[36] The accusation no doubt hurt, and this sort of evidence suggests that some real problems lay behind it. Even supposing that these internal and external criticisms were unfounded, it seems unlikely that they could even have been made in the late 1930s, when careful attention to grievances and meticulous shop steward activity were hallmarks of the left.

The key underlying problems for the CP shop stewards were the persistent decline of Party membership since 1942 and the lack of activity in factory groups. At the end of 1942 the CP claimed its peak membership of fifty-six thousand but by March 1945 their own figures showed a membership of 45,435.[37] Rapid turnover and semi-active factory groups were symptomatic of the same problem. In general only a minority of Party members were involved in political work within the factory. The author of a pamphlet written in 1943 stated for example that factory groups often consisted of a few leading members and a large number of others who did no real work.[38] That such statements did not

*Factory News*, 13 March 1944

derive merely from the Communist habit of immolatory self-criticism is shown by other evidence. In a pamphlet of 1944 another Communist wrote that the main aim in factory groups should be to establish a regular monthly meeting.[39] This minority had to do a terrific amount of work selling the *Daily Worker, New Propellor* and an enormous number of pamphlets. Some idea of just how much was done can be gained by looking at any one of a number of literature-selling campaigns organised by the CP in the second half of the war. These were often run on an inter-factory competitive basis, with factories challenging each other to see how much literature each could sell. The winner of one of these competitions in 1944 (Armstrong-Whitworth Aircraft, Baginton) sold nearly four thousand pamphlets.[40] Such sales did help in the widespread dissemination of left-wing ideas amongst the factory population, and to that extent greatly bolstered the ideological influence of the left. The CP perfected the pamphlet as a propaganda instrument in these years. Short enough to be read by workers without a great deal of time, they were also long enough to expand on particular themes in more detail than was possible in the *Daily Worker* or *New Propellor*. But it would hardly have been surprising if the people who took part in these campaigns had little time to listen attentively to workers' problems.

Notwithstanding the intensive activity of a minority of CP members, the Party's membership declined in this period. There is little doubt that part of the reason for this lay, as James Hinton has suggested, in the CP's failure to initiate another campaign such as that for JPCs, which might have created an atmosphere conducive to another tremendous upsurge in membership like that of 1941-2. Their politics, although of interest to many workers, did not really bite on industrial problems to the extent that they had earlier in the war. It was not, as Harry Pollitt later insisted, that the CP did not grow because its members did not want it to grow; nothing could have been further from the truth.[41] But the CP's politics on most domestic matters were essentially indistinguishable from those of the Labour Party, differing only on international questions. So it is hardly surprising that the CP lost ground to the Labour Party as the end of the war approached. In electoral terms, the Labour Party was infinitely more credible than the CP.

The CP had always relied on its industrial base, but found it difficult during the second half of the war to maintain the enthusiasm of the late 1941/early 1942 period because it insisted that whatever happened nothing should be done that would in any way hinder production. Towards the end of the war there were various indications that the Party's rank and file were becoming increasingly willing to modify their attitude and to initiate campaigns that might involve stoppages of work, in order to achieve important political objectives. The CP's King Street leadership suppressed these tendencies wherever possible. Within the AEU there were many full-time officers who were either members of the CP or sympathetic to it, which resulted in a nice coincidence between AEU and CP policy. An excellent example of these forces interacting occurred during the political agitation surrounding events in Greece at the end of 1944.

During the war the Greek Communist Party had put itself at the head of the liberation army, (ELAS and its political wing, EAM) which had by the end of 1944 succeeded in driving out the occupying Nazi forces. At the last minute the British forces intervened to ensure that the Communists would not be in any position to convert their predominance in the liberation armies into state power. In early December sixty thousand British troops turned on the Greek popular armies, and on Christmas Day 1944 Churchill and Eden travelled to Athens and imposed a provisional government on Greece. According to at least one historian, the intervention of the British constituted the sole reason for the failure of the Greek revolution to be realised.[42] These events had important implications for the British as well as the Greek people: up until the events in Greece there had been a broad consensus that the war was being fought as an anti-fascist crusade, for self-determination and democracy for the peoples of occupied Europe. But the British intervention had radically challenged this consensus: could the British Army be turned to similar tasks elsewhere, even in Britain itself? Not only Communists asked this question. So, too, did many ordinary workers. Although not traditionally particularly receptive to calls for international solidarity, the British labour movement showed momentary signs of responding to the CP's expressions of outrage at the Greek events. For a few weeks it seemed possible that Greece could reawaken the international consciousness of the Spanish Civil War years.

The most impressive possibilities for building a militant movement in response to the government's action appeared to centre on London. On 18 December the *Daily Worker* reported that a meeting of AEU shop stewards in the North London district had decided to call token strikes on Wednesday 20 December to protest against the government's Greek policy.[43] On making inquiries, the local official of the Ministry of Labour discovered that some of the workers in the large factories in the Brentford area had agreed to go along with this policy. The official spoke to the District Secretary of the AEU (Claude Berridge of the CP), and was informed on the Tuesday before the proposed action that a meeting of the leading shop stewards from these works was to be held in order to send a statement to the press appealing to all members to proceed in such a way as not to interfere with production. The reason given was that the German counter-offensive in the Ardennes had changed the military situation. As a result, the expected widespread token strikes became a few lunchtime meetings.[44]

There is no doubt that the military situation in Europe had indeed changed for the worse. The Germans had advanced forty-five miles in three days before they ran out of fuel. But the campaign which had started, only to be nipped in the bud, was not revived in its initial form despite the continuing fighting in Greece, which was to prove a protracted struggle. Most shop stewards' committees restricted their activities to passing resolutions against the British intervention.[45] In terms of the depth of the campaign, there was a considerable difference between the proposed strikes and the shop stewards' resolutions. The difficult decision to stop work required the active approval of large numbers of workers, whereas the shop stewards' resolutions required only their members' passive consent. In retrospect it seems clear that only an energetic crusade which had at least the potential to stop war production would have been likely to divert the government from a major decision emanating from agreements made with its allies.

The CP's overriding commitment to war production was not, however, the only reason for the stillbirth of the Greek solidarity movement. Another contributory factor was the progress of the government's plans for industrial demobilisation. Redundancies had already begun to bite in the munitions factories, and engineering workers were becoming concerned about the transition from war to peace, particularly in so far as it affected their jobs. Fear of the many consequences of the transition is the predominant feature of industrial life from the autumn of 1944 until well into 1946, but it is hardly mentioned in the official history as an industrial relations problem. The official historian, accurately reflecting the government approach at the time, presented the loss of jobs across the board as an inevitable consequence of the termination of government contracts for war materials. At the end of the war this attitude was crystallised in the introduction of the term 'redundancy' to describe the process. Passing into the popular vocabulary at this time, the term implied an inevitable occurrence, quite independent of human agency. One *became* redundant, rather than *got* 'the sack'.[46] In a sense, of course, redundancies were an inevitable concomitant of industrial demobilisation. But engineering workers did not accept the necessity of *mass* redundancies, carried out according to whether workers had been transferred or not or whether they were dilutees. The CP took up this same point in its own literature on the subject. The official argument was that those transferred or conscripted should be released as categories of worker who had been compelled to work in particular workplaces, and that any 'excess' labour could be absorbed by war production. Engineering workers sensed that this meant that not everyone who wanted to work would be able to do so; but if there was enough war work, then people could be transferred to it in the usual way.

There were two underlying fears shared by many in the industry, concerning the transitional period. The first was the possibility of a spell of unemployment while working engineers and some from the services tried to find work in a temporarily swollen labour market. The other was the anticipation that they would lose relatively well paid employment either by the change-over from government contracts to less well paid civilian work or by being forced to move to other factories.[47] And the post-war situation in the longer term was seen as largely dependent on the return of a government committed to full employment.

Many engineering workers had of course experienced unemployment 'the last time', despite promises of a 'land fit for heroes' at the end of the First World War, and were determined not to suffer a repetition of that experience. One personnel officer wrote of a shop steward in his factory who was: 'a sample of the type bred of the aftermath of the last war. He was out of work two years after the last war and it has left a permanent mark on him. . . He told our works manager that he didn't intend to suffer that this time.'[48] This experience and feeling were common to many, but amongst the skilled engineers it coexisted with a reasonable degree of confidence that there would be work for skilled men. Their confidence was well founded, because they were able to find jobs quickly. It was amongst the large numbers of dilutees, semi-skilled and women that the fear of unemployment was liveliest. The AEU's position of 'dilutees first' reinforced this division.

The CP and E&ATSSNC policy did not envisage a large-scale public campaign against mass redundancies through the *Daily Worker, New Propellor,* or pamphlets. Indeed, in the summer of 1944 the CP seemed to be specifically rejecting such an initiative as alarmist.[49] This may have been partly due to the obvious difficulties involved in dealing with an extremely complex problem, but it may also have been linked with the rising electoral ambitions of the CP and the desire to continue to be seen as a respectable and responsible party fit to be a part of an expanded Coalition. At this point the question has to remain unanswered, but it is clear that at the leadership level, initially at least, it did not regard any of the campaigns on the redundancy issue as a major priority. When initiatives did come, they came from the shop stewards themselves rather than from London.

The *Daily Worker* had never been an agitational paper, in the sense that it was descriptive rather than prescriptive; it was *New Propellor* and pamphlets that were usually used to launch such campaigns. It appears that the CP produced two items of interest. The first was a document prepared at the end of the war by the CP's Metal Advisory Committee for shop stewards; the second was a pamphlet directed towards engineering workers and entitled *Engineering Prospects and Wages.*[50] This pamphlet paid very little attention to the redundancy issue, restricting itself to remarking that redundancy should not be a 'general release of labour' that threw responsibility for finding work on individual firms, but 'a real switch over from war to peace planning'.[51] The emphasis, then, was on the government's responsibilities, and this was quite consistent with CP policy in general, which stressed the need for central planning. The only mention of what might be done was contained in an approving reference to the shop stewards' committee at Short's, which had agreed practical proposals for alternative products in cooperation with government departments. The general impression was that the CP, in so far as it reacted at all to the redundancy issue, was sucked in by its responsiveness at local level to the needs of engineering workers, rather than being prepared to lead the shop stewards from a well-planned position.

The mass release of labour from war factories posed fundamental questions about the nature of post-war British society. The Short's shop stewards had taken advantage of the close links which they had and their management had with the MAP (which had replaced the senior management only a year earlier) to obtain work for their factory which was designed to meet social needs. This work was the building of aluminium houses to meet the housing shortage which it was well known would arise after the war. Shop stewards in other factories took up this idea: mining machinery would also be needed to satisfy the very real need of the under-capitalised coal industry, household goods would be needed for the new houses, and so on. The whole 'swords into ploughshares' idea contained considerable scope for persuading workers that there need be no mass redundancies, and that there was work of great importance to be done if only the government would take the task on.

The development of these demands, and their ultimate substantial failure, owed much to the early involvement of the Ministry of Aircraft Production. It was quite possible for the shop stewards, many of whom looked on the left-wing Stafford Cripps as their ministerial ally *par excellence,* to concentrate on lobbying the sympathetic MAP rather than intensifying their propaganda and putting their arguments over to their own members. Cripps' ministry gave every indication that it was prepared to respond positively to the problem. Indeed, it had taken the initiative well before any real movement had developed in the factories. In early 1944 the MAP had adopted the policy of trying to work with the private aircraft manufacturers to decide on viable alternative projects for the large amount of spare industrial capacity which they recognised would exist at the end of the war.

Cripps himself became involved in discussions with aircraft employers on the possibility of placing government contracts to manufacture prefabricated aluminium houses at the end of the war. But an initial meeting in February 1944 between the Minister and the representatives of some aircraft firms confirmed the MAP's already well developed feelings about the firms' propensity to 'milk' their departmental contracts. Mr Bartlett of the Bristol Aircraft Co. betrayed the employers' attitude somewhat when he said that the idea of a scheme to build aluminium houses, 'as at present conceived', had as its object not so much the production of cheap houses—he added ominously that 'the aircraft industry is not a cheap producer'—as the provision of work for redundant aircraft workers. He added that an important by-product would of course be 'supplying an article that would be in short supply at any price'. The MAP representatives saw the way the employers were thinking, and were quick to retort that speed, low cost and efficiency were all a part of the same picture. The programme proposed at this meeting was at least half a million houses for the home market, plus export possibilities to the devastated countries of Europe and the colonies.[52] The cost estimates proposed by the aircraft firms deterred the MAP from pursuing this high projected total production, however, and by February 1945, when the Cabinet Housing Committee accepted Cripps' suggestion that the scheme should be implemented, its financial basis had been established and the proposed order had shrunk to just fourteen thousand houses. Some prototypes had been ordered immediately from Bristol Aircraft, who took the opportunity to point out that a large number of skilled engineers (then in short supply) would be needed to carry out re-jigging work on stamping machines jigged for aircraft sections.[53] The production 'pre-fab' was to be produced at BAC, Blackburn Aircraft at Dunbarton and Short's, Belfast, providing work at its peak in early 1946 for thirteen thousand.[54]

The Short's shop stewards had been active in pressurising their management to provide work in a town noted for its poor housing and high unemployment in the depression years, with results (as *Engineering Prospects and Wages* pointed out) that were 'very satisfactory for a large part of the workers employed'.[55] The same could not be said for the mass of engineering workers. Even when we take into account the other workers engaged on making household fittings and appliances (also under government contracts) the employment provided was strictly marginal. If the initial programme had been fully implemented—and there was no argument about the demand for the product—there would have been work for approximately half a million people. The aluminium house project had foundered on the rock of the employers' high costings for the work, and on the outright lack of interest on the part of some (Vickers, for example).[56] The engineering employers, and particularly the aircraft manufacturers, felt they would be able to find outlets for their products. They did not envisage maintaining the same levels of employment as they had during 1944. In any case, in looking towards the post-war era, they were rather more concerned with profits than providing housing.

A high proportion of the best plant within the engineering industry was in public ownership, in the form of the shadow factories clustered around Coventry, Birmingham and London.[57] Here the prospects for a determined battle to keep the works in government ownership and to produce essential goods appeared better than in the long-established privately owned plants. After all, they were already publicly owned, and were only managed for a fee by private manufacturers. Shop stewards and District Committees in London, Birmingham and Coventry, where the shadow factories were of crucial importance to engineering employment, had been making representations to the supply ministries and their managements throughout the winter of 1944-5. In Birmingham the shop stewards of the major factories coordinated their campaign and succeeded in gaining a good deal of publicity for their demand for alternative work. At a demonstration in early 1945, a leaflet distributed to workers in the Rover Nos 1 and 2 shadow factories, the City of Birmingham Aircraft Factory and the Austin Motor and Aero plants, Longbridge, set out clearly the shop stewards' arguments. The leaflet began by stating that the shop stewards of all these factories had been making 'fruitless endeavours' to secure information on plans for their works. The stewards now believed that plans were under way to utilise the factories, but 'the same attention has not been paid to the problem of the labour employed in them, because in spite of the advanced state of these plans, redundancy has been carried out full scale'. In the previous twelve months, the Austin Motor Co. had shed seven thousand of its twenty thousand workers. The authors of the leaflet rejected the ministries' arguments on the subject:

> We are being told that the labour from these factories is urgently needed elsewhere. All the evidence and experience compels us to reject this view, because we know that when the Ministry of Labour has required labour of a special scale and experience, they have invariably extracted same. But in the present case men are declared redundant first. We have asked for a list of priority vacancies for the purpose of obtaining volunteers and have been unable to get them.

The leaflet went on to point out that whole communities had been built up around the new factories, and that work should therefore be brought to the people rather than vice versa. Finally, it demanded new projects for all the

Birmingham factories, the introduction of the Meteor tank engine at the Rover No. 1, and the retention of existing labour.[58]

In London also, at the many disparate units which made up the London Aircraft Productions Group as a part of the shadow scheme, the shop stewards made representations to the ministries in November 1944 to request alternative products.[59] In Coventry meetings of shadow factory stewards elected a deputation to lobby their Executive, the supply ministries, and Labour MPs. Meanwhile, the CSEU was approached to help organise a local demonstration at the end of February. At the beginning of March local convenors recommended to the AEU District Committee that the trades council, Labour Party and CSEU be approached to hold a joint meeting on redundancy in general.[60] In Manchester, workers at a shadow factory which was to close in March 1945 presented a petition to the Lord Mayor in protest.[61] On occasions, these protests were successful in winning temporary reprieves for workers who were declared redundant. At London Aircraft Productions shadow group, for example, a demonstration of three thousand workers in November 1944 brought the withdrawal of redundancy notices the following day, as the *Daily Worker* pointed out.[62] In general, however, the campaign failed in so far as it aimed at avoiding redundancy by retaining factories under government control. There were some successes in providing alternative work, as we have seen, and the shop stewards were in many cases able to ensure that redundancies were carried out in a way which accorded with the priorities of those they represented, but the Coalition government was strongly opposed to public ownership of the shadow factories.

A large part of the problem as far as the shop stewards were concerned lay in the slow and continuous erosion of their position by the release of groups of workers during negotiations for the preservation of jobs. In short, the ground was constantly moving beneath their feet. As time went on, their position became increasingly weak. At London Aircraft Productions, for example, while discussing alternative products, the stewards had been presented with lists of those who were to be discharged. They complained to government departments that the lists contained workers who should not have been discharged and that they had not been consulted.[63] The crux of the problem is encapsulated in their case: recognising the need for an orderly rundown, if rundown there had to be, they found themselves presiding over the very event they were arguing should not be happening.

It is possible, in retrospect, to criticise the E&ATSSNC for failing to develop a more extensive and influential campaign to keep the shadow factories in public ownership, or, indeed, for failing to run bigger and better campaigns on every aspect of redundancy. But this line of criticism ignores a number of vital considerations. The first is the problem experienced by shop stewards when confronted by the state. The government had a clearly defined policy on these matters, and could argue from a position of overall control and full information. Given the relatively limited experience and perspectives which informed their activity, shop stewards were unable to challenge this policy directly. It is important to remember that they were not a political party, and that their members continued to see them as defenders of their interests in the workshops.

The government's policy on the shadow factories was clear. Although the factories were in public ownership, the Coalition government was determined that they should not remain in the state's hand; it opposed anything that might suggest post-war nationalisation of the engineering industry. The contrast with the JPC campaign could hardly be more striking, since this had been carried out in line with an existing governmental policy option.

Shop stewards confronted by well briefed politicians found it extremely difficult to dent their arguments, despite careful preparation. Their ability to argue from a position of control or comprehensive information was illustrated by the meeting held between the Birmingham shadow factory shop stewards and MPs at the end of the February 1945 demonstration mentioned earlier. At this meeting the stewards argued for the manufacture of agricultural machinery in the factories, but the MPs replied that this would call for long preparation and that in any case Dalton had not yet decided on plans for the location of industry. The MPs agreed with their request for one factory to be turned over to the manufacture of popular cars, but they maintained that there was a problem with ancillary labour, and in any case the position of one factory could not possibly be considered in isolation.[64] Here, then, was the problem. The shop stewards could not lay claim to representing the national interest, nor were they prepared to do so. They could only make representations on their members' behalf. One of the inherent limitations in shop steward activity had become painfully apparent. But there was a second consideration restraining the shop stewards—the attitude of their members in the workshops. As ever, they could only go as far as their members would allow. The shadow factories contained large numbers of 'immigrant' and transferred workers, many of whom had no wish to remain in their workplaces. In fact, many of them had little thought for anything except returning home as quickly as possible. What is remarkable under the circumstances is not so much the weakness of the campaign as the fact that one occurred at all. It is a tribute to the sense of unity that the shop stewards had managed to build up during the war years that they were able to lead demonstrations despite the important divisions of individual interest amongst their members.

By March 1945 it had become apparent that the pressure to keep the shadow factories as government plants had failed. By this time, when the Coventry AEU convenors were proposing their meeting on redundancy, the Board of Trade had allocated the majority of the factories to private firms. Both the ministries and the employers had their own good reasons for wanting the shadow factories sold off. The government's determination not to do anything which smacked of a desire to determine the post-war order under the umbrella of wartime controls has already been mentioned. There was little enthusiasm for the principle of public ownership on the part of the employers, of course, and wartime 'collectivism' had not much dented their traditional commitment to *laissez-faire* economics. They were not even particularly enthusiastic about the prospect of contracts for the aluminium house when it became apparent that the MAP intended keeping a tight rein on costs. In any case, they were often very interested in acquiring the well equipped shadow units for their own use on private commercial work in the post-war era.

For its part, the Board of Trade went out of its way to encourage motor firms to take up its offer of the shadow plants. The firms concerned were usually the wartime managing companies. Rootes, Austin, Nuffield and the Standard Motor Co. all purchased some or all of the floor space and plant offered to them. There was considerable interest in all the factories; built to modern specifications and stocked with modern (often American) machine tools, they provided excellent productive resources, frequently together with good welfare facilities. It was perhaps not surprising, then, that the amount of floor space applied for was three times the area available.[65] Political and Economic Planning later commented that the factories represented good value, and that their capital cost presented little problem for companies with 'considerable liquid assets' accumulated on government contracts.[66] A large section of the British engineering industry therefore ended the war with a tremendous productive resource in these factories, in which investment had been directed towards the development of mass production methods and up-to-date machine tools, introduced almost without thought of cost.[67] Their later fate is well known.

The shadow factories, as we have already noted, were often particularly trade-union conscious, and this was directly related to the fact that people realised they were government-owned and that the managements could lay no more claim than the trade unions to representing the owners of the plant. Their sale to private companies therefore strengthened managerial authority, as well as precipitating a loss of jobs. The trade union movement was correspondingly weakened in several important industrial centres, and needed some time to recover its former confident strength.

The sale of the shadow factories to private engineering firms undoubtedly constituted a setback in the battle to defend wartime wages, conditions and levels of employment, but many engineering workers were employed in the privately owned sector of the industry, and always had been. In these factories the shop stewards came straight up against the peacetime plans of their employers without much possibility of state intervention to save jobs. To this extent, in view of the shadow factory experience, their position was perhaps less ambiguous than their shadow factory counterparts. But there were on the other hand many acute problems facing the many left-wing shop stewards who were anxious to defend wartime gains. In the first place, as we have already noted, many women who had been forced into the industry during the war had no desire to stay, and those that did were in any case normally victims of the AEU's policy of 'dilutees first'. Many men, transferred from their homes, were equally anxious to return to them. A typical case was that of Reg Chambers, from Glynneath, South Wales, highlighted by B.L. Coombes in an article in *Picture Post* in early 1945. Reg was a member of the local football team who was certified partially incapacitated by silicosis. He had worked in a colliery timber yard, and then became an inspector in a Coventry war factory. The money was much better in Coventry, but he became homesick for his wife and children and decided to return there and make do on what he could earn by working on an outcrop coal-washing plant at home.[68] Many South Wales men, Glaswegians and Geordies felt similarly, and could hardly wait to get back to their homes despite their well paid jobs in the Midlands and South. These feelings were in many cases exacerbated by the lack of work in many factories in 1945. The rundown of the war economy created large pockets of workless people still employed in factories.[69] Long hours spent in factories with practically nothing to do drove industrious workers almost to distraction, with the result that applications for release increased. Skilled workers, too, were often keen to get on to the labour market as quickly as possible before the better jobs were snapped up.[70] Thus there were many engineering workers whose minds were already elsewhere, and who were consequently difficult to mobilise in defence either of jobs or of existing working conditions. Some activists were driven to desperation as a result of these attitudes, which they saw as prejudicial to the conditions won in wartime. The chairman of the works committee at Vickers-Armstrong, Manchester, exhorted his readers in the factory paper in no uncertain terms: 'Get off your backs. Wake up, and organise, or the time will come when your conditions will be those of the 1931 depression.'[71] Between March 1944 and March 1945, one thousand people were made redundant at this factory, leading in early 1945 to a mass march through Manchester of two thousand, shouting the slogan: 'We worked for Hitler's destruction—we can work for Britain's construction.'[72] Such mobilisations showed that, despite the problems, workers could be got 'off their backs' on the redundancy question.

Although there were some problems with the CP's industrial base (indeed, it would be difficult to find a period in which there were not), the left-wing shop stewards played an important role in propagandising against mass redundancies, and did all they could to increase their bargaining power to regulate and administer redundancies in as orderly a way as possible. In many ways the E&ATSSNC shop stewards were well placed to do this. Although they had not always succeeded in integrating the 'Red Army members' into the factory groups, they still retained their positions of influence at the head of important shop stewards' committees, and indeed were to do so for years after the end of the war. There were numerous instances at the end of the war of groups of engineers taking action to guarantee jobs, in all of which the factories concerned had an important group of left-wing shop stewards at their head. What is impressive is the way the CP stewards retained their ability to threaten and actually carry out small-scale strikes despite both the objective problems and their own anti-strike policy, as we shall see from the following cases.

At Beardmore's Parkhead Forge many of the workers in the heavy machine shops stopped work for a day in April 1945, to protest at redundancy and to draw attention to Clydeside's poor economic prospects.[73] At a big London factory at the end of 1944, a large body of shop stewards toured the city to drum up support for a collective delegation to the ministries and interested officials. At Briggs' Bodies one thousand four hundred workers stopped work in protest at the proposed sacking of some of their number due to cuts in Ministry of Aircraft Production programmes; in this case the shop stewards appear to have been better informed than the management and, knowing that redundancies were likely, took pre-emptive action. This seems to have achieved its object, as transfers to other work within the plant were agreed.[74] When one hundred and seventy were threatened with redundancy at Napier's of Acton, they were advised by the shop stewards not to register as unemployed at the local labour exchange. The management therefore applied for the Ministry of Labour's permission to discharge these people. On hearing this, shop stewards spoke to the manager of the labour exchange and threatened that if the discharges took place nine thousand of their members would stop work on 11 June 1945. Mass meetings were held in Acton, and support actively canvassed in other factories. At one such meeting at the end of May, thirteen thousand workers attended and leaflets were circulated protesting against the production cuts and the latest award of the National Arbitration Tribunal (Award 718). There were also meetings at the De Havilland factories on the same issues. All of this activity had already been highlighted in the public mind by a walk-out of four thousand six hundred workers at Napier's dispersal factories after meetings held on 17 May, following which deputations went to the House of Commons. By the beginning of the second week in June, however, this agitation seems to have subsided and the redundant workers were cooperating with labour exchange officials by giving the details they had earlier withheld. Their placement in other factories was already under way.[75]

The disputes which did arise on redundancy did not generally last any length of time—very few more than a day. They were on the whole short protest actions in which the shop stewards called on the loyalty of their members to impress on government officials and managers the strength of shop floor feeling. Many of them were primarily concerned not so much with the fact of redundancy itself as with the enforcement of agreed procedures for implementing the run-down. On the whole there were very few stoppages on this issue, but that is not to say there were not cases where managements did victimise shop stewards through unfair selection for redundancy. Several such instances are recorded. According to Jock Wallace, Bert Stacey, a shop steward at Napier's Liverpool shadow factory, was sacked in 1945 for organising an unauthorised meeting prior to leading a demonstration against redundancies into the town.[76] When one whole section, including the convenor, was made redundant at a London motor works, the shop stewards protested to the Ministry of Labour and Ministry of Manpower's local officials. Other cases could be cited in which the shop stewards were unable to call on their members to take action to defend their colleagues, who had to resort to the Essential Works Order tribunals. Bert Stacey never returned to Napier's (nor English Electric, who took the factory over); at the London motor works the management agreed to retain the convenor provided it was shown that a majority of the workforce wanted it. But the shop stewards could only muster five hundred and seventy-five signatures on their petition, which represented about a quarter of the workforce.[77] No more was heard of the matter, at least by the Ministry of Labour.

Shop stewards spent a considerable amount of time during this rundown period trying to ensure that only those members who wished to leave the factory were made redundant, and trying to find substitutes for those who did not. It was not every management that would accept consultation: the Midlands Regional Industrial Relations Officer, for example, complained that employers did not see the advantage of following the Ministry of Labour's recommendations that shop stewards be consulted, with the result that the charge of victimisation was made, as he said, 'very often with some justification'.[78] The sheer size of the shop stewards' problem brought its own difficulties: the papers of Dick Etheridge, the well known CP shop steward at Austin's Longbridge works who became its convenor at the end of the war, contain some sixty lists of redundant workers. In many cases Etheridge had arranged for substitutes for those made redundant. The amount of human-relations work involved must have been enormous, as must the good will of many of those who remained. Conflicts could often arise with the management. Hindmarsh, Dick Etheridge's wartime predecessor as

WEST PRESS SHOP.

February 23rd 1945.

It has been agreed with the Shop Convenor that the following Operators having become redundant, are now able to be finally dismissed.

MALE.

| Check No. | Name. | |
|-----------|---------|---------------------|
| 6625 | McGuiness | Press Operator. |
| 6766 | Jones | ,, ,, |
| 6766 | Harrison | Guillotine Operator. |
| 6633 | Everitt | Press Operator. |
| 6551 | Smith | Hand Press Operator. |

FEMALE.

| | | |
|------|----------|---------------------|
| 6068 | James | Hand Press Operator. |
| 6816 | Eastwood | ,, ,, ,, |
| 6064 | Bollard | Power Press Operator. |
| 6874 | Foxall | ,, ,, ,, |
| 6562 | Henlon | ,, ,, ,, |

(Sgd) R.Hindmarsh...............

Redundancy list (No. 10) from Austin Motor Co., Birmingham

convenor at Longbridge, had to deal with a case in which a member suspected that a man who had worked overtime to finish a rushed job was to have 'something done' for him by the foreman despite the fact that he was on the redundant list, while he, the member complaining, had not been offered suitable alternative work.[79] The shop steward in the member's area had already told him that no one on the redundant list was to be reinstated 'under any circumstances', and that he would refuse to sign the list if there was any tampering with it.[80] Having reluctantly accepted redundancies, the shop stewards were determined to deny foremen the opportunity of retaining only those whom they regarded as allies on the shop floor. Trade union organisation might otherwise have been substantially undermined.

Perhaps the main fear harboured by engineers at the end of the war was that redundancy, and the termination of government contracts, would be used as excuses by the employers to launch major attacks on the wages and conditions established at the peak of war production. Great steps forward had been made, and engineers were more than a little reluctant to return to the lean years of the Depression. They did not want the clock turned back, and looked forward to building on their recent gains. The employers, on the other hand, used what they saw as 'the economic realities of the situation' as their touchstones, and argued that in order to establish their competitiveness in post-war markets the 'inflated' earnings paid during the war would have to be revised downwards. For engineering industrialists, who had been well organised through the Engineering Employers' Federation since the end of the nineteenth century, it was essential to maintain a united front by insisting that the national agreements (which had become little more than a safety net for most engineers during the war) be adhered to more closely. Their own long tradition of solidarity was to some extent revived.

The various local officials of the Ministry of Labour's industrial relations department reported almost to a man that the employers were becoming more sharply aggressive in collective bargaining from about the beginning of 1945.

With the end of the war clearly in sight, they became determined to start peacetime industrial relations as they meant to carry on. To give just a few examples of the ways that the government officials saw employers' attitudes: in February, the Midlands officer reported that he observed 'a tendency on the part of some employers to assume that wage levels will fall as soon as they engage on post-war work and it seems to come as a shock to them to find that workpeople seriously resist attempted reductions'.[81] At the end of March the same official reported a strike of four thousand at the Birmingham Small Arms Co., because the firm had unilaterally imposed a five per cent cut in an output bonus and dismissed an Indian worker for 'insubordination'.[82] On the same day his Scottish counterpart reported two recent cases where employers had dismissed all the workers involved in a dispute.[83] In June the London and South Eastern Regional Industrial Relations Officer wrote that employers no longer pressed by government contracts were quite prepared to allow strikes to become trials of strength, and to wait until their employees were, as he put it, 'sobered by idleness'.[84] The new toughness became increasingly prevalent as peace approached.

Workers often felt they could detect a tendency towards a more authoritarian and in some cases almost military style of management on the shop floor. In a few instances managers provoked serious stoppages by adopting an especially abrasive attitude. Undoubtedly the most noteworthy battle on this front was a nine-day strike at the Humber Co.'s Coventry works involving five thousand people in January 1945. The cause of the dispute seems to have been tied up to a very considerable extent with the attitude of the works manager, Mr H. Pryor. At a local conference held immediately after the strike, a whole number of complaints were brought against Pryor which were adduced as evidence that he was unsuited to his position. The list of grievances against this man included sacking an older man for taking advantage of a custom allowing such men to leave the works slightly early (a privilege abolished by Pryor), refusing to allow the payment of subsistence allowance to transferred workers during working hours, adopting a negative attitude to the JPC,

341

referring to a girl who had been employed on milling and drilling work for three or four years as 'purely green labour', caging and padlocking the tea urns, adopting a 'take it or leave it' attitude to negotiations with stewards, forbidding superintendents to negotiate with stewards, remarking that, 'If I wanted my foremen to be wet nurses, I would have provided them with udders', and refusing to continue the established practice of having a short weekly meeting with shop stewards to discuss workshop questions.[85] It is hardly surprising that Jack Jones, for the TGWU, described Pryor's attitude as 'harsh, rigid and unbending'. Billy Stokes, for the AEU, attributed the manager's aggressiveness to a hardening of the firm's attitude to wartime conditions. As Stokes said:

> It is the general impression in the works, that we gathered from the meetings we attended, that it is part of an attempt to prepare for post-war conditions, and that co-operation in the industry for the successful prosecution of the war, which has been so distinct a feature of war-time relations, has now to give way to a changed atmosphere of pressure from above.[86]

As another officer put it, it appeared as if the company might want to revert to 'the old atmosphere of boss and hand'.[87] The dispute was settled when the company agreed to meet the officials at a local conference, at which a director, Mr Botwood, agreed to attend negotiations of 'major importance' within the works.[88] The problem was to recur in another, bitter strike a year later, over the sacking of almost the entire workforce at this factory. In this dispute strike action was threatened (and in some cases taken) at other factories, and by all the local sheet metal workers. As a result of this sympathetic response, the company was forced to climb down and offer jobs to the majority of the 'redundant' workers.[89]

Even more importantly, the 1946 Humber strike prevented what the Coventry-wide strike committee described as 'the first attempt to depress Coventry wages to national level' by basing piece-work rates on the nationally agreed minimum.[90] Earnings in the Midland town had soared to unprecedented levels during the war because of the high piece-work values

which had been established on war work; it was because the
Humber management tried to depress these high values that
the dispute attracted the support of shop stewards throughout the town. Their substantial success in beating off this
early initiative ensured that Coventry's reputation as a gold-
mine for semi-skilled car workers was preserved into the
1950s and 60s. But this was not merely a parochial success.
The mechanism of the Coventry Toolroom Agreement, by
which a monthly figure representing the average piece-work
earnings of skilled piece-workers throughout the town was
mutually agreed between the employers and unions, ensured
that the efforts of the shop stewards to push earnings up
from their high wartime base had national repercussions. The
Agreement's figures, which were the basis on which all local
toolmakers were paid, became a monthly beacon for piece-
work negotiators in factories all over Britain. Their almost
uninterrupted rise since the Agreement's inception was a
very considerable asset to shop stewards throughout the
British motor industry in the post-war years. The Humber
management had attempted to reassert nationally negotiated
values on behalf of engineering employers both locally and,
to a lesser extent, nationally; the failure of their attempt
ensured that it was the last for a long time.

As it happened, the hope for full post-war employment
was more or less to be realised and the fears of many trade-
unionists that the post-First World War Depression would
recur proved groundless. Indeed, it was the conviction held
by most working people that this would be so that had to
some extent undermined the militant shop stewards' attempts
to resist redundancy. But the problem did not rest there.
As we have seen, there were those trade-unionists who had
hoped to keep existing government factories in public ownership, and this campaign, carried on in the teeth of much
opposition, had failed. Indeed, it had been to some extent a
propaganda campaign designed to raise the political questions
that were coming to the fore with the impending general
election. Economically, the battles to preserve wages and
conditions had only just begun by the end of the war, and
they continued into 1946 with the Humber strike. But the
wartime experience had raised hundreds of thousands of

workers' employment expectations in terms of wages, conditions, welfare provision and, perhaps most important of all, treatment as citizens with rights which did not diminish at the factory gate. Only a major and sustained onslaught by the employers could have removed these gains, and this was not to happen. As far as the state of trade union organisation was concerned, there can be little doubt that the steward was on the shop floor to stay. In due course it became necessary for the advocates of managerial *diktat* to smear, ridicule and abuse the shop steward, in an attempt to undermine working people's growing recognition of the value of workplace representation. The end of the war did bring setbacks for union organisation which meant that the late 1940s did not inherit the shop floor organisation of 1943-4: the removal of large numbers of workers and the closing down of many plants of itself ensured this. But there was also a good deal of victimisation of shop stewards from early 1944 onwards. It is difficult to quantify the impact of this tendency but in some plants in the immediate post-war years it certainly affected the willingness of workers to come forward as nominees for election as shop stewards. The overall impression—and it has to be an impression by the very nature of the subject—is that workplace organisation was rather less strong and stable in the years of the Labour government than it had been in wartime.

Quite clearly, all of these issues were closely linked in people's minds with the post-war political order and the coming election. It was impossible for anyone to ignore the political dimensions of industrial life: the nature of reconstruction, the prospects for full employment, the possibility of nationalisation in many industries, were tied up with which party was in government. Political tension and anticipation were heightened by the fact that there had not been a general election for a decade. Ever since the mid-1930s, the Conservatives had been in control at Westminster, despite the creation of the Coalition government in 1940. In early October 1944 the Labour Party announced its intention to fight an independent election campaign, rather than continue the coalition, and the electoral debate began in earnest. The theme on the left was 'never again'; never again did anyone want to return to a situation where unemployment and the human waste and decay which went with it were the order of the day, and this was reflected in the Labour Party's manifesto, *Let Us Face The Future.* The Conservatives, on the other hand, had no such powerful groundswell of opinion behind them: they were not the party of reform, nor were they the party that had won the war. The very fact that the Churchill Cabinet refused to take any concrete action to ensure that things would be different after the war fuelled the feeling that only a Labour government would have the will and determination to reform Britain in any meaningful sense. Indeed, some Labour Party activists were not at all disappointed by Churchill's insistence on taking no reformist measures, realising that any such initiatives could well have redounded to his party's credit.

The result of the general election came as a surprise to all of the national political commentators in the major newspapers, who had disagreed solely on the size of the expected Conservative majority. On 26 July it was announced that the Labour Party had gained a majority of one hundred and fifty-eight over the Opposition. The move away from the Conservatives was particularly striking in the larger industrial towns, reflecting the strong reformist spirit reigning in these areas.[91] Even for those political commentators who had been unaware of the development of trade union organisation and had overlooked its militant reformist content, surprise at the result was hardly appropriate. The election campaign, with the deep involvement of many trade-unionists at all levels, had offered a number of clues as to the likely outcome at the polls. At the official level, the trade unions threw their weight behind the Labour Party with some vigour. In London, for example, a march of engineers to Trafalgar Square brought thousands of AEU members onto the streets with their banners flying. They were led by AEU members of the Home Guard, and shouted slogans as they marched: 'Make the Tories Redundant on July 5!' and: 'Engineers Demand the Forty-Hour Week—Vote Labour!' The engineers were addressed by the AEU's President, the ex-First World War shop stewards' leader Jack Tanner, who urged them to vote Labour; the crowd held together despite a heavy shower

of rain.[92] This sort of officially organised activity was
duplicated up and down the country, and many of the
activists were drawn into it.[93]

For the first time in the twentieth century the Labour
Party was backed up electorally by a formidable industrial
machine. Never before or since has such widespread shop
steward organisation combined with enthusiasm for Labour's
cause to such effect. There were good political reasons for
the near-unanimity of the shop stewards for Labour. The
Communists, who had become so influential amongst them,
had decided not to follow an aggressively independent
policy in the election. In a decision much criticised in the
CP Conference of November 1945, they argued for a continuation of a Coalition government after the war (with a
Labour majority) and reduced the number of Communist
candidates to twenty-one.[94] This meant that in the majority
of constituencies there was no Communist candidate, and the
efforts of the left shop stewards were generally thrown
behind the Labour contender. The E&ATSSNC and *New
Propellor* urged stewards to draw the mass of members into
the campaign and called on all shop stewards' committees
to take a lead in propaganda amongst the membership,
without spelling out who to vote for.[95] But in most cases it
had to mean voting Labour.

In an attempt to make themselves more effective in the
coming election and at the same time deal with the problem
of losing members from factory groups through redundancy,
the CP took a decision which was referred to as a serious
mistake by Harry Pollitt at an extended meeting of the CP's
Executive Committee almost eight years later.[96] Industrial
members were to be redistributed amongst area branches,
and existing industrial branches dissolved and replaced by
factory committees. The results were disastrous in the
medium term because this move led to the dissolution of
possibly the CP's greatest asset, the industrial branches.

Despite this organisational change by the CP, the shop
stewards as a whole, through their traditional report-back
meetings and factory papers, had already been agitating in
the direction indicated by *New Propellor*. While holding
meetings on matters like redundancy or the national

*New Propellor*, July 1945

engineering negotiations, they took the opportunity to point out to their members the links between the political and industrial situations, and to build political consciousness on the basis of the immediate industrial issues. At the end of May 1945 the London Regional Industrial Relations Officer remarked on just this sort of use of the unease over redundancy 'to awaken the political conscience of the workers'.[97] In West London the timing of redundancies presented the shop stewards with opportunities for political propaganda which they were not slow to seize. On 15 May the stewards at Napier's were given notice of large-scale redundancies, and within two days had organised a mass demonstration of eight to nine thousand Napier's workers outside Acton Town Hall. Deputations visited the mayor and the local MP, Captain Henry Longhurst. Harry Shaw, the convenor, and Jack Page, the night shift chairman, outlined their case, making two key points. The first was that the government should have published a plan for the changeover from war to peace production; the second was that the Acton plants should be turned over to peacetime goods. As an example they quoted the Acton No. 1 factory which was, they felt, suitable for conversion to mining-machinery production. Another had been a cosmetics factory before the war, and there was no guarantee, Shaw said, that this factory would not be returned to the same sort of work rather than to work of greater national importance.

Shaw expanded on these points to the Napier's workers, arguing that what Britain needed most urgently was decent houses, good furniture and cooking utensils, and luxuries could wait until these needs had been satisfied. Rather than announce redundancies, the government should pay workers for a forty-seven-hour week despite their having no work to do, just as they had in the early days of the war. Adding that 'this was not really a Napier's struggle, but a test case which affected all the war workers in Britain', Shaw reminded his members that they had stuck to their jobs through the flying-bomb raids, and had been the first workers in the country to set up a JPC.[98] On Tuesday 29 May the Napier's stewards held a mass meeting in Acton Park. It resolved not to accept redundancies until a satisfactory statement on the utilisation of their factories was given; opposed the recent NAT decision on engineering wages; demanded positive government plans for the changeover from war to peace production, and called for the election of a government 'based on a Labour and Progressive majority pledged to plan for the needs of the people'. The meeting was attended not only by Napier's workers but also by engineers from seventeen other London factories. The speakers included Claude Berridge, Harry Shaw, Bill Stacey, Napier's Liverpool convenor, and Ted Bramley, the prospective CP candidate for Acton.[99]

The next week, the local *Acton Post and Gazette* printed a letter from A. Doig, a toolroom worker at the No. 1 factory who had attended the meeting of 29 May, which showed a highly critical attitude to the CP's 'stage-managing' of that meeting. It is interesting both for its biting critique of CP activity and for the oblique shafts of light which it throws on the meeting. It is quoted in full:

Sir—The writer has read about Commonwealth's 'circus'; he saw the 'Communist' Party's in action in Acton Park on Tuesday evening, May 29th, the occasion of a protest meeting on 'redundancy' being used for 'putting across' Ted Bramley. Was he invited or did he just drop in in passing? I have known for some time that the policy of the CP was determined by the foreign policy of Russia; it was a new one for me to be told by Claude Berridge that Joe Stalin was 'our convenor'. During Claude's militant period he was not afraid to give the 'answers'; perhaps 'taking the can back' to the workers during the 1941-45 war has 'softened' him up a bit. What is all this nonsense we get from Harry Shaw these days about the workers backing up their 'leaders'? We do not elect leaders, we elect representatives; the former command, the latter carry out mandates. Sheep need leaders and where you have sheep you have shepherds, crooks and fleecers. Take the 4s. 6d. award. This award has the same interpretation as the 326 Award, which the *Daily Worker* and the Pollitt Parrots noised abroad was a good award. It raised the wages of the lower paid workers. When the Barrow workers put a different interpretation on it, and after negotiating for some time came out on strike, the same *DW* and *PPs* reviled them up and down the country. 'There's a war on', 'Use the negotiating machinery' was the cry. Before the war (1941-45) the CP regarded this machine as fit for the junk pile; during the war it was just what the doctor ordered; and after the war is fit for the junk pile again. However, if there is any trouble boys we can comfort ourselves with the knowledge that we will have Claude's sympathy while he is telling us to use the negotiating machinery. Here, I would appeal to the rank and file of the CP (the majority of whom I believe to be sincere in their views) to take a holiday from the Party; study other people's views and read the literature of the Party before and during the period between October 1941 and May 1945. Then consider whether you are to be taken in any longer with the nonsense, 'Changing Conditions', 'New Situation', 'Leading the Working Class', and, above all, the doctrine that 'The end justifies the means'. I know that it is a hard job to break away having done it myself, but do it before it breaks you.[100]

The writer of this letter was clearly extremely critical of the CP's political manoeuvring within industry. It seems unlikely that most workers were similarly aware of the CP's politics, let alone as sharply articulate. But within only a short time Ted Bramley, as CP candidate, having used the Napier's platform, withdrew his parliamentary candidature and placed all his electoral organisation at the disposal of the Labour Party candidate.[101] The efforts of the CP shop stewards and the public abuse which they received within the letters column of the local paper were, then, to some extent in vain. During the following week the shop stewards announced that they had in fact accepted the redundancy procedure, but insisted that they would continue to agitate to secure alternative work and the return of a 'Labour, Communist and Progressive majority' to plan the transition from a war to a peace economy.[102] A minority may have felt somewhat misled as to the true objects of the shop stewards' campaign; no doubt Mr Doig was amongst them. But for the majority, the point was well taken. It is difficult to see how even a group of factories could effectively challenge government economic policies under war conditions. On the other hand, it is not at all difficult to see how the issue could be very effectively linked to the political situation.

Captain Longhurst certainly gained very little from his involvement in the Napier's agitation. When asked about how he had voted on the proposal for an increase in service pay, at a public meeting which he held immediately before the election, he said that he resented the accusation that he voted against it: 'He sat seven hours in the House of Commons with only a ten minute break for a sandwich. . .', to which a woman replied: 'I stood seven hours in a factory that day.' Captain Longhurst was challenged to state an engineer's basic rate. When he answered, he was interrupted 'by a very grave woman's voice saying "Are you sure, Henry?"' Longhurst left to cries of 'Fore!' from local children.[103] Not surprisingly, he lost his seat at the general election. The extent to which this was due to the activities of the left shop stewards is difficult to say. It seems likely that he would have lost it in any case. Nevertheless, their efforts to exploit the large-scale local redundancies unquestionably involved large numbers of workers from a large number of local factories, and there was no doubt about their left-wing political allegiances.

It was in this way, then, that the shop stewards used the opportunities presented to them by the immediate situation: it was not so much a case of presenting abstract political arguments to their members as of drawing out the political implications of the day-to-day difficulties experienced by industrial workers. As the E&ATSSNC had for some time pointed out, the redundancies raised the wider issue of nationalisation, alternative products and full employment.[104] The shop stewards in a very large number of workplaces had a political leadership which did not hesitate to draw these issues out.

Perhaps the ultimate accolade for the shop stewards' efforts in the election was given in a report to Lord Beaverbrook which analysed the causes of Labour's landslide victory. This private report, which was far from friendly to either the left or the trade unions, pointed out the role of the stewards in no uncertain terms: 'The shop stewards were undoubtedly a tremendously valuable propaganda organisation for the Socialists during the election campaign. Where there was no Communist candidate they devoted all their energies to securing the return of the Socialist.'[105] For such a statement to have been made to the Conservative press baron, the master of political propaganda, was praise indeed.

The tasks which faced the left in wrenching control from Conservative electoral machines in many areas should not be underestimated. In Birmingham, for example, the left had a traditionally very powerful opponent in the form of the efficient Unionist organisation. The Unionists had beaten off the Labour challenge in 1935 through their control of the city corporation, their provision of motor cars to take supporters to the polls, and their control over the local press. Yet just a few years later their hold was beginning to weaken. The local Labour Party made links with the strikers at the Austin Aero factory in 1937, and by April 1938 over two thousand strikers from the Rover shadow factory were so angry with Chamberlain's refusal to intervene on their behalf that they drowned his speech to local Unionists. The electoral truce led to the decline of the Unionist machine, which went into mothballs for the duration of the war, while the left and in particular the CP stepped up its activity considerably. In 1944 the Birmingham Labour Party launched an appeal in conjunction with the trades council to obtain one shilling from every trade-unionist in the city before the general election. The shop stewards collected £525, equivalent to over ten thousand individual contributions. Over thirty-five thousand copies of a pro-Labour leaflet were distributed in the factories by the shop stewards. Factory-gate meetings were supported by the stewards at a number of local factories. It was little wonder, then, that numerous local and contemporary experts pointed to the shop stewards' and workshop organisation as a key factor in the Labour victory of 1945.[106] In the post-war Wilson Report on Labour Party organisation, the Birmingham party was cited as the classic example of effective liaison with the trade unions in general and the shop stewards' movement in particular.[107]

As the Birmingham example shows, it was not just in the immediate sense suggested in the report to Beaverbrook that the left-wing shop stewards had played their part in the election of a Labour government with an enormous majority. They also reflected and reinforced an increasing willingness on the part of workers in manufacturing industry to challenge the 'managerial prerogatives' which employers had long claimed were necessary for the running of their enterprises. This willingness was not new: its origins are to be found deep in the nineteenth century, in the activities of craft trade-unionists in engineering. What was new was the extension of these attitudes to a much wider stratum of engineering workers with no connection with the craft trade union tradition. The process of opening up work issues as matters for discussion, in which working people had a legitimate claim to voice their opinions, was not, and could not be, sealed off in a water-tight compartment away from wider social issues. For most of the AEU shop stewards, trade-unionism and the Labour Party were two sides of the same coin: one devoted to industrial and the other to political action. To recruit members was not simply to bring them into the trade unions, but also to open up the political issue by asking them to pay the political levy. The large number of new members, especially women, who agreed to pay the levy, was eloquent testimony to the shop stewards' activity in this respect. Many of the new workers came face to face for the first time with, and sometimes joined, the wider labour movement. This was not necessarily a question of joining the Labour or Communist Parties—although many did—but of adopting a commitment to social change both at work and in society at large which in many ways trans-cended the limitations of these parties. Their vote for the Labour Party at the end of the war reflected this conscious-ness, but it did not adequately articulate the hopes and aspirations of trade-unionists.

Looking back from the 1980s it is remarkable to see the extent to which the shop stewards succeeded in bringing their members politically as well as industrially behind them. It is of crucial significance here that the shop stewards stood for democracy both in the workshop and outside of it. The later Cold War rhetoric about 'shop steward dictator-ship', if put into the mouths of 1940s Conservatives, would have been greeted with derision on the shop floor. It was managements who were perceived as dictatorial; when Jock Wallace was on the platform of a mass meeting of eight thousand Napier's workers in Liverpool a manager was careless enough to protest that the meeting would have to be ended as it was political. Wallace accepted the manager's statement as a motion, and it was defeated by eight thousand votes to one.[108]

It has frequently been remarked by historians that the Army Bureau of Current Affairs, dominated by left-wing intellectuals, was vitally significant in the propaganda and educational discussions that made the British Army a socialist force. In that case, the industrial equivalent to ABCA was not its anaemic and late-born offspring the Industrial Bureau, but the shop stewards' movement led by its worker-intellectuals of the left. Communist Party activists had not 'infiltrated' the engineering unions: they had rebuilt them from the shells they had been in the Depression. Their key instrument for leading this trade union renaissance was the political-industrial newspaper, *New Propellor*, which by 1945 had been in continuous publication for a decade. By the end of the war it was complemented by numerous factory newspapers all taking up its leads and relating them to the day-to-day problems of the particular workplace. But these papers, vivid and effective though they were, were only the beginning of the political-industrial process. Selling and distributing a paper was not, the Communists had been taught, simply a matter of getting rid of as many copies as possible like an industrial newsagent. It was above all a question of using the papers as weapons, as educational and organisational tools to politicise workers through action. For many Communists it was the hard and rigorous intellectual training related to day-to-day practice and acquired within the CP which enabled them to do this. Perhaps soon a historian will be able to use Communist archives to allow us to appreciate this aspect of the CP's internal life more fully.

Yet the role of the Communist and Labour Party shop stewards through the E&ATSSNC was not simply one of political propaganda. During the course of the war, their role underwent a fundamental change. After the entry of the Soviet Union into the war, their objective of involving themselves in, leading and politicising strikes shifted to one of increasing production within which political and industrial action were to some extent counterposed to one another. Particularly after the battle for JPCs had been substantially won, political action became an alternative to industrial action through go-slows and strikes. To a very considerable extent they were successful, where they had influence, in

354

preventing strikes. Some historians who have not themselves tried to gauge the extent and intensity of discontent on the shop floor, have complained that they were not successful enough. Seen in this context, the achievement of the left shop stewards in deflecting workers from strike action (sometimes at considerable cost to their own positions, as we have seen) becomes much more substantial than they have allowed. But when the left wing deflected this industrial unrest, they did not simply suggest inactivity or blacklegging. They directed workers to the use of *political* channels for solving their problems—to lobbying MPs, making representations to the various responsible ministries and so on. It was no use, they argued, looking at the industrial situation in isolation; shop floor grievances had to be seen in the context of a world struggle against fascism, the sworn enemy of trade-unionism. The best way to settle accounts with the 'English fascists' was to settle with their foreign counterparts first. After the war was over, they argued, there would be every opportunity to turn the full strength of the labour movement firmly towards substantial reform, and to deal with the enemy at home.

At some expense to themselves, and despite losing a little ground on their left to the Militant Workers' Federation and others, the left-wing shop stewards pushed industrial discontent into parliamentary political channels in 1945. The Communists in the leadership of the E&ATSSNC, having no plans to found a revolutionary party on their political leadership of the factory movement, such as that dreamed of by the shop stewards who played an important part in forming the Communist Party, were pushed inexorably towards providing an industrial support and propaganda machine for the Labour Party. They themselves, despite their industrial successes, could not hope to translate factory leadership into electoral support. The Labour Party, on the other hand, did not have the capacity to educate and mobilise their own supporters in industry. The Labour Party had no national newspapers directed at workers in particular industries, little close involvement with their daily shop-floor problems, and only a very few factory branches (set up in imitation of those of the CP). Their great strength, of course, was the secular political shift in their direction which was sweeping them to the most impressive victory of their history. The growth of the shop stewards' movement during the war buttressed and nourished the development of the labour movement as a whole, and to this extent made a positive contribution that has been too little recognised.

Almost immediately after the war, the political leadership of the shop stewards' movement came under savage attack both industrially through sackings, redundancy and victimisation and politically through the maelstrom of the Cold War. Those who had been more than willing to call on the support of the shop stewards to prosecute the war effort turned viciously against their erstwhile allies in an attempt to decapitate the most political and active from the body of workplace trade-unionists. An enormous amount of propaganda was heaped on the heads of the stewards, who had become 'subversives' and 'extremists'. The beginnings of the process which was to lead, in the 1970s, to the full-scale deployment of the media against workplace representatives could be discerned. The process effectively buried not only the contemporary but also the historical realities.

## NOTES

1  Quoted in M. Edelman, 'Redundancy: A Threatening New Word', in *Picture Post,* 4 Aug. 1945.
2  P. Inman, op. cit., p. 393.
3  E&ATSSNC *Bulletin,* 8 May 1944. See also *Minutes* of the Coventry District Committee of the AEU (25 April 1944): 'The Committee emphatically protests. . . sufficient safeguards are already in existence to take drastic action against *agents provocateurs.* Any new regulations we consider as quite unnecessary and as an attack against the commonsense of responsible Trade Union officials and Trade Union members.'
4  M. Foot, op. cit., p. 462.
5  See R. Croucher, op. cit., p. 330.
6  5 May 1944, LAB 10/445. The strike was from 3 to 11 September (LAB 34/59).
7  26 May, 9, 30 June. LAB 10/443.
8  *DW,* 11, 13 March 1944. *Minutes* of the Manchester District Committee of the AEU, 22 Feb. 1944. Transcript of an interview with Bill Abbott by Spencer Phelan, 9 Feb. 1979.
9  *DW,* 13 March 1944. Owen had been a member of the Woolwich Arsenal shop stewards' committee in the First World War, and was sent as their delegate when the Clyde Workers' Committee members were deported. He attended Ruskin College, Oxford, where he helped to found the National Council of Labour Colleges. In 1937 he was elected to the Manchester City

Council for Labour but was expelled from the Labour Party when he took the chair at a *Daily Worker* rally in Manchester on 30 July 1940. He returned to the factory, but immediately accepted a position on the *Daily Worker* (*DW*, 8 Aug 1940).

10 Transcript of an interview with Bill Abbott by Spencer Phelan, 9 Feb. 1979.

11 *DW*, Oct. 1943-Feb. 1944. *Catholic Worker*, Feb. 1944.

12 *Catholic Worker*, Aug. 1944. 5 May 1944, LAB 10/443.

13 *DW*, 11, 13 March 1944.

14 6, 27 Oct. 1944. LAB 10/443.

15 F.H. Happold, 'A Better Way to Stop Strikes', in *Picture Post*, 6 May 1944.

16 10, 17 March 1944, LAB 10/443.

17 3, 10 Dec. 1943. LAB 10/359.

18 RCP *Industrial Bulletin*, no. 1, Nov. 1944 (Modern Records Centre, University of Warwick).

19 In October 1941 when the JPC campaign was under way, Churchill told the Cabinet that great importance should be attached to ministers following the recognised procedure of seeing trade union Executives only, despite the suggestion that it might on rare occasions be useful to see unofficial deputations (War Cabinet *Minute:* WM 104(41) *Minute* 8 in Beaverbrook Archive, D/89, 20 Oct. 1941). It was agreed at the same meeting that the Ministry of Information should take 'suitable steps' to ensure that the E&ATSSNC was not given 'undue publicity' (extract from War Cabinet conclusions, 20 Oct. 1941, in Beaverbrook Archive D/89). This policy may have softened at least after the rehabilitation of the *Daily Worker. New Propellor* advocated the E&ATSSNC's policy of seeking maximum publicity during the battles over pay at Rolls-Royce Hillington. The shop stewards 'made full use of the trade union machinery supplemented by publicity measures on the lines advocated by the E&ATSSNC, and the maintenance of working-class discipline by the workers who refused to respond to the provocation of the Trotskyite elements who wanted strike action' (*NP*, Nov. 1943).

20 *NP*, Jan. 1944.

21 Scottish shop stewards': *Open Letter* to the government and shipyard employers (n.d.). 25 Feb. 1944. LAB 10/445.

22 Ibid.

23 *NP*, 24 April 1944.

24 The paper changed its name in April 1946.

25 There are a number of important sources for the history of the battles to unionise Fords in this period, which have yet to be fully exploited by labour historians, and most of which are to be found in the Lovell papers, Marx Memorial Library. See the article by Lovell in the *Morning Star*, 18 November 1968, and the letter written by Ben Gardner to Lovell on 21 March 1946, in the Lovell papers. In a memorandum to Citrine, Feather wrote of the left shop stewards that they were 'totally unsuitable from any point of view. . . for appointment as shop stewards' (see his undated memo in TUC T.602.57.4). See also 7, 14 Jan. 1944, LAB 10/443.

26 *Catholic Worker*, Feb., March, July 1944, also carried an important series of articles on the Ford events.

27 Sweetman's sacking is mentioned in LAB 10/443, 5 May 1944. Harry Hartshorne, a CP steward and toolmaker who had worked at Fords in Manchester and Detroit, also lost his job at about the same time (*DW*, 9 Feb. 1944; *Catholic Worker*, March 1944). The role of the Irish is

mentioned in Connolly Association, *The Irish in Britain*, 1945, (Maitland-Sara collection).

28   R. Harrison, G.B. Woolven, R. Duncan, *The Warwick Guide to Labour Periodicals* (1976), entries 1091, 1436, 3376. The *Humber Clarion* is dated 1948(?) in this guide, but I have seen a copy dated 1946. The late Bill Wellings told me that the paper's predecessor was *Humber Bulletin*.

29   R. Harrison et al., entry 1331; on *Factory News* (A.V. Roe), see Spencer Phelan, *The Avro Conspiracy* (unpublished Labour Studies dissertation, Ruskin College, Oxford, 1979). Interview with Jock Wallace, 8 April 1980.

30   S. Phelan, op. cit., pp. 49–52.

31   Ibid., p. 50.

32   Ibid., p. 53.

33   On the matter of the suspensions given to some workers for lateness, *Factory News* commented: 'If the suspension for five hours was the result of coming in ten minutes late, we agree that it was an "unconscionable penalty", but we do not see events in such isolation. No-one for example. . . thinks that we declared war on Germany because Poland was invaded and for no other reason at all.'

34   *Factory News* (A.V. Roe), p. 51.

35   Discussion statement in CP, 'Party Organisation—Weapon for Victory' (1943), p. 4, Maitland-Sara collection.

36   8 Sept. 1944. LAB 10/445.

37   CP, *The CP On The Way To Win* (May 1942); *Victory, Peace, Security* (Oct. 1944); *Communist Policy for Britain* (Nov. 1945). For details of delegates, see H. Pelling, *The British Communist Party. An Historical Profile* (1958), p. 192.

38   Joe Marshall, 'Building a Factory Leadership', in *Organise To Mobilise Millions,* (n.d., early 1943), p. 4, Maitland-Sara collection.

39   CP, *Strengthen Our Organisation*, p. 5, Maitland-Sara collection.

40   Ibid., p. 11.

41   In his reply to the discussion at the Eighteenth National Congress of the CP, Harry Pollitt ended his speech: 'You can talk about objective and subjective factors as long as you like. You can talk about under-estimations and over-estimations as long as you like. But the fundamental reason why our Party does not grow is that you comrades do not want it to grow! That is the reason! The Party wants to be a narrow Party, it wants to be a Party of exclusive Marxists. It resents hundreds and thousands of members coming into the Party. Yes, I apply this test to all of you.' (*Communist Policy For Britain*, Nov. 1945, p. 35).

42   F. Claudin, *The Communist Movement. From Comintern to Cominform* (1975), p. 308.

43   *DW*, 18 Dec. 1944. At A.V. Roe's Chadderton factory the shop stewards' committee refused to take a position on the overtly political issue, and was criticised by *Factory News* (Christmas 1944): 'The lack of support which often hampers the Works Committees' activities in other directions, springs in no small measure from the Committees' failure to give leadership to the workers in every sphere.'

44   29 Dec. 1944, LAB 10/443. At the AEU's District Committee in Coventry, an hour's strike was proposed in protest at the government's policy, but an amendment proposing no action until a meeting called by the mayor had been held was passed instead (*Minutes* of the Coventry District Committee of the AEU, 19 Dec. 1944; 2 Jan. 1945).

45   Ibid.

46  See Maurice Edelman, 'Redundancy: A Threatening New Word', in *Picture Post*, 4 Aug. 1945.
47  This passage draws heavily on the remarks made by the Scottish Regional Industrial Relations Officer, 13 April 1945. LAB 10/534.
48  Cutting from 'Harrisson Report', in Industry Raw Materials, MO Archive.
49  This statement is based on a political letter now in the British Library written by R. Palme Dutt on 28 July 1944, which was brought to my attention by James Hinton through an unpublished paper entitled 'Coventry Communism: A Study of Factory Politics in the Second World War', which he kindly sent me. It has now been published under the same title in *History Workshop Journal*, no. 10, autumn 1980.
50  The Metal Advisory Committee document is referred to in CP, *Report of the EC*, Sept. 1944-Aug. 1945, Maitland-Sara collection.
51  CP, *Engineering Prospects and Wages* (1945), pp. 3, 5, Maitland-Sara collection.
52  'Notes of a Meeting with the Minister of Aircraft Production at the Ministry of Production', 16 March 1944. See also 'Note of a Meeting at the Ministry of Works', 12 April 1944. AVIA 15/3855.
53  I.F.S. Hetherington to MacLehose, 14 Feb. 1945; Hetherington to Bowyer, 17 Feb. 1945. AVIA 15/3856. *News Chronicle*, 9 Feb. 1945.
54  Hetherington to MacLehose, 14 Feb. 1945. Hetherington to Bowyer, 17 Feb. 1945.
55  CP, *Engineering Prospects and Wages* (1945), p. 5.
56  Note dated 6 Feb. 1945. AVIA 15/3856.
57  Some shop stewards were still fighting this issue after the return of the Labour government. The stewards at the Daimler No. 1 shadow factory in Coventry, for example, passed the following motion soon after the election: 'This meeting of Daimler No. 1 factory, Coventry, workers, calls upon the Government to investigate the possibilities of retaining this factory under Government control for the production of such necessary commodities as housing equipment, agricultural machinery, mining and textile machinery, etc. We point out that the record of this factory during the war, in quality, quantity and overhead costs, was second-to-none, a state of affairs due in no small measure to the co-operation of all in the factory, sponsored and maintained by the workers through their joint production committee and shop stewards' committee. In conclusion, we take this opportunity of assuring this government of our whole-hearted support. We say "Take your courage in both hands. The people of Dunkirk and the Battle of Britain are with you".' ('A Factory Switches Over', in *Picture Post*, 15 Sept. 1945).
58  Leaflet issued by representatives of Rover 1 and 2, City of Birmingham Aircraft Factory and Austin Aero and Motors workers, n.d., in Etheridge papers, Modern Records Centre, University of Warwick. See also 16 Feb. 1945, LAB 10/553.
59  3 Nov. 1944, LAB 10/443.
60  *Minutes* of the Coventry District Committee of the AEU, 13, 27 Feb., 6 March 1945.
61  *Manchester Guardian*, 3 Nov. 1944.
62  *DW*, 1, 3 Nov. 1944.
63  3 Nov. 1944, LAB 10/443.
64  *Birmingham Post*, 14 Feb. 1945.
65  *The Economist*, 24 March 1945.
66  Political and Economic Planning, 'The Motor Industry', in *Planning*, 2 July 1948, p. 25.

67 The Royal Ordnance Factories were largely run down after the war; almost half the available capacity had to be written off as useless for peace production (W. Hornby, *Factories and Plant* (1958), pp. 390–1). In this case, enormous amounts of government money had to be written off as a cost of the war.
68 B.L. Coombes, 'The Story of a Miners' Football Team', in *Picture Post*, 27 Jan. 1945.
69 6 July 1945. LAB 10/534.
70 13 April 1945. LAB 10/534.
71 *Factory News* (Vickers-Armstrong, Manchester), Dec. 1944.
72 *NP*, March 1945.
73 13 April 1945. LAB 10/534.
74 15 Dec. 1944. LAB 10/443.
75 18 May, 1, 8 June 1945. LAB 10/553.
76 Interview with Jock Wallace, 20 May 1980.
77 10 Nov. 1944. LAB 10/443. Interview with Jock Wallace, 20 May 1980.
78 9 Feb. 1945. LAB 10/554.
79 Etheridge papers, Modern Records Centre, University of Warwick.
80 Letter from W.R. Lord (AEU) to Hindmarsh, 28 Oct. 1944. Etheridge papers.
81 23 Feb. 1945. LAB 10/553.
82 30 March 1945. LAB 10/554.
83 30 March 1945. LAB 10/534.
84 8 June 1945. LAB 10/553.
85 *Minutes* of a local conference held between Engineering and Allied Employers' Coventry District Association and the AEU/CSEU, 1 Feb. 1945, pp. 2–21.
86 Ibid., p. 6.
87 This was said by J.T. Bolas to the ETU, ibid., p. 17.
88 Ibid., p. 26.
89 *DW*, 26, 27 Feb. 1946; 1, 4, 14, 15, 20 March 1946. *Coventry Evening Telegraph*, 2, 4, 11, 12, 13 March. *Minutes* of the Coventry District Committee of the AEU, 5, 12, 19 March 1946. The dispute was conducted by a Coventry-wide dispute committee, which sent a resolution to the AEU District Committee calling on it to organise district-wide strike action to defend established conditions in the town, which the Humber management, in league with the employers' association, were in their opinion trying to depress.
90 *Minutes* of the Coventry District Committee of the AEU, 5 March 1946.
91 A. Calder, op. cit., p. 672ff.
92 *DW*, 2 July 1945.
93 The large number of trade union officials drawn into the election campaign in Scotland was noted by the Regional Industrial Relations Officer there (6 July 1945. LAB 10/534).
94 J. Mahon, *Harry Pollitt* (1976), p. 305. Pollitt responded to the criticism in his reply to the discussion at the Eighteenth National Congress of the CP in November 1945. Acknowledging (apparently unlike his biographer) that a mistake had been made, Pollitt pointed out that there was a 'basic reason' why the CP was wrong about the leftward swing in the Labour movement: 'It is not unrelated to the point legitimately made about ears being closer to the ground.' (*Report* of the Eighteenth National Congress, p. 31).
95 *NP*, July 1945.
96 Pollitt reported to the meeting that: 'We have paid a heavy price for the

tendencies towards liquidation of factory organisation which we tolerated after the end of the war.' He went on to remind the meeting of a report to an extended EC meeting of February 1949, which had stated unequivocally that dissolving factory branches had been a mistake. The 1953 meeting heard that 'only slow progress' was being made in building new factory branches, 'and as a general aim it is not yet being seriously operated'. (*DW*, 14 Feb. 1953).

97   1 June 1945. LAB 10/553.
98   *Acton Post and Gazette*, 25 May 1945.
99   Ibid. 1 June.
100  Ibid., 8 June 1945.
101  Ibid., 15 June 1945.
102  Ibid., 22 June 1945.
103  Ibid., 29 June 1945.
104  E&ATSSNC, 'Report of a National Meeting held Sunday March 7, 1943 at the Conway Hall, London', p. 3 (Library of the Working-Class Movement, Manchester).
105  J.B. Wilson to Beaverbrook, 17 Aug. 1945, in Beaverbrook Archive, House of Lords Library (D/255).
106  R.P. Hastings, *The Labour Movement in Birmingham, 1927–45* (unpublished MA Dissertation, University of Birmingham, 1959), pp. 87, 94–5, 117, 172–82.
107  Ibid., p. 186.

CHAPTER 7

# CONCLUSION

In the course of this account of wartime industrial battles, some objective interpretations have been offered of the evolution of strike activity, the material and subjective reasons which underlay it, and the relationship of strikes to political agitation. In the first section of this conclusion these arguments are pulled together, summarised and, we hope, clarified. Then follows a section which revisits the official version of industrial relations during the Second World War in the light of the account which we have given. In this way it may be possible to modify the existing orthodoxy and its 'common-sense' assertions. But in itself this is not enough. Many labour and social historians deliberately avoid drawing out the contemporary consequences of the past, for a variety of reasons many of which are connected with notions of academic respectability. This often leads them to reduce the value of their own work, as they leave slabs of contemporary history suspended in mid-air at a respectable but mysterious distance from the present which often baffles even their historian colleagues. But this book sees historians as only a part of its readership; it is hoped that those shop stewards, trade union studies tutors and union officers who have an interest in examining their present practice in the light of the past will also find it useful. Because we regard this aspect as important, we have included a brief final section here which considers a few of the major bequests of the wartime movement to the shop stewards of today.

The growing confidence, strength and combativeness of engineering workers during the decade 1935-45 reflected a broad political unity and sense of purpose which we shall return to later, but it also flowed from traditions of skilled engineering trade-unionism which stretch back into the

363

nineteenth century. The desire to control work, and above all the way it was done, was crystallised in the image of the old engineer's chalk circle around his machine over which the foreman stepped at his peril. During the years after the 1922 lockout, there was very little opportunity for engineers to reassert their trade union organisation at workshop level because of the ever-present threat of the sack. The AEU itself drifted towards conservative policies and leadership, while the left was confined to publishing small ephemeral papèrs and railing against the Executive. Meanwhile, the industry was undergoing radical restructuring, concentration of ownership and rationalisation, which further weakened the job-control of the working engineer.

It was not until the arms-led economic upturn of the mid-1930s that engineers were able to reassert their collective identity through their workshop organisation. When the revival came, the rank and file were quick to elect shop stewards and to push them into conflict with managements, a situation tailor-made for the left within the engineering unions. At first, the most sophisticated organisation of shop stewards sprang up in the aircraft industry around *New Propellor* and the Aircraft Shop Stewards' National Council, but it was not long before the general unions too began to organise themselves. Before the war, the TGWU in particular had established itself within the industry, picking up where the Workers' Union had left off.

The most notable battle of the immediate pre-war period was fought neither by the skilled nor by the semi-skilled, however. It was the apprentices, the victims of 'rationalisation', who took up the cudgels with the employers in a series of strikes which for sheer enthusiasm and organisation invite comparison with the industrial upsurges in France and America in the same year. 1937 was the great turning point, as the apprentices won considerable increases and the right to some degree of trade union representation. The AEU had been attempting to win these concessions from the employers for some years without success; but as the union's President himself acknowledged, it was the boys themselves who had forced the employers' hand by their dogged single-mindedness. The apprentices radically changed the atmosphere in the factories and showed the way to the adults in the industry in a tremendous burst of militancy. The skilled engineers themselves had always doubted the ability of either the apprentices or the semi-skilled men or women to generate effective union organisation from within their own ranks. They were proved wrong, but continued to look to their own traditions of gradual erosion of managerial prerogatives through continuous organisation and union democracy as the key to progress in the factories.

The clearest indication of the continuing importance of the struggle to push back the 'frontier of control' occurred during the campaign to establish Joint Production Committees in late 1941. Although some saw this agitation as the top of a slippery slope which would end in shop stewards becoming integrated into management's perspectives, for many it represented (at first, at least) a genuine assault on the 'Colonel Chinstrap' type of manager ridiculed by Tommy Handley on the radio.[1] Yet the actual establishment of the Committees proved more effective as an assault on managements than their later uneven operation as working bodies. It very rapidly became apparent that JPCs were only the first step towards the democratisation of British industry, and that many of the old problems remained.

For most of the engineers in the factories the burning grievance remained their Depression wages, which lived on long after the economic argument for them had disappeared. The skilled AEU men of the 'ASE mentality' working in the northern shipyards and factories harboured considerable resentment, and blamed not only the employers but also their own officials for concentrating on production at the expense of their wages. As the JPC campaign came to an end, the wage front was opened.

During the Total Time dispute, the Tyneside AEU men demonstrated in no uncertain terms what they thought of the conduct of their local officials and District Committees. Their demand that all officials should consult them over any change in their working conditions, however apparently trivial, carried powerful echoes of the pre-First World War disputes about 'local autonomy'. Their demonstration showed how the conciliatory spirit which some employers and government

365

itself had intended to bring about through the establishment of JPCs had effectively failed to bind the north-easterners to their employers in quite the way which had been hoped. The discontent shown by the Total Time strikers with their local lay and full-time union officials, and articulated by some of their own shop stewards, was only duplicated in the Barrow dispute in so far as the Communists who tried to introduce politics to end the strike received short shrift. While the Barrow dispute again manifested attitudes hostile to those current in the Peckham Road, at the same time it represented something more serious: the rejection of an award by the National Arbitration Tribunal. It was this, as much as the very sharp criticism received by the Executive itself for defending the award, that gave rise to such concern within the union that the Executive decided to hold only the second Special Conference of the AEU's history. In due course the AEU adapted itself to the problems, and through the efforts of its full-time officers it restored a measure of stability and EC control in these districts. But the skilled men had also been agitating amongst other members of the workshop community by trying to recruit apprentices and women to the union and demanding the 'rate for the job'. The women and apprentices presented problems that could not be significantly affected by internal manoeuvring within the union, because the great majority of them remained non-members.

The apprentices and women who came so much to the forefront of industrial militancy in the winter of 1943-4 did so in the face of considerable pressures in the opposite direction. They found themselves ranged above all against the government and its various wartime agencies. Confronted by the activities of the Special Branch and MI5 (whose work we have only been able to glimpse through the available records, but whose presence often lurks unmistakably in the background), and by the possibility of prosecution and conscription, they had every reason to fear for their personal freedom. Moreover, the government had by this time become aware of the Trotskyist involvement in strikes, and began to use this as a propaganda lever. Trotskyists had also been active around the Total Time and Barrow disputes, but it was not until the winter of 1943-4 that Bevin was to draw attention to their activities in public speeches, and not until the apprentices' strikes of 1944 that the full weight of the media was thrown against the strikers and their political allies.

The women and apprentices were also, of course, faced with the opposition of the TUC, the engineering unions at official level, and the CP and E&ATSSNC. Yet this opposition was in some respects formal. As far as the unions were concerned, they could not exert the sort of pressure against the strikers that they had done in earlier disputes simply because the majority of those concerned were not their members. The apprentices had a history of hostility to intervention by trade union officials which the newly built Junior Workers' Committees had only just begun to erode. The left-wing shop stewards, as we have seen, took sizeable collections on behalf of both the women and the apprentices in the major factories of the Clyde and Tyne. The majority of left shop stewards seem to have adopted an attitude which can only be described as 'benevolent neutrality' to the women and apprentices on strike. As is so often the case in labour history, the national appearance did not reflect the local reality.

The battle for equal pay gathered momentum during the Second World War, having begun (unlike its counterpart of the First World War) at the very outbreak of hostilities, and reached its climax in 1943-4. By the summer of 1944 it had been defused as a national campaign, with the defeat of several strikes on the issue and the establishment of the Royal Commission on Equal Pay. It lived on in the form of innumerable local and individual cases taken up at shop floor level which continued beyond the end of the war. But it was the apprentices' strike of 1944 which brought the industrial relations situation to crisis point as far as the government was concerned, by implicitly challenging at a crucial point in the military timetable the right of the state to direct labour wherever it saw fit.

Even before this strike, Bevin had been faced with wide-spread industrial unrest not only in engineering, but also in coal mining, which had drawn him to the conclusion that legislative action was required to deal with the situation.

The existing law, and its practical application through selective prosecutions, had its limitations and dangers. In particular it had been shown early in the war, both at Betteshanger and elsewhere, that prosecution could not be used effectively against large bodies of determined strikers. In addition, there was the issue of political involvement by the extreme left in the form of the Militant Workers' Federation, the Clyde Workers' Committee, the RCP, ILP and others. Now Bevin had a personal history of ruthless suppression of political 'agitators' during strikes, which had shown itself during the busmen's 1937 Coronation dispute, and he moved with comparable severity against the extreme left in 1944. It was this combination of factors, occurring in the context of the imminent invasion of occupied Europe, that pushed the government to the point of straining the close alliance between itself and trade union executives which had existed since 1940. Regulation 1AA put pressure on this relationship because senior trade union officials felt that it was not entirely clear whether the regulation was directed at official and 'constitutional' activity by their unions or at 'irresponsible elements'. Bevin's response was quite simple: the regulation's objective was to strengthen their hands in dealing with 'irresponsible elements' and they should therefore welcome it. Jack Tanner, amongst others, was later to regret not having opposed the regulation openly, but nevertheless agreed to it when faced squarely by a determined Bevin.

Regulation 1AA gave further impetus to the managerial counter-attack which was gathering momentum in early 1944, and which was to swing the industrial balance of power further towards the state and employers even before the end of the war. The first prong in this two-pronged attack was the traditional weapon of victimisation. As we have shown, quite a large number of prominent shop stewards lost their jobs in early 1944. This was due not only to sackings carried out under the misconduct clause of the Essential Works Order, but also to transfers to other war work ordered by National Service Officers. Many trade-unionists therefore suspected state collusion with managements in their removal. Be that as it may, the second prong in the attack on workplace organisation flowed directly from governmental negotiations with the USA designed to shift an increasing amount of productive responsibility to American industry during the last phase of the war. As British industry began to run down from the summer of 1944 onwards, many large-scale redundancies took place with wartime regulations still in full force. These redundancies undoubtedly undermined the collective strength of the shop floor trade union organisation built up over the previous decade. Under the cover of economic inevitability, crystallised in the emergence of the new word itself, existing work groups with their networks of mutual loyalty could be broken up, shop stewards transferred or declared redundant and women sent back to the home.

The prospect of returning to a 'free' labour market was greeted with apprehension by many of the semi- and un-skilled, recalling as they did the long years of the Depression which had followed the brief post-First World War boom. Despite their partial unionisation by the general unions, the semi-skilled found themselves in a very difficult position at the end of the war, and their shop stewards were often reduced to simply administering redundancy amongst their members. They were confronted not only by the political presentation of redundancy as 'inevitable', but also by the attitudes of the skilled men. For the AEU, redundancy meant immediate implementation of the policy of 'dilutees first'. The old gulf along the skill divide had reappeared. Despite the growth of the general unions during the war, the industry was still dominated in 1945 by the skilled men and their union, and they intended to guarantee their sectional interests above all else. Although they were in many cases opposed to the prospect of returning the shadow factories to private ownership, wanted full employment in the post-war era and so on, they also took the overriding view that if anyone had to go, then it would be the 'dilutee' before the skilled AEU member.

Industrial demobilisation posed questions of workplace trade union organisation which it was substantially unable to answer. While the shop stewards had been able to push back the frontier of control in the factories, had established many democratic rights within industry and improved many aspects of their members' working conditions, they met with difficulties when they needed to change the direction of their activities. The prerequisite of an orderly change in direction was some form of coordination through the E&ATSSNC. But the CP, which constituted the political core of the E&ATSSNC, had decided not to conduct a campaign over redundancy. The demand for alternative products was not used mainly to raise workers' confidence to fight redundancy in their own factory—to do so appeared to them to be taking on the government single-handed—but rather as a political weapon in the run-up to the general election of 1945.

The left-wing shop stewards did succeed in some cases in enforcing an orderly return to peacetime production with acceptable guarantees for their members. But perhaps their most important contribution lay in the national political field. If they could not prevent mass redundancies then they could at least indicate clearly to their members exactly what was going on; and they pointed the way towards a Labour government committed to a programme of nationalisation and a planned economy. Mass meetings, leaflets, demonstrations and so on were all deployed to ensure that the members were fully politically aware when they cast their votes. But the left shop stewards also created the conditions in which the Labour Party could expect the much wider vote of industrial workers. The stewards had consistently exerted political pressure on MPs and Cabinet ministers as a way of dealing with their own industrial problems. They thus deflected the rising wave of militancy amongst their members into political channels and towards public politics, arguing all the time for socialist solutions to the problems they encountered. By contrast, the Labour Party itself had no equivalent industrial organisation through which it could propagandise amongst or mobilise factory workers. This was provided for them by the CP at the end of the war, since the CP consistently deferred to the Labour Party in electoral terms. In other words, the CP had become the industrial arm of the Labour Party, even though its direct role in terms of canvassing in 1945 may not have been especially vital.

At the beginning of this book, we set ourselves the task

of critically examining the interpretations of the history of wartime industrial relations offered by the official historian. It seems appropriate now to re-examine the main thrust of this most influential work in the light of the evidence presented here. Mrs Inman, as we have seen, recognised the existence of industrial conflict despite the opposition of the E&ATSSNC to strikes and the establishment of Joint Production Committees. But in doing so, she made an assumption about the E&ATSSNC and an untestable counter-factual assertion concerning JPCs. As far as the E&ATSSNC is concerned, she adopts the judgement of K.G.J.C. Knowles, who convicts the Communists involved of 'agitational incompetence' since, although they opposed strikes, the strike rate rose rather than declined.

The question of the relationship between the left shop stewards and their members cannot be adequately dealt with in so facetious a way, however. What has to be examined is just how far the shop stewards tried to prevent, head off and end strikes and, at the same time, how strong were the pressures from their rank and file not to do so. While it is possible to accuse the CP stewards of agitational incompetence, it has also to be recognised that shop stewards were above all representatives of their trade union members. While they might also be Communists, members of the Labour Party, or activists in any other political party, their priority was to heed the industrial wishes of their constituents in the factory.

How far, then, did the shop stewards exert themselves in preventing strikes after the invasion of the Soviet Union? This question clearly raises important issues concerning the nature of the political allegiances of the left shop stewards of the time. The answers have at this point to be general and tentative since the available documentation does not allow anything else, but certain points can be made with the evidence we do have. First, it is clear that there was some shift in the attitude of the CP stewards during the war, under a certain amount of pressure from their own party and its politics on the one hand and from their members on the other. During the Total Time strike of 1942, for example, even local Catholics had to admit that the Tyneside Communists had never actually supported the strike nor agitated for it. As a result, a number of them lost their shop stewards' credentials in the elections held immediately after the end of the dispute. This particular strike, no doubt partly because the *Daily Worker* had only just been allowed to recommence publication, was roundly condemned by the Communist paper. By the end of the war, the attitude of the CP in the factories appeared to be undergoing a subtle change. During the apprentices' strikes the *Daily Worker* and *New Propellor* did not attack the reasons for the stoppage but, on the basis of reports from activists in the localities, preferred instead to attack the Trotskyists for 'duping' the boys. By the end of 1944, CP stewards in London had to be prevented from striking over the Greek issue by the intervention of their Communist district officer.

Second, the CP shop stewards do not always appear to have put political priorities before industrial grievances. The prolonged go-slow conducted by a north-western aircraft factory after a 'production week', the threatened district-wide stoppages in Coventry and Manchester in 1943, the collections held throughout the Clyde factories in support of both the women and apprentice strikers of 1943-4—all these instances prompt us to ask whether the CP shop stewards disassociated themselves from these actions. Given the Communist pre-eminence in the areas concerned, such instances seem to point inevitably to only one possible answer. Many CP stewards, it would appear, preferred not to lose their steward's cards as some of their comrades had done and, faced with the uncomfortable choice between their political and industrial loyalties, adopted positions of varying degrees of ambiguity. Certainly, it is quite wrong to assume that CP shop stewards put the King Street line. Many of them had joined the CP and E&ATSSNC primarily on the strength of their trade union activity rather than the overtly political part of their work, and were reluctant to abandon industrial action 'for the duration'. Finally, it is important to remember that although the political leadership of the E&ATSSNC was Communist, the organisation was not entirely uniform in its political make-up. Even during the debate on JPCs, the voice of opposition was raised within the Council itself, while one speaker who argued for JPCs testified to the value of industrial action in obtaining one at his workplace!

The argument put forward by the official historian in respect to JPCs is in some ways more important than the assumption she makes about the CP, as it relates to the attitudes of engineering workers rather than those of a political minority. The argument here runs counter to her own evidence in that it asserts the role played by the JPCs in preventing an even greater increase in the strike rate than actually took place. Now this argument may be correct, but it certainly does not run in the same direction as the facts. The problem here is that the JPCs did not *in themselves* achieve the result ascribed to them. The JPCs, as we have argued above, could hardly have fulfilled such an important role since a very high proportion of them met only once, while others were not in any sense representative bodies. Sections of skilled workers on occasion completely rejected them as irrelevant to their concerns, while JPCs largely left untouched the large numbers of women and apprentices working in the industry. Because of the almost total exclusion of women and boys from the committees, almost half the engineering workforce was not involved in their deliberations at the peak of industrial mobilisation.

Industrial conflict arose from a wide range of circumstances relating to the industrial interests of particular groups of workers; it did not arise because of any substantial political opposition to the Second World War itself. Unlike the First World War, the Second was seen by the political leadership of the shop stewards' movement to be an essential and entirely justifiable fight to save the world from the nightmare of fascism. It was this consciousness on the part of the E&ATSSNC which ensured that industrial disputes could not turn into the basis for a campaign to end the war itself, as they had momentarily during the First World War. Sooner than tax the CP shop stewards with agitational incompetence, the official historian should have recognised the enormous debt owed by the British governing class to their ostensible political enemies. In case this should be doubted, we would point out that, in alliance with the rank and file and in the most adverse political conditions imaginable, the CP shop stewards had in 1940 conducted prolonged and determined strikes to defend victimised shop stewards. They had, in addition, played a part in the apprentices' strike of 1941 which had forced the government to play the prosecution card which it was so reluctant to use. By contrast, all the major strikes of the 1942-5 period were defeated, while the prosecution weapon had to be deployed remarkably rarely. Moreover, in general terms, time lost through industrial action amounted to less than one day per worker throughout the war. This was not due, as we have shown, to a shortage of industrial grievances, but rather to the fact that the CP shop stewards generally opposed strikes and, perhaps even more importantly, to the fact that the government was fully aware that this was so. Others will point, no doubt, to the role played by the unions at official level in opposing strikes. After all, were they not more consistent in their opposition than the Communists? Yet the value to the government in having a national organisation of shop stewards arguing a no-strike line on the shop floor can hardly be overestimated. As the shop stewards of the First World War had shown, the integration of the unions at official level into the state war machinery could easily lead to a situation in which a dangerous vacuum was left at local level. In the First World War the burgeoning militant district and national organisations of shop stewards had stepped into this vacuum, creating serious problems for the government. Since then the British trade unions had remained, by international standards, very short of full-time officers. The shop stewards were therefore relatively important within the unions as a whole. Moreover, the shop stewards in question had a collective record of fighting employers and indeed, on occasion, the government itself. Who better to argue a no-strike policy and hope to be heeded by the rank and file?

Joint Production Committees, although supported by the CP, were not notably successful in providing a safety valve for grievances. They were, on the other hand, indirectly effective in reinforcing the left shop stewards' opposition to anything which might tend to hinder production. The left

374

shop stewards found it difficult to argue for JPCs, and then only shortly afterwards to argue for a determined fight against managerial priorities. While on one level the JPCs constituted an attack on managerial prerogatives, they were also a recognition of the centrality of management's priority, which—however CP propagandists might deny it—was production. This political orientation within the factory ensured that the shop stewards did not produce any theory of workers' control to rival J.T. Murphy's *The Worker's Committee* (1917). The idea of workers' control was, of course, a highly subversive one, building as it did a theory of the possible reorganisation of society through workplace representation. Shop stewards were presented as the potential midwives of a new, socialist society. The contrast with the Second World War is striking. The nearest equivalent to Murphy's idea in the Second World War is that of the tripartite regulation of industry by government, employers and trade unions. The theory reflected the pervasive influence of the JPC idea.

The official historian, then, and as a consequence many of those who have followed her, failed to examine the extent and importance of political trends within the shop stewards' movement and therefore underestimated the role of left shop stewards in limiting and diverting the rising tide of militancy. In common with many others, she was also much taken by the view that British workers were willing to prosecute the war at no matter what cost and under any authority however incompetent and hostile to their interests. This view, of course, does not comprehend the dual nature of wartime militancy as anti-fascist *and* anti-managerial. The Second World War, it is true, did not give rise to the sharply defined class conflicts which characterised the First; but, on the other hand, the political climate was markedly less jingoistic and 'white-feather' patriotic. Because this contradictory duality was not grasped (and perhaps could not be in an official history), Mrs Inman was rather too ready to assume that the opposition of the trade unions at official level, combined with the existence of consultation machinery, was enough to explain the low strike rate of the Second World War when compared to the First.

To demonstrate the inadequacy of the official argument, we may perhaps be allowed a semi-rhetorical counter-factual question of our own: what might have happened had the CP supported strikes, or even adopted an attitude of selective support in pursuit of certain key political objectives? The question only assumes importance in the light of the evidence of unrest which we have produced, of course, and the answers to it would be quite speculative. Yet one thing is almost certain—that British society in wartime would have changed even more radically.

In this final section of our conclusion, we try to draw out some of the consequences of the history which we have described. As working people become interested once again in their own past, it is very important to try to compare and contrast with the present, so that history can become a useful tool for today's trade-unionists. It is essential that activists consistently question the direction of their own individual and collective activity, and this can only be done by constantly looking back at what has been achieved and what mistakes have been made. But this assessment of the past is not only a matter of looking at what happened last week, month or year. The development of shop steward history is much clearer over periods of, say, ten years, than it can ever be over one or two. Only in this way is it possible to see the way forward.

It is in this spirit that we examine the history of shop-floor industrial relations in the 1935-45 period and compare it with the 1970s. Both periods are considered in a critical way which perhaps overlooks the strengths of trade union organisation over the last half-century. But sharp criticism can do no harm; without it, we shall simply slip back into the sort of labour history which claims that workers, unions and parties in the past never made mistakes, never stored up problems for the future, and always progressed. To put this kind of 'history' forward is to make sure that history will in fact be useless. Trade-unionists immediately sense that such history is little more than a pep talk; daily experience tells us all that this type of account of the past is a fraud. It is with this in mind that we approach our comparison between past and present.

We begin the comparison by looking at the shop floor organisation of the rearmament and war years, and contrasting it with the organisation of the 1970s. Then we consider the political direction of the shop stewards' movement of the war years and its legacy to the present.

What is meant, at factory level, by the phrase 'good trade union organisation'? If the words mean anything, then they must surely mean not just full trade union membership but, above all, good communications between the members and their representatives. Confronted by united managements using all the resources at their disposal to make the workforce adopt their objectives as their own, trade-unionists have to try to achieve unity in their own ranks. But for the union the problem is always harder than it is for management, since many more people are involved.

Judged in this way, the factory trade union organisation of the 1935-45 years was in many respects stronger than that of the 1970s. Although a lower proportion of the workforce in engineering was unionised at that time, communications between the shop stewards and their members were generally better. What evidence is there for this? First, it is important to recall that in the 1935-45 period we are dealing with a shop stewards' *movement*; there is no real equivalent to that movement today. That shop stewards' movement had a large-circulation newspaper which, in its early days at least, played a vital part in building up trade-unionism, encouraged workers to contribute articles and letters, supported strikes, and so on. Had it not been for the wartime paper restrictions on *New Propellor,* it seems likely that a very high proportion of the engineering workforce would have seen it once a fortnight; as it was, the paper was available in large quantities in almost all of the larger factories. Second, local factory papers were also more common than they are today. Through these papers the shop stewards carried on a dialogue with their members which ensured that they remained closely in touch. The whole culture of workplace meetings was more deeply rooted; regular meetings helped to ensure that all workers were drawn into the discussion of their working lives, and that this was not something left to the shop steward. This right had to be defended against wartime legislation which

377

tried to restrict meetings in 'protected places', but defended it largely was. Finally, it is important to point out the very wide range of ways in which the wartime shop steward helped his membership. This was partly because it was difficult to separate 'personal', 'domestic', 'family' and 'social' problems from 'work' ones. If a member had a relative on leave from the services, or had been bombed out of the house, then this could raise issues at work which could not always be left to the management. But it was also partly because some shop stewards recognised here not just an extra responsibility, but a new opportunity to be of service to members. Making allies in this way could be of great value.

Shop steward organisation in the 1970s has not been as close to the membership. Numerous managements have adopted the tactic of appealing to the workforce over the heads of shop stewards, in a constant attempt to undermine the position of the stewards by showing that they do not adequately reflect the views of their members. This gap has opened up for a number of reasons. Perhaps the most important is the general political offensive against trade-unionism conducted through the media and to which there has been (in comparison with the earlier period, when the *Daily Herald, Daily Worker* and *New Propellor* were widely read) very little reply. But there are other reasons which are industrial in origin and are almost as important. The 'check-off' system, under which companies deduct union subscriptions automatically from pay, is one. Although this system has the attraction of freeing the steward from the time-consuming job of collecting dues, it has the much bigger disadvantage of allowing stewards to neglect certain individuals or even whole groups and their problems. Stewards no longer undergo the discipline of having to justify union membership to their members every week. Another important means whereby this gap has developed is through the written agreement. In the 1935-45 period, very few agreements were in writing. Almost everything was determined by custom and practice, by making small gains and then hanging on to them. As far as managements are concerned, written agreements have slowed this process down considerably. Although they often serve a useful purpose to less well organised sections in factories, written agreements can tie down and demoralise previously well organised ones whose stewards are constantly confronted by a convenor or trade union officer enforcing agreements. The abolition of piece-work has had similar effects. Under piece-work, the shop steward was constantly pushed into hourly and daily battles with the rate-fixer to establish good piece-work earnings. In this way, managements found, wages 'drifted' upwards. During the 1970s, piece-work was therefore phased out in favour of various 'measured day work' systems. Stewards were relieved of their old hourly battles and, in many cases, of much of their activity. In some cases the argument shifted to manning levels; but more than a few stewards were lost on the way. Finally, the intervention of legislation, by 'giving' rights to workers 'unfairly' dismissed and to shop stewards to conduct their industrial relations duties, has very often led to members being sacked and then attempting to gain compensation through the legal process rather than keeping their jobs through collective action at the workplace, and to senior stewards and convenors spending long periods away from their workmates and from the views and feelings of the shop floor. A good deal of this 'pro-union' legislation has had damaging effects on workplace organisation.

All of these issues have been dealt with in great detail by industrial relations academics in a much more thorough way. There is no doubt that shop floor trade-unionism in engineering faces very serious internal problems. Whether the trend towards an increasing gap between stewards (and especially full-time convenors and senior stewards) and their members can be reversed remains an open question. The problem is, of course, that the whole context of shop steward activity has changed dramatically since the war. The political environment, as we have already pointed out, is far more inhospitable to trade-unionists. The level of unemployment has been consistently higher throughout the 1970s. Capital has become far more international. The unfavourable climate has hampered the much expanded body of shop stewards who are now trying to operate not only in engineering but throughout industry in both manufacturing and the public services.

As the 1970s have given way to the 1980s and the ravages of a Conservative government committed to 'monetarist' policies, the question of fighting redundancies has become *the* issue which faces workplace trade union organisation. The experience of the decade of rearmament and war is not especially helpful here. The shop stewards' movement of that period was built on rising or full employment and the expectation of full employment. These were the conditions (and in some ways the preconditions) for its growth and development. All of its methods of doing battle and its organisational structures were based on a favourable labour market. It was only at the end of the war that the possibility of unemployment had to be confronted. It is all too clear that the legacy of this period has not been particularly positive, as the dimensions of present-day stewards' failure to stop the slide into mass unemployment become apparent.

This is perhaps at first surprising. In certain respects the shop stewards of the shadow factories had begun to lay the foundations for contesting redundancies. They had been quite successful in organising combine committees which straddled the different plants owned by the same company, for example. They had also begun to develop the idea of alternative products for arms factories, which was to be taken up (knowingly or otherwise) by the Lucas Aerospace shop stewards in the 1970s to persuade their members that redundancies were far from inevitable. It could be argued that here was a promising beginning, if not more.

Yet the battles of 1944-5 against redundancies brought few lasting gains, and for a number of reasons. The first was the fundamental acceptance of economic realities as expounded by the government. The Coalition government had promised full employment, and since the war was ending, there was no further need for war workers; for the overwhelming majority of trade-unionists, these arguments were quite sound. As long as there was full employment, producing useful goods was not the main criterion. We shall return to this point shortly. Second, although the shop stewards of 1935-45 have been characterised as close to their members, this has to be qualified in one major way: they were close to their male, skilled members. In fact, the AEU stewards quite unashamedly turned their organisation against the continued presence of women in the factories in 1944-5, and insisted on the removal of all 'dilutees' (male or female) as and when they were able to do so. They were principally concerned with men's jobs, and in particular the position of the returning servicemen. Thus although the wartime shop stewards had succeeded in improving their organisation by establishing combine committees, and thereby theoretically increased the possibility of resisting job loss in any given plant, they nevertheless remained locked into governmental economic 'rationality' on the one hand and an outmoded and male-oriented form of trade-unionism on the other.

This legacy was not helpful during the battles against redundancy in the British Motor Corporation in 1956, the Upper Clyde Shipbuilders' occupation of the early 1970s or, more importantly, in the many closures that were *not* fought. Moreover, with conditions generally far less favourable, unemployment has reached levels unknown since the 1930s. The Redundancy Payments Act of 1965, initiated by Ray Gunter, has radically altered the way redundancies appear to most workers, by allowing them to 'buy' jobs. This has brought about a situation in which many workers are even demanding of their shop stewards that they be made redundant. It has been possible, because of this legislation, for managements to introduce the idea of 'voluntary' redundancy, a large proportion of job loss becoming, through this stratagem, almost acceptable. This continues to be a major stumbling block in workplace organisation, as it has drastically weakened workers' overall position in the labour market. Also, with capital becoming far more international than it was at the end of the war, companies have strengthened themselves enormously vis-à-vis their employees and national governments. By dual-sourcing components, for example, Fords have been able to isolate strikes whether in Halewood, Dagenham, Saarlouis, Valencia, or anywhere else. There are many other advantages to management in internationalisation; their increased control has not been matched by international shop floor trade union solidarity, however. Shop stewards continue to think of such solidarity as an exotic luxury or a utopian impossibility. To these developments has recently been added another, in many ways equally important one—micro-processor technology, which opens up tremendous possibilities for managements in terms of 'rationalisation' and subsequent job loss, while at the same time increasing top managements' control over the productive process. These three crucial developments have made the shop steward's job incomparably more difficult than it was at the end of the war. In some ways, the unsolved problems of the past have come back in even more serious forms.

During the second half of the 1930s it had appeared that the Communist party was beginning to build a political leadership amongst the shop stewards. An organisation had been set up which used industrial disputes in one key section of the engineering industry from which to draw political conclusions. This was an important development: such groups have always been difficult to politicise in Britain because of the rigid distinction traditionally drawn in the labour movement between 'industrial' and 'political' questions. One can only speak of the beginnings of such a development, but nevertheless, whatever its problems and limitations, beginnings there were. The shop stewards' movement was strongly anti-government, facing up squarely to the Baldwin and Chamberlain administrations and opposing their policies at home and abroad as pro-fascist. During the 'Imperialist War' period, up until the invasion of the Soviet Union, the CP stewards generally refrained from overt political agitation and concentrated on industrial grievances. With the arrival of the 'People's War' period, the CP could once again reassert their political priorities. From the first, as we have shown, their demands fell within the general scope which the Coalition government was prepared to countenance and even at times tacitly support. The establishment of JPCs was an important episode in this connection, because it showed the CP stewards concerting their strength to achieve government aims at the same time as attacking managerial prerogatives. Within the factory, managements were under attack; but this was in line with the state's political perspectives. During the 'Imperialist War' period a similar move to establish factory consultative committees by the government had been fiercely denounced by the *Daily Worker,* but the invasion of Russia had completely changed the CP's relationship to the state.

From the end of the JPC campaign at about the end of 1942, to the end of the war, the CP veered towards advocating political policies which related much more closely to the conduct of the war itself than to the immediate interests of workers. It organised factory meetings on opening the second front (a campaign which could hardly be called a notable success except in so far as a second front was eventually established) rather than, for example, on the immediate implementation of Beveridge's proposals. By 1945 it had even gone so far as to advocate the continuation of the coalition into peacetime with the CP as a part of the alliance, whereas the Labour Party came out for a general election. Thus, while CP policy became increasingly divorced from the activities of workers and more intently focused on pressing its claims as a potential member of a coalition, CP membership fell from its historical peak. Far from achieving a fusion between its policies and workers' daily industrial concerns, the CP reached a position where the two streams were moving in diametrically opposite directions.

Whether any voices within the CP actively canvassed a more sensitive reaction to industrial disputes is unknown, and must remain substantially unknown until the CP opens its archive to historians. But it is clear that by the post-war period there were serious problems in their political orientation. To take just one central example: they continued to advocate the establishment of JPCs in the post-war period, only to find them opposed by managements and largely ignored by industrial workers. The task of building a political movement in industry had proved too great for the CP. Its hold on factory trade-unionism became increasingly organisational rather than organically linked to the mass of workers; Cold War purges made this problem even more apparent than it otherwise might have been. But the most important result lay in the subsequent direction that the shop stewards' organisation was to take.

Clearly, it would be idealistic to expect the CP to have demolished at one blow the division between political and industrial activity within the British working class. But the general direction of their policies from October 1941 reinforced the idea already current amongst workers that the state could be called in to redress the balance of power between themselves and management. Under certain circumstances this had some application, but in others it could have disastrous results. During the years of Labour government from 1964, so-called pro-union legislation has concealed potential dangers to unions and their membership as we have already suggested. Similarly, during the 1970s the tendency to look towards the National Enterprise Board for salvation during plant closures has only recently begun to be criticised as counter-productive within the trade union movement, and then only on its fringes.[2]

The war period represented a tremendous opportunity to establish certain traditions within workplace organisation and to abolish others. The shop stewards' movement was very young and extremely plastic in its structure, and had large numbers of new members to represent. One could say that factories, unions and the labour movement went into the crucible of war for recasting. The positive results were considerable. Having shaken off the demoralisation of the Depression, shop floor union organisation emerged as a powerful force; the first majority Labour government was elected; the left was at an historical high point in many unions. Yet the nature of this left dominance in itself represented a problem for the British working class. The CP in particular had encouraged a naive attitude to the state, which echoed that of the Labour Party. This naiveté, always dangerous in a country with such a sophisticated governing class as Britain, proved especially hazardous as Britain moved into a phase of rapid economic decline, for which working people have been asked to pay. It is in this context that the course of the political movement amongst the shop stewards of the war years has been examined: not only as a history worthy of interest in its own right, but as an experience vital to an understanding of the shop steward organisation of the present.

## NOTES

1 See Ted Kavanagh, *Tommy Handley* (1949), ch. 15. ITMA's humorous reflections on factory life were based on time they spent at a Chester aircraft factory (ibid., p. 160).
2 Coventry, Liverpool, Newcastle, N. Tyneside Trades Councils, *State Intervention in Industry. A Workers' Inquiry* (Newcastle, 1980).

# BIBLIOGRAPHICAL NOTE

The purpose of this note is twofold: to indicate to historians the nature and location of some of the most important sources used in writing this book, and to suggest the most useful ways of approaching the subject to trade-unionists interested in the past. No attempt has been made to list every archival and printed source, as the result would be little more than a catalogue in which vital works were lost among numerous publications of no more than peripheral interest. Readers with particular concerns are referred to the footnotes.

## 1 *Archives*
The *Public Record Office*, now housed at Kew, provided by far the most substantial source material. The main classes of documents are listed below, in descending order of importance:

a)    LAB 8 and LAB 10. These two classes of files are central to any research on wartime industrial relations. LAB 8 is generally concerned with labour matters which touch on industrial relations, for example dilution, the transfer of labour, provision of canteens, and so on, while LAB 10 contains the extremely useful weekly reports of the regional conciliation officers, special reports filed during times of unrest, strikes, etc., together with Headquarters files, ministerial and other memoranda.

b)    LAB 34. These Ministry of Labour disputes books record all stoppages notified to the Ministry of Labour. While they are not entirely accurate, they are the most faithful and comprehensive record yet available.

c)    INF 1. Ministry of Information documents relating to home security, 'fifth-column' activities, home morale.

d)    AVIA 15 and 22. Records of the Ministry of Air-craft Production. These are rather difficult to use because of the non-consecutive numbering used in the indices, and the tendency for industrial relations material to be mixed with technical files. They are nevertheless occasionally very useful when dealing with labour difficulties experienced by MAP contractors.

e)    CAB 65, WM series. Minutes of the War Cabinet, which may be used with the help of a subject index. CAB 98.18 (Minutes of the War Cabinet Committee on Communist Activities) was especially interesting. Unfortunately, many potentially useful records relating to 'subversive activities' have been kept closed to historians under one of the Public Record Office's restrictive rules.

f)    Various files from the SUPP (Ministry of Supply), MEPOL (Metropolitan Police), ADM (Admiralty) and MH (Ministry of Health). Some MH files contain interesting material on nursery provision and women's welfare. The Admiralty used to take a close interest in industrial rela-tions in its contractors' workplaces, but here again much material is closed to historians. Nevertheless, ADM 178/162-3 (Dismissal of Communists from War Department and Navy Department, 1927-37) is of some use, and is open without restriction. ADM 197 contains Admiralty Whitley Council papers.

After the PRO files, the most informative archival source for this book was the *Mass Observation Archive* run by the Social Science Research Council at the University of Sussex, which is most interesting for the light it can throw on popular attitudes during the Second World War, although the increasingly official role of MO's information-gathering for the Ministry of Information has to be borne in mind. The records are still to be comprehensively catalogued, and offer most under the headings File Reports and Industry Files. File Reports are detailed reports written up on a particular topic (such as Clydeside industrial morale in 1941), while industry files are collections of material sent in by observers relevant to a particular industry. The archive also contains diaries sent in more or less regularly, as well as numerous other types of raw material collected for future publication or simply out of general interest.

*The Beaverbrook Papers* in the House of Lords Record Office. These papers were most useful in Series D (eighty-eight boxes). Unfortunately, the entire collection was in a chaotic state in 1975-6, despite the claims made in the official guide (*A Guide to the Political Papers, 1874-1970* compiled by the first Beaverbrook Foundation. House of Lords Record Office, Memo no. 54, 1975). Nevertheless, there are some interesting documents from shop floor workers requesting Beaverbrook's intervention in various matters.

Amongst the most important sources on managerial attitudes and policies were the fortnightly and monthly *Minutes of the Coventry Engineering Employers' Association,* which were made available to me during 1972 at the Association's office in Davenport Road, Coventry. Also useful were a few documents sent to me by the Engineering Employers' Federation, although I was refused access to their records as a whole.

Many sets of trade union documents were used, of which only the most important are listed below:

a)     Minutes of the General Executive Council, TGWU, 1935-45 (Modern Records Centre, University of Warwick). Printed records of decisions.

b)     Minutes of the Coventry and Manchester District Committees of the AEU, at their respective offices. These are very informative and often contain Head Office circulars, memoranda, letters, and so on.

c)     Minutes of the Glasgow Trades Council, Mitchell Library, Glasgow.

d)     Minutes of the Manchester Trades Council, including Minutes of the Metal Trades Group of the Council, 1930-46, at the Central Reference Library, Manchester.

e)     Minutes and Correspondence of the Newcastle District Committee of the AEU, including very interesting handwritten notes by district officials. These were kindly made available to me by Ray Challinor of Newcastle Polytechnic.

f)     Minutes and papers of the TUC Organisation Committee, in the TUC Library.

g)     Minutes of Works and Local Conferences in Coventry,

in the Modern Records Centre, University of Warwick.

h) Etheridge Papers, Modern Records Centre. These voluminous records belonging to Dick Etheridge, shop steward and then convenor at Austin Longbridge, begin about 1944 and contain a good deal of useful information. Len Powell's papers have not been used in this study, as they were only deposited there as this book went to print.

i) Minutes of the Oxford Branch Committee NUVB, and various papers relating to Pressed Steel Fisher, Oxford, including interesting management documents and TGWU records. These were kindly made available to me by Roger Seeley, who works at Pressed Steel and is preparing a history of the TGWU branch there.

j) Minutes of the EC of the Electrical Trades Union, TUC Library.

k) Minutes of the EC of the National Union of Foundry Workers, Modern Records Centre.

## 2 *Magazines and newspapers*

National and local newspapers were rather less important to this study than they have been to most comparable books, largely because of a widespread editorial desire to play down industrial disputes as far as possible. This self-censorship only begins to lift with the apprentices' strike of 1944, from which point local newspapers become increasingly willing to cover industrial conflict.

The most useful source of this type is undoubtedly the leftward-leaning *Picture Post,* which was not afraid to point to the causes and motivations of industrial unrest in both its written and pictorial content.

Other useful sources include the many factory papers which sprang up from the middle of the war, of which there is an excellent collection at the Library of the Working Class Movement, 111 King's Road, Manchester. These papers are often parochial but they can also be very revealing of the attitudes of engineering workers themselves. The best available collection of *New Propellor* is also available at the same excellent library.

Managerial journals, in particular *Industrial Welfare* and *Labour Management,* also contain a considerable amount of material of great interest which is often quite sympathetic to working-class points of view.

The *Daily Worker, New Leader, Socialist Appeal* and *War Commentary* offered industrial news from their respective political viewpoints. Needless to say, these newspapers often engaged in fierce polemic, at times bewildering but at others quite revealing. Their detailed coverage of factory affairs obliges serious historians to use them despite the very real difficulties involved; no other newspapers were remotely as interested in these questions.

One source which has been almost completely ignored by historians is the very informative *Catholic Worker.* This paper gave excellent coverage of industrial matters at certain points, and was especially well informed on Fords Dagenham and Rolls-Royce Hillington. At times it can provide a useful control over the newspapers of the extreme left.

Finally, *Labour's Northern Voice,* newspaper of the Manchester Trades Council, can frequently be very helpful in its general coverage of industrial matters.

## 3 *Pamphlets*

Historians interested in twentieth-century left-wing politics have good reason to be thankful for the zeal with which Sara and Maitland collected pamphlets from all left groups, which are now deposited in the University of Warwick Library. Although it is only arranged under the most general headings, the collection is especially useful for the 1930s and 1940s.

The Marx Memorial Library also has a small collection of pamphlets relating to the campaign for the People's Convention.

The Second World War revived the British tradition of the political pamphlet, in which arguments could be developed without the restrictions typical of newspaper articles and which remained short enough to retain a large readership. They are a major source for the political history of the period.

## 4 *Books, articles and theses*

There are no books which provide a satisfactory overview of shop steward history; nor are there any which deal in depth with industrial relations in wartime as seen from below. Readers interested in a general picture of social and industrial conditions during the Second World War could not do better than to read Angus Calder's still engaging and vivid book *The People's War* (1971). Those interested in developments in industry should read the drier official history by Mrs P. Inman, *Labour in the Munitions Industries* (1957). Unfortunately, the first is long and the second tedious. To catch the flavour of the period quickly, look at the documents in K. Coates and T. Topham, *Industrial Democracy in Great Britain* (1967).

Readers concerned with the coal industry should look at the excellent history of the South Wales Miners' Federation by Hywel Francis and David Smith, *The Fed* (1980). It is a pity that other areas of the Miners' Federation do not have equivalent histories.

There are some useful articles in various issues of *History Workshop Journal,* including those by Arthur Exell of Morris Motors, Oxford, and James Hinton on Coventry during the war. There is also an item by Jonathan Zeitlin entitled 'The Emergence of Shop Steward Organisation and Job Control in the British Car Industry: A Review Essay' in *History Workshop Journal* no. 10, Autumn 1980.

The recollections of Doris White, an ex-factory worker at Wolverton's railway works, have now been published under the title *D for Doris, V for Victory* (Oakleaf Books, Milton Keynes, 1981). This is a very valuable set of recollections of wartime factory life.

Although a good deal of the published material lacks the liveliness of Doris White's book, there are some unpublished theses which offer at least as much in terms of real insight plus an ability to hold the reader's interest. I do not include amongst them my own thesis 'Communist Politics and Shop Stewards in Engineering, 1935–46', Warwick PhD., 1977 written as it was under a variety of academic and personal pressures and butchered by order of examiners. One very useful thesis is Robert Hastings' 'The Labour Movement in Birmingham, 1927-45' (Birmingham MA, 1959), an excellent study of its subject. Another useful dissertation which contains interesting information on the development of an aircraft company and the workers within it is by Spencer Phelan, 'The Avro Conspiracy. The Origins and Development of Labour Relations in an Aircraft Firm 1906-1945' (Ruskin College Labour Studies dissertation, 1979).

## 5 *Oral sources*

One of the most important sources for this study has been the personal reminiscences of trade-unionists active during the war years. I have always used them in an essentially secondary way, because of the problems involved in recalling events at a minimum range of twenty-five years. Many of these discussions could not be dignified with the title 'interview', and many were not tape-recorded. Their influence on my interpretations will nevertheless be clear to those who were kind enough to talk to me. Some of the most important interviews were taped, including those with Harold Taylor (Coventry), Jock Wallace (London and Liverpool), the late Bill Wellings, Jack Williams and Billy Stokes (Coventry and Birmingham). The deaths of these last three activists since my research was begun underlines the importance of recording older trade-unionists' memories while they are still available to us.

# INDEX

Abbott, Bill, 34, 310
accident rates, 15, 78
Addison, Paul, viii
AEC Co., 62
Aeroplastics Co., 290
aircraft companies, 4, 121, 328
air raids, 107–112
Aircraft Shop Stewards National Council, 41, 112–3
Albion Motors Co., 85, 104, 293
Allaun, Frank, 317
Alvis Co., 95
aluminium houses, 327–9
Amalgamated Society of Engineers, 19–21
Amalgamated Engineering Union
Executive Committee, 37–8, 44–5, 46, 62, 93, 98, 101, 102, 218, 220–4, 232, 288
District Committees, 113, 132, 232–3
National Committee, 131
*Monthly Journal*, 59
full-time officers, 64–5
Special Conference, 221, 224–6
formation of, 21
leadership in inter-war years, 28
anti-fascist activity, 65
objections to Essential Works order, 116–7
Western Area -Organising Committee (London), 80
and apprentices strikes (1941), 127
Trotskyists, 175, 178, 230
and CP, 144, 323
and JPCs, 150–3, 155, 174
craft membership, 168–9
Regulation 1AA, 309
combine committees, 207–8
Women's Conferences, 1943–5, 266, 276

women workers, 269–75, 277–9, 284–5, 287
Rolls-Royce Hillington, 287–8, 291
women's redundancies, 299
'dilutees first' policy, 326
1945 General Election, 345
anarchists, 177
apprenticeship, 9
apprentices strike
1937, 45–57
1941, 123–31
1944, 230–5
arms firms, 1–5
Armstrong-Siddeley Co., 11
Armstrong-Whitworth Aircraft Co., 24, 55, 56, 60, 85, 97, 163, 322
Austin, Longbridge, 81, 213, 330–1, 338
Avery Co., 110

Barr and Stroud Co., 51, 290
strike (1943), 292–3
Barrow, 127
AEU District Committee, 220–4, 226
strike (1943), 218–26
Bartlett, 328
Beardmore's Parkhead Forge, 83, 104–5, 172, 173, 215–6, 229, 336
Bedaux system, 10
Berridge, Claude, 65, 312, 324
Betteshanger Colliery strike (1942), 217
Beveridge Report, 198–9
Bevin, Ernest, 14, 17, 74, 87–9, 102, 115–6, 145, 153, 161, 223, 231, 238–43, 252, 264, 265, 296, 314
Bifurcated and Tubular Rivet Co., 262–3
Birch, Reg, 310
Birmingham, 49, 75, 81, 121, 154,

395

and Trade Union Report, 173
and women workers, 253–4, 260
Mather and Platt Co., 54, 276
McAndrew, Hector, 102
McArdle, Paul, 183
McElroy, 287
McLaren, Sir Charles, 281
McLearie, 278
McShane, Harry, 237–8
Menzies, Charlie, 292–3
Metropolitan-Vickers Co., 34, 310
Middle Docks and Engineering Co., 273
Militant Workers Federation, 228–30
Ministry of Aircraft Production, 150, 158, 200–1, 202–3, 254, 327
Minton, Dr., 18–19
Mitchell, J.W., 184
Morgan, J.G., 185
Morris Co., 75, 81, 128–30, 267
motor industry, 58
Munro, W.J., 54
Murphy, J.T., 257–8, 271–2, 375

Napier Co., 152, 157–8, 317, 337, 348–51
National Arbitration Tribunal, 222, 241
National Unemployed Workers Movement, 33, 39
National Union of Foundry Workers, 276, 278
National Union of General and Municipal Workers, 150–274, 276
National Union of Vehicle Builders, 30, 31, 45, 60, 61
Neptune (Swan Hunter) strike (1943), 205–6
*New Leader,* 176–7
*New Propellor,* 40–3, 47, 93, 110, 113–4, 202, 289, 346
Nokes, Gertie and Freda, 81
North British Locomotive Co., 6, 104, 187–9, 229, 257, 290
North East Marine Engineering Co., 233
Nuffield Co., 334
nurseries, 263–4

Official History of the Second World War (Civil series), vi–vii, 371–6
Order 1305, 88–9, 128, 217, 241
Owen, Jack, 247, 310

Page, Jack, 348
Park Royal Coachworks, 312
Parsons Co., 236
payment by results, 11, 158–9, 179
People's Convention, 112
Perryman, John, 86
Piggot, L. 122
Pitter's Tool and Gauge Co., 32
Pollitt, Harry, 74, 86, 322, 346
Pott, Ellis, 318
Pressed Steel Co., 75
  strike (1934), 128–30
Priestley, J.B., v
production methods, 7–9, 76–7, 201
Pryor, H., 341–2

Reading, Lady, 263–4
redundancy, 310, 325–40
Regulation 58A, 88
Regulation 54CA, 202
Regulation 1AA, 240–3, 308, 309
Renold Chain Co., 299
Revolutionary Communist Party, 235–7, 239, 313
Roberts, Tom, 40
Roe, A.V. Co., 4, 54, 60, 85, 127–8, 208, 228, 259–60, 265, 318–20
Rolls-Royce Hillington plant, 83, 104
  strike (1943), 290–1
Rootes and Rootes Securities Co., 6, 9, 76, 78, 200
Rover No. 2 plant, 154
Royal Commission on Equal Pay, 295–6
Royal Ordnance Factories, 75, 76, 173–4, 263, 270–1
Royal Society for the Prevention of Accidents, 18
Ryan, Rachel, 153

sabotage, 90–1
Salford Electrical Instruments Co., 35, 57
Samuels, Miss, 296
Scott, Joe, 65, 225
Scott, Reg, 113
Scottish Trades Union Congress, 269–70
shadow factories, 4, 75–7, 329–332, 334–5
Shaw, Harry, 348–9
Sheffield, 28
Sheeley, Paddy, 56

(1941), 253
nature of work, 254, 261–3
and management, 258–9
shopping, 264–6
absenteeism, 266–7
and trade unions, 271–5
earnings, 282–3
equal pay, 283–4, 295–7
redundancy, 299–300
Woolwich Arsenal, 90–1, 211–12

Workers International League, 175–6, 228
Workers Open Forum, 238
workshop ritual, 83–4

Yarrow Co., 125
Young Communist League, 45, 50, 53, 125, 130–1

Zinkin, Peter, 41